Library of
Davidson College

ND CARUSO

ENRICO CARUSO

A BIOGRAPHY

BY

PIERRE V. R. KEY

In Collaboration with BRUNO ZIRATO

With illustrations

NEW YORK
VIENNA HOUSE
1972

© 1922 by Little, Brown, and Company.

This 1972 VIENNA HOUSE edition is reprinted
by arrangement with Little, Brown, and Company.
International Standard Book Number: 0-8443-0074-8
Library of Congress Catalogue Number: 72-81091
Manufactured in the United States of America

927.8
C32A

73-7776

To

HIS GREAT PUBLIC

PREFACE

THE purpose of this book is to present a portraiture of Enrico Caruso and to set down essential facts touching his career and private life which belong properly in a biography. It is doubtful if any other music artist attained so widespread a popularity; on the side of interpretative art he has been accorded, almost unanimously, a supreme place. In an age wherein personalities are not few, Enrico Caruso appears in an outstanding light; he was one whose name and photograph were instantly identified and recognized wherever civilization prevailed.

To secure and detail facts, and to permit the individuality of the man to reveal itself as it was, have been the aim of author and collaborator. Neither time nor effort was spared to obtain from every authoritative source possible information which it was felt should have representation in this volume. Members of the Caruso family, intimate friends, persons associated with the singer in his professional activities have assisted to make the work as complete as possible. This aid came from the United States, Italy, England, France, Germany, Mexico, Cuba, and South America.

In a letter written to the author, on November 15, 1921, Mrs. Enrico Caruso stated, "It is most gratifying to me that you have consented to write the biography of my husband. Mr. Caruso told you so much of his life-story when you and he prepared that comprehensive series of articles two years ago. And, as you know, he had planned to collaborate with you in writing his biography for publication as a book, a volume that would stand as a permanent record of his career as an artist and a man.

"I will, of course, give you full access to all the letters, papers, and other data which belonged to Mr. Caruso; and I will assist you in every manner possible, for your book will be the only authentic biography. I am happy that Bruno Zirato is to assist you as collaborator."

Giovanni Caruso, only living brother to the singer, wrote to the author in a letter dated November 20, 1921, "I am sending the data you wanted, and will arrange to confer with you and Zirato as often as may be necessary, during my stay in America. Your book of Enrico will be *the only book*, the one he had told me he expected you and he would write together."

For all their deep interest, both Mrs. Caruso and Giovanni Caruso realized that the value of the biography would rest in its fidelity to fact. Enrico Caruso was human; he therefore had shortcomings as well as virtues. To disclose them as they existed has been the constant purpose of the author. He has sought, as far as possible, to let experiences tell the story.

To the reader it must be apparent that integrity and industry were no less responsible for the achievements of Enrico Caruso than his vocal and artistic gifts. The development of the man was such as to be little short of amazing; one has only to read to appreciate the growth and unfolding of his finer qualities, which carried him from the beginning (a youth of humble parentage, having the slenderest of early opportunities) to an ultimate position of justly earned admiration and respect.

Despite the generous physical proportions of this volume, it has not been possible to use everything available for publication. Much that was at hand could not be incorporated in its pages; excellent and interesting incidents — if non-essential from a biographically historic standpoint — were omitted with regret.

The gathering and assembling of the necessary material represents a huge and exacting task. No one else was so well fitted for it as Bruno Zirato, secretary to Enrico Caruso throughout the closing years of his life; and Zirato's constant and helpful suggestions to the author during the writing of the text form a large part in its accomplishment.

Grateful acknowledgment by author and collaborator is made to the following persons, who coöperated in supplying information — without which the book as it stands could not have been made:

Gabriel Astruc, Vittorio Arimondi, Pasquale Amato, Frances Alda, Camillo Antona-Traversi, A. F. Adams, Henry Bassano, Richard Barthélemy, Giovanni Bellezza, L. Barcellona, Elena Bianchini-Cappelli, Francesco Cilea, Francis C. Coppicus, Ricardo Cabrera, Richard S. Copley, Federico Candida,

PREFACE

Roberto Ciappa, Feodor I. Chaliapin, Maria Castaldi-Caruso, Amedeo Canessa, Calvin G. Child, Martino Ceccanti, Gino Castro, Nicola Daspuro, Giuseppe de Luca, Menotti Delfino, Eugene H. Danziger, Carlo d'Ormeville, Andres de Segurola, Carlo d'Amato, Luis P. Figueras, Vittorio Ferraguti, Mario Fantini, Giulio Gatti-Casazza, Filippo Galante, William J. Guard, Fabian Garcia, Giuseppe Grassi, Giovanni Gatto, Cesare Gravina, Frank Garlichs, Otto Gutekunst, Giuseppe Jaricci, Giuseppe Lusardi, Michele Lauria, Enrico Lorello, Mario P. Marafioti, Leopoldo Mugnone, Antonio Mazzarella, Alberto A. Macieira, Lionel Mapleson, Herman Mishkin, Vincenzo Morichini, Carl E. Peck, Giacomo Puccini, Percy Pitt, Graziella Pareto, Angelo Ruspini, Titta Ruffo, Antonio Scotti, Antonio Stella, Enrico Santini, Louise Saer, Sadie M. Strauss, Alfred F. Seligsberg, Pasquale Simonelli, Marziale Sisca, Arturo Scaramella, Joseph Tonello, Egisto Tromben, Enrico Usiglio, Henry Uterhart, Beatrice Vergine, Gianni and Gina Viafora, G. B. Vitelli, Edward Ziegler. The Municipalities of Genoa, Treviso, Trieste, Naples, Palermo, Livorno. The Metropolitan Opera Company of New York,. The Colon Theater of Buenos Aires. The San Carlo Theater of Naples. The Covent Garden of London. The Vittorio Emanuele Theater of Palermo. The Alla Scala Theater of Milano. The Cimarosa Theater of Caserta.

P. V. R. K.

CONTENTS

CHAPTER		PAGE
I	Introductory	1
II	Youth	10
III	Working Days	20
IV	Débuts	41
V	Realizations	81
VI	Climbing	154
VII	Established	200
VIII	Trying Days	245
IX	A New Period	275
X	Golden Days	305
XI	Twilight	343
XII	The End	388
	Appendices Compiled by Bruno Zirato	393
	Index	443

ILLUSTRATIONS

ENRICO CARUSO . . . . . *Frontispiece in Photogravure*	
THE HOUSE WHERE CARUSO WAS BORN	10
ANNA BALDINI-CARUSO, MOTHER OF ENRICO . . .	22
ASSUNTA CARUSO, ONLY SISTER OF ENRICO . . .	34
MARCELLINO CARUSO, FATHER OF ENRICO . . .	34
CARUSO AS TURIDDU, WITH ELENA BIANCHINI-CAPPELLI AS SANTUZZA, IN "CAVALLERIA RUSTICANA" . . .	50
A CARD TO DON ANTONIO MAZZARELLA, OF CASERTA, AT A PERIOD WHEN CARUSO WAS STRUGGLING FOR A LIVING	58
REDUCED FACSIMILE OF THE PROGRAM OF THE TEATRO MUNICIPALE IN SALERNO FOR THE PERFORMANCE OF "LA GIOCONDA" GIVEN IN HONOR OF CARUSO, APRIL 30, 1897	74
ENRICO CARUSO IN 1896	78
A PAGE OF CARUSO'S MANUSCRIPT	122
How he studied the rôle of Samson	
CARUSO AS RODOLFO IN "LA BOHÈME"	134
CARUSO AS THE DUKE IN "RIGOLETTO"	158
CARICATURES OF CARUSO AND UMBERTO GIORDANO, AUTHOR OF "FEDORA," MADE BY CARUSO, PARIS, MAY 5, 1905	194
GARDEN AND REAR ENTRANCE TO CARUSO'S "VILLA BELLOSGUARDO," AT LASTRA A SIGNA, FLORENCE .	198

ILLUSTRATIONS

Caricatures of Caruso, drawn by Himself on a Typewriter	202
Puccini Counts on Caruso's Collaboration for the Success of the London Première of his "Madama Butterfly"	208
The Author of "Fedora" to Caruso after the Première at the Metropolitan Opera House	236
An Appreciation by "Ciccio" Tosti, after hearing his own "Ideale," recorded by Caruso	242
Marble Bas-relief, by the Master of the Marble Madonnas, XV. Century, in the Caruso Collection	246
Eighteenth Century Gold Watches, Enameled and Jeweled, in the Caruso Collection	250
How Madame Réjane appreciated a Caruso Performance	272
One of Caruso's Last Pen-and-ink Caricatures	276
Caruso's Pencil Sketch of Little Gloria when she was Nine Months Old	276
Caruso as Dick Johnson in "The Girl of the Golden West"	284
Caruso as he appeared in "The Splendid Romance," a Film made in America but never Produced	292
Caruso in 1913, the Year which marked the Beginning of his Ascendancy	298
Caruso as Samson in "Samson et Dalila"	312
A Page of the Score of "Samson et Dalila" copied by Caruso	316
Mrs. Enrico Caruso	324
Caruso as Eleazar in "La Juive"	346
Gloria	350
A Page from Secchi's "Love Me or Not," illustrating Caruso's Original Method of Teaching himself how to Sing in English	370

ILLUSTRATIONS

Caruso as Canio in "I Pagliacci" 376
Voucher of Check received from the Metropolitan Opera House, for Caruso's Last Performance, "La Juive," Dec. 24, 1920 384
The Last Picture. Taken at Hotel Victoria, Sorrento, Italy, July, 1921 388

ENRICO CARUSO

CHAPTER ONE

INTRODUCTORY

LOOKING back to that particular Saturday, I can see now how virile a thing is hope; how easily it may thrust reason aside as too assertive. I am not likely to forget either the date — May 28, 1921 — or the hour — one o'clock in the afternoon—commemorative in these pages of my last meeting with Enrico Caruso.

He was seated in a room high above the rumble of New York streets, which is imaged still in the mind. His chair was drawn close to a slender-legged table topped with an oblong of thick glass. Without a coat, his vest partly unbuttoned, he was guiding stiffly with the fingers of his gloved right hand a pen. Through the south window shone the sun; the spring air suggested approaching summer. On other such days had he been thus engrossed; though with body and spirit less wasted. He had come, very slowly, back to the period of convalescence known now to have been part of the danger period of his sickness.

Traversing mentally the events which have followed since that day leaves a bewildered feeling of an opportunity neglected. So much might have been said — in place of the inconsequential talk seemingly befitting the occasion. Others no doubt are conscious on their part of a similar omission. Perhaps it was just as well that no such special attitude of mind was allowed.

As Edward Ziegler and I were admitted to the Caruso apartment in the Hotel Vanderbilt we caught sight of the tenor — down the long hallway which led to the room where he worked. Bruno Zirato, Caruso's faithful secretary, was kneeling on the floor opposite the singer, who was dictating some instructions as he laboriously wielded his pen: the disposition of some final matters prior to the departure for the steamship *Presidente Wilson*. Only a few hours hovered before the voyage eastward from New York toward the land of his birth, which for two years he had not seen.

There was no sense of impending tragedy in that walk along the hallway. It was more a moment of rejoicing that death had been beaten off; that health, if by no means yet attained, lay at no great distance. Trustworthy physicians had approved the proposed journey. Well! Anxious days almost past and gone. Danger may not have wholly withdrawn, but it seemed a danger shrunken and dwindled away to something too puny for a successfully renewed attack.

Some boxes and stripped walls indicated a change of abode for the Caruso household. Expecting our arrival, Caruso had raised his head when Mario, one of his two valets, admitted Ziegler and me. He smiled as we crossed the threshold of his workroom, and extended a greeting with partly lifted arm and a word.

"Halloo!" he said.

The speaking voice was subdued and lacking its accustomed sonority. For an instant, until he spoke again in slightly firmer tones and smiled with a trace of the old-time humor, a sudden oppression held. Zirato rose and pulled out chairs, while the tenor continued with what developed to be a caricature of his secretary — the last drawing he ever made in this country, and one of the last anywhere.

All the while Zirato chattered on — alternately in English and Italian — and Caruso plied his pen and occasionally interjected a monosyllabic word. A fancied repressed nervousness in the secretary's manner was contradicted by his smiling countenance; he too (as he has since admitted) felt buoyed by hopes which heartened so many others.

I remember, though, how touched by illness was the singer's face. Beneath the loosened waistcoat the arched chest of previous days was no more; the whole frame appeared shrunken, and the loss in weight very many pounds. Considering all he had undergone one marveled that he had survived at all.

He still appeared, on that May afternoon, a very sick man; but who would have sensed the outcome that lay only a few weeks off? Such external evidences as were to be observed of the long fight with disease must gradually depart. Two months, three possibly, under the sun at Sorrento; further rest in a climate which helps to heal such cases, and care. Even the gloved right hand conveyed none of the significance it should. I was aware, too, that the arm had been stricken by the pressure of lying upon it for days when Caruso had remained unconscious, holding to life by a shred of his tenacious vitality. It had left the hand incapable of grasping with firmness any object; so a glove was used to give support and purchase to the fingers.

The mental process of comparing the physical Caruso of the moment with the Caruso of six months before had passed when Zirato finished making notations on the tags attached to the various keys he held. They fitted trunks containing the tenor's costumes, stored at the time in the Metropolitan Opera House; and at Caruso's direction Zirato passed to assistant general manager Ziegler these keys, voicing the singer's desire for their safe keeping.

What a series of pictures the thought of Caruso's costumes suggested! Seventeen consecutive years of triumphs — and the arrested eighteenth season. Would he don again any one of those costumes? It was impossible to repress the unspoken question. I looked across at the figure at the desk, with drooped head crowned by thinning hair. Caruso was still making marks with his pen on the paper before him. Perhaps he also was thinking of some of his great nights. Underneath the table the tenor's legs — their slenderness ill concealed by trousered coverings — could be seen stretched out in customary fashion when he sat thus, with ankles crossed. He looked up at that moment and put aside his pen.

INTRODUCTORY

There followed then some further commonplace conversation in which we all joined. Caruso gathered cheerfulness, possibly from some mysterious sources he himself did not know. He received with little exclamations of pleasure some messages from friends we had brought him, and leaning back in his chair looked at us out of wistful eyes. In them I caught now and again the distant expression which comes when one projects the mind through great spaces; and I have no doubt that at these moments he had anticipated by a fortnight the voyage of the *Presidente Wilson,* and was already in Sorrento — across the bay from his beloved Naples — and was perhaps getting some of the good of it.

The desire to linger was put resolutely away and I rose to leave; there was a realization of what a tax upon a none too abundant strength would be the experiences at sailing time.

I wish I might know what thought Caruso held as we clasped hands in what I did not suspect was the long farewell. Hope — virile Hope — continued on guard even at that precious instant.

At the end of the passageway, preparatory to stepping into the hotel corridor, I turned; and Caruso lifted slightly his gloved hand. He was still seated before the slender-legged table, gazing down the hallway, as I drew the door shut after me.

Five hours later found the singer on the deck of his ship, Mrs. Caruso standing by his side, with Baby Gloria seated on the rail between them. A throng of people swarmed the dock; many among those faithful hundreds had remained patiently waiting for more than half the day. They waved hands and hats and handkerchiefs as the *Presidente Wilson* moved away from her slip. It was America's unconscious farewell to its best loved singer.

II

An estimate of a great man may come in his lifetime, but only when he is gone forever is the true evaluation reached. There seemed at Enrico Caruso's death an immediate realization of a world loss, — due to the affection felt for him. Indeed, it was from the pleasure his singing gave that Caruso became in a way the property of the people. He always said that he belonged to the public; and what a vast public it was! But the sadness which touched so many those August days of 1921 must have dulled the perceptions. Not until months later did there arise a full consciousness of the gap he has left.

Through "the machine" (as he termed the phonograph) he was available to multitudes who could by no other means feel the spell of his voice and art. It seems a fitting medium, now, to help keep our memory of him fresh: we have only to close our eyes — listening to his reproduced singing — to have him almost with us.

Preparing this volume was not easy; Caruso had expected to share the work. He first spoke of it toward the end of numerous meetings we had, during which he supplied the material for a series of articles covering experiences in his life. As the story grew, so did Caruso's interest warm to the idea of expanding and rewriting the whole into a book. He believed this should be leisurely done, with respect for facts. The undertaking, he knew, would be laborious: securing much data from the countries where he had appeared, then arranging this chronologically with other data. To select what we felt should go to make the text of some forty thousand words had been trying enough. The singer's appreciation of this deterred him from the more elaborate and painstaking effort; yet he did not dismiss completely the thought, for, now and again, at some unexpected moment, he would refer to it.

No effort is necessary to picture him as he appeared the evening we finished the last of these articles. It was Caruso's 1920 name day, July 15. He sat in his workroom in a rented villa at Easthampton, Long Island, cutting strips of Manila paper to be made into huge envelopes. Such work he enjoyed, just as it pleased him to gather the accumulation of newspaper clippings and put them in these homemade receptacles. Afterward he would paste the cuttings, with meticulous care, in scrapbooks. Idleness he disliked; rarely was he satisfied to confine himself to a single task if he could perform simultaneously another. As he grew older he guarded carefully his time; there were few waking hours he did not turn to profitable account. During his final years there was the almost constant companionship with Mrs. Caruso, and the eagerly seized playtime moments with Baby Gloria.

Much that follows in these pages was jotted down

when Mrs. Caruso was actually present, or near by. That first day, in the singer's Knickerbocker Hotel suite (February, 1920), automatically revisualizes itself: a wintry afternoon in New York, as dusk approached, with the narrator modeling on a clay bust of himself as Eleazar in "La Juive"; Mrs. Caruso clicking a small typewriter in one corner of the room.

These were moments for studying the man, his face, his figure, his habiliments, his inherent simplicity. He spoke always with a resonant enough tone, though it was seldom loud or suggestive of a singer, except to music experts aware of the significance of a speaking voice concentrated where nose and forehead join. Caruso's speech was rarely hurried. Deliberation, of a sort which reflected thoroughness, attached to whatever he said and to nearly every movement he made. While seated he had a way of occasionally leaning forward; massive from the waist up, his high-curved, barrel-like chest indicated its store of breathing space and power.

On this February day Caruso was all but ready for the street; he need only have exchanged his dark lounging robe for the customary sack coat. As usual, he was immaculate from head to shoes; the singer particularized in such matters. Surveying one side of Eleazar's nose which had eluded his modeling skill, he half-shut his eyes as though preparing for some mental journey. Having diverted his attention from the rebellious bit of clay, he sat with body relaxed, the stick he had been using protruding from the heavy fingers of his right hand. Directly he put it on the stand before him, to fit a cigarette into a long holder. That done, he began puffing, his head tilted to one side, his shoulders showing square and wide and high under the loose folds of his gown.

At that instant he appeared a Somebody. Authority which he had been acquiring gradually for years was in those days of his life so natural that in such a situation he seemed splendidly aloof. Even the Caruso voice was subservient to this authority, which made him the singer he could not have become with voice alone, though it were this rather special voice.

When Caruso recalled his thoughts to his surroundings that wintry afternoon, it was with a perceptible flexing of his body. Resuming work upon the imperfect side of Eleazar's nose he began his narrative.

CHAPTER TWO

Youth

ENRICO CARUSO was born in Naples, Italy, February 27, 1873, on the first floor of a house at Number 7 via San Giovannello agli Otto Calli. He was the eighteenth son. His parents were both born in Piedimonte d'Alife: Marcellino Caruso on March 8, 1840, Anna Baldini on May 29, 1838.

It is difficult to reconcile the foregoing dates, and no birth records are available to substantiate them. Caruso and his brother Giovanni — speaking on different occasions — were in agreement as to the ages of their father and mother; each stated that there were twenty Caruso boys and one girl.

None of the seventeen children had survived infancy, so, as Enrico thrived and approached his third year, a new happiness crept into the Caruso household. January 8, 1876, gave it a fresh impetus, when Giovanni was brought into the world; but between him and Enrico another son had come "without the strength to live." Assunta, the only girl, followed Giovanni on August 10, 1882, the twenty-first Caruso child. She died June 2, 1915, adoring her brother Enrico who, apart from providing for her every comfort, had shown her a constant tenderness throughout her somewhat melancholy life.

Anna Caruso had been too ill to nurse her Enrico. Signora Rosa Baretti, a woman of gentle birth living

THE HOUSE WHERE CARUSO WAS BORN

The cross over the third window from the left marks the room where Caruso was born. Immediately adjoining the house stands the church where he was baptized. The house is No. 7 via San Giovannello agli Otto Calli, Naples.

Photo L. Grassi, Napoli.

YOUTH 11

in the same house, was the one who volunteered to save a life. In later years Caruso insisted that it was she who had put into him some of her own bigheartedness.

When he was six, and the family moved to Number 54 via San Cosmo e Damiano, Enrico was sent to a kindergarten, where he remained for two years. At the time his father had employment as a mechanic in the factory of a Signor Francesco Meuricoffre, being advanced, about 1881, to superintendent. In this year his employer gave him the use of a house in Sant' Anna alle Paludi, which belonged to the factory. So once again the Caruso family transferred their belongings, — to a more permanent abode; they remained in it until Enrico Caruso reached manhood and began seriously his professional career.

From this home, at the age of eight, the boy Enrico made his first acquaintance with a public school. No emphasis was put upon it in the narrative, although it is on record that he was required to wear a black cap circled with a blue band, — a sort of insignia of this school. It is known too that he was industrious: he had an eagerness to learn, and even then he was a most considerate son. For his mother he showed his love in those practical ways not always displayed by children older: he was always ready to help her about the house, to do errands; and often he hovered beside her bed when she fell ill, for, after the birth of Assunta, Mrs. Caruso never completely regained her health.

This devotion so intensified the bond between

mother and son that there grew between them a deep and sympathetic understanding. "If you were to go into the neighborhood where we then lived," Caruso once said, "and ask of the old-time residents for Marcellino's son, none would know who was wanted; but an inquiry for 'the treasure of Marcellino's family' would bring the instant answer: 'Oh! you mean Enrico Caruso.'"

The treasure of the family developed early responsibilities affecting his mother's welfare. If not the actual head of the house, he served somewhat regularly in that capacity. Marcellino Caruso was fond of wine, and his not infrequent absence of evenings put upon Enrico, as eldest child, certain duties.

It was inevitable that this companionship should have had its effect upon an impressionable nature. Giovanni Caruso spoke of it when he arrived in New York, from Naples, three months after the death of his brother. Mrs. Caruso has told of little things her husband unconsciously let drop which sketched intimate word pictures.

An insistence for neatness and order and personal immaculateness, which possessed the tenor during later periods of his life, took root during his childhood. There was no grumbling at having to carry upstairs pails of water for his bath; every such opportunity was more than casually welcomed, — one appears to have been made on any pretext possible. To keep himself fresh, his hair brushed, his clothes free from dust and spots — these were matters the boy refused to neglect. And pride was

YOUTH

stirred in the mother when she gazed on her slender son and beheld his efforts which did her credit. For all his tenderness and devotion, however, the then future great artist was nevertheless a boy; pretty much all boy, and at times a capricious one. Such manifestations became noticeable soon after he joined a school where boys were trained to sing in church choirs, which was conducted evenings at Number 33 via Postica Maddalena by Father Giuseppe Bronzetti. Giovanni Gatto, a sort of tutor and brother-in-law to Bronzetti (who died in 1893 with the devoted Caruso at his bedside), spoke in 1921 of incidents touching the little Enrico not long after he entered this school, at the age of six. Gatto — one of a considerable number of Italians who later owed many of their life comforts to the singer's bounty — had Enrico in charge; he called him Carusiello. He remembered well occasions when the youthful singer (a moment approaching for him to contribute a contralto solo in some music performance in the church where the sessions were held) was as difficult to manage as a prima donna displeased over some magnified triviality. "He could be coaxed, by appealing to his gentler nature," explained Gatto, "but meeting his opposition with force seldom succeeded." One exception he related found the boy's father playing a stern rôle, after Enrico, in a fit of temper, had torn from his coat two silver medals given him for singing excellence, and thrown them at the feet of Bronzetti. Administering a slap to Enrico his parent said, "Kneel down, and kiss Father Bronzetti's hands and feet!"

— and the boy did so. Thereupon he went almost immediately before the people who sat waiting, "to sing like an angel", declared Gatto.

Caruso's first training in singing and music was received from Maestro Alessandro Fasanaro, who discovered his gifts of voice and expressiveness while teaching his pupil his school hymns. It was Fasanaro who encouraged the little dark-skinned lad; Fasanaro who guided and stimulated him, and by studying his nature appealed to that side of it which could be so easily reached by one willing to exert the patience. A charge of five *lire* a month was paid, at the beginning, by Mrs. Marcellino Caruso for the privilege of having her son attend the school; later, as he progressed, Bronzetti refused to take this money. Punctuality, neatness, and industry carried Enrico along. By hard work he finally became the principal soloist of the chorus.

In Naples every church is called upon to participate in various ceremonies. One of them is a religious procession through the streets, which takes on importance through the joining of choirs from different churches. Father Bronzetti's choir was greatly sought during the period Enrico Caruso served as a member. Maestro Fasanaro, receiving fees from the churches which he visited with his charges, rewarded them with pennies. To his contralto soloist, who always attracted the most notice and favor by his singing, Fasanaro was more liberal; for Carusiello there was generally several *lire*. With presents of candy, and sometimes a coin or two from admiring priests, the boy's earnings were enough to make him happy. Yet he seldom kept them; "the hole in the Caruso pocket" had developed even thus early.

His position in the Bronzetti school appears to have been easily and completely taken. He craved companionship, and won it. He could, and did, invite the affection of his elders because of a character they were unable to resist. He was playful and serious, in turn — often unexpectedly so. Gatto tells of suddenly developed moods, when an appearance to sing impended, or had passed; moods which presented the tranquil and lovable Carusiello with an unyielding front, — a strange little person, standing firmly upon a dignity that might have been the more amusing but for its disturbing consequences.

On one occasion, returning to Naples from Amalfi, a neighboring town where the choir had gone to sing the Mercadante Mass in the Church of St. Andrea, Enrico declined obstinately to enter a coach with his mentor and his companions; he would ride on the box with the coachman. And ride he did, until Gatto, observing that his charge had dropped fast asleep and fearing he might fall under the horses, transferred him bodily to the interior of the coach — where he continued for the remainder of the journey to slumber placidly.

These evening sessions at the Bronzetti school were fruitful to Carusiello in other respects than music. If Fasanaro and others of the small faculty did their share, there was one of a different calling who must not be overlooked, Giuseppe Spasiano, the penmanship teacher. Quite early during the little pupil's attendance, Spasiano made his particular discovery: here was a boy with a natural facility to use either pen or pencil. No urging was needed to win his interest; he took to drawing as happily as does the proverbial duck to water. And Spasiano suggested, and corrected, and dropped the necessary words to induce the substitution of pains for speed. Hunched over his desk Carusiello would forget — temporarily, at least — about music. As he acquired skill Spasiano gave him manuscripts to copy, which skill — highly developed in his mature years — came to be of practical use. For it is a curious fact that Caruso learned the words and notes of his opera rôles by copying them. He explained that the process assisted materially in impressing them on his memory.

The influence of his instructors in this unpretentious institution appears to have affected the youthful Caruso very positively, in ways that held even after he passed actively out of it, about 1887. Before that he had been taught by Alfredo Campanelli and Domenico Amitrano, pianists and coaches in the Bronzetti school; and by Giovanni Gatto's daughter, Amelia, an excellent musician and pianiste. There is some hint that she formed for Caruso a violent attachment, though he was much her junior; but nothing ever came of it. With her the boy studied *solfeggi*, also solo compositions he was preparing for appearances outside the school.

Eager in his pursuit of knowledge of music and singing, Caruso did not hesitate to accept whatever instruction offered, some of it from sources other than were available at Bronzetti's. He was only ten

YOUTH

when he met Ernesto Schirardi, a pianist, and Maestro Raffaele de Lutio; little more than a baby, yet even then regularly employed for pay. He had bidden farewell to the public school, turning from teachers and comrades to the mechanical laboratory of Salvatore de Luca. His wages were two *soldi* an hour. Schirardi and de Lutio gave the small Caruso advice as to how he should use his voice, and together they taught him some arias from operas.

During these days he revealed those industrious leanings which, years later, became almost an obsession. He would come home, dead tired, from work; then set himself to some musical task. First, however, he always made himself clean; and he has related how, wishing to surprise his mother, he once bought with some treasured pennies a large sheet of stiff white paper, and cut it into a shirt bosom, which he tucked inside his coat.

Developing ambition, and setting a higher value upon his services shortly after his eleventh birthday, Caruso suggested to his superior in the de Luca laboratory that he be given more money. A refusal was his answer. Was it possible? Could it be that all his energy and faithfulness were to go unrewarded? He stiffened his slender body, and with much seriousness resigned. He took himself then to the establishment of Giuseppe Palmieri, where iron drinking-fountains designed for public use were manufactured. One of these drinking fountains, which he had built, he always visited when, years afterward, he returned during his vacations to Naples. For two years he continued in helping to quench the people's thirst; he admitted, however, that his heart and mind were all for music. More than one evening found him earning a *lira* or two for singing a serenade under the window of some Italian maid — while her suitor stood near, looking upwards for some recognition of the vocal tribute he had paid to have bestowed. It was an avocation that generally called forth remonstrances from Carusiello's Bronzetti instructors for taxing his precious voice. Occasionally the enterprising contralto would find some small engagement to participate at a social affair, or in some religious service; he was born to be an artist and no day's labor at the shop left him lacking in either will or desire to accept with enthusiasm whatever fell in his way.

If Marcellino Caruso manifested no great interest in his son's semi-professional progress, his wife supplied enough. But she was wise. The praise a sensitive boy needs to encourage him was never denied. She was generally present, when the occasion was one making it proper for her to appear; afterward Enrico would go to her for his most cherished reward. These were proud moments for both mother and son. She no doubt saw farther into his future than others could have seen. The maternal instinct is a wonderous thing. Yet she was careful never to say too much; hers seems to have been a far-seeing course, tempered with judicious restraint. So the boy, for all his small successes, acquired no egotistical poses. If they perhaps smoldered within him, they were lovingly smothered. The best, and that alone, was nurtured by the woman who had so little yet so very much to give this son she had borne. The years were few allowed her for her task; still, in some ways, they were enough. The memory of them, and of her, never slipped from the mind of the one who was thus fortunate in the molding his nature then received. Who can estimate what effect it had upon his future work! Caruso undertook once to do so. But words would not come.

CHAPTER THREE

WORKING DAYS

WHEN Caruso was nearly fifteen he was given his final opportunity for scholastic study. It came at private hands. Signorina Amelia Tibaldi Niola, sister of Doctor Raffaele Niola, who had attended Mrs. Marcellino Caruso during her illnesses, was Enrico's tutor. She was a cultivated woman, strict in the Italian speech. Her set purpose in one direction was to break her pupil of his habit of a too free use of the Neapolitan dialect; and it was this insistence, and the boy's carelessness one evening, that brought him a slap so hard as to end forever his school days.

"The next night," said the tenor in relating the incident, "I took my books and left home as usual — though not for my lesson. The railway yards were near. I played there each evening for two weeks, with my boy friends, until time to go home.

"One day my father met Doctor Niola, who wished to know why I had stopped going to his sister.

"'He does go,' said my father, 'regularly.'

"'Then he must lose his way,' replied the doctor.

"The following evening my father appeared while I was playing, and took me home for punishment I still remember. Soon after he put me at work with him at the Meuricoffre plant."

Although official records disclose Caruso as having made his opera début, when twenty-one, in "L'Amico Francesco", his first appearance actually took place nearly seven years before. It was at the Bronzetti school, in a work written by Maestri Campanelli and Fasanaro to secure funds for that institution. Considerable opposition was offered to the proposal to give an operatic piece in a church, but it was finally overcome. "I briganti nel giardino di don Raffaele" was the title of this opera. It was quasi-comic and not too difficult for the boys to sing. Carusiello, being the comedian of the school, was cast for the rôle of a *bidello* — a sort of janitor — don Tommaso. Peppino Villani, the solemnest youth of all, assumed the part of Lulu, a girl. The performance developed into a success; but it did not foreshadow with accuracy the future careers of the two young singers who carried off chief honors, though many who were present ventured predictions. Years afterward, Villani became one of Italy's most celebrated comedians, while Caruso was engaged oftenest with tragic rôles.

His time apportioned to work, singing, and play, Caruso followed each with an intensity characteristic. Indifference touched no part of him; he seems almost never to have approached anything, whether out of necessity or choice, in half-hearted fashion. No regular contributions to the family exchequer, slender though it was, were exacted of him. His earnings were regarded as his own, and he spent them as he saw fit: for apparel, of which he was boyishly fond; the theater; and, since it was the custom for the Neapolitan boys of his acquaintance to play occasional games of chance, some of his money was lost to luckier playmates.

Free-handed and sunny; respecting with almost stiff-necked rigidity a promise or obligation, he was, for all his temperamental moments, sensitive to the good opinion of others. Shrinking from disputes, Caruso gave evidence all through his youth of that disposition, so marked in maturity, to avoid the unpleasant. To make and retain friendships, to lend a helping hand when he could, or a word of cheer — that was his nature; and, if it was not a consciously courted popularity, he found himself generally inviting a welcome wherever he went. Enhancing these qualities were his strain of comedy-making and his voice, — a combination rare enough to set him apart from others.

As he continued more and more to sing in different places his reputation gradually widened. He grew, after a time, to be known as the little divo, Errico, a name in point of fact, which was his own; Enrico did not evolve until the tenor became very well known. Although he walked onward in those days, it was for this Italian boy no flowery path; there were hidden thorns to prick his sensitiveness.

No formal declaration of preparing him for a singing career was ever voiced; no family powwow, no laying of plans, nor house-top shouting. Events shaped the Caruso future, and with them he moved, grateful for what might follow. He seized with fervor, however, every new opportunity, putting into

ANNA BALDINI-CARUSO, MOTHER OF ENRICO
From a pastel drawing which stood at Caruso's bedside.

each effort — as he did to the very last — every resource he had.

About the time he entered the employ of the Meuricoffre establishment, Caruso had become sought after to sing in the May church celebrations which abound in Naples. Mary's month, it is called; and always is it set apart by the populace to pay homage to the Blessed Virgin. The music festivals that close these celebrations were pretentious; there was scarcely a good singer but got his chance. The one which knocked at the Caruso door on June 1, 1888, found a boy wavering in a distressed mood, because his mother lay seriously ill. He did not wish to leave her, but she insisted; and thus urged, though with misgivings, he trudged gloomily to the Church of St. Severino, there to perform his part in the festival of the Corpus Domini holiday, in which Maestro Amitrano was to conduct the music. He would lift his contralto voice, he argued to himself, pouring forth his heart in thanks for such a mother.

In the midst of the service came an interruption. People who had seen the father emerge weeping from his house came looking for Enrico. Anna Caruso had gone on her final exploration while the son she adored was engaged in the work which she loved best to have him do.

II

The work at the Meuricoffre plant served well, at this juncture, for a sorrowing boy incapable of finding any heart for his cherished song. Serenading could not woo him — nor even the church choir.

Affairs in the motherless Caruso home suffered confusion, with soberly eaten meals; but such a condition could not be expected to continue indefinitely. Marcellino Caruso ministered as best he knew how to his brood of three, helped by the manful Enrico. After a time, the practical side of life persisting, a bit of sunshine appeared. Then, as the weeks slipped by, the natural buoyancy of youth prevailed.

Work at Meuricoffre's continued, and, presently, Enrico experienced again the desire to sing. True, his mother was gone, yet she at least no longer suffered; and had she not taken a deep joy in his music? So the inevitable happened, bringing the boy, by gradual processes, back to that longing which was his master. Even Marcellino Caruso acquiesced; he was not unwilling that his son should indulge his voice. Perhaps he also, by this time, had some premonition of what was to come; possibly the occasional nightly earnings helped the paternal decision.

In the meantime, however, Enrico Caruso's voice had undergone a change from a boyish contralto into a tenor — a somewhat thin one, yet, for all that, a tenor. There being a demand for even thin-voiced tenors, provided they could sing, Enrico knew little idleness. Church music was his recognized forte, and it brought him moderate rewards. The religious festivals came oftener to be attended by the sound of his youthful tenor; and as he continued to sing the Caruso name was more frequently mentioned.

There were, in the nature of things, transitions in the Caruso family. Enrico, sobered by cares, strove to meet the situation, but Giovanni was still a child, and Assunta could not, because of infirmities, be called on to assume even slight responsibilities or domestic duties. The need of a mother for his children must have dwelt in the heart of Marcellino Caruso when he journeyed to Aversa, some four months after the death of his wife, to install in a factory owned by a Baron Ricciardi machinery he had purchased from Signor Meuricoffre.

It developed that the lodging secured for Marcellino Caruso during his stay in Aversa was in the home of Maria Castaldi. A widow, she apparently found matters of common interest to herself and her temporary widower guest. And there is every indication that the two came without much delay to an understanding, for they were married on November 18, 1888, within a few weeks after their first meeting.

No mother could have been tenderer than this new one which the Church and law gave to the Caruso children, and who was brought into their home within six months after Anna Baldini Caruso had been laid at rest. She was gentle; she had patience; and she bestowed upon her small charges an affection which gradually brought to them what they unconsciously sought. To Enrico was she especially drawn; something in his nature seemed to cry out that he needed her most. For her he was almost a model child; quite the opposite of Giovanni, whose irresponsible ways were a source of annoyance. "Whatever Enrico did was always right," recently declared Giovanni, "but I was forever getting into trouble of my own making." The singer, to his very last days, loved and revered his stepmother. It always disturbed him that — despite his repeated urging to the contrary — she preferred to continue living modestly.

III

The working days of the young Enrico Caruso continued in the Meuricoffre establishment even after it had been partly denuded of its mechanical equipment, for it was a business having several sides. There was one department given over to the manufacture of cotton oil; another for purifying cream of tartar; and a third, which was a warehouse. Raw and finished material, after being inventoried, would be stored in it, and against this merchandise warehouse certificates were issued and deposited with banks as collateral for loans.

Business having receded to a threatening point when Enrico Caruso had passed his sixteenth birthday, and a reduction of the working force becoming necessary, Signor Meuricoffre proposed to the elder Caruso that his son be made a sort of accountant in charge of the records of such materials as might be received for refining purposes, and also of records covering whatever was stored in the warehouse. Approached in the matter, the boy appeared to doubt his ability to perform duties of such responsibility, but his employer soon discovered in his new accountant and receiving clerk abilities of an unusual sort. Enrico came early each morning to his desk; he kept his sets of figures accurately; and he saw

WORKING DAYS

to it that the Meuricoffre property was safeguarded from petty thefts. It was work that called for accuracy, alertness, and a shrewd mind; and required many hours of each day to complete. There were periods, however, when a lessening of business activities enabled the young singer to accept out-of-town engagements; and he had his vacation days, also.

It was during one of these recreation terms, in the summer of 1890, that patrons of cafés heard between dances the Caruso voice. One Saturday night the tenor attracted the notice of a man who, as Caruso expressed it, "liked my voice if not my way of using it."

"You do not sing correctly," observed the critic; "you should study." "But," answered the tenor, "I have no money." "Never mind about the money, my brother is a teacher of singing; I will take you to him."

Caruso went for a time to this teacher, climbing five flights of stairs to the studio, which he always reached out of breath. Convinced after the eleventh lesson that the "covering" of his high tones in the manner advocated was injuring them, Caruso paused in his vocal studies as suddenly as he had begun them. For one year he continued in his former technical ways; then came the unexpected.

He had joined forces with a young pianist to entertain bathers at the Risorgimento Baths, in via Caracciolo, in Naples. During the previous summer the tenor had had similar opportunities to display his vocal gifts for such pieces of money as generously inclined persons had seen fit to bestow. "Come here and sing," the owner of the baths had said. "What my patrons give to you you may keep; I will take no percentage." A like arrangement existed at the baths during the few weeks in the summer of 1891, which found Caruso singing often without receiving a solitary *lira*. He has admitted that those days were pleasant to remember; that they brought him no real unhappiness. Toward the end of the summer he met Eduardo Missiano, a baritone singer in comfortable circumstances, whose interest in the struggling tenor was to influence so vitally his future career. Relating his first meeting with Missiano, who was preparing for a career, Caruso said his new acquaintance asked him if he were studying. "I explained that I had no money for study." "Never mind," encouraged Missiano, "you have a fine voice; I will take you to my maestro Guglielmo Vergine, and somehow arrange for him to teach you."

But Vergine displayed less enthusiasm for the Caruso voice and its possibilities than his pupil had shown. He thought it a small voice which sounded "like the wind whistling through a window." Dejectedly silent, Caruso waited while his newly found friend argued with the seemingly disinterested Vergine (for subsequent developments lead to the belief that the maestro may have chosen to conceal his real feelings). At length Vergine said, "Very well, come back in eight days, and I will hear him again." Reluctantly consenting, after this second trial, to accept Caruso as a pupil, Vergine declared warningly, "but don't expect too much of yourself." He proceeded then to drawing a contract — one of those remarkable documents which continue to be made between impecunious singers and avaricious teachers — which provided that Caruso should pay Vergine twenty-five per cent of his total earnings for *five years of actual singing*. This was the "joker" clause in the contract. It would have taken the tenor many times five years in his profession to have fulfilled the terms; and an Italian court tried for two years to reach a decision. In 1899, when Caruso was singing in Rome, Vergine went to him. A reconciliation was effected, an understanding brought about, and on the payment to Vergine of twenty thousand *lire* the contract was torn up.

The lessons began shortly after arrangements had been reached, though they were rather unusual lessons. Vergine taught in classes. It was his practice to assemble his pupils in a large room, and then to call on various ones to sing specific technical exercises and arias. He would admonish and approve; he would call for criticisms from members of the class; and passing from one pupil to another, each found an opportunity to be heard and enlightened. Throughout several of these class-lessons Caruso was not surprised at being ignored; he considered himself as undergoing a preparatory period valuable for what it offered one to hear and observe. But as weeks passed without his being called on to sing, the tenor grew anxious. One day he volunteered to sing some phrases to illustrate a point Vergine had explained generally to the class, whereupon Vergine exclaimed, "What, are you still here?"

Persistence, however, brought its reward. Or it may have been — as it doubtless was — Vergine's way of protecting his pupil from developing a suspected overconfidence. Permitted, at length, to sing, Caruso found the hand of restraint laid heavily upon any aspirations he may have had to use his full voice. He listened to other tenors with tones stronger than his. He heard the maestro's favorable comments of their efforts. Often, as he has confessed, he thought slightingly of his own chances as compared with those colleagues who delivered ringing high tones, which sounded many times more effective than his own voice of "the whistling wind." Yet, for all the discouragement, the subdued pupil progressed. It may have been a slow growth, but it appears to have been sure. And the tenor always insisted that he was taught with infinite care and skill. "It was Vergine," he once explained, "who emphasized the necessity of singing as nature intended, and who constantly warned — 'Don't let the public know that you work.'"

Such instruction had a tendency to keep the Caruso voice light. It was not until some six years after those first Vergine lessons, when he came under the influence of Vincenzo Lombardi, that Caruso really allowed his voice to come free, with the natural power back of it which was necessary for the disclosure of its fullest beauty and resource. To force the tone is unquestionably a grave error for any singer to commit, yet an equally grave error is to baby the voice by a repression of energy.

This practice of vocal restraint was responsible

for much of the criticism visited upon the public endeavors of the then young artist. It was undoubtedly to some extent the cause of his inability — for all the natural facility he possessed — to sing high notes with fullness and ease. Had he persisted in those earlier technical ways he might have continued longer to "break" on high A-flats and B-flats, as was his not infrequent custom even after he had achieved considerable recognition on the operatic stage.

Established at last in the studio of a maestro he respected, Caruso directed his efforts toward improving his opportunities. His perfect trust in Vergine is reflected in the calmness he showed under criticism for not using more voice. He was content to follow instructions and advice; and if he failed to please completely all his hearers, there were enough who approved of his singing to confirm his belief that Vergine's way was perhaps the best.

Occupied all day long at Meuricoffre's, Caruso had little time after working hours for more than vocal practice and such singing as fell his way. He never studied any instrument, or music on its scientific side. Though musical in an unusual degree, he was never a musician. He sang, when he developed into an artist, in a more musicianly manner than some singers who were musicians; but such subjects as harmony were destined, to the end of his days, to remain to him a mystery. This lack of intimate understanding of music on its higher side was not, however, to prove a handicap. The singer had an unerring feeling for accuracy of pitch; his sense of time and of rhythm must from the beginning have been exceptional; and he once said that he learned thoroughly with reasonable quickness. Still, even these attributes, and a studious nature, could not overcome the handicaps imposed in those days when the greater part of the young singer's time was passed at a desk or in some part of the Meuricoffre plant. Not until he was twenty-one, upon his return from his brief military service at Rieti, did Caruso forsake business and give himself wholly to his musical career. The period from 1891 to the spring of 1894 was passed in going to and from his daily labors; in frequent lessons at Vergine's studio; in singing when and where he could find an opportunity; and in snatching some leisure moments for companionship with his youthful friends.

Permitted by Signor Meuricoffre to absent himself from business for any church festival engagements, Caruso experienced, about 1891, a certain demand for his services during festival times. Some of these festivals were in neighboring towns; and attending them were occasional incidents to be remembered. One in particular, which occurred in the village of Majori, seemed to have impressed the tenor in an unforgettable way. He had been engaged at a fee of ten *lire* ($2) a service by a contractor who was supplying all the musicians for this particular church. On the final evening of his Majori engagement, his churchly duties over, Caruso was preparing to leave for the fifteen-mile journey to Naples, when the contractor called to him. "Your work is not finished," he said, "you must go with

WORKING DAYS 33

me to sing at a reception in the home of Baron Zezza, the mayor." The young singer could but comply. He had no other course, after he had once sung for the mayor's guests, than to sing whenever he was asked — which proved to be often and long continued, for it was six o'clock the next morning when he learned that he might depart.

Enthusiastic over the young tenor's voice and singing, Baron Zezza insisted on escorting Caruso to the door; but instead of the mild temperature of the evening before, they found the air biting and raw. It would never do to risk catching cold on the stage ride to Naples, so the mayor procured for the singer an old shooting jacket, which he insisted Caruso should keep as a remembrance of that particular occasion.

It was in 1913, while he was filling an engagement in Covent Garden, London, that Caruso was reminded of the incident in a letter from Baron Zezza which read, "If you are the Enrico Caruso who sang more than twenty years ago in one of the Majori church festivals, I wish to know why you did not return to me the overcoat I then loaned you. If you are that one, please return to me the overcoat."

To this communication the tenor replied, "I am the Enrico Caruso who sang in the city at the time you mention; but I did not intend to preserve for the remainder of my life the overcoat which you offered as a souvenir. I cannot return it, since I do not know what has become of it. But if you desire to have an overcoat, or the value of one, you must first send me the amount of money for the work I did in your house, because I was not paid for it. Such amount must be what I receive to-day, which is $2000. This is a special favor, for twenty years ago my voice was the same voice of to-day, with the difference that I now sing only three hours. In your house I sang for eight hours. You must also add the interest for twenty years."

Baron Zezza's answer was, "I had not the slightest intention of annoying you about the coat. I merely wished to learn if that boy who sang at my house is the Enrico Caruso who is having such a wonderful career. I am content to have as my souvenir his autograph." He got it, an inscribed photograph of the singer, in a frame, and also a silver hunting flask.

At twenty, Caruso was summoned to be physically examined for military service. This official communication all but threw him into a panic. Visions possible only to such an imagination as was his sent him in search of friends, and they in turn found a man of influence who reassured them. This influential person doubted, he said, whether the young Caruso would pass the physician's test. He was slender; his very appearance suggested a delicate constitution. The matter, in any event, need cause them no concern; there were ways of bringing about the rejection of a prospective soldier. But when the tenor in trepidation presented himself to the military examining board, he was pronounced mentally and physically fit to serve his country. Thereupon he was given written notice to prepare

ASSUNTA CARUSO, ONLY SISTER OF ENRICO   MARCELLINO CARUSO, FATHER OF ENRICO

After photographs by H. Mishkin, N. Y., from a medallion in the possession of Giovanni Caruso, brother of Enrico.

WORKING DAYS

for a regimental call which might come at any hour after his twenty-first birthday.

The story which Caruso himself told the writer of his military experiences is perhaps the most vivid one possible to record. It was in late February of 1894 when he bade farewell to his father and stepmother, and to Giovanni and Assunta, and "set out for Rieti, by way of Rome — where I was to join my regiment, the Thirteenth Artillery. During the eight days of my stay in Rome I met with harsh treatment from the junior lieutenant of my battery, who, for reasons I have never learned, took a violent dislike to me. Discovering that I was a poor horseback rider, he seized every occasion when I was mounted to make me more uncomfortable. He would come to my side and roughly turn my feet to bring them into the proper positions. Often he would hit me across the legs with a quirt. When we finally reached Rieti his persecution ceased.

"Wishing to take advantage of the free time, from four in the afternoon to eight, to exercise my voice, I searched for a suitable place and found it in the large drill hall. The day we were settled in the Rieti camp I was doing my exercises when a corporal came into the hall and called to me. 'Quickly!' called the corporal. 'The major wants to see you.' I asked, 'What does he want?' The corporal answered, 'I don't know; maybe he has some letters for you from your family, or maybe he wishes to speak to you about your singing.'

"I hoped the major had a letter from my father; I was short of money. Then I thought that perhaps he might wish to compliment me about my voice. I followed the corporal to the door of the major's office, which adjoined the drill hall. Standing there for a few moments without being commanded to enter I asked, 'May I come in?'

"A hard voice answered, 'Yes, come in.'

"I took off my cap as I entered the office and raised my hand in a salute. The major sat before his desk, writing; he did not glance up at me, but that did not prevent him from seeing. He had sharp eyes, Major Nagliati. Finally, after what seemed a long time, he raised his head.

"I stood embarrassed as he looked me all over, and was more embarrassed when he said, 'You must be a stupid one.'

"I didn't answer; it is the rule in the Italian army that a soldier may not answer his superior unless requested to. But why did he call me a stupid one? I quickly found out.

"'Why do you salute when you have no cap on?' demanded the major. 'Don't you know it isn't regulation?' I replied that I was but for eight days a soldier.

"'What name?' snapped the major in his curt, rough voice.

"I told him, 'My name is Caruso, Enrico Caruso.'

"'Oh!' he replied, though it wasn't exactly a reply, but more a sort of involuntary ejaculation, to which I soon discovered he was given.

"'Where from?' he inquired. I said I was from Naples.

"'Why do you bother me, making so much noise?'

"I answered, 'I exercise.'
"'Exercise what?'
"'Exercise my voice,' I replied.
"'Oh!'
"'What did you do before you became a soldier?' he wished to know.
"I explained that I had studied to become a singer.
"'A singer! What for?'
"'For the theater,' I answered.
"'Oh!'
"'How long,' he inquired next, 'must you be a soldier?'
"I said, 'Three years.' He knew this; I wondered why he asked.
"'Three years a soldier, eh? After three years — good night voice.'
"Following a long pause the major stared at me with that first stern look and said, 'I don't want to be annoyed any more with your exercising your voice; I have to work in the afternoons. Now go away.'
"I put on my cap (remembering what he had told me of the regulation) and saluted and went out. The corporal, curious, was waiting for me.
"'What did he want?' demanded the corporal.
"I said, 'He's crazy.'
"But to my surprise, two days later, when Major Nagliati was passing me, he stopped and said, 'What are you doing this afternoon during the free time?'
"'I want to exercise my voice.' I took, somehow, a sudden courage.

"'Well,' he said, 'after you exercise, meet me at the café, at five o'clock.'

"My comrades who had witnessed the incident rushed up to me as soon as Major Nagliati was out of distance. They were eager to learn what had prompted a commissioned officer to stop me after such fashion. Upon being told of the summons to appear that afternoon at the little café popular at that time with the officers, the soldiers began to speculate on what might happen to me.

"'He will try to send you to prison,' predicted one of them; then he walked off, whistling.

"Promptly at five o'clock I arrived at the café, but I took care not to enter; a private soldier in the Italian army was not permitted to enter such a place when he knew his superior officer was there. Looking through the doorway I could see Major Nagliati seated at a small table at the rear of the café. He was reading a newspaper and smoking a cigarette. I walked up and down before the entrance, pausing occasionally to glance within and hoping thereby to attract the major's notice; but he only continued to read and smoke. Finally he summoned a waiter (he had seen me the moment I arrived), and I heard him say, 'Tell that soldier outside to come in.' I entered the café and walked to the table where the major sat. He had a bad face, but a good heart.

"'Have you had lunch?' asked Major Nagliati.

"'Yes,' I replied.

"'You say you are a Neapolitan; then you must like coffee. Smoke?' He offered me a cigarette and ordered coffee, after which he returned to his newspaper and ignored me. All the time I tried to guess why he had summoned me there; the major was a strange man. Finally he put down his paper and took out his watch.

"'I think I have found something for you,' he said. 'In this town is a baron who loves music. I have spoken to him about you, and asked that he let you go to his house to exercise your voice. The baron is coming here shortly.'

"In this the major was mistaken, for instead of the baron came his brother — explaining that the baron, unable to keep the appointment, had sent him in his place.

"'Oh!' ejaculated Major Nagliati. 'Well, this is the boy I have spoken of to your brother. Let us go to his house.'

"So we all departed, but the baron was not at home, being still detained with his appointment. The following day, however, I was commanded to go back and I found the baron a kind man. He proved to be a musician and pianist; and he seemed to enjoy playing for me to sing, and correcting my mistakes. I was made happy at this opportunity the major had given me, yet I dared not thank him. I knew he would not have liked that. It was enough for him to know that he had arranged matters as he had; probably he got from the baron reports of me.

"We worked on, and in the first five days with the baron I learned the entire rôle of Turiddu in 'Cavalleria Rusticana.' By this time the whole regiment had learned what was happening. I was taken by my comrades to the drill hall during some of the free time, to sing for them — many songs. But after a few such experiences Major Nagliati appeared, one afternoon, and stopped me. 'How many times must I tell you not to annoy me with your singing?' he demanded. It was his consideration for my voice that caused him to interfere; he realized it might be harmful for me to sing continuously for those soldiers; so he made it impossible for them to continue asking me to do so.

"Twenty days later the major sent for me again.

"'You cannot be a soldier and also a singer,' he informed me. 'I have arranged that your brother Giovanni shall come here at once to take your place.'

"Major Nagliati would not allow me to express the gratitude which overwhelmed me. And on the next day came Giovanni, to be my substitute."

CHAPTER FOUR

Débuts

THIS sudden and unexpected release from military service sent the singer's thoughts soaring. He had emerged from threatened obscurity into the sunlight, and the almost fortuitous touch attached to it moved him deeply. He wished immediately to return home; he wished with a strange intensity to embrace his father and stepmother; but he was not without other desires to which his nature was susceptible. Some celebration seemed proper. At Rome, where he was detained during the formalities of his discharge, and after receiving his pay for having been thirty days a soldier, Caruso found this opportunity. A close friend, Sergeant Angelo Arachite, participated in the farewell dinner, which left the tenor with just two pennies in his pocket. It was perhaps fortunate that the Italian Government had provided the transportation from Rome to Naples, otherwise the journey might have been slower than that made by a train which halted for periods longer than was consumed in the actual time of running. Some bread purchased with the two pennies was all the food Caruso had from midnight on a Saturday until late evening of the next day, Easter Sunday. Bursting joyously in upon his slumbering parents, who knew nothing of his coming, he went happily to bed. But morning brought to him serious thoughts. Work of any sort other than singing had been resolutely put out of his mind. His career was waiting to be made, and the tenor set himself in those limited ways then at his command to attain it.

Church singing, soirée engagements, and the somewhat frequent serenade brought him small sums of money. It was not enough however to meet Caruso's every need. There came also one opportunity to appear in an amateur representation of "Cavalleria Rusticana", given in a small Naples theater for the entertainment of people "who did not pay to go in." This appearance was not considered to have constituted a début; Caruso regarded it as an experience too trivial to detail. In fact, nothing of significance occurred during the summer that followed. It was for the singer an existence of routine, with the lessons in Vergine's classes and rather more study than had previously been possible consuming a fair portion of the time. But work did not seize completely this Neapolitan youth who had just entered man's estate. His fondness for the companionship of his friends sent him regularly into their midst; and the card games in the little cafés continued to hold their fascination for him. Nor was he insensible to feminine charms, or to passing some of his leisure hours in the society of young women toward whom he was drawn. Fortunately he had no serious love affairs, although he was slender of figure, and — as photographs taken of him at the time show — romantic enough in appearance to render him eligible.

The summer of 1894 passed. Autumn, however,

brought a light in the sky of Enrico Caruso's hopes. This light was reflected by Nicola Daspuro, one of the foremost newspapermen of Italy, a respected writer, and — by no means least of all — the general representative for the south of the Milan music-publishing house of Sonzogno. Daspuro had obtained in 1893 from the municipality of Naples the concession to operate for twenty-five years the Theater Mercadante (better known as the Fondo). And he had at once arranged with Edoardo Sonzogno, head of his firm, to supply the Mercadante for three consecutive years a season of opera and ballet. After having his theater remodeled and redecorated, Daspuro reopened the Mercadante doors on December 6, 1893, with an inaugural representation by the Sonzogno organization. That season is still talked about in Naples. It compelled by the brilliancy of its achievements the closing of the San Carlo Theater, and no wonder! Sonzogno had engaged an unique company in which there were nine celebrated tenors (among them Roberto Stagno, Francesco Tamagno, and Angelo Masini), twenty-two prime donne (including Gemma Bellincioni, wife of Stagno, and Adelina Stehle), and three widely known ballerine, Mlle. Danesi, Mlle. Cerri, and la Côte d'Or, from the Vienna Opera House. In such circumstances it was natural that Daspuro, occupying so conspicuous a position in the lyric world of Italy, should have subsequently been sought out by singing maestri anxious to place in the Sonzogno Company their most proficient pupils.

"In the fall of 1894," said Daspuro, "Maestro

Guglielmo Vergine, a very good singing teacher whom I knew, called on me and recommended warmly a young tenor then studying with him — a certain Caruso — whose voice he declared to be of exceptional beauty and angelic sweetness. I expressed my regret at being unable to satisfy Vergine's desire to have his pupil appear during the approaching Mercadante season, since my company was *au complet;* but instead of discouraging the maestro, my refusal only moved him to renew his assurances — with a color of expressiveness to be found only in a Neapolitan soul — of the celestial qualities of his pupil, whose voice Vergine insisted was absolutely phenomenal. He continued begging me as a god — invoking the names of all my dead — to at least give this young tenor a hearing. To be rid of this insistent person I at length said, 'All right; bring this tenor with you, and let me hear his phenomenal voice.'

"The next morning Vergine and Caruso appeared at the Mercadante and Caruso sang for me. I liked him immensely. His voice was really beautiful. What impressed me most was his clear enunciation, and an accent full of warmth. I congratulated him and Vergine as well; and thereupon promised to try to arrange to have Caruso sing in one of the matinée performances within the next few months, although he had thus far never appeared publicly on any stage. When my first conductor, Maestro Giovanni Zuccani, came some time later to Naples to begin his preliminary duties for the 1894–1895 Mercadante season, I summoned Vergine. He brought Caruso for a second audition. Zuccani liked his voice so much that we agreed to have the tenor appear at a matinée representation of Ambrose Thomas's "Mignon"; and we asked him to make ready for a piano rehearsal. The day finally arrived; but alas! what a different Caruso. The extreme sensitiveness of his temperament, the nervous excitement caused by finding himself surrounded by singers and maestri of repute and his lack of complete familiarity with his rôle seemed almost to have paralyzed Caruso's mental faculties and to have tightened his throat. Maestro Zuccani and I sought fruitlessly to encourage him. He only confused the words of his text, began and finished phrases out of *tempi*, and, beyond all these and other mistakes, his voice cracked and broke to pieces on all his high notes. Maestro Zuccani was patient and kind until he wearied of correcting the struggling Caruso. Then my conductor lost his temper, and turning to me declared that it was impossible to take this tenor to the footlights. Vergine and Caruso, furiously angry with Zuccani, left the theater in tears. After this experience I did not hear from them for a long time."

For all the discouragement which fell so heavily upon Caruso through his failure to grasp an alluring opportunity to appear in an opera house of the first rank, the tenor was not defeated. Soon after his experience with Daspuro and Zuccani he was approached by a professor of the contrabass who had played often with Caruso in church. He spoke to his younger friend of "a very good chance to make a début." A young maestro, of considerable financial means, Mario Morelli by name, had written his first opera and was planning to present it before privately invited audiences. The opera was in four acts, with the tenor character serving as the protagonist. "You would have nearly two months in which to study your part," explained the contrabass professor, "and the appointment would bring you eighty *lire* for not less than four performances. I advise you to accept." Himself unwilling to decide, Caruso replied, "Go to Vergine; whatever he tells me to do I will do." Vergine examined the music of the tenor rôle, and instantly recommended his pupil to accept the proposal. Caruso studied his part in the opera, "L'Amico Francesco," which presented him as a man of about fifty. He was amused that Signor Ciabò, the baritone engaged to appear in the character of the tenor's adopted son, was nearly sixty years old. Nothing interfered with the progress of preparations until the night of the general rehearsal. Then, while Caruso was dressing, he discovered that he was lacking shoes and stockings, and also a scarf which it was necessary to have tied about his neck. A request for these articles brought from the costumer no more than a laugh. A few moments later the *regisseur* entered the tenor's dressing room and inquired, "Are you ready?" "Yes," replied Caruso, "if you like." Departing in anger the *regisseur* returned presently with Morelli, who demanded, "Why are you without the necessary parts of your costume? I paid you." Caruso answered that he considered eighty *lire* to be no more than money enough to buy a good dinner before each of the four performances, an opinion in which the composer at length concurred. So Morelli sent out for the needed wearing apparel, and the general rehearsal commenced.

Some music experts, who were not friendly to the young Caruso, had expressed doubts that he would be able to finish the four performances of "L'Amico Francesco." Stories of the tenor's light voice, and Vergine's method of cultivating it, had gotten abroad. The music was looked upon as being too strong for Caruso. So these experts sat back in their seats, in the Nuovo Theater, on a November evening, 1894, expecting a fiasco, and hoping, after the manner of their kind, that it would occur. Events, however, brought no such outcome. That first representation went rather well for the tenor, vindicating the judgment of his maestro, who predicted for his pupil in the second performance of the opera, two evenings later, a more pronounced success.

Neither "L'Amico Francesco" nor its tenor protagonist moved many who were present at the two performances on November 16 and 18 to enthuse. In fact, so slight was the impression caused by the opera that its composer and patron abandoned the proposed two final representations. Whatever disappointment he may have felt, Morelli's gratitude for what Caruso had done prompted him to present the tenor, in addition to his guaranteed *cachet*, with a bonus of fifty *lire*. Moreover, the composer assured Caruso that he might expect an invitation to sing in the première of his next opera, on which he was then at work. It was never given, for, not long afterward, Morelli died.

For Caruso, however, those appearances in "L'Amico Francesco" held potential rewards. He had achieved a début with moderate success; and his singing during the second representation enlisted the increased favor of at least two persons who were in positions to aid in advancing him in his career. One was a famous theatrical agent, Francesco Zucchi; the other Carlo Ferrara, impresario of the Cimarosa Theater, at Caserta, who had journeyed to Naples in search of a tenor for a season of opera he planned to hold during the Quaresima, in 1895. Zucchi, who had followed closely the endeavors of the tenor débutant, became convinced after his second appearance that he possessed the qualities of a future great artist. To Zucchi, the singer became at once the *nicu* Caruso (*nicu*, in the Sicilian dialect, means "little"); and going to him the agent proceeded, with the sweeping authority for which he was noted, to place him under his protecting wings.

Zucchi was at that time a sort of character. He had retired from the stage because of advancing years; but he still had left his old-time aggressiveness, and a loyalty which had drawn about him a host of second-rate artists who looked upon him as their firm protector. The agent had a sort of headquarters in the unpretentious *Caffé dei Fiori*, situated in Naples's via del Municipio; and here he ministered to his followers ruling, if with rough ways, out of a kindly heart.

DÉBUTS 49

Tall, with square shoulders *à la* Tamagno (though thinner than the celebrated tenor), Zucchi had dyed to a deep henna a moustache which bristled upwards towards his freckled cheeks. His appearance was accentuated in ferocity by fluffy hair, which he wore after the manner of Raffaello Sanzio. Zucchi was ever ready, as a good Sicilian, to defend his charges against the claws of the Milanese agents. He always sat at the head of the presiding table; and in every controversy he was the first and the last one to speak. When an impresario from any near-by mountain community came to Naples to form an opera company, Zucchi was prepared to supply a tenor who could spin out the tone like Gayarre, or one who had three such C's as Tamagno possessed. If a prima donna were sought, the singer Zucchi offered had high notes which would put to shame those of Adelina Patti herself; while his bassos — if bassos happened at the moment to be specifically in demand — had low F's that boomed as loud as the big gun mounted on adjacent castle walls. To an impresario who solely needed a *comprimario* singer, Zucchi would say, "I have no second-rôle artists, but to accommodate you, my good friend, I will have one of my first tenors — who usually receives one thousand *lire* a performance — save the situation by singing, for this time only, a secondary part." The first tenor in question might later sign with the impresario for ten *lire* an appearance (happy of this chance to be certain of eating during the ensuing few months); but momentarily his honor had been preserved — by the protecting Zucchi.

II

The contract for Caruso's first appearance in Caserta was negotiated between acts during one of the performances of "L'Amico Francesco." He was visited, while dressing, by Impresario Ferrara of the Cimarosa Theater, and his attorney; and within a few minutes all the arrangements had been made. The tenor once told of the thrill this experience had brought him. He was impressionable; his imagination moved him to peer into the future; but he did not visualize overwell. He was taking his first professional steps; who can blame him if he did not perceive a few that might falter. He sang promiscuously between November and April, in which month was the opening of the Cimarosa Theater season; then, with a light heart, he boarded a train. This engagement, the tenor believed, would send his artistic value either up or down.

"Cavalleria Rusticana" introduced the young singer to Caserta — with Mme. Elena Bianchini-Cappelli, as Santuzza, and Enrico Pignataro in the rôle of Alfio. In their reviews of the next day the newspaper writers commented upon a conflict between the voice of Caruso and his music; his acting they pronounced "awful." There was not much praise for his Faust in the Gounod opera of that name, in which he had as principal associates Mme. Moscati-Ferrara for the Marguerite, Pignataro, the baritone, and a basso named Sternajuoli. An unknown opera, "Camoens", by a Maestro Musoni, was also performed, and soon after forgotten. The slender

DÉBUTS 51

audiences did not make for enthusiasm, nor always for enough money to permit every artist to be paid. On more than one occasion the young tenor was obliged, before he could eat breakfast, to ask Impresario Ferrara for his ten *lire cachet* he had earned the night before. This poor business brought the season to a somewhat abrupt end, sending Caruso homewards with twelve cents to show for his four weeks' work.

The singer, however, was not seriously disturbed by this small misfortune, and June found him, one bright afternoon, waiting like Micawber for something to turn up. In the midst of a game of cards, at which he was engaged in Bella Napoli alla Ferrovia — a little restaurant which he haunted not far from his Sant' Anna alle Paludi home — the singer was interrupted by hearing his name called aloud. He looked up; there stood the impresario of the Bellini Theater, who had come in search of him. It appeared that the tenor who had been engaged to sing in a special Sunday evening performance of "Faust" had suddenly fallen ill. Pignataro, the baritone, who had sung with Caruso during the Caserta season, had suggested his name; so here was another opportunity, a better one than any that had gone before. The fee was twenty-five *lire* — the highest Caruso had yet received — and it was pressed upon him by an anxious manager, gratified perhaps thus to show his relief over an averted disaster to his advertised performance. There was no further card game that day for Enrico Caruso. He departed almost on the heels of the impresario; and within the hour had purchased a pair of white silk trousers as well as a pair of white kid shoes. The next day, Sunday, he strode forth — "the envy of my less well-garbed comrades."

That special Faust representation brought the tenor a success greater than he had expected. After the *Salve Dimora Casta e Pura* romanza of the third act his name was on many a tongue. At the close of the opera the impresario offered him a four weeks' engagement for the approaching autumn, at the same theater. The tenor was happy, for at the age of twenty-two he found himself assured of regular appearances and *cachets* in a season which was virtually certain to go through to the end. Nor was that all, for, after a Bellini Theater appearance in "Rigoletto", in July, Caruso received an invitation to sing for one month in Cairo, Egypt, at the then to him astounding figure of six hundred *lire*. (Enrico Santini, impresario of the Esbekieh Theater, of Cairo, has placed the amount at the somewhat lower figure of sixteen pounds.)

"I made the voyage on an English boat," declared Caruso. "By the second day out from Naples everybody on board knew that they had with them a tenor, so a concert was arranged. The consequences were not unlike those which happened after I had first sung for my regimental comrades in Rieti. I was asked to sing oftener than I thought was good for my voice. Going one night to the bar for a glass of wine, I found the room noisy with the laughter of a group of young Englishmen. They greeted me with enthusiasm and loudly demanded a song.

CARUSO AS TURIDDU, WITH ELENA BIANCHINI-CAPPELLI AS SANTUZZA, IN "CAVALLERIA RUSTICANA"

His first appearance in standard opera, Cimarosa Theater, Caserta, 1895.

'No, if you please,' I answered. 'I have come for my wine, then I must retire.' I started toward the bar, only to be surrounded by these young men — some laughing, others merely smiling, though all of the one mind that I should sing them a song. They continued good-naturedly to urge, and I as good-naturedly asked to be excused. Finally one of their number said to me, 'You will sing for us just one song, and then we will make you a nice present; if you don't sing we will let you take a bath in the Suez Canal.' I of course preferred to sing — not the solitary song requested, but several times. Immediately after my last song the young man who had been the spokesman took his hat and went around to his companions; and into that hat these Englishmen dropped many pounds sterling, until one hundred of these banknotes had been gathered. I was much pleased and made to feel rich. Never before had I had at one time so large a sum. I am not ashamed to say that now (1920), for at that time one hundred pounds was like $100,000 to me to-day."

Egypt offered to the tenor new opportunities, which he dutifully seized. One of them was a first appearance in the "Manon Lescaut" of Puccini, a rôle he had learned with Maestro Enrico Santini, a nephew of the impresario. Caruso sang also in "Cavalleria Rusticana", "Rigoletto", and "La Gioconda", under the bâton of Conductor Alfredo Sarmiento. It was Sarmiento who afterward became his accompanist and prepared him for his introductory "L'Elisir d'Amore" in which, during 1901 at La Scala, he overwhelmed a captious audience.

Mme. Bianchini-Cappelli and Vittorio Ferraguti, a baritone, were members of the Cairo company. Other matters than singing, however, found attraction for the tenor. It was summer; the skies were clear; and two feminine vaudeville singers consumed some of the leisure moments he and Ferraguti had to spare. The situation, though, was odd; for the women could not speak Italian, nor were Caruso and the baritone able to converse in any language than their own. So the couples communicated with one another by making signs. Once, attending a representation of "Rigoletto", the Egyptian entertainers fell into ecstasies over the costumes of their "adored" ones — their voices interested them least of all.

Signora Bianchini-Cappelli, who had been a fellow student of Caruso in the Vergine studios, relates an experience she had with the tenor at his Cairo première of "Manon Lescaut." Only five days had been given them to learn the Puccini score, and Caruso had found difficulty in memorizing the final act. At the performance all went reasonably well until the scene where Manon lies on the ground dying, and begs Des Grieux to go in search of water for her.

"Enrico had gone off the stage, according to the action required," explained Signora Bianchini-Cappelli. "I was suddenly startled to hear him call to me from the wings, 'Don't move; I am going to put the score against your back — otherwise I cannot proceed.' Then he returned to where I was lying, the score of the opera concealed from the audience's view. Never have I felt such embarrassment before the public. I was supposed to be dying, and had gestures to make and movements of my body. But with that score propped against my shoulders, and realizing what it meant to Enrico, I was helpless to do more than hold as still as possible, serving as a human music rack for my comrade. And what did the rascal do? He was bursting to laugh! I could feel that he was, and the thought made me furious; for I had to die lying quite still, and with no chance to make any effect. When the curtain fell I rose and chased Enrico, and threw the score at him, which he had dropped in his flight. Later we made up. Of course, there came a good laugh — not only over that situation but over the mistakes we had made with the words, and the new music we had sung instead of what Puccini had written — which had quite gone from our heads."

There were also other experiences of a different sort: sight-seeing excursions, visits to unusual spots, and a trip on the Nile to the famous pyramids. This last was made with Maestro Santini, in a small boat that, accidentally capsizing, deposited the occupants in murky waters from which both were rescued with mud plastered to their clothing. In their plight the singer and his companions sought a carriage, though without success. Fearful that the muddy garments would leave marks on the seat cushions, each driver refused stonily the pleadings of the would-be fares. Two donkeys finally had to serve Caruso and Santini. Astride these small animals they rode through streets, to the great amusement of beholders.

Caruso did not return to Naples on board an English steamer. He engaged passage on an Italian boat, and, as he expressed it, "in the nice, rich suite which was steerage — because my poor one hundred pounds had been so maltreated during my first days in Cairo that it flew completely away." Good fortune, though, had not departed with it. No sooner had the steamer been made fast at its dock than a representative of the impresario of the Mercadante Theater greeted Caruso, and offered him seven hundred and fifty *lire* a month to sing during the coming winter. Here was news to offset the illness of a rough passage from Egypt.

October came soon enough, bringing the Bellini Theater season into the foreground. Stories of Caruso had been traveling about; so there was some special interest in the "Rigoletto" opening for which the tenor was cast to sing the rôle of the Duke. Hazardous indeed was the task any tenor undertook in those days. Small jealousies were ever loose; a singer had to be judged by others than certain envious companions. It proved to be so in this instance, — as Caruso discovered when he walked out upon the stage, and toward the foot-lights. For there, occupying the entire first row where he could easily see them, were all the best tenors Naples possessed at that time. The position was both trying and exasperating. When the representation was finished, the victim of this quasi-cabal went solemnly home. What did it mean? In the morning he found out. In all the music circles of the city there hovered a principal theme: Caruso was the great fake of the artistic world, a mere nothing in comparison with each tenor who posed as his judge.

"Faust" brought the singer no better fortune. He was easily dispirited; and brooding over this ill-fortune did him no good. His engagement concluded, he experienced a degree of solitude, so far as attracting the attention of impresari was concerned. None went to see him; it was a question in the tenor's mind whether any would care to seek again his services until opportunity came to correct in some measure the poor impression he had caused. So the months slipped by, until the Mercadante season arrived—when the wheel of circumstance once more took a propitious turn.

There had been no formal announcement of Caruso's engagement; his name had no place in the prospectus. Through the courtesy of Federico Candida, of Naples (who provided the information from the manuscript of his book on the history of opera in the theaters of Italy, soon to be published), it seems that not until November 29, 1895, did the name "Caruso" appear on a poster outside the Mercadante Theater — announcing him for an appearance in "La Traviata", with Mme. Kate Bensberg as Violetta, and Ludovico Magni in the part of Germont. This same opera had opened the season only six nights before, with Signor Potenza as Alfredo and Maestro Sebastiani conducting. Reading the name of a new tenor, some of the people exclaimed, "Who is this Caruso?" The question was answered a few hours later to an audience which pronounced him passable.

In those days the singer had no opportunity to coddle his voice. During later years, after it had become precious to both impresari and public, two appearances in any week — three at the most — came to be regarded as a maximum to impose upon it. That season at the Mercadante was for Caruso one of strenuous work; he occasionally sang *twice on the same day.*

He did this on December 15, 1895, appearing in a matinée performance of Bellini's "Romeo e Giulietta" and, that evening, in "La Traviata." December 26 presented the tenor first in "Rigoletto", then in "Romeo e Giulietta." Within twenty-four hours he was called upon for an afternoon representation of "Traviata", and after he had eaten dinner he proceeded to the theater to be heard as the Duke in "Rigoletto." Two days intervened, whereupon — having nothing else to do — Caruso sang a New Year's Day matinée in "Traviata" and a night performance of "Rigoletto." It would have been a task with sufficient rest in between, but this was not possible; every week day was a singing day for the struggling Neapolitan. He wanted the experience of routine; well, he was getting it.

Caruso made enough of his numerous opportunities to move the critics to commend his voice as fresh, clear, and of penetrating effect. He sang in "La Traviata" fifteen times before his engagement was concluded; the opera "Rigoletto" required his services on ten occasions; in "Romeo e Giulietta"

A CARD TO DON ANTONIO MAZZARELLA, OF CASERTA, AT A PERIOD WHEN CARUSO WAS STRUGGLING FOR A LIVING

Naples, 31 January 1895

My dear Don Antonio,

Answering your invitation I inform you that I accept, but with the condition of the fee of L. 15 and the railroad fares. I make this price only for you and because you have remembered me, otherwise they should have to pay me 28 Lire.

Today I will go around to find that piece of music by Paisiello and as soon as I find it I will study it and then I will send it to you.

If you wish to send me the piece you have, rush it to me and let me know the train I shall take to come there.

Thanking you I salute you

Respectfully,

Enrico Caruso

he appeared in the rôle of Tebaldo before fifteen audiences; while in "Faust", essayed for the first time in this season on January 11, 1896 (with Signore Franco and Riso, Signori Bonini and Rossato, and with Vincenzo Galassi conducting), Caruso had three appearances. He finished his endeavors there on February 18, as the Duke. His associates in "Rigoletto" had been Signora Franco as Gilda and Vittorio Ferraguti as the Jester, and, for conductor, Maestro Galassi. Under the bâton of Maestro Sebastiani, "Romeo e Giulietta" had enlisted as Romeo the services of Signora Emma Carelli, who has since become the celebrated impresaria (at the Costanzi, of Rome) of to-day, while Signora Franco sang the Giulietta.

That Mercadante season went on until the final day of the Carnevale, in February, 1896. Several other operas had been performed, "Il Trovatore", "Ugonotti", "La Forza del Destino", "Fra Diavolo", "Il Matrimonio Segreto", "Giannina e Bernardone", and "La Favorita",—in none of which had Caruso appeared. His progress had nevertheless been marked. And in "Faust", particularly, were his accomplishments held to have been the most serious he had achieved.

Also in February the Sicilian agent, Zucchi, undertook to give some special performances of "Faust" in Caserta. He had invited Caruso to be one of the company members, with results disastrous to him and all the others too. Most of these Caserta audiences were peasants. They did not appreciate the artistic value of *bel canto* singing, so with characteristic vehemence they objected — after the second act of the opening presentation — to each of the artists — and with such fury that the season, then and there, met an unexpected demise.

No sooner had Caruso returned to Naples than Impresario Giulio Staffelli put the tenor into a short season at the Bellini Theater. There he sang in "La Traviata", "Rigoletto", "Faust", and "La Favorita" under Maestro Siracusa, striving with seriousness and energy to make every phrase tell. He also sang in a new opera "Mariedda", by Gianni Bucceri.

He was rewarded, after one of these Bellini Theater performances, by receiving an offer from Signor Cavallaro, one of the best-known tournée impresari of that time, who wished to make a several months' tour through Sicily, of a place in his company. The fee was to have been six hundred *lire* a month, a sum which was still tempting enough to the tenor to induce him to accept. He was troubled at the time. The departure of his brother Giovanni with his regiment, for Massaua (Africa), to engage in the Italian-Abyssinian War so depressed Caruso that his impresario feared he could not sing the Mercadante performance on that — February 8 — night. But he did. He finished the remaining appearances scheduled for him; and boarding ship sailed for the island to the south.

The opening of the Sicilian tour was scheduled for Trapani, in the Municipal Theater of that particular town. Caruso found the home of Enrico Pignataro, a baritone member of the company, an

DÉBUTS 61

inexpensive place in which to live; and he sang well enough the preliminary rehearsals of "Lucia di Lammermoor" to satisfy those mainly concerned. Then came the day for the general rehearsal. At two o'clock that afternoon Caruso sat down with his baritone friend for the dinner which must serve until after the evening performance should be over. He drank no more, he declared, than the amount to which he had been accustomed at home; what he apparently failed to take into account was the heavier character of Sicilian wine, for when he at length attempted to rise from the table the tenor discovered that both his legs and his head were unsteady. Insisting that a walk in the air would help, the baritone took his younger companion out of doors. Perhaps had he been content to cease his ministrations all might have gone well. Instead, however, a bracer was mixed for the still dizzy Caruso — and that settled matters completely. He was forced to lie down. Hours passed; eight o'clock arrived, an audience assembled in the municipal theater, and an infuriated impresario, learning of the non-arrival of his principal tenor, sought an explanation of the baritone. Then the truth came out. Caruso was still asleep when theater attachés reached him. It was nearly one hour afterward when he walked upon the stage, his head by no means so clear as it should have been for the important task of a début.

The opening scene progressed well enough before the audience whose annoyance over the long wait had almost subsided. Caruso's voice was responding; only the text was less clearly fixed in his mind than the music. Presently came the words, *Le Sorti della Scozia* (the fate of Scotland). Why he should have sung *Le Volpi della Scozia* (the Foxes of Scotland) the tenor was never able to explain. No sooner had the words been delivered than there ensued mingled murmurings, which gradually swelled into a tumult. In vain the impresario sought to restore order. The curtain had to be rung down, and thereupon excuses were made for the singer, who, it was announced, had not recovered from the effects of his sea voyage. When the opera performance proceeded, it was without a tenor.

Despite this incident, and to his surprise, he was allowed to appear in the first public presentation of "Lucia di Lammermoor", on the following night. It is perhaps not to be wondered at that he barely managed to get through. Nor was it an evening devoid of incident. Beginning to sing, Caruso was heartened by the encouragement called out by some of the friendly disposed members of the audience. But no sooner was it proffered than persons otherwise disposed voiced their protests. "*Le Volpi della Scozia!*" they shouted; and instantly there were created two factions, each striving in its clamor to outdo the other. Throughout each act it continued until, his courage broken, Caruso finished his part with his voice weak and almost out of control.

He was startled upon emerging from the theater to discover a group of young men gathered about the stage-door entrance. Caruso hesitated, fearful that physical violence was to be done him. In this, however, he was mistaken, for immediately the leader spoke, saying, "What is the matter? We tried to encourage you, and you took no notice." Then these Trapani supporters escorted their tenor to his lodging, urging him to "be prepared for tomorrow", although realizing that by their injudicious applause they had not helped his cause.

Morning came; and after breakfasting in a little café Caruso caught sight of the impresario. To the tenor's salute and inquiry Cavallaro replied briefly, then walked away. Wondering what this might mean, the singer sought his baritone friend, who excused himself hurriedly on the pretext of an appointment. By this time genuinely troubled Caruso walked toward the theater. On the way he met different members of the company, all of whom appeared distant and reserved. Finally he met the opera company secretary. "Hah!" exclaimed the latter, "I was looking for you. I have a letter."

Caruso opened the communication. It was from Trapani's opera commission, formally protesting him as a singer. He walked dazedly to the home of the baritone and showed him the letter.

"There is nothing to do," he said, "but to go back."

"Then," answered Caruso, "you must find a way; I have no money. You are responsible for my position. If you had not allowed me to oversleep, I should not have been late at the general rehearsal, and all these things could not have happened" The baritone departed and returned later to explain that he had made arrangements for passage to Naples with the sailing master of a vessel. The passage would be only eight *lire;* but since such ships were prohibited from carrying passengers Caruso was cautioned not to go aboard until after nine o'clock that evening.

He was preparing to leave when, from the courtyard below, his name was loudly called. It was Secretary Seciutto, dispatched by his impresario after the failure of the company's dramatic tenor in "Lucia di Lammermoor", to order Caruso to remain in Trapani. There had been an uproar, it seemed, as soon as the audience discovered that instead of Caruso they were listening to the dramatic tenor whom he resembled. Then the people had shouted: "No! No! the Fox of Scotland is the better one." Though permitted to remain, Caruso had to consent to accept a reduction in his fee to two hundred *lire.* "For," explained the impresario, "I must engage another tenor for the place of this one who goes."

At the second performance of "Lucia di Lammermoor", in which Signor Oddo, the new tenor appeared, Caruso decided to be present in order that he might see for himself what would happen. He paid two and a half *lire* for a seat in the fourth row. "It was reassuring to hear the things spoken about me by the people near by," said Caruso. "But the surprise was to come. No sooner was my presence discovered than I was taken from my chair and pushed up and upon the stage. And standing there, I was unwillingly compelled to see this young

DÉBUTS 65

tenor (who had a very beautiful voice) led from the stage. I finished his part in the opera — apparently to the satisfaction of the audience."

The remainder of the Trapani engagement was attended by no further disturbing episodes. One result, however, was this: Caruso received his six hundred *lire* a month; and fifteen years later, when he chanced again to be passing through Trapani, the people recognized him and greeted him with cries of "*Le Volpi della Scozia*."

III

The arrival in Naples was attended with some measure of triumph. Favorable as well as unfavorable reports had preceded Caruso. The impresari, the maestri, the opera singers themselves, and the students preparing hopefully to be of their number, all knew more or less of the tenor's Sicily tour. They were curious to discover, through the next appearances of this young artist, whether he had in truth advanced. This speculation was put speedily to an end in two public achievements — made possible by the ever faithful Zucchi. The mayor of Salerno, preparing for his city's celebration in 1896 of Italy's Independence Day (the first Sunday in June), had ordered two presentations of "Rigoletto." Commissioned to supply the artists, Zucchi had insisted that his *u' beddu nicu* (fine-looking little boy) should be intrusted with the rôle of the Duke.

Salerno's opera-going public had never heard of Enrico Caruso until the Saturday evening which marked the beginning of the celebration of 1896. With the mayor and his staff among those present, the singer went before them. He was seen and heard and — although his voice broke on the high B-flat near the end of the duet, *'E il sol dell' anima* — conquered. He was quite as favorably received the following evening by a Salerno throng which discounted a troublesome top note in such a voice. Admirers of the unknown tenor immediately sprang up, one of whom was Enrico Lorello. To this music enthusiast, who could not forcibly enough express his regard for the Neapolitan, Enrico Caruso was "the coming world's greatest tenor." Lorello repeated his prediction to every one he met, including Caruso himself, to whom he said, "You will one day be the greatest of the greatest." To this the tenor had smilingly answered, "Well Lorello, if that be so, then you shall be my secretary."

Among those best fitted to estimate Caruso's qualities aright was Maestro Vincenzo Lombardi, — the same Lombardi who afterward became a famous teacher of singing, and whose opinions commanded such widespread respect. Lombardi was then distinguished as musician and conductor. When he spoke, others obeyed; wherefore, summoned by the maestro, Caruso presented himself without delay.

Dismissing preliminaries of any sort, Lombardi asked the tenor if he had ever sung in "I Puritani", which it was his intention to give during the Salerno season to be opened during the next two months.

"I explained to Lombardi," to use Caruso's own words, "that I had never attempted to sing the tenor rôle in 'Puritani' because my voice was too short" (lacking in the extreme high notes). "The manner of Lombardi was not altered by what I had said. 'If you accept for the money we can pay, I will make "longer" the voice — because you do not know *how* to sing.'

"I was surprised at these words, yet I knew Lombardi to be a great maestro; so I was glad to accept at once his offer of seven hundred *lire* for a two and a half months' season. I began very soon to study with Lombardi. He got me to put more power behind my tones; and although I did not, until much later, get the top notes as I should, I was finally able, through his instruction, to give all those in the 'Puritani' music which the tenor must sing."

The Salerno opening at length arrived. Impresario Visciani chose the Verdi Theater, and prepared well; "I Puritani" was presented and under Lombardi's conductorship won a merited success. Apart from all the principals who participated in it stood one clearly revealed. All the hardships and heartaches, all the yearnings and sacrifices were compensated for in this first "Puritani" that Enrico Caruso sang. The news was flashed quickly to Milan; then with almost similar speed came a letter from Milan's La Scala impresario inviting the singer to create the tenor part in the opera "Il Signor di Pourceaugnac", by Baron Franchetti. Well aware of the value of his "find", Visciani would not release him when the request was made. Perhaps it was just as well. Certainly Caruso suffered nothing in his career through having to defer his La Scala début. And he had the satisfaction — after one "Puritani" representation — of being visited in his dressing room by the then tenor-idol of Italy, Fernando de Lucia who, learning of the Caruso acclaim, had come from Cava specially to hear for himself what this possible successor might be like. De Lucia was not disappointed; and, tenor though he was, he congratulated his confrère and begged him to consider well, for his future, the need of study.

"I Puritani" was followed by "Cavalleria Rusticana", also with Caruso; an opera in which he failed to equal the vocal and artistic accomplishments attained in the former work. Still, this did not appear to influence his popularity with the public. He began to attract the attention of people outside the theater, and they, wishing to pay him special consideration, disputed among themselves which should have him for this occasion or that. One admirer, destined for a time to be conspicuous among all who stalked after Caruso during his waking hours, was don Peppo Grassi. An elderly impresario — rotund, smiling, and having the gift of delicately sarcastic speech which prevails even now in the columns of *La Frusta*, of which he is proprietor-editor — Grassi fell completely under the Caruso spell. His daughter Josephine, studying singing at the same time with Lombardi, did still more than that. Her malady was love, which affected her at first sight of the young tenor. She was not, it appeared, to endure that malady quite alone; Caruso too was stricken with it, with the result —

DÉBUTS 69

somewhat later — that the two became engaged to be married.

All this, together with the singer's increasing favor, prompted the vigorous don Peppo Grassi to bestir himself. What could so effectively fan this Carusiana flame as a company organized for a special Salerno season? With Lombardi and Vergine as partners, Grassi decided to present at the Comunale Theater during October and November of 1896 twenty performances of opera. Preliminaries passed; the première took place; a fresh impetus was imparted to the Caruso boom. " La Traviata", "La Favorita", "Carmen", "I Pagliacci", and "A San Francisco" — the last mentioned having been popular because of its librettist and composer, Salvatore di Giacomo and Maestro Sebastiani — were the operas performed. Signor Pagani was the alternate tenor; Signora Annina Franco wore prima donna laurels; Signora Masola was the mezzo-soprano; and the ever-present Pignataro sang leading baritone parts. With Lombardi conducting, the organization seemed artistically secure. The audiences were large and enthusiastic; everybody who was anybody at all attended the performances with appropriate regularity, and unpretentious folk went as well. Many of these occasions, by reason of Salerno's opera fashion of the moment, took on a gala touch. Multicolored feminine costumes dotted the audiences which assembled in the Comunale; supper parties followed every performance, and the season bore on with Caruso growing steadily in the public's regard.

Considering some of his vocal shortcomings at that time, it may cause curiosity. A favorite he unquestionably was with the Salerno populace; but a reliable singer he had by no means then become. Despite the ingratiating quality of his voice, and a style of singing undeniably smooth, the tenor was still uncertain of his highest tones. With some arias he experienced great difficulty, and one of these was the Flower song in "Carmen." Invariably, when attempting to sing the top B-flat which marks the climax near the close of this number, Caruso's voice broke. It would occur, clock-like, during every performance of the Bizet opera, to the discomfiture of the singer and don Peppo Grassi's despair. So concerned was don Peppo over his protegé, that as often as the Flower song approached he would station himself in the wings, gazing upon Caruso in a manner that seemed to say, "You must not break on the B-flat." Then would come the fateful phrase — *Te riveder, Carmen* — and the splintering of the top note. Unfailingly, on every such occasion, don Peppo would jump backward, run his fingers wildly through his hair, and knock his head against one of the wings — which fortunately was of paper.

Such behavior, even though practiced by his impresario, jarred the singer's nerves. His first protests being of no avail Caruso finally rushed into the wings after the act of one of the performances and cried, "Listen! if you stand here again while I am singing the aria, I will leave the company. You are my *jettatore* (hoodoo)."

"I, *jettatore!*" exclaimed don Peppo. "How is that possible?"

"Because there is no worse *jettatore* than one who is interested in or who has affection for one he wishes well."

"Very good," answered the impresario, calming himself. "When next you sing the aria, I will go outside and smoke a cigar."

Although Grassi kept his word, Caruso's Flower song B-flat continued to break whenever he attempted to deliver it — and, according to don Peppo (though he admitted not having heard) even worse than before. Yet the people appeared not to care. They became more devoted to their tenor, with the result that the box-office receipts were large whenever he sang. Invitations to the best Salerno homes continued to be too numerous for him to accept them all.

Caruso's vocal trouble on the high notes, if unimportant to these particular listeners, nevertheless gave him grave concern. He realized that if he were ever to become great he must conquer this shortcoming. Lombardi did also; and together they worked, harder than ever to make the upper voice secure. The maestro appreciated, as his pupil did not, that a constricted throat while attempting to sing high notes was chiefly responsible for the breaking of his tones. In order to cause the tone to "pass" properly when the higher pitches were reached, Lombardi — after explaining carefully those essentials with respect to proper breath support, and a loose lower jaw — would make Caruso drop his head, then place it firmly against a wall. In this position he would command, "Now sing — with strength." Persistence brought some reward; before the conclusion of that Salerno season the tenor's top notes began to come more freely, and it was not many months afterward that the "breaking" habit almost totally disappeared. Caruso's peculiarity of "setting" a top note with lowered head may be remembered by those who heard him during the height of his fame. To the last he followed this practice: attacking a high tone in the manner explained, one foot extended well in advance of the other, then — with the tone focused — occasionally throwing back his head, to let the tone soar as only a Caruso tone could.

Toward the end of the Salerno season at the Comunale, Caruso gave the first-known evidences of the vocal endurance and dependableness he was, later in his career, so convincingly to disclose. "A San Francisco" was scheduled for its première, with Caruso in the leading tenor rôle; and since it was a short opera the bill included for its closing portion "I Pagliacci." The former opera had been received enthusiastically, largely because of the popularity of composer and librettist. Indications were pointing to another notable Comunale night when the indisposition of the tenor (a Signor Pagani), cast to sing Canio, filled the management with alarm. What if Pagani were unable to finish? With diplomatic forethought don Peppo Grassi, preparing in advance for the emergency his experience whispered threatened, repaired with Lom-

DÉBUTS

bardi to Caruso's dressing room where the singer was changing into street attire.

"Undress," said don Peppo, "but do not leave the theater."

"Why," demanded the astonished tenor.

"Because if Pagani does not go well in 'Pagliacci' you will have to sing. Not a word more."

Observing that Lombardi approved of the impresario's intention, Caruso became furious. "You are both crazy!" he cried. "I am starving, and I shall go out to get some food."

"Do not worry," admonished Lombardi. "Signor Grassi has arranged to have you served at once with a fine dinner here in your dressing room."

"And Caruso," said Salvatore di Giacomo (librettist of "A San Francisco") who was present, "ate a large dish of spaghetti, two pork chops, and drank almost a liter of wine." Soon afterward, as "Pagliacci" was progressing, the theater auditorium rang with cries of: "Enough! Enough!" for Pagani, as he had feared, was in very bad voice. By this time Caruso had donned his clown's costume and painted his face white. It was perhaps a hazardous thing to have thus used his voice so soon after a hearty meal, but the singing of the tenor for the remainder of "Pagliacci" seems not to have suffered. The performance closed with the audience expressing in almost frantic applause its whole-hearted approval.

The period between the finish of the Comunale special season in late November, and the December opening of the Bellini Theater, in Naples, was short.

It nevertheless enabled Caruso to improve still further, through the application of Lombardi's principles, his coveted high tones. Appearing during this season of Santo Stefano in "La Gioconda" and "Ugonotti", the tenor was recognized as never before by the people of his native city. The critics wrote of his progress; they commented upon his admirable diction; his voice, all declared, had acquired both color and warmth. One reviewer went so far as to assert that "Caruso sings *à la* De Lucia", and as De Lucia was for the Neapolitans almost a god, he could scarcely have said more.

January of 1897 brought the young tenor another opportunity to appear in the Mercadante Theater of Naples. The season was under the impresa of Alberto Landi and Baron Mascia, the operas assigned Caruso being "La Gioconda", "La Traviata", and "Dramma in Vendemmia", a new work by Vincenzo Fornari. Signora Penchi, soprano; Mme. Domprowitch, contralto; and Signori Guarini and Brancaleone, baritone and basso respectively, appeared with the tenor in "La Gioconda", which was conducted by Maestro Scalise. Fornari directed his own opera, "Dramma in Vendemmia."

Although Antonio Scotti was also a Neapolitan, his engagements during the earlier period of Caruso's career had prevented his ever having heard his younger fellow townsman. During this Mercadante season Scotti was singing in "Falstaff" at the Argentina Theater, in Rome. Camillo Bonetti — famous now as impresario of the Colon Theater, in Buenos Aires — was then secretary to Signora Fer-

REDUCED FACSIMILE OF THE PROGRAM OF THE TEATRO MUNICIPALE IN SALERNO FOR THE PERFORMANCE OF "LA GIOCONDA" GIVEN IN HONOR OF CARUSO, APRIL 30, 1897

The copy from which this reduced facsimile was made, was furnished through the courtesy of Nicola Daspuro, Naples. Note announcement of the singer's Christian name as Errico, not Enrico.

rari, in those days a South American impresaria. During a visit with Scotti in Rome, the baritone spoke to Bonetti of a tenor, by name Caruso, who was then appearing at the Fondo (Mercadante) of Naples. "I would suggest," Scotti said to Bonetti, "that you go to hear him." This the latter did; but his report did not bear out the fine reports circulated on all sides. "That Caruso," declared Bonetti, "is no more than a mediocre tenor; so mediocre as to be of the third class." Not until 1899 did these two men, who were to become such fast friends, meet. On May 24, 1902, at London, in a Covent Garden performance of "La Bohème" these two artists, who afterward appeared together in so many representations, sang with each other for the first time.

IV

Experience had been having its effect upon the young Neapolitan tenor. Though still vocally and artistically immature, he was beginning to reflect in his operatic appearances the value of a moderate routine gained in troublous grooves. The hard knocks had not been endured without the learning of valuable lessons; for each one fitted Caruso the better to meet whatever next might come. Health had blessed him. Fortune seemed to have approached somewhat nearer. The career, if yet in the distance, was nevertheless a discernible thing. Like the ship which trembles under the impact of deep waters, the singer was beginning instinctively to brace himself to meet responsibilities that then increased. A slip or false move would have invited more serious consequences than if made even half a year before. Having accomplished more, more was expected of him. He played during his leisure moments as he had played in the past: the world was looming larger, brighter, and altogether a more desirable place in which to live. But the need of work, of applying himself to each task with that thoroughness which helps to bring mastery, appears at this period to have been borne in upon the man. Indeed, Caruso could not have added to his repertory to the extent that he did short of much labor. His Bronzetti school training began to break through, and with pen or pencil he would copy the notes and text of some opera part, fixing both, through this method, securely in his mind. His increasing favor with those of the public who heard him had begun to develop in him some self-confidence; and this was perhaps responsible for the poise he commenced to acquire.

These manifestations of growth were not confined solely to the singer's artistic side. Having become a man, he turned toward man's inclinations, one of which was his discovery that he could not much longer live conveniently in his former home. So a few months later he bade a farewell to that dwelling in Sant' Anna alle Paludi which had so long sheltered him. He returned whenever possible for visits with his father and stepmother; but after the year 1897 he was master in whatever place he was privileged to call his house.

Having been engaged for the new Salerno season

DÉBUTS

at the Comunale Theater, Caruso presented himself well in advance of the opening date of March 1, 1897. He was to receive one thousand *lire* for an engagement which was to continue, as it did, until the following May 4. In the company were Signora Zucchi-Ferrigni, soprano; Mme. Masola, mezzo-soprano; Enrico Pignataro, baritone, and Signor de Falco, basso. Maestro Vincenzo Lombardi was the conductor. The operas in which Caruso appeared were "La Gioconda", "Manon Lescaut", "La Traviata", and "Profeta Velato", a new work by Maestro Daniele Napolitano. The tenor started his appearances under a favorable star. With each fresh effort he found such an added ease that the people rose to him. When it became evident to the watchful Vergine that his pupil was more than holding his own, the singing master left for the long-anticipated return call on Nicola Daspuro — once again to tell of the accomplishments of his favorite tenor, who alone needed the "famous push" to send him to the "pinnacle of glory."

To Vergine's pleadings that Daspuro consent to make the journey from Naples to Salerno the latter roughly replied, "I go to Salerno? You are crazy."

"Yes," answered the teacher, "but please come."

"I had never beheld such faith in a pupil as this maestro showed for Caruso," declared Daspuro. "He touched me. To myself I said, 'Perhaps this man speaks the truth. Anyhow, I could have a friendly chat with my friend don Peppo Grassi, the impresario; and by going I will be rid for always of this maniac.' 'Very well, Maestro,' I consented. 'But if I find, instead of a divo, a dog, then — poor you!'"

Daspuro reached the Comunale, where Vergine awaited him with still another request. He must not, begged the teacher, be seen by the sensitive Caruso before the performance. "He would instantly recall his experience with you and Zuccani, perhaps lose his head, and then — good night!"

The opera was "La Gioconda" and in it Daspuro avers that Caruso sang with a voice full of warmth and power, and with much style. So impressed was the Sonzogno manager that, following the audience's acclaim of the tenor, he promised Vergine, between acts, to engage Caruso for a Lirico Theater season, in Milan. After the performance there was a supper at which Caruso, the then overjoyed Vergine, and Daspuro gathered.

"How much," inquired Daspuro of Caruso, "do you receive for an appearance?"

"Twenty *lire*."

"Then how do you manage to eat?"

"Oh! that is easy," replied the tenor. "The people like me. I sing wherever I am asked; and in return I am given luncheons, dinners, and sometimes presents."

"Eat well," said Daspuro, "but do not be too generous with your voice," to which Caruso smilingly answered, "Don't worry about that. I can give voice to all the world."

This response nettled Daspuro, who feared the tenor was developing conceit. So, Neapolitan fash-

ENRICO CARUSO IN 1896

The original photograph, framed in silver, was given by Caruso, in London, to his son Enrico, Jr., as a birthday present. The photograph has suffered evident injury, but the portrait is of interest as representative of the transitionary period between the singer's youth and maturity.

ion, he admonished him: "*Guagliò* (young man), be careful not to lose your head."

There is no evidence that Caruso was propelled through the public's attention into the loss of his head. What he did lose was his cherished moustache, which he sacrificed in order that he might more fittingly suggest Chevalier des Grieux in Puccini's "Manon Lescaut." Although a long and vocally arduous rôle, the tenor appears to have sustained it without fatigue. His powers of resistance were steadily developing; and it was well for him that such was the case, otherwise — since he was appearing in almost every opera — he would not have performed so physically exacting a task.

The final portion of the Salerno season brought renewed recognition for Caruso. Such was its proportion that word of it drifted to Milan. Confirmation of this recognition by Maestro Leopoldo Mugnone, who had heard the tenor, was such that very shortly a Signor Argenti, theatrical agent, telegraphed the tenor inviting him to accept an invitation to participate in the inauguration of the Massimo Theater of Palermo. He offered two thousand seven hundred and fifty *lire* for forty-five days, a fee larger than any the singer had then received. Fate appeared finally to have showered its bounty upon the young artist. Through Lombardi and Commendatore De Leo, Mayor of Salerno, Caruso had asked don Peppo Grassi for the hand of his daughter in marriage. He had received Grassi's consent joyously; there had been some sort of celebration in honor of the engagement; the ceremony had been set for the following year. In the midst of all this happiness there crossed its path a shadow in the person of one of the twelve ballerinas who, by their dancing, had captivated Salerno. She fascinated the tenor with such completeness that his feelings toward Josephine Grassi experienced a sudden change. Whether he ever really loved her may be open to question; the fact remains that when the final curtain fell on that Salerno season Caruso departed for Palermo taking with him the pretty ballet girl. In this contest of hearts Terpsichore had defeated Euterpe.

CHAPTER FIVE

REALIZATIONS

CARUSO missed the honor of participating in the formal opening of Palermo's Massimo Theater in May, 1897. "Falstaff", with Leopoldo Mugnone conducting, was the opera chosen — without the tenor whose hopes had been fixed on sharing in the event. Puccini's "La Bohème" followed, then came "La Gioconda" and the Caruso début before a Palermo audience. The singer has related how he arrived "on the *piazza*" (as Italian singers are wont to express it) only to find Mugnone less friendly disposed than at the time he had recommended him for the Massimo engagement. Caruso felt Mugnone's coldness to have been due to reasons scarcely fair (each, it seems, had formed an attachment for the one who had seen fit to bestow her favor upon the younger man). Still, whether fair or not in the stand he took, Mugnone, according to the tenor, made his rehearsals of "Gioconda" most unpleasant affairs. Summoned on occasions to appear at the theater as early as nine o'clock in the morning, Caruso has described how difficult he found each attempt to reach the high notes of his part. A change in this maestro's attitude was brought about during the general rehearsal of the opera, when the tenor sang with such fervor that Mugnone himself, exclaiming "bravo", rapped approvingly with his bâton on the conductor's stand. The trouble period, though, was not safely passed. The Sicilian artists of the company were angry that one of their compatriot tenors had not been engaged for so prominent a post; and there also was the threatened danger of protestation from the theater commission, which it could exercise up to and including Caruso's third appearance in the opera of his début. No such protest was ever exercised. The tenor's third Enzo was evidently too satisfactory an achievement. So he continued to the end of the season, in June, singing in twelve representations of "La Gioconda", with Signora Nedea Borelli, soprano; Signore Borlinetto and Paolicchi-Mugnone, contralti; and Signor Terzi, baritone. Under the management of Commendatore Ignazio Florio and Cavalier C. di Giorgio, that opening Massimo season was a distinguished success. It sent Caruso to his Sant' Anna alle Paludi home with much money in his pockets, a part of which he spent freely in the purchase of new clothing. Then it was that the tenor acquired his first frock coat; and arrayed in his newly bought garments, and wearing a derby hat, he strode forth to astonish the neighbors with his fine apparel.

His Palermo experiences had further strengthened the Caruso resources, and they likewise increased Nicola Daspuro's faith that the tenor was to achieve a great career. Meeting Edoardo Sonzogno in Rome, to attend with him the première at the Costanzi Theater of "Andrea Chenier", Daspuro informed his chief of Caruso's Palermo success.

"'Signor Edoardo,'" Daspuro began, "'we have

REALIZATIONS 83

in Naples a young man, Enrico Caruso, a youthful plant of a tenor. He has a voice a trifle short, but with a center that is round, velvety, and reminding one of Masini in his prime.'
"'You really like him?' inquired Sonzogno, to which I answered, 'Enormously.' 'Then engage him,' directed Sonzogno, 'for the next autumn at the Lirico' (Milan).
"'I will do better,'" declared Daspuro. "'I will make with him a contract for only the autumn but orally for the three seasons of fall, Lent, and Carnevale. You will see that when Caruso sings Milan will take flight to the sky.'
"'Go easy,' cautioned Sonzogno; but I was confident, and said 'you will see.' 'Then do as you like,' remarked Sonzogno, indulging in one of his incredulous smiles.
"Returning to Naples," continued Daspuro, "I summoned Vergine and Caruso, and proposed a contract for the tenor to sing at the Lirico at five hundred *lire* a month, from October 1 to December 10. The right was reserved, however, for Sonzogno to engage Caruso for the following Lenten and Carnevale seasons. We met next morning at the Galleria, and proceeded to the little telegraph office near the San Carlo Theater. I signed for Sonzogno, and Vergine and Caruso for themselves." It was agreed that the tenor should study three operas which at the time were new to him: "Voto", by Giordano, the "Arlesiana" of Cilea, and Leoncavallo's "La Bohème." Later, after an examination of these scores, Vergine recommended to his pupil that he

refuse the last one. A reconciliation having been effected with Mugnone, near the end of Caruso's Palermo engagement, the conductor had suggested to Impresario Arturo Lisciarelli, of Livorno, that he secure the tenor for one month of the season he was planning to give, beginning in August, 1897.

"I can state very definitely," Caruso once declared, "that from the time of my Livorno engagement began the fortunate period of my career—from which I have had much pleasure, success — and sorrow. Perhaps I might separate that career into four distinct parts:

"The first period ended in June, 1897, at Palermo.

"The second covered the ten years between 1898 and 1908.

"The third part extended from 1909 to 1918.

"The fourth section, which began in 1919, will continue for — I cannot say how long!"

At his first Livorno appearance, as Alfredo in "La Traviata", Caruso impressed vividly his hearers and manager. Upon the singer this reacted in beneficial ways, stimulating him with such confidence that at each reappearance he sang with finer vocalism and art. There entered in his mind at this period a firm belief in himself. He perhaps might stumble, but he was convinced that never again would he be destined to fall.

It was at this juncture that the publishing house of Ricordi, anxious to present in Livorno some performances of the then recently produced — and successful — "La Bohème" of Giacomo Puccini, had arranged with Lisciarelli to that end. The project promised difficulties, for Livorno was the birthplace of Pietro Mascagni, whose operas were being fostered by Sonzogno, chief publishing rival of Ricordi. Realizing the natural skepticism with which the Livornese would regard any work by a composer other than their beloved Mascagni, the Ricordi firm were proceeding with extreme care. They had consented to the choice of Signora Ada Giachetti for the rôle of Mimì; Antonio Pini-Corsi was acceptable for the Marcello; but where to find an adequate Rodolfo these publishers did not know. There were many tenors, yet only the best one would do. The problem was: Where was he to be found?

Lisciarelli had every confidence that Caruso was the tenor sought, and he so stated in a letter dispatched to the Ricordis, in Milan, from which he anticipated a favorable reply. The answer, however, conveyed more than a feeling of doubt, for it read, "Who is this Caruso?" To the tenor, thus summarily rejected, this communication came as a slap in the face. Lisciarelli had promised him for the "Bohème" appearances one thousand *lire* for an extra month of singing; and, besides, he wished keenly to appear in a new rôle. The music Caruso already knew; this chance to sing it he determined to seize. So when the impresario suggested that he go to Puccini, who was stopping at the time in his country place on the shore of Torre del Lago, he was ready to acquiesce. The distance from Livorno was not far.

"If Puccini approves of you," declared the impresario, "the business is fixed." Caruso had further ideas in the matter, of a monetary sort.

"All right," he replied, "only — if he recommends

me, you must pay me one thousand *lire* for each 'Bohème' appearance. Should you wish me to appear anyway, without Puccini's consent, I am willing to agree to sing for just my living expenses alone — fifteen *lire* a day." This proposal Lisciarelli flatly refused, the subject was dropped, and Caruso soon forgot about it.

One Sunday morning some ten days later the tenor was awakened from his sleep by a friend who knocked loudly on his door. "Get up!" came the command, "and come with me out to the country for some shooting." Caruso approved of the suggestion. An hour afterwards he and his companion were riding in a train that ran alongside the shores of Torre del Lago. They had not gone far when, Caruso's attention having been attracted to a picturesque looking dwelling, his friend suggested that they get out the better to see it. Caruso walked toward the house with his companion, who led the way across the lawn, up to the doorway, and directly the two entered the hall. Advancing to meet them came a man whom the tenor instantly recognized, from photographs he had seen, as Puccini himself. The composer, who seemed to know perfectly well Caruso's guide, made the tenor welcome. At their host's suggestion all three thereupon went out upon the lake, secured a bag of game, then returned to the picturesque little house. Comfortably settled once more, Puccini turned to the singer and said, "Signor Caruso, people have told me much about you, but never have I heard you sing. Do you know my 'Bohème'?"

The answer came quickly. "Yes, Maestro; I can sing for you the romanza, but please do not ask me to put in the high C."

"Perhaps you have not looked well at the score," reproved Puccini, "else you would have seen that the marking shows the singer may, or may not, take the C at his pleasure."

"Oh, yes," agreed Caruso. "But it is the custom to put it in."

"Never mind; sing me well the aria and I will not care for the high C. Generally the tenors sing all the music badly in order to save themselves for that one note."

Directly Caruso had finished singing the *Che gelida manina* Puccini turned to the friend who had brought him, saying, "Tell Lisciarelli that I approve the appearance of Signor Caruso in my 'Bohème.'"

"I was made twice glad," declared the tenor, "for besides being able to add another opera to my repertoire, there were the large *cachets* which I could use very well. My friend and I returned to Livorno; that same evening I saw Lisciarelli, who had already received Puccini's message. 'To-morrow,' he informed me, 'we will begin rehearsals.' 'Yes,' I agreed, 'but please remember to make the new contract.' 'Naturally. You will sing Rodolfo in "Bohème" for one month, at the price of your living expenses — fifteen *lire* a day.'

"I was astonished. What of our agreement? It developed that Lisciarelli barricaded himself behind the argument that, since he had rejected my proposal, *he* had not actually sent me to Puccini. If I had chosen to go there of my own accord, it was no concern of his, even though the maestro himself had approved of me to sing in his 'Bohème.' It was of course a clever trick, in which, to serve this impresario's selfish end, my friend had been innocently used. I had nothing to do but accept on those unfair terms to me, yet I was not sorry because another success came to me."

Such was its success that the opera was performed in Livorno during August of that year on twenty-six occasions, each time with Caruso as Rodolfo. All did not go smoothly, in spite of outward evidences to the contrary. Intrigue wormed its way into the ranks of Lisciarelli's company, as it so often does into the ranks of many another. A new tenor had been summoned; and he attempted, by devious machinations, to undermine Caruso in order that he might sing Rodolfo in his place. To an extent he succeeded; though he got no farther than part of a single appearance, in which he was treated to much the same experience of that young tenor at Trapani who had suffered the humiliation of having been led from the stage.

This unpleasantness, nor the strange insistence of Lisciarelli in limiting the *cachet* of his popular tenor to fifteen *lire* a day, disturbed scarcely at all the easy-going Caruso. He foresaw, even before it actually came, the outcome likely to follow the overextension of the Livorno season; the town was scarcely large or prosperous enough to support so much opera. Also his heart had been made happy, some time before, by an affection that had arisen between

REALIZATIONS

him and Ada Giachetti, the prima donna whose Mimì provided such substantial support to his first Rodolfo. More experienced operatically then he, Signora Giachetti was also a well-schooled musician and pianiste. Nature had given her comeliness and a quick mind; and being herself of a sensitive disposition, her understanding of the unaffected and direct Caruso helped to establish between them a very close bond. Out of her broader knowledge of opera routine, and her superior years, she was able to counsel and direct. The technic of singing, too, she had grasped and ultimately mastered. What was more natural then — in a land and in a profession where such alliances so often obtain — that Enrico Caruso and Ada Giachetti should have combined their fortunes. For eleven years that relationship continued; and she is the mother of his two boys, Rodolfo and Enrico Jr.

II

That Livorno season "died", just as Caruso had anticipated, leaving him with scarcely funds enough for the journey to Florence where friends made him welcome in their home for eight days. This same family loaned him fifty *lire* to go on to Milan in search of other friends who, the tenor felt confident, would aid him in his pecuniary dilemma. He arrived at the Galleria — the famous meeting place of opera singers, conductors, and impresari where most of their business is transacted — and sought one after another of those whose assistance he had counted upon. But each person Caruso approached to ask for money either refused, or else demanded an interest rate of fifty per cent. Three days passed before the tenor summoned courage to present himself to Edoardo Sonzogno, to ask, diffidently, for part of his "advance" on account of his forthcoming engagement at the Lirico Theater. Sonzogno did more than to receive Caruso with kindliness; he considerately paid to him the entire "advance", which at that time he need not have done. Relieved in being able to return at once the fifty *lire* borrowed money, Caruso accepted an opportunity to sing in a single representation of Puccini's "La Bohème" at the Verdi Theater, in Fiume, and then prepared to rest.

In mid-September, when the tenor returned to Milan to make ready for the October first opening of the Lirico season, those oscillating clouds which seemed destined never to leave his skies again reappeared. Unfavorable reports of Caruso began to reach the ears of Sonzogno, and curious to learn what Daspuro might have to offer, he wrote him a letter.

"Dear Daspuro," it began, "I thank you for the present you have made me by engaging a baritone instead of a tenor." Instantly came the following reply.

"Dear Signor Edoardo:

Before judging it is essential to hear and see. Anyhow, if Caruso is a baritone De Lucia is a basso profundo. Wait; and in the meantime do not lend your ears to jealous and wicked tongues.

Nicola Daspuro."

REALIZATIONS

The reaction of uncertainty upon such a nature as Caruso's was damaging to his artistic powers. Realizing through not having been summoned for rehearsal that something was wrong, the tenor had no alternative than to wait and hold his peace. The season was going on; other artists were busy; yet he, though a member of the Sonzogno company, was having no active part in it. About October 15, 1897, he was summoned before the director and asked, "Are you ready with the three operas I sent your master, Vergine?"

"I am ready with two of them," answered Caruso, "but not with Leoncavallo's 'Bohème.'"

"Well," inquired Sonzogno, "why?"

"Because my teacher said it was too strong for my voice."

"In spite of what your teacher says," retorted the director, "I suggest, since you have nothing to do, that you try to learn this part with an accompanist I will send to you."

That very afternoon work was begun on the Leoncavallo score; and the singing continued, day after day, through the remainder of October and on through a part of November. Sonzogno had not exercised his option in his contract with Caruso to engage him for the Carnevale season, and the singer "saw black" for his future as the weeks passed with nothing to reassure him. This apprehension was ended suddenly the middle of November when, without previous intimation of any sort, Caruso received from Sonzogno a letter confirming him for that Lirico's coming Carnevale season. Then the discovery was made that the accompanist — under orders from his superior — had been reporting regularly upon the tenor's abilities and progress. Although this respite had come at a moment sorely needed, it was by no means assured that the immediate future was secure. Before that there must come an actual début, in which a critical and exacting public, and a still more critical and exacting impresario, would render two vital decisions. In the midst of worrying over that coveted Lirico first appearance, the tenor was ordered to report to Sonzogno.

In his almost irritatingly slow speech the director asked: "Are you ready with 'La Navarraise'?" to which Caruso answered, "Who is she?"

"What!" ejaculated Sonzogno, "you don't know the opera 'Navarraise'?" The tenor answered that he did not.

"Well," observed the impresario, "you have five days in which to learn it." Caruso was all but stunned at the thought of this seemingly impossible task. It appeared to him to be so unjust an ultimatum that he made no attempt to reply. Sonzogno went on to explain that "La Navarraise" was in only one act; and giving the tenor the score he commanded, "Now go; and be ready day after tomorrow to rehearse."

Troubled, Caruso assuredly was over this make-or-break situation. He "worked and worked" for two days for the rehearsal. When it came his singing so discouraged Conductor Ferrari that the latter addressed Sonzogno, who was seated near by, and

REALIZATIONS

said, "I cannot go on. He (meaning Caruso) doesn't know anything."

Sonzogno appeared less doubtful. "Well, Maestro, we mustn't expect too much of him, and anyway the public wishes most of all to hear 'Navarraise'."

Another forty-eight hours brought the company to the general rehearsal, at which the handicapped tenor encountered further trouble in the person of Signora De Nuovina, the soprano prima donna. His mind concentrated upon the music and action of his part, Caruso had neglected to remove his hat, which so infuriated the arrogant singer that snatching it from her associate's head and throwing it upon the stage, she cried, "When you sing with a lady take off your hat." There may have been some justification, but she could not have really known the feelings of her sensitive comrade, for he admitted — in relating the incident — that he "swallowed the wrong way", and was made to feel quite unhappy. Other mishaps occurred during that rehearsal, so serious, it appeared, that Sonzogno was prompted to remark that "To-morrow at the performance, we will assist at a triumph for Signora De Nuovina and a fiasco for this young Boo!"

How far from what happened was the director's prediction! A triumph there was, though not for the soprano. Instead, it veered from the screaming of Signora De Nuovina which the public disliked, and was placed before the new tenor whose voice — though light — and smooth singing carried him into favor that was destined to hold. "Signora De Nuovina had encouraged Sonzogno and Ferrari in the idea that I would not do," declared Caruso. "She disliked the suggestion of a change of tenors, for with Caruso she felt her success would be relatively easy. It was with dread that I went out upon the stage at my beginning in the performance. Hisses and screams greeted me. I later learned that when I attacked the aria many people thought I would have a fiasco. When I triumphed I was told it was due to the 'grace and charm' of my singing." From that night, Caruso was never again to experience any difficulties in singing the Sonzogno repertoire. In his lodgings at the Pension Gasperini he studied new rôles, and the many dark hours he had passed there were supplanted by brighter ones. Cilea, composer of "Arlesiana", was immediately desirous that the Araguil of "La Navarraise" should be the Federico of his new opera. And on November 27, 1897, it so happened; with a twofold recognition for Cilea, who conducted, and for singer. Some experts felt at the time that in the *Lament* of Federico the real voice of Caruso was first disclosed.

In spite of the very evident direction the wind was blowing for Caruso, he was not accepted on every side as an established artist. There was still the inclination on the part of many who heard him to withhold any considerable approval, while others — who received and weighed such reports as reached them from a distance — were no less conservatively inclined. Ada Giachetti, aiding in ways she was so well able to, gave him her encouragement and support. The weeks passed, January came, and on the twentieth day of that month, 1898, the tenor made his Genoa début at the Carlo Felice Theater. Sonzogno had sent him there, to Giovanni Massa, the impresario. Oddly enough, it was as Marcello, in Leoncavallo "La Bohème" (the opera Vergine had pronounced too strong for his pupil's voice) that the first appearance took place.

Artists whom the people of the United States have often heard were members of that cast. Besides Pini-Corsi, who sang Schaunard, Genoa greeted Giuseppe de Luca in the part of Colline. Rosina Storchio was the Mimì, Emilia Corsi had the character of Musetta, and Signor Angelini appeared as Rodolfo. Alessandro Pomé sat in the conductor's chair, as he did also when "The Pearl Fishers" introduced Caruso, on that occasion, in his first appearance in the rôle of Nadir. Regina Pinkert, a member of Oscar Hammerstein's New York Manhattan Opera Company during its opening 1906-1907 season, was the soprano of that cast, and Signori de Luca and Carozzi had principal parts.

There was work enough to absorb much of Caruso's time, but he found hours for recreation — away from the theater, and all thought of it, with the comrades of whom he was fond. Signor de Luca, later to be associated with the tenor in many New York Metropolitan presentations, recalls incidents of that season when both singers were struggling to get on.

"I met Caruso for the first time at that Carlo Felice season, in Genoa. He received five thousand *lire* for the entire season of about three months; and we lived together at the Pension Mancinelli, in via Assarotti. Caruso had a parlor as well as a bedroom, while I — with no more than seven hundred fifty *lire* for those three months — had to be content with a small room in which to sleep. Our friendship having grown, I was allowed on occasions to use Caruso's parlor . . . when I was visited by persons wishing to borrow a *lira* or two, or who desired tickets for the opera.

"The prices we paid included meals as well as lodgings, but it was not food either of us cared to eat. So we visited the restaurants. On fine days we preferred riding out to the Righi, situated in the Ligurian hills, from which one might gaze at the magnificent panorama view all about. If not just like Naples, it suggested the country that Caruso loved; and often out of the joy that filled his heart he would sing, standing there, the popular songs of the people.

"Following an evening performance at the Carlo Felice, Caruso liked to go for supper to Peppo, a restaurant in the Galleria. Always when it was finished, the six or seven artists who usually made up the party would stand at a given point in preparation for a foot-race across the Galleria to the Café Zolesi at the further end. It was understood that the one who finished last must pay for the coffee — and it was very often Caruso. He had begun then to lose his slender figure; he was putting on weight."

The Genoa season ended, after the final performance, with a small celebration at Righi's. Caruso was host at that supper which attracted the attention of other diners who had recognized the tenor. Urged to induce Caruso to sing for them the proprietor made known to his guest their wishes; and he responded with that good-natured willingness which, during his early career, was in such instances a noticeable trait. He gave, first, the Flower song from "Carmen", and then, with de Luca, the duet for tenor and baritone from "The Pearl Fishers." When Proprietor Righi presented the check Caruso nodded his head.

"You have served us with an excellent dinner," he informed the *restaurateur*, "and to prove my entire satisfaction with it I will be reasonable in the charge for the songs Signor de Luca and I provided for your guests. Your bill is one hundred eighty *lire;* ours to you I will put at the reasonable amount of three hundred *lire*. All you owe me, therefore, is one hundred twenty *lire*."

The astounded Righi stood speechless — until Caruso relieved the situation with his laughter. It was typical of the jokes Caruso enjoyed indulging in until some time after he had established his American reputation, when, having become preëminent in his art, he shaped his public conduct accordingly.

Caruso departed from Genoa with pleasurable recollections. And he carried with him a bust of himself, modeled by Achille Canessa, a Genoese sculptor. Canessa had invited the tenor to look upon a bust he had made from a death mask of Roberto Stagno, who had passed away in April of that year. Impressed by the character of the artistry, Caruso had assented to Canessa's suggestion that the singer sit for him. Although it was the intention of Impresario Massa to present to Caruso his own bust, in recognition of his Carlo Felice services, Canessa never was paid. Massa forgot about the matter, and Caruso, unaware of the incident, remained ignorant of it ever afterwards. The sculptor — perhaps through artistic sensitiveness — never made the facts known. They came to light only a short time ago.

Anxious now to preserve without subsequent faltering the artistic advances he had made, the singer plunged still more seriously into his work. Had he been conscientious before? He would guard with a deeper sense of appreciation the hours of study. Friends had proved their loyalty; other persons whom he had never known had become friends also, and proffered their support. Then there was the public which had encouraged him; the public he toiled to please and must continue to please if he were to hold its confidence. Springtime passed into summer, and June 26, 1898, carried Caruso to Trento where, at the Sociale Theater, he appeared in several performances of "I Pagliacci", and the "Saffo" of Massenet, which brought *cachets* of five hundred *lire* each. July found the tenor once more in Livorno, this time to remain for two months at the Politeama Livornese (still under the control of Sonzogno) where he was to reap a joy from his operatic singing of "I Pagliacci" in a degree theretofore untasted.

Sonzogno himself had, by his fairness, been responsible for the first part of this joy; for when Caruso had tendered to the impresario his Genoa earnings (which under the terms of his agreement he was in duty bound to do) Sonzogno had said, "No, I don't do business in that way. You worked hard for the money; keep it."

III

The preparations for the première of Umberto Giordano's "La Fedora" had engaged the consuming interest of the operatic world. Roberto Stagno, in whose house in Florence the composer had penned many pages of his score, had been the choice for the Loris Ipanoff; and Gemma Bellincioni, Stagno's wife, had been nominated to sing Fedora. The death of the great tenor compelled the selection of another to take his place, one so difficult to fill that few persons, if any, believed such a thing to be possible. In the midst of deliberations by Giordano and Sonzogno, Signora Bellincioni was asked to aid with her professional advice. From her Livorno villa, at the composer's request, she had gone to a Politeama performance of "Pagliacci" especially to hear Enrico Caruso sing. The entire score of "La Fedora" was almost as familiar to her as her own part. She was acquainted with the requirements of Loris; her ability to pass upon the resources of any tenor candidate was regarded by the composer as almost equal to his own. After hearing Caruso she wrote to Giordano:

"You know that 'Pagliacci' is an opera entirely different from your 'Fedora', and that Canio is not a bit like Loris. In spite of this difference it is my opinion that Caruso has the voice and the intelligence to make him an assured success in the rôle."

The judgment of this distinguished artiste was apparently all that Giordano required to move him to a decision. He himself had heard Caruso during the "Arlesiana" première in which he had sung the preceding November in Milan; so he hesitated no longer. The singer who only four years before had yearned eagerly for a chance to be heard was thereupon invited to create a new rôle. And hard upon this stimulating information came other news — on July 2, 1898 — to bring to the tenor further consciousness of his growing responsibilities. A son had been born to him in Milan; and soon afterward, his Livorno duties disposed of, he hastened to his home at Number 1 via Velasca to be with the boy and its mother. Caruso and Ada Giachetti named this boy Rodolfo, in remembrance of the rôle the father had sung in Puccini's "La Bohème"; but he grew up as Fofò, and, among his intimates, Fofò he still is.

The 1898 Lirico season at Milan opened, under Edoardo Sonzogno's sponsorship, on October 22 with a revival of "Arlesiana." Caruso appeared, meeting with much the same moderate reception he had experienced before. Federico Candida, a Neapolitan journalist who still resides in Milan, has written that the singer's "fair success of 1897" was substantially repeated, pointing out the tendency of Milan's practice of conservatism in bestowing its approval on any newcomer artist. In Leoncavallo's Bohème, given at the Lirico November 8, 1898, Caruso's performance prompted no reviewer to write in glowing terms. He was, it appeared, only one of

REALIZATIONS

the cast — which included Signore Bel Sorel and Santarelli. But what a change was wrought in both public and critical opinion on the evening of November 17, 1898, when he appeared under the bâton of Composer Umberto Giordano, and with Gemma Bellincioni as Fedora. Delfino Menotti in the part of De Sirieux, and Signora Anita Baroni singing Countess Olga.

In a rôle (Loris Ipanoff) which some have declared could not have suited him better had it been specially written for him, Caruso appeared at his best in that world première of "La Fedora." The envious might continue to speak slightingly of this Neapolitan tenor; associates who chafed because he had outstripped them were certain to follow their previous course of circulating untruthful reports of his alleged shortcomings; but unprejudiced people considered in Caruso's accomplishments of that night only what their ears told them. It was as though his voice and art had burst suddenly through an obscuring haze. After the *Amor ti vieta* aria the spark of a new glory was kindled, and news of it flashed over the telegraph wires to many European cities. The following day there was enough in the newspaper reviews to convince even the conservative that a great singer was being made. One celebrated critic, in the course of his comments wrote: "*Caruso cantó in Fedora e la fè d'oro*" (Caruso sang in Fedora, making it of gold).

"After that night," Caruso once said, "the contracts descended on me like a heavy rainstorm. Of course, many friends crowded about me. I liked best of all, though, the present from Sonzogno — a copy of each opera score he had thus far edited."

One of these contracts offered was from Russia, and since both the prestige and emolument (six thousand *lire* a month) were regarded as offering the greatest rewards, Caruso prepared for his departure northwards. He sang "Saffo" with Signora Bellincioni, before leaving Milan near the end of that December; and there was a twofold sadness in the departing, for Ada Giachetti sailed at almost the same time to fulfill a South American engagement. Little Fofò alone remained amidst the scenes of his father's triumphs, in the care of his aunt — Rina Giachetti.

The Petrograd of to-day was St. Petersburg at the time Enrico Caruso first arrived there, in late December of 1898. A city different from any he had previously visited, the tenor relaxed without delay in a round of sightseeing which yielded an added interest through the conditions in which he then found himself. Relatively he was in comfortable circumstances. He could poke about with the consciousness of a financial security never before felt, and this rather heightened the pleasure of such excursions. The people were new to him; the climate, if not altogether to the liking of his Italian nature, at least supplied an element of novelty; it was all quite wonderful in its way and lent its effects to this observant man. Travel brings its advantages in ways of enlightenment, as Caruso was eventually to learn. Here was an environment of a character worth absorbing — one fairly teeming

REALIZATIONS 103

with art — and the tenor, as events later proved, was to be the gainer.

That 1898–1899 season of the Grand Théâtre du Conservatoire in Petrograd included among its lists of principals a number of illustrious artists. One was Signora Luisa Tetrazzini, another Mme. Sigrid Arnoldson, and a third the great baritone, Mattia Battistini. The basso Vittorio Arimondi, whom United States opera-goers know so well, was also of that company — huge of body and ever generous with his helpful advice to his newly made and younger tenor friend. Here was an array of artists who were above petty jealousies or intrigue. Each one performed his or her duties; there was present always a spirit of *camaraderie;* life for them during that Petrograd season was one devoted with evident profit to both their art and leisure.

In this beneficial atmosphere Caruso's singing thrived. His début rôle was Rodolfo in Puccini's "La Bohème." Mme. Arnoldson appeared as Mimì; Signora Tetrazzini was Musetta; Signor Brombera had the part of Marcello, and Arimondi was the Colline. The lyric beauty of the Caruso voice and his ease of singing commanded instantaneous and approving notice from the Russians. Correspondingly favorable attention was attracted by the tenor when he appeared next in "I Pagliacci," with Mme. Arnoldson and Battistini. Donizetti's "Maria di Rohan" was the third opera in which Caruso appeared, and thereafter came "Cavalleria Rusticana", and "La Traviata."

Changes were gradually marking this singer who

was moving forward, step by step, in his career. He was some distance from being a man of the world (he was just approaching his twenty-sixth year, and the advantages which help to make such men had not as then arrived), but those who knew him at the time noted signs that he was maturing. At this juncture, with his name published frequently in Russian newspapers, Caruso awoke one morning to find a summons to appear at a special concert which was to be given before the then Czar Nicholas II of Russia, in his Petrograd palace.

He describes the czar — to whom he was presented at the conclusion of the concert — as a "small, almost insignificant-looking man with an anxious face. Royalty was to me something to be regarded from a distance. The scene was brilliant. Such color, together with the beauty of the women and the bearing of the men — assembled in so large a space — was wholly new to me. I recall having felt a sense of gratitude for that opportunity, and wondered if there was to be another — and when and where. I could feel people staring as I was received by the czar, who said, 'Thank you very much,' and then presented me with a pair of gold cuff buttons set with diamonds."

In February Caruso returned from Russia to Milan. He arrived with the consciousness of having progressed; of being equipped more completely to resume his place at the Lirico during the Carnevale season then about to begin. Prior to his departure from Milan in 1898 a contract for his first South American engagement had been negotiated. Perhaps the thought of this added to the spirit of confidence which was commencing to glow within him. Carlo d'Ormeville, dean of the Italian managers, who was responsible for this particular contract, recently related some incidents connected with it.

"I had been one of the intimate friends of Caruso from the start of his glorious career at Milan to those last days of his premature death. No one can ever fill the emptiness he has left in the lyric world. Apart from his great voice and talent, he was acclaimed as an artist scrupulous to the last detail in fulfilling his engagements. As a man he was of golden character and so generous that many times his left hand did not know what his right hand was giving.

"I had the honor of engaging him for the 1899 season in South America to appear under Impresaria Ferrari. Caruso was then no celebrated tenor. The contract (for twelve thousand *lire* a month) was signed November 16, 1898, on the eve of his notable first performance in 'Fedora.' The day after the première Caruso was declared by not a few to be the greatest of tenors. Meeting him twenty-four hours later, he expressed disappointment over the terms of the contract. Some of his friends, made acquainted with the conditions, had become furious.

"'Tell me,' I asked, 'what did any of your friends offer you before the 'Fedora' performance? Nothing! Isn't that true? Well, you signed with Signora Ferrari before that performance, and I am sure you will keep your written agreement.'

"'Ah! my dear Carlo,' answered Caruso, 'I would rather die than to break a contract.'

"Caruso went to Buenos Aires. He won. And he was engaged for future seasons on more advantageous financial terms."

Before he sailed, however, there were some rumors to be silenced; rumors to the effect that the tenor, while in Russia, had lost his voice. These reports were not without their damaging influence, for soon after he reached Milan Caruso was invited by Signora Ferrari to call upon her. Despite his assurances that he was in vocally excellent condition the impresaria continued skeptical; she wished some tangible evidence that he was still the reputedly excellent tenor she had engaged. Returning to his home after this disconcerting interview, Caruso found there a letter from Sonzogno. It read: "I hear that you have lost your voice — somewhere in Russia. Well, my theater is wide open to you to sing any opera at any time."

The Carnevale season of 1899, which began at the Lirico in late February, brought Caruso once more before the people of Milan. No part of the opera circles of the city was without a feeling of excitement. A large attendance was assured; the public would be there — in the spirit of any public — ready to applaud or condemn. A canvass would probably have returned for the one whose ability was being questioned a majority vote of confidence. Such, at any rate, must be the conclusion drawn from the occurrences of that opening Carnevale performance of "Fedora" at the Lirico when Caruso, singing with

Signora Bellincioni, triumphed as he never had before. Thus was another canard disposed of. Before the close of that Carnevale season the malicious workings of the tenor's enemies had, by his achievements, been smothered.

Caruso sailed in April, aboard the SS *Regina Margherita*, for Buenos Aires, where he arrived May 7, 1899. Another task lay ahead. Seven days after he went ashore, in the Théâtre La Opera, the tenor performed it. "Fedora" was to introduce him to a South American audience; and he felt a sense of security in having as a comrade Signora Bellincioni. But one of those storm-clouds appeared again in the Caruso skies. A baritone — one Caruson by name — who had sung in Buenos Aires had not left any too excellent an impression. Some misunderstanding on the part of certain newspaper writers having caused a confusion of the two singers, through the similarity of their names, the public was led by published articles to anticipate a possible baritone singer in the place of an expected tenor.

The opening night of May 14, 1899, arrived, and before the first South American assemblage he had ever faced Caruso sang Loris Ipanoff. Delfino Menotti was also of the cast; Maestro Mascheroni conducted, and a scene similar to scenes Milan had caused when "Fedora" had been given there was enacted. After the performance, which fired the temperamental listeners to make a demonstration, Impresaria Ferrari embraced her tenor; then she urged him to put his signature to a contract for the three seasons following at twenty-five thousand, thirty-five thousand, and forty-five thousand *lire* a month respectively, only two of which — the first and third — he fulfilled.

"La Traviata", in which Caruso and Signora Bellincioni appeared as Alfredo and Violetta, was performed on May 24. A second "Fedora", during which the fervor of the audience duplicated that which had attended the first one, was given on May 27. With Signora Bellincioni, the tenor sang on June 4, in "Saffo"; but the opera displeased the South American public, and it has been asserted that this perfomance was a fiasco. Other operas then were presented, in a steady succession: "La Gioconda", on June 8, with Signore Elisa Petri and Elvira Lorini in the cast; Mascagni's "Iris", on June 22, with Signora Maria de Lerma; "Regina di Saba", on July 4, with Signore de Lerma and Lorini, and Signori Taboyo and Leonardi (in which one critic declared that it was Caruso's opera, not Goldmark's); "Jupanki", by Arturo Berutti, a South American maestro, which had only two subsequent presentations after its July 25 première; and "Cavalleria Rusticana", which marked Caruso's 1899 farewell, on August 8, with Signora Petri singing the Santuzza. The Buenos Aires public had already bestowed upon Caruso the title *divo;* and at this performance he was made to repeat the *Brindisi* (Drinking song) three times. One other, and unlooked-for "Cavalleria Rusticana" came before the tenor sailed for Italy. It was a benefit performance, given for the refugees of the Rio Negro flood.

IV

Accounts of the Caruso accomplishments in South America began at this period to intensify managerial desires to have the tenor's name appear in the pages of their prospectuses. Invitations were awaiting him on his arrival in his own country to accept various alluring contracts. Each letter was ingratiatingly phrased; for within a comparatively brief period he had emerged from the realm of uncertainty into one of promise. It was often "Caro Enrico" — to be followed by a jogging of the singer's memory to recall some service rendered him, or an assertion that *always* had the writer held firm in his faith in *Caro Enrico's* future. The handwriting appeared plainly upon the wall, and impresari were not slow in heeding its indications. More than one progressive impresario waited on the tenor in person; those managers who could not, or were not yet ready to bring themselves to so doing, dispatched emissaries in efforts to win the singer's consent to signing a contract.

Caruso himself has described his own feelings at that time. "I liked, just then, to reflect on those bad days already gone which had brought me hardships and heartaches. It was nice to be back in Naples, with my father and stepmother, and among old friends. They had much to tell me of what the Neapolitans had had to say of my career.

"'He goes on,' they had said, in effect, 'and the public accepts him; perhaps some day he will become a great tenor.' It was clear to me that my fellow citizens wanted me to gain success, but feared the time had not yet come to insure it.

"This special home-coming was different from any other of mine. Besides plenty of money in my pocket I had also my South American contract — which meant more money for the future. I had to smile at the thought of how different everything had been only two years before. Then my professed Neapolitan friends had found excuses to deny me small loans when I had asked them, in the Milan Galleria. These friends would have been glad to let me have any reasonable sum I might then have requested — which was not necessary since I had enough money of my own."

Caruso did not stop for long in Naples. Milan was a desired objective, to consider what engagement from among those offered it would be most desirable to accept. "I was almost as eager to meet my former fellow artists," explained the tenor, "as to sign a piece of paper which would mean that I should be certain of opportunities to sing in a given number of performances at respectable *cachets*. All the way from Naples to Milan I continued to wonder, 'What will they say? How will they act?' I looked a good deal through the car window without seeing as much of the country as on other similar journeys.

"I went quickly to the Galleria from the railway station, not stopping to find a place to live while I should stay in Milan. Everybody was so glad to see me when I went in that I at once knew my South American engagement had been enough of a success. Soon afterward I decided upon the contract offered me to appear during the coming autumn season at the Costanzi Theater, in Rome, at fifteen hundred *lire* for each of the first ten appearances, and twelve hundred fifty *lire* for every appearance that might follow."

There were a number of reasons for Caruso's choice, one being that the Costanzi's impresario — Vincenzo Morichini — was idolized by the Romans.

The Neapolitan singer, who was sensing more and more the opportunities opening before him, was nevertheless willing, during those September days spent in Milan, to relax in play. In the home he had established for his baby Fofò and its mother he spent happy hours. It was no longer, as it had been at the outset, a tax upon his finances to maintain it. There during afternoons and evenings his friends gathered and also those acquaintances who showed an anxious desire to be counted as friends. Any tenor standing upon the threshold of success is a magnet. Marked long before for his generosity, Caruso could not escape those who flocked toward him out of motives calculated to serve their own ends. He was courted and waited upon by scores of persons he barely knew. If his course took him to the Galleria, he was sure to find there innumerable persons — whose faces he scarcely remembered having seen — calling out compliments to him as he passed. It was the old story; and if new to the singer at that time it was destined to run on. The gossip of the theaters intrigued him; the lowliest Neapolitan, stopping him in the street, could engage his ear. He took delight in selecting his dress for various occasions with minutest care; indeed, Caruso was becoming conspicuous for his dress — a dress not then so conservative as it became in later years.

Autumn came and with it the important business of preparing for the approaching season at Rome. He repaired there, attending personally to the choice of a place in which to live. The quarters selected were located in the dwelling at Number 79 via Napoli, but satisfactory as they proved in all physical requirements, one element appeared to be missing. With the accumulation of work due to his advancing artistic position it became evident to the singer that assistance was required. He needed, in short, a secretary; so, faithful to the promise he had given four years before, he offered the post to Enrico Lorello, of Salerno. Lorello accepted, joined his employer in Rome, and thus was the first of the several who were ultimately to serve Caruso in that capacity.

The Costanzi season held potentialities for the rising singer, one being the stipulation in his contract with Impresario Morichini that he should create the tenor rôle in a new opera by a well-known composer.

"I understood what the opera was to be ('Tosca') and who was its composer (Puccini), and I felt a pride in the nomination," declared Caruso. "I speak of this as a prelude to what I shall say to show that one's career is neither so brilliant nor so easy as may seem to the casual eyes of the public. For it developed that in spite of a crescendo of successes attending my appearances in Buenos Aires, and the later ones in Treviso, I was to experience a setback in Rome.

REALIZATIONS 113

"My happy anticipations were checked, upon reaching the Costanzi, to be informed by Morichini that for me there was to be no new opera. To my inquiries I was given no satisfactory enlightenment (it is astonishing to observe how little opera executives sometimes appear to know). Searching my own mind I discovered, what I believed, to have been the reason for the refusal to allow me to create Cavaradossi in 'Tosca.' During the first season of Sonzogno — exactly five months before I sailed for South America — many artists, conductors, and composers had been present at each of my Lirico appearances. Some of them had not agreed with most of the critics and the public as to my abilities; these objectors holding the same unfavorable opinion of those tenors who had heard me in 'Rigoletto' at the Mercadante in 1895. I could have argued the matter with Morichini. Perhaps, had I been insistent, something might have happened, for at Livorno Puccini had declared me capable of singing Rodolfo in his 'Bohème.' A better and more experienced artist at the time of my Costanzi début, there seemed enough justification to intrust to me the rôle of Cavaradossi."

Caruso's reasoning appears to have been sound enough. Only recently Puccini said, in speaking of the tenor's accomplishment during that Livorno season of 1897, "I do not remember so well to-day the incident of 'La Bohème' with my dear friend Caruso. But I do remember that those performances revealed the treasure of a magnificent voice, and that the success was memorable. Caruso then found the Racconto of the first act a little heavy for him, although he did not confide it to me at the time. He mentioned it to me in after years, when we had become more friendly; and he added that he would like to have had the aria lowered a half-tone. He interpreted also my 'Manon Lescaut.' As Des Grieux he is unforgettable. Always will I remember the finale of the third act, as he used to sing it."

Still it was Puccini himself who took from Caruso the coveted opportunity of being the first Cavaradossi and gave it to Emilio de Marchi. Whatever Puccini's objections to Caruso as the creator of Cavaradossi at the time of its world première at the Costanzi, he admitted to the tenor — when he appeared in the rôle one year later in Bologna — that never had he heard the music better sung.

Although wounded in his feelings, the tenor "did not fuss or complain." He endeavored, as later, "to avoid trouble . . . a course that always seemed, in time, to bring compensation." "Iris" being the opera chosen for the Caruso début at the Costanzi, a host of Mascagni admirers was present to observe what the artist would do. Among those associated with him that 1899 season in Rome were Signore Emma Carelli, Mary Dalniero, and Monti-Baldini, and Signori Silla Carobbi and Borucchia; the redoubtable and then friendly Leopoldo Mugnone occupied the conductor's chair. The chagrin Caruso felt over the "Tosca" episode may have exerted some effect upon his Costanzi première appearance, but he began well and continued thus to the end of the performance. The result appears to have been doubly fortunate, for between the tenor and his former maestro Vergine there was effected a reconciliation, following their differences, several years previous, over the interpretation of the terms of the contract made in 1893. A court decision having dragged on with no apparent end in sight, Caruso proposed to Vergine that he pay him a lump sum of twenty thousand *lire*, which the latter accepted under an agreement that the contract should be annulled. This adjustment no doubt relieved the singer's mind. He continued even to the end of his days to hold in esteem the man who had been his first singing guide. Some persons have contended that Vergine deserved less credit for developing the Caruso voice than others who during later periods proffered expert advice. They may be right; indeed there is evidence gathered here and there to support the belief that from Lombardi and various additional sources the tenor received suggestions most profitably applied. At the time of that Costanzi season it is questionable if Caruso would have admitted this to have been true, or ever likely to be true.

Nevertheless the singer's voice in those days was not the freely produced voice into which it was later to develop. Although it had gained in roundness and substance, and soared less reluctantly to the top notes, there could scarcely have existed the strength and the brilliancy which were to be its ultimate characteristics. Careful at all times to restrain any tendency towards forcing, Caruso charmed more at that time by the smoothness and purity of his singing than by any *tour de force*.

Boito's "Mefistofele" followed "Iris." The presence of Arrigo Boito, the composer and librettist, was enough to bestir the artists. On the day of the presentation the singer, as was his custom, went to the Hotel Laurati for luncheon, in a happy frame of mind; but how quickly it was to be dispelled. Informed by the waiter who served him of the presence of Boito himself, the singer lapsed into diffidence over the consciousness that soon he might be moving along the path of disgrace. He was "discouraged because of the proximity of the maestro", although he need not have been. For that evening his Faust sent Boito to his hotel in a satisfied frame of mind.

Meeting Caruso next morning the composer said to him, "I came to Rome especially to hear you sing in my opera and I am happy to shake your hand. I did not visit you in your dressing room last evening because I wished to save you further emotion and keep myself free to form a deliberate judgment upon your performance. Your voice has in it a quality that touches my heart; your singing possesses an instinctive virtue I will not attempt to describe. I congratulate you; and from my heart and my mind I thank you for the enjoyment you gave to both."

To the unexpected tribute Caruso was able to make only some conventional response. He stood, as Boito walked deliberately off, looking after him out of eyes that bespoke the gratitude his tongue could not express. Thus encouraged, it was only natural that the singer's subsequent opera appearances should have gained through the stimulus of a respected judgment. "La Gioconda" carried him a rung higher up the ladder on which he climbed; each new effort awakened a keener consciousness of the possibilities which lay ahead; he plodded onward, hoping, dreaming, for the cherished ultimate reward.

The season wore on, with the end (December 15) approaching. Well enough established, the tenor found his favor extending. It was heightened, shortly before his farewell appearance, when, invited to sing at a special gathering, he attracted to his cause many members of Rome's press of that day. This affair was a reception arranged by the Associazione della Stampa, planned by Attilio Luzzatto, its then president and editor of the influential daily newspaper *La Tribuna*. The audience which listened to Caruso's interpretation of the *Lament* of Federico from Cilea's "Arlesiana" was comprised largely of aristocrats who resided in the Italian capital. Assisted by Mugnone, who played the pianoforte, the result was even more pronounced than either Caruso or Mugnone had expected. Three times was the aria repeated, the applause on each occasion reaching a point quite uncommon to auditors of that sort.

V

Rome had provided compensations enough to assuage the hurt Caruso had felt over his missed honor to create the rôle of Cavaradossi. He was willing that it should be dropped into the bag of past experiences, there, so far as was possible, to be forgotten. Christmas time was approaching; and immediately thereafter his engagements demanded his presence, for a second time, in Petrograd.

What an array of artists with whom to sing! For soprani there were Signora Luisa Tetrazzini, Mme. Sigrid Arnoldson, and Mme. Salomea Krusheniska; the great tenor Angelo Masini, and the equally distinguished baritone Mattia Battistini, were to be regularly in the casts; another celebrated tenor of that day, Francesco Marconi (better known as Checco), also was of the company which had as its leading basso Vittorio Arimondi, and as mezzo-soprani Signore Cucini and Carotini. The first conductor was Vittorio Podesti, afterward one of the maestri at New York's Metropolitan Opera House.

Settled in Apartment 88 in the Hotel on the Grand Moskaja, Caruso prepared for the Petrograd première performance "Aïda." He had never sung in this opera because, apart from its intricate *tessitura*, it had been considered too heavy for his voice. Again the resourcefulness of the maturing artist was disclosed as the representation progressed, and the result left the audience of one mind. From all accounts it must have been a triumph; the arias were delivered smoothly and not without the needed dramatic emphasis, and for the first time in any public endeavor Caruso sang a satisfactory high B-flat. In his own estimation "Much of the growth I gained at that time I attribute to the singing of Radames. The rôle was of much help because it developed and consolidated my voice and aided toward making secure my top C, which I had previously been afraid to attempt."

REALIZATIONS

Having resumed the friendship of the previous year, Arimondi was almost constantly with his younger associate. "To win as Caruso won then was exceedingly difficult," declared Arimondi, "and an achievement to be remembered. In those times every opera was put up by the impresario with a cast of such excellence that, even had there been among them none of the celebrities present, personal success could be gained only through the disclosure of real gifts. In the 'Aïda' performance which Podesti conducted was Mme. Krusheniska in the title rôle; Signora Cucini sang the Amneris, Battistini was Amonasro, and I appeared as Ramphis. It was Caruso's night; a night to have stirred an artist older and more experienced than he, and the forerunner as well of more than one other of the same sort.

"Presently came the tenor's first opportunity to appear in 'Il Ballo in Maschera', with Mme. Krusheniska, Signora Cucini, Battistini, and myself; and he took another forward step. The Petrograd public had by this time accepted Caruso completely. When he sang they were happy. Appearance was succeeded by appearance, and before long he sang Faust in 'Mefistofele' for the first time in Russia. Mme. Krusheniska and Signore Carotini and Cucini, and I were of the cast, which labored under trying circumstances.

"Mme. Arimondi and Mme. Giachetti, having decided to join us, had left Milan together on a train due to arrive in Petrograd at eight o'clock on the morning of the date set for the 'Mefistofele' première.

Lorello had been dispatched to receive them and we were both waiting when the secretary returned with the disturbing information that the train had not arrived. His inability to obtain any explanation for the delay was causing us further anxiety when a telegram from my wife, written in Russian, was delivered to me. I knew she did not know one word of that language; so Caruso and I hurried forth to have it translated. But nobody could interpret clearly its meaning, which made us desperate.

"By this time it was midday, yet neither Caruso nor I thought of stopping for lunch. We could only pace excitedly the floor of my room, talking loudly to each other until our voices began to get hoarse. Caruso at length left me; in half an hour or so Lorello came in to say that his master had gone out — without putting on the overshoes which are necessary in Russia if one is to go about safely in a temperature thirty degrees below zero. I tempered my desire to scold when Caruso returned with the news that the train had been derailed in the open country, though without injury to any passenger. At three that afternoon Mme. Arimondi and Mme. Giachetti reached Petrograd on board the relief-train, both suffering from exposure — Mme. Arimondi seriously so. The performance of 'Mefistofele' took place that evening but at what a cost! Caruso developed bronchopneumonia the following day and was ill in bed for one month."

Those days of suffering and restless tossing gave way finally to days more tranquil. There was enough for the patient to think seriously on: of what had gone by during those doubtful earlier years of the career; the gradual ascent to more propitious moments; and the recent efforts so productive of rewards. Mme. Giachetti was always near at hand; there were remembrances and messages from solicitous persons, and even personages; time began to hang less heavily. Toward the end of the illness, when Caruso found strength returning to him, he discovered a more pronounced leaning in the direction of really serious study to which he had begun to turn in the autumn of 1899. Success had impressed him with the importance of treating it with that consideration which compels — from any opera artist — a deal of work. He had become aware of the advantages accruing from methodical habits; during the season at Rome the tenor had decided that a daily schedule would perhaps help. So, on the back of an envelope taken from one of his pockets, he had jotted down the hours of each day and the purposes to which he intended to put them.

"There was one," he had explained, "for rising; another for the breakfast; still another for the exercising of my voice — and so on. Afterward, when I happened to oversleep one morning after a hard night at the opera, I altered the schedule. But it somehow grew until, after a considerable time, it became a sort of fixture. Occasionally some of these resolutions were overcome when a friend would come to take me out for a game of cards; or when several of my companions would drop into my rooms. I was generally ready to reconstruct the schedule, especially on waking late from my rest following some overindulgence at cards that had cost me money. In such moments I was forced to admit that I might be wasting time.

"Not being a musician, I wished, in order that any conductor should find me well prepared, to learn perfectly the words and the notes of my parts. It helped, I discovered, to write both on the pages of a book small enough to be conveniently carried in the pocket. One day a fellow artist came in upon me when I was engaged in copying a part. He chaffed me, and I answered; finally he warned: 'Look out you do not make a mistake in copying and become a composer.'"

That practice Caruso adhered to right to the end of his career; and while riding on a train, aboard a boat, or in any other conveyance, he would take from some coat pocket one of his handy little books out of which he either refreshed his memory or fixed his mind upon matters to be learned.

During the Lenten period of 1900 the company which had been appearing in the Petrograd Conservatory Theater journeyed to Moscow, and, installed in the Grand Theater, began another season. It was in Gounod's "Faust", which Caruso regarded as the "opera grammar" of young tenors, that he came before the public of that city. Not having sung the rôle for several seasons, he made a gratifying discovery; it was much easier for him to sing than at any previous time. Mme. De Lerma was the Marguerite of that Moscow cast, and the others included Signora Carotini, and Battistini and Arimondi.

Samson et Dalila
Premier acte
Scène I

Samson est parmi les Hébreux sur la place publique de la ville de Gaza en Palestine

Apres le corale des Hébreux qui finisse avec les mots " Divins serments par nos aieux reçus?. et précisement sur les huit mesures de musique jouée par l'orchestre, Samson sortant de la foule dis :

Arrêtez | ♪ ô mes frères | ♪ Et benissez le
arrêtté   ô mès frèré   é benissé lé
nom Du Dieu saint de nos | pères! |
nõ   du dié   sẽn   di   no   pèrè
| 2 | ♪ Car l'heure du pardon Est peut-
       car   l'eurè   du par-dõ èt pèt-
être arri-|vée! — | — Oui, j'en-
ètrè   ar-ri-vèè   ui   sj ãn-

A PAGE OF CARUSO'S MANUSCRIPT

How he studied the rôle of Samson. Note the spelling of the French diction just beneath the words of the score, in which the French pronunciation is Italianized.

REALIZATIONS

In this city the tenor renewed his studies in practical ways eminently valuable. For there is so much more, he has contended, beyond the sort of study a singer may do in the studio with a maestro, or at home. Many times he learned that one way of singing a phrase was either a right way or a wrong. Observing his audience, Caruso would note upon them the effect of some particular manner of delivering his voice; if they were pleased, he would remember that he might repeat the effort at some future time, and he likewise took pains to fix in his mind what did not please. He had not yet arrived at the point of unfailingly seizing each opportunity to add to his store of vocal and operatic knowledge, but he was trying. Youth still held; experience and years were to add to his apprehension of what it was necessary for him to know before he could apply such knowledge to enlarging his resources. Nevertheless, the singer had grasped the fundamentals which are essential in any drive toward a worthy goal. At least he appreciated that other things matter for an opera singer besides a fine voice, well used. Such must be the estimate, else he would have been content to rely more than he ever was willing to rely upon the appealing qualities of such tones as he was then beginning to command.

The Moscow season went over, spring hovered, and with renewed confidence Caruso returned to Milan for a visit with his son Fofò and a brief stay with his father and stepmother before he should sail on the SS *Regina Margherita* for his second South American season. He was not met this time with any false rumors about a voice "lost in Russia." The Caruso star was ascending where it could be more clearly seen; Italians were gradually admitting among themselves that it was growing brighter.

Mme. Ferrari, impresaria of La Opera, welcomed her tenor with widespread arms. He would make his season's début in "Mefistofele", with the always dependable Mme. Carelli, the basso Signor Ercolani, and Maestro V. Mingardi conducting. All would be fine, the success enormous, was the picture sketched by this energetic manager. How different it actually proved. Instead Buenos Aires received Caruso so coldly that the nervousness he felt at the beginning of that May 10 performance increased until he found difficulty in finishing the evening. In the morning, at the studio of his artist friend, Filippo Galante, the singer declared that if at the next "Mefistofele" performance the public failed to accord to him the recognition he sought, he would return straightway to Italy.

What a difference that second "Mefistofele" wrought, just two nights after the first one. Caruso may have excelled his previous endeavor; it may possibly have been the temper of a South American audience, which is known to be sometimes moved by seemingly trivial details. Regardless of the cause, it is a fact that after the first aria the public stormed in applause and would not let the performance go on. It wished, it demanded with emotional violence, a repetition of the aria from the singer who had been well nigh ignored forty-eight hours earlier. It is to such a slender thread that the fate of an opera artist may occasionally hang. No encore was forthcoming, but the tenor came many times before the footlights, satisfied then at being restored to the position which had been his during his introductory Buenos Aires season, one year before.

Caruso thereupon relaxed, as was his habit when matters affecting his career took a favorable turn. With his expanding powers he was developing his sensitive side; and while he reacted with a smile to any approval by his public, he was even more susceptible to expressions of ill will. Coldness hurt him more than any outburst of disfavor, and a chilly-disposed assemblage could plunge him into moroseness from which nothing could rescue him save the subsequent warming of his critics, — and on occasions not even that.

Caruso repaired after the second "Mefistofele" appearance to the studio of Galante. Each day's leisure during that 1900 South American stay found him with his artist friend; and the two chatted and worked together, the tenor alternately painting and modeling, under the guidance of his master. He went abroad, too, in the streets of Buenos Aires, either walking or driving, as suited his pleasure. For it cannot be gainsaid that Caruso liked admiration. He may have chosen to maintain outward unconcern, yet he was not unaware of the act of some passer-by who, recognizing him, chose effusively to make known his presence.

"Iris", on May 17, was the second work in which the tenor appeared at La Opera during that second Buenos Aires season. Success had touched him during the previous year; it returned again, although the press expatiated upon the immoral spots in the opera and urged the public not to patronize future performances of it. No attention was paid this advice; indeed, at the next presentation the attendance was even larger than before and, with Signora Carelli and Signori Angelini and Ercolani in the cast, Caruso discovered his popularity increasing and his singing of the serenade of *Yor* redemanded.

All was then momentarily well. Restored to his best humor the tenor continued to fill regularly his announced appearances. Besides repetitions of the operas mentioned he sang in "La Regina di Saba" with Signora Carrera and Signori Mendiorez and Giraldoni; his introductory "La Bohème" in South America was sung on June 23, and on July 12 he appeared for the first time that year in "Cavalleria Rusticana." Even before he went upon the stage, to sing with Signore Carelli and Ida Rappini and Signor Pacini, Caruso captivated his listeners; the *Siciliana*, sung behind the scenes before the curtain rises, had to be repeated. Just two weeks later, through the illness of Emilio De Marchi, another first tenor, Caruso was called upon for a Des Grieux in the "Manon" of Massenet. Singing as he was then singing, he could but satisfy his auditors. They let themselves go with no effort at restraint; it was for the tenor an evening to look back upon.

The way thereafter was a steady triumphant march and it was capped at the farewell when Caruso bade his adieu as Rodolfo in "La Bohème." He sang twice on special occasions before sailing for Montevideo aboard the SS *Sirio*, the first time at a memorial service held on August 9 in the Buenos Aires Catholic cathedral in honor of the assassinated King Humbert of Italy, and again on August 12 in a concert held at the Progress Club for the Dames of Charities. Finishing the shorter season in Montevideo, where a part of the Buenos Aires répertoire was given, Caruso departed for Genoa.

September found him back once more in his Milan apartment in via Velasca, where he turned for one month from everything connected with singing. How quickly those few weeks flew past. It seemed to the tenor that he had barely set foot upon his native soil before he must report at Treviso, that lovely city near the Austrian border, where he had been engaged to appear at the Sociale Theater. There was something to look forward to in the association he was to have in "Tosca" with Ada Giachetti. At least they would not be separated so soon again after their long absence of the previous spring and summer. Together they journeyed to Treviso; they sang in the rehearsals to the delight of Impresario Enrico Corti; they worked at home over details that might make their performances the smoother; and at the première of October 23 each found the reward. Egisto Tango — who afterward spent one season as a conductor at the New York Metropolitan — led the presentation; Antonio Magini-Coletti was the Baron Scarpia. If that Treviso season was not long, it led to some desirable friendships, one of them being that with Antonio Guarnieri, then the first 'cellist of the Sociale Theater orchestra, who later became a celebrated opera conductor. And on each of the twelve occasions when he sang in "Tosca" between October 23 and the following November 11 the tenor met with no serious mishap.

Appearances at the Comunale of Bologna were to come next, — appearances likely to give Caruso some concern because of the interest that had already been created through the announced engagements of Giuseppe Borgatti and Alessandro Bonci, two other tenors more firmly intrenched than he. Bonci was perhaps the more formidable one; the same Bonci who had created the tenor character in "Il Signor di Pourceaugnac" at its April 10, 1897, La Scala première, which Caruso had been unable to accept. Older than Caruso and more experienced, Bonci held the advantage. He was established at the Politeama when Caruso and Borgatti joined the Comunale, and the Bonci adherents were to be counted on to do their part. For the public it was a situation to be desired; competition generally brings the best from those competing. But for Caruso it was a situation of quite another sort. If not actually afraid, he was at least fearful of an outcome he could not afford to lose. A lessening of such prestige as was then his might harm him in any number of ways; recovering from a setback is often harder than the original gaining of the position itself.

Nerved for what was in truth an ordeal, Caruso stepped before the Bologna public in his opening appearance. Ada Giachetti and the baritone Giraldoni were two of the stalwarts on either side of the tenor. Mugnone was at the conductor's desk. The public would be sure to get the utmost possible from Caruso if his support was an element to be counted upon. "Tosca" and "Iris" were the two operas which lifted the newcomer into a place near the spotlight, contriving to keep him sufficiently near the rays to be seen with that distinctness necessary to attract attention. It was, though, a pivoting spotlight which, sweeping in a circle, touched first one then another of the three tenors who were contesting for popular favor. One night it would be Caruso; the next Bonci had his innings; whereupon Borgatti's turn came. For several weeks this triangular race continued, the adherents of each proclaiming at every opportunity the supremacy of their favorite. Finally the tide rolled the majority opinion in one direction, — toward Caruso, youngest tenor of the three, who was declared to have gained the palm.

VI

After Bologna there was to come for Caruso his début at Teatro alla Scala — "the terrible La Scala of Milan which scares all artists." Its general director at that time was Giulio Gatti-Casazza, who since 1908 has been the executive head of New York's Metropolitan. The first conductor was Arturo Toscanini, even then known throughout Italy as a disciplinarian of the severest type. The goal of every lyric artist, La Scala nevertheless loomed before each new arrival — formidable, pitiless, severe. To win there was to be carried to the heights; to lose was to be swept away into the limbo of oblivion.

"I did not know what caused it, but almost immediately I realized that the feeling was against me," declared Caruso. "First came the untraceable rumor that I was 'not well.' Then somebody else was 'not sure' of my ability. Somebody else remarked that the fifty thousand *lire* I was to receive for the three months' season was 'an enormous sum' for such a singer as Caruso. It was in such an atmosphere that I began a most critical period in my career.

"I had been notified that I would make my début in 'Bohème', on the second night of the season; Wagner's 'Siegfried' was to be the opening opera. Since the public was eager about 'Bohème' it was sure to be well prepared; the discipline at La Scala was strict. Emma Carelli was to be the Mimì, Alessandro Arcangeli and Oreste Luppi were to have the rôles of Marcello and Colline. Toscanini was of course to conduct.

"The first rehearsal finally began, with the other principals of the company and specially permitted visitors listening to my every tone and watching every move I made. How little the public realizes what the artist must endure to present well the music and action of a character. It may have taken blood from one's heart to attain the excellence which sends an audience from the theater, satisfied. When in this rehearsal we reached the tenor's romanza of the opening act, I sang in full voice every note of the aria excepting the high C; this I gave falsetto.

"I noticed some of the artists looking at one another, for in Italy the use of the falsetto is not a mark of good singing. At the end of the romanza Toscanini asked me if I could give the high C a little stronger; and I answered, 'yes.' He then asked to hear, to which I replied that I did not wish to give the tone strong so early in the day. I feared this might displease Toscanini, but an artist must do what he thinks is best and right; and feeling certain of my high C when it was necessary to sing it in the performance, it seemed unwise to risk singing a poor tone at a time when a good tone was what was wanted.

"At the third rehearsal, when I continued because of the same reasons to sing the high C falsetto, Toscanini said he was afraid to let me go on without hearing how I would give the note from the chest; and he suggested that the aria be transposed a half-tone lower. To this I did not object; it did not however remove the obstacle, for at the next rehearsal when we arrived at the high B natural I sang that note falsetto.

"At last came the date for the general rehearsal which at La Scala begins at nine in the evening with a large audience; it is almost a regular performance. The day had not gone far — it was, I remember, only nine in the morning — when the man who summons the principals to the theater (the *avvisatore*) arrived at my house to inform me of a 'small' rehearsal. Both the composer and the librettist had attended all the rehearsals; many changes had been made; now some one had thought of new changes.

"Shortly after I reached the theater we began with the third act of 'Bohème.' There were many stops; many suggestions; finally we finished and took up the fourth act. After a time I began to wonder when this 'small' rehearsal would end. At half-past one we were still at work and no mention had been made of lunch, nor was there any when this act had been disposed of, for immediately we began on act one. By this time I was becoming angry over the thought that my soup at home was getting cold. I began to sing this first act with all my voice and continued in this through the romanza, including the much disputed high note near the close. When I gave it without any vocal restraint Toscanini (and everybody else also) appeared relieved. For a reward we were put to work upon the second act, in which I also used all the tone I had. Having sung with complete strength the entire opera, I was astounded when the *avvisatore* called out, 'Signore, Signori — to-night at nine o'clock the general rehearsal.'

"It was my intention to object, and I should have done so had not the soprano stopped me. 'Don't worry,' she said, 'to-night we will sing in only half-voice.'

"Having reached home at five o'clock I had little rest when, at seven-thirty, the *avvisatore* called with a carriage to take me to the theater. There was present an invited audience of distinguished persons: the critics, privileged subscribers, La Scala artists who were not taking part in the performance, and some of their friends. I began the opening act in demi-voice. Presently I noticed that the soprano who had told me in the afternoon that we would all sing that way was using her entire voice. At the

REALIZATIONS 133

first opportunity I inquired why she did so. She answered, 'I want to put the part in my throat.' I was surprised at the finish of the act to notice that there was no applause. While I was resting in my dressing room don Giulio (Gatti-Casazza) entered and requested me to give in the next act a little more voice. I begged him to excuse me, explaining that I was singing too soon after having eaten to give all my voice with comfort to my digestion.

"Don Giulio's request upset me and made me so nervous that in the second act I could scarcely find even this demi-voice I had used in the opening scenes. In a few moments I heard a rapping noise; immediately the orchestra ceased playing. Then Toscanini pointed at me with his bâton and said, 'If you don't sing, I can't go on.' I urged, for the same reason I had given don Giulio, that he excuse me, but instead of answering he laid down his bâton and left the orchestra pit; then the curtain came down.

"I went to my dressing room feeling that I should give back my advance money and leave La Scala. In all probability I should have done so, if the Duke of Modrone, president of the La Scala board of directors, had not come to me. When he heard what I had to say, he urged that I resume my singing in whatever way I felt physically able. We finally took up the opera, with Toscanini conducting, and at one o'clock in the morning the general rehearsal finished."

Caruso was so dispirited when he reached home that he considered again the advisability of asking to be released from his contract. When he awoke later in the day he was more firmly of that mind, for he had contracted fever. Matters now had become serious. Attended by a physician, his grievances magnified by illness, the world had become suddenly forbidding. What was the use of it all? Enmity was everywhere about him; he wished to be rid of the whole sickening business.

But suddenly the sun broke through the clouds when, on the day set for the La Scala opening, Gatti-Casazza visited his tenor to inform him that "Siegfried" was not well enough prepared to be presented. "La Bohème" had been decided as a substitute; here was Caruso's opportunity. In vain did the still stricken singer protest; for two hours Gatti-Casazza argued, to ultimate success. Caruso capitulated. He consented to sing. And sing he did, on the evening of December 26, 1900; and despite the handicaps imposed by the illness from which he had not fully recovered, victory came to him. He was not entirely clear of the woods; he had still a little way farther to go. But that "Bohème" appearance restored his wavering courage and enabled him to collect his resources. He was not far from a goal just around the corner; a glorious goal.

Gatti and Toscanini were too well seasoned not to have immediately discovered the quality of this new tenor. Shortcomings he undeniably had; maturity of voice and powers were yet to come. It seemed the part of wisdom to both to nurse this singing plant, and the first step to that end was to allow him to rest. Headaches which years later were to torment him had already begun to appear; nor was he by any means wholly recovered from his touch of fever. A

Copyright Mishkin, N. Y.

CARUSO AS RODOLFO IN "LA BOHÈME"

REALIZATIONS

rest of eight days, during which an eased mind proved no insignificant factor, sent Caruso up for his second Rodolfo in condition to do himself justice. At the conclusion of the tenth appearance public confidence had been won; and on January 17, 1901, the tenor created the rôle of Florindo in Mascagni's then new opera "Le Maschere", his principal associates in the cast being Signore Emma Carelli and Linda Brambilla, and Signori Arcangeli and Luppi.

What might have happened if "Le Maschere" — produced simultaneously in seven different opera houses of Italy — had succeeded at La Scala must be conjectured. Indifferently received after its third Milan presentation, Gatti-Casazza was put to it to find a substitute. During this period Director Gatti-Casazza and Conductor Toscanini fell to meeting of evenings to consider what opera could be found to replace "Le Maschere."

"On one of these evenings," related Gatti-Casazza, "I went with Arturo Toscanini to the Caffé Cova in the neighborhood of the theater. I had remembered having heard while a child 'L'Elisir d'Amore', that charming opera buffa which Donizetti had written in fourteen days. Some of the traditions were yet fresh in my mind: the dispute Donizetti had with Romani the librettist over the introduction as a tenor romanza of a special piece of concert music he had composed — *Una furtiva lagrima* — during which dispute Romani had exclaimed, 'What! a pathetic wail by a stupid fellow when all should be festive and gay?' And then the dedication of the opera to the ladies, when Donizetti had written,

'Who more than they know how to distill love? Who better than they know how to dispense it?' At various times since its première on May 12, 1832, at the Teatro della Canobbiana (now the Lirico) 'L'Elisir d'Amore' had been revived with recurring success.

"During one of the many pauses in our conversation on this particular evening," continued Gatti, "when Toscanini and I had each vainly suggested one work after another, I at length said,'Suppose we try to put together "L'Elisir d'Amore", an opera always fresh even if almost forgotten.' 'I would be delighted to try,' answered Toscanini, 'but the company? We have Caruso, who would do admirably as Nemorino; we have no Adina, although one could be found; but my dear Gatti, what we have not, and what I doubt we can find, is a Dulcamara suitable for La Scala. It is a difficult rôle, and buffos of good style are no longer to be had.' We separated to go to our respective homes.

"The next day, after a rehearsal, the conversation was resumed. Toscanini (I can visualize him now) was seated before a piano and playing from 'L'Elisir d'Amore' the duet of Adina and Dulcamara. He was playing half-unconsciously, looking upwards, and repeating in a far-away manner: 'Where — can we find — a Dulcamara? — There is — none.'

"Maestro Sormani, one of the assistant conductors who chanced to hear this curious chant, immediately inquired, 'Why not the buffo Carbonetti?'

"Toscanini paused, swung round in his chair, and exclaimed, 'Carbonetti? But the voice?'

"'The voice of Carbonetti, which I heard last year,' replied Sormani with quiet assurance, 'is a voice no worse than other voices we have since heard right here in La Scala.'

"'Very well,' declared Toscanini, with his characteristic quickness, 'then let us get Carbonetti and try "L'Elisir."' We decided at once to do so; that very night, between acts during a performance of 'Bohème', I spoke to Caruso about Nemorino.

"'I know only *Una furtiva lagrima*,' he informed me, 'but if you wish I will begin to-morrow to learn the entire rôle.' Soon I engaged for the Adina Signora Regina Pinkert; Magini-Coletti was cast for Sergeant Belcore, and Federico Carbonetti journeyed to Milan from the provinces, where he had been passing such a wretched existence that he presented himself at La Scala without an overcoat, and carrying a valise tied up with a bit of string. But he had a spirit not in the least curbed by his fortunes. 'They say I am getting old!' he declared. 'That is a calumny! I still defy all the youngsters to travel around Italy in the winter as I do, without an overcoat.' Then he hurried off to report to Toscanini, who had to be severe with the enthusiastic buffo to prevent his introducing in parts of his music top notes not written in the score.

"Reports that La Scala was to revive 'L'Elisir d'Amore' were not so favorably received by the public; and I began to receive letters intimating that I was about to turn La Scala into a provincial theater and would soon be punished with a fiasco more decisive than any I had known. These warnings did not interfere with our preparations for the première of the revival. The painters started work on the three scenes, and my much loved president of the board, Duke Visconti di Modrone, made a personal search among the Milan carriage makers until he had found a 'berlin' which he had adapted for use by Doctor Dulcamara.

"The rehearsals were not strictly joyous affairs. The voice of Carbonetti irritated Toscanini intensely; and never have I seen him in such ill humor as he was on the morning of February 17, 1901, which had been fixed for 'L'Elisir' première. Perhaps he sensed the quality of the audience which gathered that evening; for it was moderate in size and made no pretense of its mind to teach a lesson to Toscanini, to me, and — if necessary — to the memory of Donizetti.

"Toscanini's face was still forbidding when he walked to his conductor's desk in the orchestra pit. The opera began; the chorus sang its strophes; Adina related with grace the story of the love of Queen Isolde; Nemorino sighed delightfully in his song — but the audience took not the slightest interest. Not even Belcore — which Magini-Coletti was interpreting masterfully — could soften the stern faces of the terrible subscribers. The concertato of Adina, Nemorino, and Belcore, with the chorus, was followed by a chilling silence which traveled to where I was standing back stage, causing my blood to freeze with the fear that after all the evening would end disastrously.

"Presently the duet of the soprano and tenor commenced. Signora Pinkert delivered her opening phrases delightfully; and when she had finished, I caught some subdued murmurs of approval. Then Caruso began. Who that heard him will not remember? Calm and conscious that at this point lay the fate of the performance he uttered his response (*Chiedi al rio*) to the soprano in a voice of such warmth, and with such art of sentiment, that I cannot describe its effect. Gradually he melted the icy reserve with which the auditors had invested themselves; little by little he compelled their attention; and when he arrived at the cadenza he swept on to a climax with such fervor that none in the theater could resist. Such a tempest of applause can be appreciated only by one who knows an Italian audience — and more particularly a discriminating La Scala audience. So uproariously did that assemblage demand a repetition that Toscanini, notwithstanding his aversion to granting encores, had to submit. The curtain fell with an ovation for Adina and Nemorino when they came thrice before the curtain.

"My nervousness was such at this point that I could not remain upon the stage; I went beneath it. I feared to observe how Carbonetti would fare with this critical audience. When I fancied his cavatina should have been finished, I approached the prompter's box to inquire. Marchesi (the same prompter now at the Metropolitan) whispered to me that Carbonetti 'went well,' having caused many to laugh who wished not to. That settled matters; if the old voice of Carbonetti had met with favor, then the ship was indeed safely in port.

"From that point on, approval greeted every

number. And when Caruso sang *Una furtiva lagrima* he was made to repeat it, with a third delivery of the aria almost compelled. That settled everything. I was limp, but content. When Toscanini came back stage to go before the curtain with the artists, he embraced Caruso, then turned to me and said, '*Per dio! Se questo Napoletano continua a cantare così, farà parlare di sè il mondo intero.*' (By Heaven! If this Neapolitan continues to sing like this, he will make the world talk about him.)

"It was after a representation of 'Marta' at the New York Metropolitan one evening during the season of 1916 that Otto H. Kahn remarked to me, 'With Caruso in such admirable form why shouldn't we revive "L'Elisir d'Amore"?' This was, as we say in Italy, 'inviting a goose to drink.' I accepted with enthusiasm Mr. Kahn's suggestion. 'L'Elisir d'Amore' is one of the very few *amori di teatro* (stage's love) of which I am the faithful slave — 'L'Elisir' with Caruso, be it understood.

"Perhaps this may explain my feelings toward him whenever he sang Nemorino, and which moved me to say to him after one of those 1916 'L'Elisir' performances: 'Caro don Enrico — I and many others have become less young; but you must truly have drunk of the elixir of love because your voice and your art, constantly advancing toward perfection, have preserved the charm and the wonderful resources of that memorable night at La Scala. To you and your art may the gods grant as much youth and glory as still smile upon the "Elisir" of the great Italian master.'"

REALIZATIONS 141

After that "L'Elisir d'Amore" revival première at La Scala there was a sudden lifting of the unpleasant atmosphere which had surrounded the Neapolitan tenor. Difficulties were of course to be expected so long as the career continued; and at twenty-eight one can scarcely be more than well started along the highway. Such was Caruso's viewpoint expressed at the time to Ada Giachetti; he likewise communicated his feelings in the matter to other of his intimates. Still, the hostility manifested in the underhanded fashion that was no new experience instilled within the singer a feeling of sadness rather than resentment. By nature friendly, he disliked any unfriendly thoughts others might have for him. His success was resting far too easily upon his widening shoulders to cause on his part any display of irritating egotism: he forbore to speak overmuch of himself, of his voice, or his singing, and there is no evidence to indicate that he developed at that time any offensive mannerisms. Perhaps no particular credit belongs to Caruso for such restraint; it apparently was no part of his make-up to lord it over a fellow artist. But for all his open-heartedness he unquestionably was learning to look more closely at the companion across the table; and under it also, lest his toes be surreptitiously trodden upon.

Although "Le Maschere" had caused the public to upturn its music nose the tenor music gave Caruso a real opportunity. In the rôle of Florindo he had found such congenial moments that the complete turning of the La Scala tide in his direction dates from the time of that opera's première. A miscellaneous performance, given in La Scala February 1 in commemoration of Giuseppe Verdi (one week following his death) presented Caruso in the quartet from "Rigoletto" with Signore Brambilla and Ghibaudo and Signor Arcangeli. With "L'Elisir d'Amore" firmly established in the favor of the Milan public, preparations were begun on "Mefistofele," in which the distinguished Chaliapin was to appear.

The Russian basso had an experience with Toscanini at his first rehearsal similar to that of Caruso during his "Bohème." Chaliapin could not understand why he should be asked to sing full voice when the other artists were permitted to suppress their tones. A stranger to him until that meeting, Caruso explained to Chaliapin that Toscanini had reasons for wishing to hear a voice then new to him. "He knows," said the tenor, "just what the rest of us can do. You have not to worry. Toscanini is like one of these dogs who bark and do not bite." The basso felt that Caruso had "the face of goodness", and a voice which was "the ideal" Chaliapin had been "waiting years to hear." Those nine La Scala "Mefistofele" presentations, the first of which took place March 16, 1901, included in the cast Signore Carelli and Pinto. But the artists talked about by the public were Caruso and Chaliapin.

The tenor bade au revoir to La Scala with the consciousness of a securer place in the world which was then beginning to open its arms. April, 1901, brought the sailing time for South America, and when the SS *Orione* docked in the Buenos Aires harbor on May 10 Caruso disembarked with Toscanini, Mme.

REALIZATIONS 143

Ericlea Darclée, Signore Amelia Pinto and Alice Cucini; the tenors Borgatti and Mariacher; Giraldoni and Sammarco, baritones, and the bassos de Segurola, Ercolani, and La Puma. There was no enthusiastic Mme. Ferrari to greet the little group of artists; the impresaria had died several months before. In her place was Camillo Bonetti, her former secretary, who had engaged the Theater of La Opera and was bent on making that season an extraordinary affair. He felt elated in having such a maestro as Toscanini, a personage by reputation even though he had never conducted in Buenos Aires. And he needed a Toscanini, for there would be no Emma Carelli and no Emilio de Marchi in the "Tosca" première. Mme. Darclée and Caruso might actually surpass these missing favorites yet fail to stir so favorable a public response. It was therefore a somewhat delicate situation which waited for its turning upon a capricious South American public.

The test was not long coming. On May 16 a dress rehearsal was given before an invited audience which included the critics. Two nights later brought the public performance and a gathering by no means happy in the absence of their adored Carelli and de Marchi. That first act of "Tosca" was performed before auditors concerned chiefly in making comparisons between the tenor and soprano before them on the opera stage, and those two artists the listeners felt should be there. In the same atmosphere the second scene was begun, but before such singing coldness could not prevail, and when Caruso delivered his *Vittoria! Vittoria!* cry of defiance to the

Scarpia of Giraldoni, all oppressiveness disappeared. No South American assemblage was able to sit unmoved by such tones, and the capitulation was immediate. Later came the *E lucevan le stelle*, and an uproar akin to a riot. In vain did Toscanini protest the demand for a repetition; it had to be granted, just as de Marchi thereafter was forced into a place secondary to the one he had hitherto held. The same opera was presented on the next evening (Sunday) and the Thursday following; so far as public desire was concerned, "Tosca" might have gone indefinitely, with that especial cast.

Time and experience must have carried Caruso materially forward in both voice and art during the year of his absence from Buenos Aires, for in each fresh rôle he was vehemently acclaimed. These demonstrations had their beneficial effects. Stimulated by them the tenor spared nothing he could give as an adequate return. On June 1, 1901, he appeared with Signora Pinto in "Regina di Saba"; and eight days later, in "Rigoletto", he sang the Duke to her Gilda. All the forces within him must have leaped out on this occasion, else followers of the great Masini could not have allowed themselves to concede Caruso to have been "a wonderful Duke."

Those were sunny days indeed for the tenor. He had won the people; he was earning thirty-five thousand *lire* a month; he could look ahead, then, and actually smile over the spotty past. One could of course never be quite sure of what might lurk in the distance, but the present was a glorious enough present to be enjoyed to the full, — with his comrades of the opera, with those notables of the city who insisted he accept their hospitality, and with the always sympathetic Galante whose friendship and studio continued to be sources of attraction to the singer's artistic heart. And visible signs of this material and mental prosperity were beginning to appear. The former slenderness of figure had given way to one manifestly stocky; no longer was the anxious, eager-to-please look to be found upon the tenor's round face. Never given to bodily exercise, and able at that time to eat whatever and as much as he pleased, Caruso was entering willingly the period of self-indulgence. He smoked cigarettes, he laughed when asked if he were not afraid they might affect his voice, and kept such hours as it pleased him to keep. In short, he was acquiring the ways of one gripping hard to success and developing out of it the sort of confidence necessary to retain that hold. There was time enough also for good reading had Caruso been so inclined; but he never was. For him a book was something to be looked at rather than into. His knowledge was a knowledge gathered principally from observation and word-of-mouth communication, — if exception be made of such study as was brought to the learning and refreshing of his opera rôles. His later years did not bring a development in that direction, for when his wife, who devours books voraciously, asked him why he did not read, he dismissed the subject with the terse rejoinder, "I learn from life, not from books."

"L'Elisir d'Amore", "Iris", "La Traviata", and "Lohengrin" — sung in Italian — were other works in which Caruso appeared during this South American sojourn. The tenor rôle in the latter opera must never have appealed to him; it is a question if at that time its qualities of knightly dignity were suited to his inclinations and style. In the final period of his career — when he added to his repertory such parts as John of Leyden in "Le Prophète"; Samson in "Samson et Dalila"; and Eleazar in "La Juive" — "Lohengrin" might have disclosed him upon no less eminent an artistic plane. Reports of the two Buenos Aires "Lohengrin" appearances go no further than that he sang with "considerable success." Since Caruso never afterward essayed the character of the Knight of the Grail it may be assumed that it brought him no laurels. For Caruso possessed a sense of values, and whatever could assist materially his career was seldom overlooked.

On July 29 the tenor sang in a performance of Rossini's "Stabat Mater" given as a memorial to King Humbert of Italy; and August 17 marked his Buenos Aires farewell in the same work which had opened the season. The next day, on board the SS *Manilla*, he sailed for Italy. Two years elapsed before he returned to those audiences which had reserved for him an especial place.

Independent enough upon his return home to indulge in a rest, Caruso declined every contract offered for an autumn engagement. He had money; what more natural after his periods of struggling that he should avail himself of some leisure with which to enjoy it! The Galleria of Milan saw him regularly each day, as did those other places frequented by the workers of the opera. Conspicuously clothed, the tenor was a familiar figure and one not to be missed. Amid friends and scenes that warmed his Italian heart, the weeks drove all too swiftly toward that late December day which was to carry him back to the public of his native city for his début at the celebrated San Carlo Theater. There were only two interruptions. The first one took the tenor to Bologna, where he sang in "Rigoletto." The second interruption came in the form of a request from the Associazione Italiana di Beneficenza, of Trieste, urging Caruso to sing in two charity performances of "L'Elisir d'Amore" to be given at the Politeama Rossetti.

Those evenings of December 14 and 15, 1901, remain memorable. Signora Adelina Padovani was the Adina; Signorina Emma Trentini sang Gianetta; G. Caruson and Signor Borelli appeared respectively as Belcore and Dulcamara, and Maestro Gialdino Gialdini conducted. A souvenir of those days during which Trieste bowed under Austria's rule now reposes in the Trieste City Hall. It is a phonograph "proof" record (then unpublished) of the song *La Campana di San Giusto*, presented by the tenor to those first members of the Parliament which, after so many years of waiting, swerved from Vienna to Rome. This presentation took place in New York, during a visit made by the Parliament members to deliver a series of lectures.

Trieste had served as a sort of operatic warming-up for the vastly more serious business of the San Carlo début. How often in his youth had Caruso paused before that stately building, hoping he might — and wondering if he would — one day sing there. Among opera houses of the world the San Carlo ranked high; certainly no other in Southern Italy held for the artists so strong an allure. Having conquered in outside fields, the singer returned joyously for the effort he then believed would prove the supremely happy one of his life. All the honors reaped in those other centers of operatic art could scarcely compare with the single honor he hoped Naples would bestow upon a native son. For he did hope, with a confidence born of those recent successes gained before people quite as critical as the Neapolitans.

Perhaps, had there been no intrigue to combat, a different story might be told. Naples assuredly was eager to welcome within the halls of its beloved San Carlo its rising singer. And had the power remained solely with the populace the record would doubtless have run according to the adage. But operatic Naples was swayed at that time by violent prejudices; and out of these prejudices there had grown the famous *patiti*, — as the enthusiasts of the opera were then termed. Each of these enthusiasts, affirms no less an authority than Nicola Daspuro, assumed the right to constitute a legitimate guardian of the artistic traditions of San Carlo. In reality, however, this assumption of authority had been seized by the followers of two impresari during an earlier feud, their numbers being later swelled by the adherents of various teachers of singing whose approval or disapproval of an artist was sufficient to make him happy or forlorn. Then there were the pessimists who still hugged to their breasts disappointed ambition. A motley assortment, those Naples *patiti*, yet an all powerful one where any singer was concerned.

That turbulent group has been called by Signor Mormone, the eminent music reviewer for the newspaper *Roma*, the *sicofanti*. Sycophants they unquestionably were. They might have had their own opinions; doubtless they did hold them. But they were ready to be subdued under such orders as might be issued by the leaders, in the manner customary for these leaders to display in the presence of any San Carlo audience.

The stamping ground of the *sicofanti* (or *patiti*) was the orchestra pit of the San Carlo. On the right they sat, assuming all the airs of maestri and professori, and with such a seriousness as prevailed in the Grecian Areopagus. "Monaciello" — as they called Cavalier Alfredo Monaco — was one of the leaders, and many artists had experienced evenings of woe for failure to have previously paid homage either to Monaco or his co-leader, Prince Adolfo di Castagneto, who from his historical seat in the first row, right, of the orchestra pit would assume the airs of a modern Diocletian.

At every première, just before the curtain rose, the prince would enter the theater. If the soprano or tenor or other artist about to début had not previously called to pay him personal homage, it proved an oversight serious in its effects. For the prince liked to feel that his protection was a valued thing.

When it had not been sought he would stalk to his seat, observing audibly, "Who is this new and unknown celebrity? We will hear. We will be rigid critics, yet we will be just." These were the stereotyped words, so well known to a San Carlo audience. Equally stereotyped would be the action, manner, and words of the Prince di Castagneto if the newcomer singer had won the audience's applause. He would rise ceremoniously from his seat, adjust his monocle, and with the pose of a censor from whose edict there could be no appeal he would declare, "Bad — *very* bad!"

This ultimatum was the invariable signal for a riot in which the "Rights" stood arrayed against the public, seated in the other parts of the house. Such dissension, started thus in the theater, would extend into the foyer and corridors of the San Carlo, thence to the streets, and later it would drift into and be continued within the fashionable club called the Casino dell' Unione, and amongst those who gathered in coffee houses, restaurants, and newspaper offices.

Did Gayarre sing, the Stagno devotees maintained that Gayarre forced his voice. For those who bowed to Gayarre's art Stagno was no more than a bleating goat. Masini — to those opposing him — spoke rather than sang; de Lucia had to stamp his feet against the stage in order to produce his high tones and Tamagno was a *strillazzaro* (fruit vendor). These and other comments, uttered by the excitable Neapolitan opera *sicofanti* in judgment of artists of renown, bespoke no symptom of merciful consideration for any young singer ready to come before them.

REALIZATIONS

Caruso was well aware of this existing situation when he signed the San Carlo contract Impresario Roberto de Sanna had prepared. He knew on his arrival in Naples, several days prior to the night of his début in "L'Elisir d'Amore" on December 30, 1901, that a visit to Prince di Castagneto or to Chev. Monaco would help to gain for him a likely success. A visiting card sent to each of the newspaper music critics also might have enlisted tempered pens.

But such practises had not been Caruso practises; he never turned to them at any time in his career. Quite possibly he wished to win — if it were to be so decreed — by virtue of accomplishment unaided by favor of any kind. He was young; he had become reasonably sure of himself; he believed his townsfolk would at least deal out justice to him. Daspuro was of that San Carlo assemblage which attended Caruso's fateful début. "I have him before my eyes," he declared, "when he advanced toward the footlights to sing the *Quanto è bella, quanto è cara.* His friends sought to salute and to reassure him with some slight applause, whereupon the sound of hisses intermingled. It was the registered objection of the ever-observant San Carlo *patiti* at the right of the orchestra pit and that of the public elsewhere. Immediately came cries of 'Wait! let us judge him.'"

Stricken momentarily dumb by this reception, Caruso stood hesitant. Near him was Signora Regina Pinkert, the Adina of the night. Just below, with poised bâton, sat Maestro Edoardo Mascheroni. Beyond, clearly visible, were the faces of the malcontents who sat shoulder to shoulder, ready *en masse* to squelch any further efforts to encourage an artist who should pass them lightly by.

For a few moments this tenseness held. It needed some immediate and exceptional effort to rescue the tenor from his position of defense. He put out of his mind whatever previous plan he may have had to win by slow methods and sure. It was then or (possibly) never; and into the accomplishment of this task he threw every resource he could summon. To shift, if only slightly, the attitude of the opposition was a thing he must do. In part he succeeded. As the performance wore on the majority listeners responded to efforts put forth from a heart of lead. Caruso sung himself to a triumph, though not an overwhelming one. For in the newspapers of the next day it was said of him that while his voice was "beautiful — very beautiful", it was scarcely adapted to the idyllic character of "L'Elisir." Baron Saverio Procida, critic for *Il Pungolo*, wrote that for the *Una furtiva lagrima* aria it was necessary to have a tenor-like timbre of voice, not a baritone. Other reviewers were of the opinion that Caruso's acting "left much to be desired."

The three days intervening between the "L'Elisir" première and its second representation were sufficient to restore Caruso's equilibrium. He no longer cared to win his compatriots for the joy it should give him. What he sought was revenge; and he meant to have it — in his own peculiar fashion. It was a dead-cold Caruso who appeared as Nemorino in the San Carlo on January 2, 1902. Signora Pinkert noticed it; Signori Bucalo and Borelli, also of that cast, noted the fact. So too, it appears, did the *patiti*, and the very public which had joined with it in resisting the endeavors of a young artist to win on merit alone.

Between that night and the following January 21, 1902, Caruso sang four additional times in "L'Elisir d'Amore"; and made four appearances in Massenet's "Manon", with Signorina Rina Giachetti, Emanuele Bucalo and Constantino Thos. Those were the last ten appearances the tenor ever made in the city of his birth. His Des Grieux in "Manon" — particularly the intrepretation of the *Dream Aria* of the third act — won over the last of the dissenters. It was sweet revenge, but for Caruso there was to be one still sweeter to comfort his wounded soul. During the final days of that San Carlo engagement he said to his friend Daspuro, "Daspuro, I will never again come to Naples to sing; it will be only to eat a plate of spaghetti."

Impresari and friends of the tenor sought at various times during the years that followed to induce him to break his vow. Vain endeavors! He never would. Much as he loved Naples, he was operatically finished with it forever on the night of January 21, 1902.

CHAPTER SIX

CLIMBING

WHATEVER reception his fellow Neapolitans may have chosen to extend him as an artist before his voice and singing at length disposed of their ill-timed opposition, Caruso must have found comfort in the consciousness of his growing importance in the opera world. From time to time negotiations had been tentatively begun for his appearances in London and the United States. As early as December, 1899, Henry V. Higgins, chairman of the board at Covent Garden, had requested Antonio Scotti to make overtures to Caruso to appear in London; and it was about that time also that an Italian agent, representing the New York Metropolitan Opera Company, had made an offer to the tenor. A Monte Carlo engagement had likewise been tendered, and from other European opera houses solicitations for his services, both direct and indirect, had reached him.

Following his Naples "farewell" Caruso was pledged to sing some special appearances at Monte Carlo; then to resume his place at La Scala. Thereafter Covent Garden audiences were to hear for the first time this much talked-about voice. The tenor had signed the Covent Garden contract upon recommendation of Scotti, with whom he had become acquainted at Milan, in March, 1899. Caruso had drawn back from the two thousand *lire* an appearance offer of Chairman Higgins, made through Scotti. "Per Dio, I receive twenty-five hundred at La Scala; why should I accept less to go to London?" The baritone emphasized the advantages which a Covent Garden engagement would bring, and his arguments at length prevailed. Caruso accepted the terms, which provided for twenty-five hundred *lire* an appearance throughout the second season, three thousand *lire* for the third, and thirty-five hundred *lire* and four thousand *lire* respectively an appearance for the fourth and fifth seasons.

Not until 1913 did Caruso receive what he felt to have been his "price", and a figure "higher than had ever been paid an artist in Europe." The stumbling block that placed four thousand nine hundred and ninety-nine *lire* the limit for a Caruso appearance during his sixth and seventh Covent Garden seasons was a contract then in force with Mme. Nellie Melba, which stipulated that she alone should receive as much as a thousand dollars (five thousand *lire*) an appearance.

Caruso departed for Monte Carlo looking ahead and upwards — even though the hurt Naples had dealt him was still felt in his heart. Those days spent with friends following the San Carlo engagement had not been altogether happy ones, although those cleaving to the tenor had sought to make them so. For, creeping in during the card games and the promenades and the gatherings of evening, which consumed much of Caruso's time during the approach of his leave-taking, would come the thought of what he held to have been the injustice dealt him as an artist by his fellow citizens. En route northwards Caruso stopped off in Milan, where he participated in several rehearsals of Baron Alberto Franchetti's "Germania", in which he was to create the tenor rôle.

Monte Carlo was different from Naples. Plunged into an atmosphere of gayety, and among people whose sole existence appeared to center in the indulging of luxurious taste, Caruso caught his first glimpse of another corner of the world. He rather liked it. The cosmopolitanism of the gatherings held his attention; and he began to note, among other things, that taste in dress was governed by other elements than conspicuousness of cut and design. The Casino attracted his interest; nor did he attempt to resist the desire to chance a few *francs* on some of the tables which silently beckoned him. The soft air, the romanticism of the place, and the clear skies appealed to his warm Italian nature. He was glad to have come to this spot; and before he left he signed a contract with Impresario Raoul Gunsbourg to return for several successive seasons.

It was at this Monte Carlo début that Caruso first sang with Mme. Melba. The opera was Puccini's "La Bohéme," Maestro Arturo Vigna conducted, and Miss Mary Royer was the Musetta. Seasoned by the constant routine he had undergone for more than five years, and enlightened at last as to the appeal and responsiveness of his voice, Caruso seems to have expanded in the capacity to sing with that degree of authority which is one of the distinguishing marks of the artist. He was accepted instantly by an audience which had heard opera in all parts of the world; by an audience well enough versed to discriminate intelligently.

"Rigoletto" presented the tenor who was destined to become a fixed star in subsequent Monte Carlo seasons in a no less favorable light, — even though he had as associates in the cast Mme. Melba and the great baritone, Maurice Renaud, then at the zenith of his powers. These two operas were alternated throughout the 1902 Monte Carlo season, and at its conclusion Caruso went forth to Milan, surer than ever of himself and the better equipped for the larger efforts to come. He had been chosen to create the tenor character of Loewe in Franchetti's "Germania", which was to be produced that March 11 at La Scala, and he took up eagerly the preliminary rehearsals.

How friendly Milan seemed to the tenor as he passed through its streets to the little family of two which awaited him at via Velasca; how different from the Milan of the year before, during those trying moments when La Scala appeared about to be snatched from him. From Fofò and Ada Giachetti he went to the Galleria posthaste — as every artist is moved to go immediately upon reaching this city — and there he received the congratulations of his comrades over the Monte Carlo success, the news of which had preceded him. So far as could be seen all serious opposition had been routed; the way into the future lay clearly enough defined; and the realization of these matters, subtle though they doubtless were, nevertheless gave back a fortifying reaction. Indeed from that time forth there was little questioning that

Caruso was certain to shortly become — if not actually at that time — the world's foremost tenor. The few who disputed his place never interfered seriously with his progress. Some circumstances arose which slightly retarded it, but such an artist could not long be kept from arriving at his predestined goal.

"Germania" went up (as opera people express the presentation of an opera) with Toscanini conducting, and a cast consisting of Caruso, Signore Amelia Pinto, Jane Bathori, Teresa Ferraris, and the baritone Mario Sammarco, who afterward became a favorite with the patrons of Oscar Hammerstein's Manhattan Opera Company. After fourteen performances of this work Caruso left for London. Here was a new center for his widening activities; a people to sing to quite different in tastes and temperament from any he had yet known. A victory in such circumstances meant an almost assured future. The tenor was almost boyishly eager for the test.

Caruso has referred to the attitude of the Covent Garden management as that of a housewife endeavoring, by the "feel" of a watermelon, to determine whether it is ripe enough to buy. "I was in a somewhat uncertain position, for the impresa wished to be convinced that I was thoroughly ripe. I accepted the conditions of the contract because I was almost sure that my voice had something of the 'red ripeness' in it."

Such was the tenor's frame of mind when he first set foot in London, where forever afterwards he was

CARUSO AS THE DUKE IN "RIGOLETTO"

to become one of its popular singers. Indeed, he became in time unique; his appearance in public was instantly attended by the gathering of a throng of people, — on the streets or indoors. He was just beginning to acquire an ease of manner which some choose to interpret as self-conceit; and his promenading may have had in it something of that air, for he walked with a short and scarcely graceful stride, his head held high, his upturned moustache bearing evidences of careful tending. All this was of course enough to be seized upon by those born with gossipy tongues. But it mattered little after Caruso had impressed Londoners with the quality of his voice and his singing.

"Rigoletto" was the opera which presented him to a Covent Garden audience, on May 14, 1902, in a cast which included Mme. Melba and Maurice Renaud and Marcel Journet. The auditorium was quite filled. With as much interest as a Covent Garden assemblage of that period would permit itself to show, the listeners gave their attention to the new tenor. His stocky frame, his chubby face and the traditional operatic bearing affected by most tenors of his time and physical characteristics, combined to give him an individual air. Whatever Caruso may have lacked as an actor, he supplied vocally. His acceptance was instantaneous and complete; and the newspapers commented on the following day in a single vein. The voice, declared one of the critics, had in it "the richness of rare velvet." The *Pall Mall Gazette* reviewer declared that "Signor Caruso sang to perfection. He is the embodiment of the finest epoch of Italian *bel canto*, and his ringing tones were marked both by an essential gift of music and by a fineness of timbre which you will not find easily surpassed." Conspicuous in the critique appearing in the *Daily Telegraph* was the sentence, "By his magnificent singing Signor Caruso evoked a demonstration that is rare here, after the clock has struck eleven."

The clock unquestionably was preparing to strike twelve for the tenor. For here was an Anglo-Saxon people as completely enthralled by his vocal resources as had been any Latin public. He could turn his eyes, after such a reception, toward the United States with expectation of enlisting favorable consideration from a nation that does not invariably approve every foreign music artist.

After "Rigoletto" Caruso appeared in *La Bohème*, again with Mme. Melba singing the leading soprano rôle and with Scotti and Journet among the Bohemians of the cast. Then came "Lucia di Lammermoor", with Signora Pacini, and the ever-present Scotti and Journet. "Aïda" followed, and on this occasion Mme. Lillian Nordica was the soprano, and Scotti, Plançon, and Journet also appeared. The Caruso vogue had begun. He was a magnet of attraction, and when he sang Turiddu in "Cavalleria Rusticana" to the Santuzza of Mme. Emma Calvé, his London future appeared to have become assured. He was warmly received in "La Traviata", with Mme. Melba, and his next new rôle was in "Don Giovanni", when he had as associate artists Mme. Fritzi Scheff and Renaud and Journet. His Nemorino, in "L'Elisir d'Amore", also won the London public.

Before the final appearance in "Rigoletto", on July 28, during which time he had sung twenty-four times, Caruso had made the acquaintance of Maurice Grau. There had been some prior negotiations looking towards the singer's possible engagement at the New York Metropolitan Opera House, of which Grau was at that time impresario. In the year 1900, Scotti had inquired if Caruso would consider signing a contract, but when the tenor had mentioned seven thousand *lire* an appearance as his *cachet* nothing came of the matter. The first Metropolitan nibble however, had come in the late winter of 1899, just after Caruso had returned to Milan from his first Petrograd engagement, and while he was singing at the Lirico Theater in "Fedora."

During one of his daily visits to the Galleria, Caruso was introduced to Maestro Vincenzo Bevignani who had been for several seasons one of the first conductors at the Metropolitan; and the conversation turning naturally into the channel of the theater Bevignani suddenly said, "You young boys who are starting hard careers should not let your heads be swelled by a few successes."

Caruso has expressed himself as having been surprised, and to have felt that he was unfairly criticized. Asking Bevignani what he meant by such remarks the tenor was informed. "There was a chance for you to go to the first theater of the world," declared the maestro, "a chance you lost through your swelled head — which caused you to ask for too much money."

"Do you think," answered Caruso, "that forty pounds a week was too much to have asked at a time when I was receiving nearly half that amount for a single appearance?"

"What!" exclaimed Bevignani, "I was told that you asked to go to America twenty-five thousand *lire* a week."

"Then you were not told the truth, because I said I would accept the forty pounds a week offer; but the contract never came." Later Caruso explained that Bevignani's silence indicated that he had been, in that particular case, "a good pear for two people."

These matters were still firmly impressed in the tenor's mind when Maurice Grau said to him one day during Caruso's London engagement, "So you don't want to come to America?"

"I replied in effect," said the tenor, "Well, it is up to you."

"In that case," observed the impresario, "I will say that I should like to have you at the Metropolitan, and I hope you will come to see me at my home that we may arrange something."

A few days later Caruso called upon Grau. He explained his disinclination to deal through an agent, to which the impresario said, "Very well, we will do this business ourselves."

"Mr. Grau," said the tenor, "I don't like to sign contracts in the way some persons do. It is enough to have one letter in which is specified the length of the engagement, the money, and the operas — because I respect my signature, and I expect the other to respect his too."

To this Grau answered that he held similar views. He thereupon wrote down the necessary matter which he felt should be incorporated in the contract, and handing the paper to Caruso said, "Please put what we have agreed upon into a letter and get two copies and bring them to me in two or three days. We will then sign together, and you will be with me next year."

"I went away gratified," explained Caruso, "because I wished to have no interference from any agent's source. Three days later I called at the Grau London residence, only to be informed by the porter who opened the door that Mr. Grau was in Wiesbaden. I explained the nature of my visit, whereupon the porter said, 'Just give me whatever you have, I am charged by Mr. Grau to forward his mail.'

"Leaving with the porter the original letter and the copies I had made, I returned to my hotel, expecting shortly to hear from Mr. Grau. Days passed, yet no word came. When the London season finished I went to my Florence home to rest; still no letter came from Mr. Grau. It seemed strange.

"It was some time during that August, while I was in Salsomaggiore, that I received a visit from the son of an agent who had said that unless I dealt with him I would never see the land of America. The moment he appeared I understood instantly what had prompted his call. No sooner had he greeted me than he pompously announced that he had been authorized by Mr. Grau to negotiate for my services. My reply to this surprising statement was, 'But Mr. Grau must have forgotten that he has a contract we agreed on, and which I signed; he must send me back that contract and the two duplicates which I left for him at his London home.'

"My visitor informed me that he was empowered to arrange all such, and other details; my mind, though, was made up, and I told the agent that I did not wish his participation in the completion of any contract Mr. Grau and I might make. To this my visitor replied, 'If you don't pass through our agency, you will never sing in America.'

"My reply was — 'You can go to Hell! I shall never sing in America if it has to be through any contract you arrange.'

"This man left — not for the place I had suggested — but to the nearest telegraph office, to cable to Mr. Grau the result of our interview. He must have included something else, for the following day I received from Mr. Grau a cablegram urging me to accept a contract through this agent.

"I considered the matter for some hours before reaching a decision. To agree meant conceding what I disliked to concede. In the end it seemed the most sensible thing to do; so for the first time — and also the last during my career — I passed under the *forche caudine*. The *forche*, as events were to prove, were never made complete.

"The contract, for a period of five years, finally was concluded; and within a few days everybody in the music business had learned of it. Letters of congratulation (as well as some worded quite the opposite) poured in upon me."

The difficulties surrounding a United States contract were not, as later developed, quite disposed of. Caruso thought they were, and continued with his vacation in high spirits until late October, when he prepared for his next operatic task, — the creation of the rôle of Maurizio in Francesco Cilea's new work, "Adriana de Lecouvreur." He arrived at the Lirico, in Milan, eager to do fullest justice to helping make successful another creation by the composer whose "Arlesiana" had given him one of his first important opportunities in this very theater, in 1897. On November 6, 1902, the première took place; and with Signora Angelica Pandolfini and Giuseppe de Luca, the performance moved to success under the bâton of Cleofonte Campanini, who was later to become so important an opera figure in the United States.

The public and critics insisted that much of the credit for the achievement during that first "Adriana de Lecouvreur" was due to the fervent singing of Caruso. It must have been for the tenor a labor of gratitude, for he could never forget what Sonzogno had done for him; nor, for that matter, his Milan reception in "Arlesiana." Sonzogno, when inviting Caruso to create Maurizio, had begged that he treat him as a friend, and the singer had replied, "Yes, and I will sing in as many performances as you wish — with the proviso that I am not to be paid one *lira*." Sonzogno was grateful, but he could not bring himself to consent to this generous proposal. In the end an agreement was reached that the tenor should receive three thousand *lire* for six appearances, and the impresario reluctantly permitted Caruso to provide his own costumes — for which he expended exactly twice the amount he received for this engagement.

Nicola Daspuro, who was among those present at the "Adriana de Lecouvreur" première, has related the reception extended Caruso and his associates in the cast. "I went to see Caruso in his dressing room during the first *entr'acte*," said Daspuro. "After we had talked for a few minutes I reminded him of those early days of his.

"Do you remember the time when you could not reach a high A-natural without breaking the note in pieces?"

"How *well* do I remember," replied the tenor.

"What did you do," inquired Daspuro, "to find an impostation which has made so secure and formidable your high notes?"

"Do you want the truth?" demanded Caruso. "Well, I will give it to you. Instead of following all the suggestions of my teachers, I did just the opposite. I found the impostation of the whole voice all by myself."

"Poor Vergine! Poor Lombardi!" murmured Daspuro. Yet he insists that Caruso was largely in the right, and that his accomplishment was due to his own "natural, unique, and unquestionably tremendous vocal and artistic instinct."

It is doubtful that Caruso or Daspuro wholly believed all they said. The tenor was given to taking to himself whatever credit was due for his advancement. He probably did not wish to deprive any one of just recognition for service rendered him, yet it is a fact that he was generally loath to concede that others had been of substantial aid to him. With him it was "I did this" or that; and it was manifested in other ways. Hearing a good story related by some one else, he would later revamp it and tell it as his very own.

From Milan the tenor journeyed to Trieste, there to sing in a second charity undertaking (as he had done once before) for the Trieste Benevolent Association. He appeared in two performances of "Rigoletto" on December 10 and 11, 1902, with Signore Fanny Torresella and Benvenuti, and Signori Arcangeli and Lucente, Maestro Gialdino Gialdini again serving as conductor.

The next task was to be a more arduous one: the big season at the Costanzi in Rome was then to be faced. Thence Caruso repaired, with sensations altogether different from those he had felt during his previous engagement in this theater, when he had been deprived of his "right" to create Cavaradossi in "Tosca." Judging from the newspaper comment following his first reappearance in "Rigoletto", the tenor's growth must have been extraordinary. The past — during that season of no more than two years since — seemed for the public a thing to have been quite forgotten. The Gilda of Signora Torresella, the Rigoletto of Signor Pacini, even the conducting of Edoardo Vitale, were overshadowed by the Duke of Caruso. He had returned to the Romans an artist; their artist, now, and how the public flocked to the Costanzi to hear him sing.

It was shortly after this début on December 26, 1902, that the tenor received from the agent who had negotiated his New York Metropolitan Opera House contract a laconic telegram. It merely stated that because of Grau's retirement from the management of that institution Caruso might consider his contract as automatically canceled.

To the tenor this information made him feel that "the star of the north would not shine" for him. "I nevertheless tried to get at the truth of the matter," he said, "by communicating with two friends then in New York: one, whom I knew very well (Antonio Scotti, then a Metropolitan principal); the other (Signor Giovanni Simonelli) whose acquaintance and subsequent friendship had been developed through correspondence.

"In response to my inquiry this first friend advised me that Mr. Grau had been ill, and would soon leave the Metropolitan. Directly, too, the news got out and was spread by some 'friends' (the sort of 'friends' who seem to enjoy such small practices) that after all Caruso would not go to America. No harm was done me. On the contrary, many proposals came to me to sing in different European cities."

However dim Caruso's "star of the north" might be, his star in Rome suffered no eclipse. It continued to shine when he appeared in repetitions of "Rigoletto"; and when on January 10, 1903, he sang with Signora Fausta Labia and Signor Borucchia in "Mefistofele." Nor was there any diminution of the tenor's popularity at his first appearance in "Manon Lescaut", with Signora Lina Pasini-Vitale, and again, on January 31, during his endeavors in "Aïda" — conducted, as had been the other operas,

CLIMBING 169

by Maestro Vitale, and with a cast including Signore Labia and Elisa Bruno and Signori Spoto and Pacini. Caruso could return to Rome whenever he chose; but he had none too much time after the close of his Costanzi season on February 8, to reach Lisbon for his introductory appearance on February 14 at the San Carlos Theater, at that time under the management of José Pacini. The opera selected for the Caruso presentation to a Portugal public was "Fedora"; Campanini was prepared to conduct, the Fedora was to be Signora Pandolfini. The Lisbon press appears to have been of the same mind regarding Caruso as was the public. The emphasis placed upon the timbre of the newcomer's voice, its emission, flexibility, and volume amounted almost to glorification. In one night the tenor had conquered a new people; he continued, in "Aïda", "Tosca","Adriana de Lecouvreur", "Lucrezia Borgia", and "Rigoletto" a triumphant march which lasted until March 19. He had sung with Signore Pandolfini, Darclée, Regina Pacini, and Virginia Guerrini, and Signori Maurizio Bensaude, Riccardo Stracciari, and Giulio Rossi; and the roster of artists also included Signora Eva Tetrazzini (sister of Luisa Tetrazzini) — one of the foremost dramatic soprani of that time — and Signori Fiorello Giraud, Antonio Pini-Corsi, Gaudio Mansueto, and Eugenio Giraldoni. Portugal made of the Caruso farewell an event: His *La donna é mobile* had to be sung three times, and the tenor even was persuaded by the management to restore the third act aria, which usually is omitted. Perhaps there was good reason for Caruso's enthusiastic farewell —

just as it may have aided in enabling him to appear on six successive evenings in as many different rôles. For something had happened to bring into a more favorable light his "star of the north."

Barely one week after Caruso reached Lisbon he received from Simonelli a cablegram containing a formal offer from Conried; and there was then begun a series of exchanged communications which, predicating the outcome, finally resulted in an agreement that would take the tenor to the Metropolitan the following season.

Pasquale Simonelli, an Italian banker residing in New York, relates the details concerning the negotiation in which he participated that led up to the signing of Caruso's first Metropolitan contract. "On January 30, 1903," stated Mr. Simonelli, "my brother John received a letter from Caruso dated from Rome. In it he wrote that Maurice Grau had informed him that he was sorry to have to dissolve the contract made, as he would not continue to be the general manager of the Metropolitan Opera House. In his letter to my brother, Caruso expressed his deep disappointment over the loss of his chance to come to America; and although invited to appear in many other opera houses throughout the world, he expressed his preference for the Metropolitan.

"Caruso asked my brother if he would communicate with the Metropolitan's new manager in an endeavor to see what might be done. My brother John was so occupied with his own affairs that he charged me to undertake the commission. When, on February 19, 1903, newspaper announcements informed the public that Heinrich Conried had been appointed to the management of the Metropolitan, I went that very afternoon to see him in his office at the Irving Place Theater of which he was then director.

"We spoke at length of artists, and Conried informed me that he was in communication with Alessandro Bonci and doubted whether he wished to avail himself of the contract Grau had signed with Caruso. As the tenor was young and unknown in America, Conried was fearful to engage him — as Grau had engaged him — for forty appearances. At length, after an extended discussion, Conried directed me to wire Caruso, guaranteeing him twenty appearances, with the assurance of additional ones should the public like him.

"I thereupon cabled Caruso, who was then singing in Lisbon, 'New impresario would accept Grau contract reducing first year half the number of appearances; prolongation depending on your success with the public.' Caruso cabled me a message I received on February 23 which read, 'I will accept proposal if new management deposits in my bank in Milan, not later than April 5, an advance covering five appearances and will guarantee me twenty-five appearances from November 20, 1903, to February 10, 1904.' That same day, after I had spoken of these matters to Conried, I wired to Caruso, 'Conried will respect the Grau contract except for the first year's appearances, giving you twenty-five, twice weekly, beginning November 23. Cable me at once as Conried wishes an answer by next Tuesday.' And on

February 25 Caruso wired me that he would accept; Conried verified his acceptance, and I again wired, 'Conried accepts. Wire me acceptance reduction to twenty-five appearances first season.'

"On March 26 Conried himself dictated a cablegram to Caruso, who was then singing in a few performances of 'Tosca' at Monte Carlo, the following: 'I accept your contract with Grau. Only change forty to twenty-five appearances first year your engagement. Will make deposit April 5 as agreed through Simonelli. Acknowledge receipt.' To this Caruso made immediate acknowledgment."

The contract made between the Metropolitan Opera Company and Caruso was readjusted during the middle of his first New York season, and a new one prepared for the four years to come. It provided, in each new year, for an increased *cachet* for each appearance, and Simonelli, apart from the three per cent commission due him under his arrangement with the tenor, was also to profit at subsequent renewals of the contract. A misunderstanding on Caruso's part of a personal matter between them caused the singer, when the time came to renew his contract, to insist that Simonelli should receive no further commissions. Nor could he be moved, at the time, to alter his decision. His mind was made up; he would not budge from his position. Several years later, however, when he learned of certain facts hitherto unknown to him, he went courageously to Simonelli and admitted that he had been in the wrong.

Before proceeding to Genoa, after his Monte Carlo

appearances, Caruso paused at Florence. The tenor had become obsessed, ever since he had begun to accumulate money, with the desire to acquire a villa; and since he had received from Impresario Conried an advance of twenty-five thousand *lire* for his first Metropolitan season, he felt he could afford this new luxury. He wished some place which would be completely his own. The Tuscan country was one he had always loved; something about the Florence atmosphere called to him that spring of 1903 more irresistibly than ever. It is true that Caruso was still unformed in many ways at that time, and that the step he then took must have enlisted on the part of some people a covert smile. A villa for a tenor not yet thirty, and barely coming into recognition? What presumptuousness! Who was this Caruso? An overdressed Neapolitan; uneducated as the world knows education, and already given to a stoutness which hinted at too much time spent at table. But for all the uncouthness he may have suggested to the critically inclined, Caruso possessed the feeling for better things. Deprived in his youth and by birth of advantages others had had, he wished to improve. And pray how was one to get on without breaking the ice which barred the way to the voyage upstream? He negotiated for and purchased the place he had set his heart on owning: the Villa alle Panche, in Castello near Florence.

A swift journey to Genoa was necessary, after Caruso acquired his Villa, to enable him to catch the SS *Venezuela* which was to carry him to South America, where his next engagement awaited him.

Many noteworthy singers were his companions of that voyage: Signore Ericlea Darclée, Rosina Storchio, Salomea Krusheniska, and Maria Farneti, and Signori Giovanni Zenatello, Florencio Constantino, Giuseppe de Luca, Eugenio Giraldoni, and Vittorio Arimondi. Toscanini was also a ship's passenger.

Caruso has said that this trip was one of the most enjoyable he had ever known. Amid companionable confrères, his heart then soaring at the constant thought of that secure Metropolitan contract, the tenor behaved like a schoolboy, as he was wont to do whenever the wind blew fair for him. During this voyage Caruso taught to Giuseppe de Luca the American game of poker; and for a time he delighted in the steady losses sustained by the baritone, who was slower in gaining some familiarity with certain essentials governing the value of hands. Before Buenos Aires had been reached de Luca progressed at such a rate that Caruso at length found excuses to occupy himself in other ways.

Chosen for the première performance from those first tenors Camillo Bonetti had engaged for that 1903 La Opera Theater season, Caruso came before a South American audience for his third year in "Tosca." Toscanini presided in the orchestra pit; on the stage with the tenor were Signora Maria Figner Mey, and Giraldoni and Ercolani. Those two years that had slipped by since Caruso had last been heard in Buenos Aires served in other ways than to move that first-night gathering to welcome back an artist to whom they had said au revoir with expressions of regret. He had been their favorite tenor then; returned with such improved voice and art, his Mario sent those listeners into their own peculiar seventh heaven, — where they continued to remain for so long as that season lasted.

The position, nevertheless, was by no means so secure that Caruso could view the situation with a complacent mien. It was true that he had popularity; in most respects he held the advantage over his first-tenor comrades who, friendly though they might seem, were still anxious to shine under the spotlight which flooded this young artist to whom the gods had been so kind. There was necessary every moment the keenest maneuvering to retain the upper hand; and Caruso applied himself diligently to every performance in which he was to appear, preparing his words and music of each rôle with the utmost care.

Even the cablegram from Simonelli, urging him to grant an extension of his first year's Metropolitan contract, did not prompt the singer to relax his vigilance. He was discounting no success; the future was something to be considered gravely. It was this attitude which caused Caruso to decline to appear in "Zauberflöte", "Fra Diavolo", "Don Giovanni", and "Marta", — his explanation being that he considered the music of the tenor parts in these operas to be too light for his voice. "Furthermore, I do not know a note of any one of them," he wrote Simonelli, "and I have no time to study rôles." He did, however, learn Lionel in "Marta", which not only brought him instant favor at the Metropolitan at his first appearance in the opera, but became one of his most successful characters.

"Adriana de Lecouvreur" and "Iris" followed "Tosca", at La Opera of Buenos Aires; and in the former work Caruso appeared with Signore Maria Figner and Virginia Guerrini, and Giuseppe de Luca, — the latter work presenting him with Maria Farneti. The public was standing firmly by its tenor, and at each new appearance he enhanced his prestige. The cost was not small. It meant hours and hours of patient studying; of extreme care of a precious voice, and of closing his ears to small gossip which, to an artist, is always unnerving.

In "Germania" Caruso sang with Signora Farneti, and de Luca; in "L'Elisir" he appeared with Signora Clasenti and de Luca; his associates in "Mefistofele" were Signore Farneti and Guerrini, and Arimondi.

The steadying hand of Toscanini was continually present; the season waned, and at the close the tenor had the satisfaction of being able to look back upon a further gain in his art.

Providence continued to touch the singer lavishly upon his shoulder. Buenos Aires had been more than kind. Montevideo — where Caruso went with the same company and management to appear for a less extensive season at the Teatro Solis — took the tenor almost as completely to its heart. There, in addition to having appeared in the same répertoire presented in Buenos Aires, Caruso sang a sterling performance of Des Grieux in "Manon Lescaut." If less comfortable for his tenor comrades, the achievement enhanced still further his renown. And the second move, to the Pedro II Theater at Rio de Janeiro, presented him before the public of that city on eight different occasions in "Rigoletto", "Tosca", "Manon Lescaut", and "Iris."

Late August found the tenor once more aboard a steamer, homeward bound, with visions of North America dancing in his mind. He went thereafter to Milan, there to rest for a few weeks before embarking upon the most important phase of his career.

II

The Caruso who first set foot on United States soil on November eleventh 1903 was very different from the Caruso its public was later to know so well. He made the voyage from Italy on board the SS *Sardegna*. His instincts and affections were ineradicably Italian; he was still, for all his travel and varied experiences, essentially of the people and sharing their inherent tastes. Much newspaper *réclame* having been made for him as the singer upon whom the mantle of the revered Jean de Reszke was likely to fall, much naturally was expected of him. It could scarcely have been a more intricate situation — with the inevitable comparisons certain to be made between the two tenors by the fastidious parterre-tier Metropolitan boxholders — for where de Reszke was aristocratic, Caruso decidedly was not; there was the widest possible physical difference in the two men, and, finally, the one was undertaking in the middle period of his career to succeed a consummately finished artist, — perhaps the greatest exponent of the highly polished intellectual school of tenors the world has known.

But for all these disadvantages, certain counterbalancing elements lay in the scales. In Caruso the United States was truly to have a tenor of the type it loved best. How completely he was to be accepted remained to be learned. His appearance was decidedly plebeian: he was undeniably fat; his manners had not in them everything to commend; he was handicapped, because of his unfamiliarity with the English language, by an inability to appear wholly at ease among strangers who spoke another tongue.

In London, with a less weighty outcome hanging in the balance, it had been altogether different. Whereas England was a part of Europe, New York belonged to the new world; and there other customs ruled which the tenor, perhaps better than any one else, understood he must assimilate before he might hope to be estimated at his true worth. He himself said, "I realized that the Metropolitan Opera House was the first in all the world. Many of the most celebrated and finest artists had appeared there; besides, the organization was the largest, its season the longest, and its répertoire the most extensive of any similar institution anywhere."

Caruso was thus well aware of the importance of the task confronting him. An indifferent reception, regardless of other fields which still called to him, could not be set imperialistically aside. Whether just or unjust, anything short of an unqualified success in this new sphere of his activities would tarnish a hard-won prestige. To win was therefore necessary;

not moderately as many another fine artist had won before him, but so emphatically that the Caruso name would be cabled around the globe as having been finally hoisted to the peak of the staff.

The attentions even of the press held a significance; for regarded as a singing personage, and besieged for interviews immediately upon his arrival in New York, Caruso was well aware that there was being created for him in the public print a position he must achieve and maintain.

He had gone at once to the Hotel Majestic, where a suite had been arranged for him in advance of his coming. Ada Giachetti was with him — as Mrs. Caruso. There, hard by Central Park, the tenor received the newspaper reporters. Pasquale Simonelli was present to introduce the writers and photographers to his friend, and to act also as interpreter. News and feature stories concerning the Metropolitan's new tenor had been freely published months before; since he was actually in the United States, he was legitimate material to be "played up", and this is what occurred, swiftly and with all the graphic touches characteristic of the New York dailies. Something about this Neapolitan appealed to the newspapermen who at first met him; and when he fell to sketching cartoons they fought for them, and every editor saw that the sketches were reproduced — to further enlighten their readers as to the personality of this newcomer to the Metropolitan who was soon to sing before them.

The newspaper fraternity were by no means the only callers who descended upon the Caruso apartment in the Majestic Hotel. Many of his countrymen, residents of New York, swarmed about his doors. They were of various classes, not a few being of the poorer sort, who went with begging intent. Destined to the end of his days to be pursued by compatriots seeking to make use of his purse, the tenor found no comfort in turning them away. He was of that peculiar Italian nature which understood the impulses of these gratuity seekers. If opposed to acquiescing to every demand, he at least seems to have sympathized with the needy. He gave — by no means freely or pleasantly in every instance — but he gave. Oftentimes he appears to have been actuated by some intangible fear that he must give; that a "no", regardless of the justice of such decision, would be interpreted only to his own disadvantage. So the Caruso hand went often into his pocket; and just as often did he consent to some proposal which he would have preferred not to have entertained, yet was to cost him either money or the lending of his time or name to what would bring money to others.

Therefore, that 1903 New York settling period was for Caruso a wearying affair. Still, he appears to have made the best of it with as much good humor as possible. And there were of course some genuinely pleasurable moments, gathered from visits of worthwhile persons, the majority of whom were his own countrymen. Members of the clergy, as well as representative members of the laity, were made welcome in the Caruso apartment. He took time to see them all; he extended his hospitality with characteristic thoughtfulness; through those days prior to his New York début on November 23, 1903, there was little time outside his professional duties which was not almost completely taken up by others.

Caruso's first meeting with Heinrich Conried took place in the impresario's office, in the southwest part of the Metropolitan Opera House on the ground floor. He was introduced to the impresario by Pasquale Simonelli, who acted as interpreter, since Caruso could speak neither English nor German and Conried no Italian or French. The tenor had long been "curious" as to "the sort of man" Conried would prove to be. He had learned of Conried's unfamiliarity with opera and opera artists. Thus, when Simonelli had taken a small machine and a disc of *Vesti la giubba*, as recorded by Caruso, and presented himself to Conried in the Irving Place Theater, he made it possible for the Metropolitan's new manager to gather some idea of the voice and singing style of his tenor. The record had been made only with pianoforte accompaniment, yet the impression made upon the impresario was unforgetable.

"'If that Caruso can sing as well in the Metropolitan as he sang to make that record,'" Simonelli quotes Conried as having said, "'his success is assured.' Conried made no attempt to conceal his disappointment in not having engaged the tenor for forty instead of the twenty-five appearances the contract (already concluded) called for. At his request I cabled Caruso, who was singing in Buenos Aires, but it was too late; he had already accepted an offer to appear in Monte Carlo during the 1904 season," said Simonelli.

Caruso was taken by Conried into the auditorium of the opera house, which he admired, just as he admired the stage, which, in those days, was more modern and serviceable for large productions than it now is. The singer sensed the atmosphere as one stimulating to an artist; he was likewise favorably impressed with what he observed in other quarters of the opera house. Everything appeared to be systematically conducted; and everywhere was neatness. There would be few discords here, he hoped, a feeling which ultimately was to be borne out by developments. For the tenor had reached the Metropolitan at an opportune time: Conried, utterly inexperienced in matters operatic and musically untutored, was just preparing to take up the reins of management; the singer himself was steadily advancing in voice and singing prowess, and there was none other in the organization who was his equal. Whether it was destiny, such were the facts. The pendulum was swinging across a propitious arc; Caruso, sensitive in the extreme, may have subconsciously gathered some faint foreshadowing of what was to come. Whatever their source, there was nothing save encouragement in the sensations the tenor experienced during that first visit to the opera house where he was to rise steadily to untouched heights, and in it was to pass the greatest number and happiest hours of his future appearances before the public. He returned to the hotel home; and soon he began in earnest his preparations for his début.

That night of the 23rd of November, 1903, was not

peculiarly different from previous nights which the Metropolitan Opera House organization and audience had both known. Other first appearances had been quite as successfully accomplished as was Caruso's. There is no record of any specially marked or prolonged enthusiasm, — if one may except the natural demonstrations some few Italians permitted themselves. What the assemblage saw was a stocky and scarcely graceful figure appearing as the Duke in Verdi's "Rigoletto"; a tenor proceeding in his acting along the conventional lines of Italian artists who had been seen before him in the same and similar rôles. What they heard was a fresh, clear tenor voice; a voice neither exceptionally powerful nor sensational in its qualities, yet one with an ingratiating quality. That it was well used was readily apparent, particularly to those who had given attention to singing. Virtually all who were present were willing enough to concede that here was an artist who seemed sure of himself; and if anticipation had led them to expect something more, there was enough to be grateful for in one who sang so easily, with such charm, and with what unmistakably was an authoritative manner. But neither with his voice nor his singing did Caruso sweep to its feet any considerable part of that gathering. Even the critics tempered their comments, and, published in the New York newspapers of the following day, they found space enough also to consider those other artists of the night — Mme. Marcella Sembrich and Antonio Scotti — who had participated in the production conducted by Arturo Vigna.

Save for a line mentioning Caruso as a newcomer there was no comment in the New York *Tribune* which touched upon his qualifications as a singer or his achievement. The New York *Times* commentator wrote of Caruso, "He made a highly favorable impression and he went far to substantiate the reputation that had preceded him to this country. His voice is purely a tenor in its quality, and is of large power, but inclined to take on the 'white' quality in its upper ranges when he lets it forth. In *mezza voce* it has expressiveness and flexibility, and when so used its beauty is most apparent. Mr. Caruso last evening appeared capable of intelligence and passion in both singing and acting."

The New York *Sun* reviewer was of the opinion that, "Mr. Caruso, the new tenor, made a thoroughly favorable impression and will probably grow into firm favor with his public. He has a pure tenor voice of fine quality and sufficient range and power. It is a smooth and mellow voice and is without the typical Italian bleat. Mr. Caruso has a natural and free delivery and his voice carries well without forcing. He phrased his music tastefully and showed considerable refinement of style. His clear and pealing high tones set the bravos wild with delight, but the connoisseurs of singing saw more promise for the season in his *mezza voce* and manliness. He is a good-looking man and acts with dignity if with no great distinction. But the Duke gives little opportunity for the exhibition of histrionic powers."

Nothing in these reviews to indicate that the critics had been swept from their feet; surely little hint that this new tenor was soon to become *the* tenor of his time.

In the New York *Sun* of December 1, 1903, in the critique dealing with the Metropolitan's "Aïda" of the previous evening in which Mme. Johanna Gadski and Scotti and Plançon participated, reference was made to Caruso's recovery from an attack of tonsillitis. The writer felt that the singer "confirmed the good impression he made at his début. He saved himself a good deal in the early part of the opera, which was wise in view of his recent indisposition. He sang the aria (*Celeste Aïda*) quietly but tastefully, and with good effect. In the Nile scene he let himself out."

The *Times* chronicler stated that, "He proved the remarkable mastery he possessed over his organ; he materially deepened the favorable impression he made at his first appearance. The quality, the flexibility, and the expressive capacity of his voice beautified everything he did. There were passion and conviction in his interpretation of the fated lover, and everywhere the marks of the adept in stagecraft."

The *Tribune* recorder wrote that "Caruso was plainly still suffering from the indisposition. But his skill in overcoming the drawbacks helped to a keen appreciation of his knowledge of the art of singing, and invited still further admiration for the superb beauty of his voice. The pleasure which his singing gives is exquisite, scarcely leaving room for curious questionings touching his limitations. He is to be accepted for what he is, with gratitude, and no one who loves the art of song ought to miss the opportunities which his presence at the Metropolitan offers."

Two days later, after the tenor's first Metropolitan appearance in "Tosca", the *Tribune* stated, "Signor Caruso filled the music of Cavaradossi with sensuous splendor, but acted the part with far less fire and distinction than his predecessor, De Marchi. Signor Caruso is primarily a singer, that is now evident. His musical instincts are as perfect as his voice is luscious, but neither his instincts nor his voice is at the service of that dramatic characterization."

The *Sun* critic also found some elements lacking in the tenor's acting, and stated that " his Cavaradossi was bourgeois. It was difficult to believe in the ardent passion of the aristocratic Tosca for this painter of hack portraits at job prices. His clothes were without distinction. The tenor seemed to be in a better state of voice than he was on Monday night and sang well, as he certainly can."

These opinions of Caruso's bearing, action and dress were shared by the *Times* reviewer, upon whom he made "indeed the deepest impression so far as his singing was concerned. Caruso displays Cavaradossi in a more bourgeois air than his predecessor (De Marchi), with little distinction of bearing and with small intensity of feeling; it is not until the scene of his impending doom that he sounds a note of elemental power in his outpouring of despair and longing for his love. . . . This he did with magnificent eloquence and a nobility of song that deeply stirred the audience."

CLIMBING 187

Evidences were beginning then to appear which foreshadowed a growing favor of the tenor newcomer. He had already made a first appearance with the Metropolitan Company at Philadelphia (in "Rigoletto" on December 29, following his indisposition which had kept him from two New York representations of "Bohème" and "Rigoletto"), and his recovery from the attack of tonsillitis and the warming attitude of the newspaper music critics were encouraging. After his introductory "Bohème", on December 5, there no longer appeared any doubt as to Caruso's full acceptance by New York as a singer. If he unconsciously suggested the plebeian, and in his acting fell short of those standards set up through the traditions of de Reszke and others who excelled on the dramatic side, in voice and song Caruso had no need to apologize. In their reviews the critics really enthused.

The strain of the première appearances over, the singer gave more thought to the matters of personal inclinations. Unable to accustom himself wholly to American cooking, Caruso wished for his own establishment where he at least might have his own kitchen. His desire made known, friends began a search for a suitable apartment, and Mrs. Gina Viafora at length found one in the Murray Hill district, near Lexington Avenue. Here Caruso and Ada Giachetti moved within a few weeks after their arrival in the United States, and it became the point of attraction for the tenor's friends and followers during his first season in this country. Often Caruso prepared spaghetti for numerous guests; he was fond of this particular dish and had a special way of cooking it. But he developed a liking for the old Café Martin — situated then at Broadway and Twenty-sixth Street — which he not infrequently patronized for luncheon, to the delight of the proprietor and patrons.

The New World having shown a pleasing responsiveness to his operatic efforts, Caruso began to regard it as a sort of future home. He was impressed by the city and its people; the bustle appealed to him, and also those evidences of resources which were reflected everywhere. And there was also the rest of this huge country which eventually he felt he should come to know. It was all very comforting, and back of this thought lay another; a fortune was by no means beyond the reach of this Neapolitan singer, who was discovering the advantages which wealth can provide.

There were a host of experiences which interested or amused the tenor, some of them supplied by Herr Director Conried who had considerable to learn in an unfamiliar field. Summoned to the impresario's office after the general rehearsal of "La Traviata", Caruso was informed that there was too little singing for him to do in the rôle of Alfredo. In order to give the public a sort of "good measure", Conried suggested to the tenor that between the third and fourth acts of the opera he might introduce several romanzas. To this amazing proposal Caruso answered, "'If I do not sing enough music in "Traviata" to suit you that is not my fault, but the fault of Mr. Verdi, who wrote the work.' Imagine what would have happened to me had I consented to this request! For I had to fight to win and keep the respect of the critics and public. Almost every time I sang some one of these critics would write, 'Yes — a beautiful voice, wonderful quality, velvet, everything which is to be expected from an Italian voice, but — Jean.'"

This velvet voice was by no means restricted to being heard only at the opera. As soon as the Caruso success became unquestioned he was sought to appear in private musicales given in fashionable homes. Mrs. W. Payne Whitney was the one to have the distinction of first presenting the tenor to a gathering of friends, on the evening of January 14, 1904; and just one week later Caruso sang for a similar assemblage who were the guests of Mrs. Orme Wilson. The fee in each instance was much larger than the $960 (five thousand *lire*) the singer actually received, but by the terms of the contract Conried had the right to Caruso's services in concert as well as opera — at the stipulated *cachet*, the difference going to swell the Metropolitan treasury.

Between November 23, 1903, and February 10, 1904, the tenor appeared twenty-nine times, — twenty-five times in New York, and on four occasions in Philadelphia. Besides those operas previously mentioned he was heard also in "Pagliacci", "Lucia di Lammermoor", and "L'Elisir d'Amore." The farewell was made in "Lucia", with Mme. Sembrich and Giuseppe Campanari, the baritone.

From the deck of the steamer which carried him in the direction of Monte Carlo Caruso looked back on the city it had been so difficult for him to reach.

What an unsuspected future it possessed for him; what a vast store of triumphs, of happiness — and of sadness and tragedy as well.

III

Monte Carlo was more attractive than ever to the Caruso who presented himself to Impresario Raoul Gunsbourg for the 1904 season of the Casino. It was not so much that Monte Carlo had improved as that Caruso was getting on. His "north star" was shining; his fame was spreading; he was beginning to experience some of the sensations which come to one who is becoming a success.

"Aïda" opened the Monte Carlo operatic festivities. Maestro Vigna, who had also come from the New York Metropolitan, conducted the performance which included Signora Giannina Russ as Aïda, Signora Virginia Guerrini in the character of Amneris, Maurice Renaud appearing as Amonasro, and Vittorio Arimondi singing Ramphis. New York had exerted upon Caruso the precise benefits he had anticipated. Apart from the broadened experience of appearing before audiences different in temperament and tastes from the majority to which he had been accustomed, the engagement had enhanced the singer's prestige. The name Caruso was beginning to have a very definite professional value; and it was also reacting upon its owner. He appreciated what it meant and how well he must guard the name which was coming more readily to peoples' tongues whenever opera was discussed, and almost wherever. Under this artistic popularity the tenor appraised with a new keenness those essentials he was wise enough to discern might be steadily turned to profitable ends. He was only thirty-one; the career less than ten years of age; but what a future was opening before him! Work he was accepting with no unwilling spirit, but he had, in the nature of things, to have his time of play. In the theater, and concerning all that pertained to it, he was serious; out of it the singer was indulging his fondness for the lighter things of which his still boyish heart was fond.

It amused him to play pranks upon his comrades, whose discomfiture gave him a peculiar glee; and he delighted in sketching, — any one, anywhere, and the more publicly conspicuous the better. It attracted attention to him, and this he may have liked, but the probabilities are that his exuberance chiefly prompted him to a practice which was a harmless enough recreation.

Vittorio Arimondi relates how Caruso, as well as other principals of the Monte Carlo company, would commission the tenor's secretary to go during an opera performance to the Casino gaming tables in efforts to win at roulette. Lorello had been succeeded by another secretary — a Signor Giordano — and he invariably departed with one hundred francs, — and as invariably came back without them. His reappearance was the signal of a general shouting of his name, to no purpose. But it was diverting, without any considerable cost.

While in Monte Carlo Caruso received from Ruggero Leoncavallo, composer of "I Pagliacci", the following letter.

Dear Enrico:

    I come with my heart in my hands to ask if you will do for me what you have already done for Giordano and Cilea — to create the tenor rôle in my new opera, "Rolando", which I have just finished. The music is written *for you*, with your voice of paradise still in my ears and in my heart. The few who have heard the score judge it to be my masterpiece, and believe the tessitura and inflections of the canto have been created for your intentions. I am sure that if you could hear the music that you, with that high feeling which is part of your heart, would not refuse me the favor I am asking. You never will find a rôle including every emotion — the humorous, the pathetic, the loving, and the tragic — to the extent as does the rôle of Henning in "Rolando." Hear it, please, and decide.

    The opera will be given in Germany for the first time — in Berlin, during October. I wish to arrange the Italy première, in Rome, in November, or during the first fortnight of December, as you may choose. The rôle of the baritone will be sung by Battistini, the prima donna is to be Emma Carelli. The ensemble will be worthy of you, and the Italian première should be of unique interest. I hope that you will not refuse, *to me only*, what you granted to other confrères. I count upon your friendship, on your goodness of heart, and I tell you it would be a great sorrow for me if you refuse to do what I ask.

    Sonzogno will write you also on the subject. I wanted to be the first to ask you. Now I salute you with the hope of receiving a favorable reply.

                  Your admirer and friend,
                        Ruggero Leoncavallo.

    Caruso replied that he would prefer to hear the opera before deciding; and to this the composer wrote, "Thank you. There is in your letter a thread of hope. In two or three days I must be in Nizza to assist at the première of 'Zaza' there. Being so near I will come to Monte Carlo and lunch with you, and at the same time I will speak with you about the informal proposal I have received to go to New York and conduct my 'Rolando' there. Naturally, you must create Henning."

"Rolando" had its Berlin première, as Leoncavallo expected, on December 13, 1904, though with less success than the public had anticipated. Whether this, or Caruso's own judgment of the tenor rôle, influenced him in his decision to refuse Leoncavallo's request seems not to have developed; it is merely a fact that he did not sing in the Naples première of the opera.

Another new country — Spain — prepared to welcome Caruso for the first time, at the close of his Monte Carlo engagement. After some haggling, Doctor Albert Bernis, impresario of the Liceo Theater, of Barcelona, at length had consented to pay the tenor his fee. To the manager it appeared exorbitant, and he did not hesitate to make known his opinion; but he had promised the Barcelona public to bring Caruso to them "at any price", so there was no alternative. Once he had appeared, some readjustment might be possible (such, at any rate, is the belief of Luis Piera Figueras, a music enthusiast and patron who was present in Barcelona at the time).

The singer reached his destination on April 17, 1904; three evenings later he faced a Liceo audience, in

"Rigoletto." His principal associates were Mme. Esperanza Clasenti and Enrico Berriel, and Maestro Giuseppe Baroni conducted. Figueras has explained that such was the vocal freedom and artistry disclosed by Caruso in the *Questa o quella* cabaletta of the first act that the assemblage shouted aloud, "Viva Caruso!" Quite different was the attitude when the *E il sol dell' anima* duet with the soprano was reached, in the second act. It had not gone far when from the gallery was heard the unmistakable sound of hisses. Coming so unexpectedly, after the previous manifestation of approval, the tenor was half-tempted to stop singing. At the conclusion of the act Caruso was informed that he had been hissed for having sung out of tune. Expert opinion challenged this assertion; it maintains that the tenor's virtually perfect pitch had differed with that of the soprano because she had sung flat.

Inwardly raging, yet determined to perform his duty, Caruso continued with his part of the performance. So well did he progress that his delivery of the *La donna è mobile* aroused his hearers to frenzy. They shrieked their Vivas! and demanded no less vociferously a repetition of the aria; but the singer, piqued by those hisses during the earlier scene, would only bow. In the midst of the uproar, and while Caruso stood coldly facing it, the galleryites called loudly, "He is discourteous not to sing it again!" The performance was concluded amid silence. There were no curtain calls for the artist; an impasse had been reached between Caruso and his auditors.

Such discord gave to Impresario Bernis his oppor-

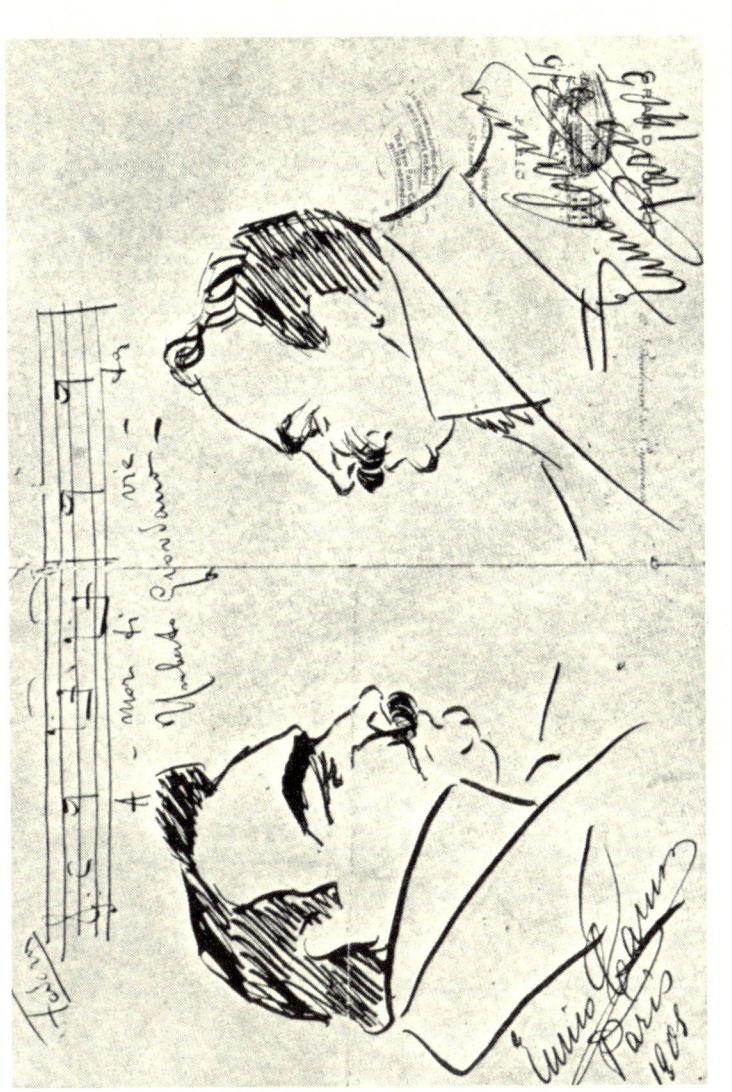

CARICATURES OF CARUSO AND UMBERTO GIORDANO, AUTHOR OF "FEDORA," MADE BY CARUSO, PARIS, MAY 5, 1905

The original drawing is in the possession of Señor Luis P. Figueras, of Barcelona. Caruso, having decided against returning to Spain after his experiences in Barcelona, many friends visited Paris to hear him. Among them was the faithful Figueras, and Caruso, to reward him for the long journey, gave him this caricature, which bears the autograph line and signature of Giordano himself. The line "Amor ti vieta" is taken from the famous tenor's aria in "Fedora."

tunity, and waiting upon the tenor he said, "You were not liked by the Barcelona public, so I cannot have you continue unless you agree to sing at half the price we agreed upon." It was a futile effort. "Not one penny less than my fee will I accept," returned the tenor. "You have announced me to appear in 'Rigoletto' on next Saturday, therefore I will sing; afterward I will leave." True to his word, Caruso sang in the Liceo for a second time "Rigoletto." After the *Questa o quella*, during the duet with the soprano, and following the *La donna è mobile* the identical scenes of the previous representation took place; it had somewhat the appearance of having been rehearsed.

Word of the difficulty having reached the mayor of Barcelona, he requested the tenor to reconsider his decision to depart before the end of his engagement. He and the cultivated music lovers of the city, the mayor explained, disapproved of what had happened. If Caruso would only consent to remain — even this appeal had no effect upon the singer.

In after years Bernis explained to Andres de Segurola, the basso, that the tenor actually had sung off pitch, and that the public had been justified in hissing him. The impresario believed that if Caruso had treated the hisses less seriously and had responded to the demands for an encore of the fourth act aria, all would have been well. His attitude in having received the applause with such coldness and evidences of superiority had, Bernis felt, been unfortunate. Many flattering proposals were afterward received by the tenor from Barcelona, but he always refused them. Nor could Madrid (a city in which he never sang) successfully woo him. And all subsequent managerial appeals were, to quote the words of Figueras, "*Todo fue tiempo perdido para los impresarios.*" (It was time lost to the impresari.)

Caruso shook the dust of Spain from his shoes, traveled to Paris, and prepared for his first appearance there in one special performance of "Rigoletto", which it was the intention to give to aid Russian soldiers wounded in the Russian-Japanese War. Although it was unusual for a singer to début in circumstances other than might attach to a regular season, Caruso, while at Monte Carlo, had yielded to the persuasions of the Paris Russian ambassador who was sojourning there.

Ample time was afforded the singer to rest and indulge in some recreation in a city which held for him a strong fascination. Parisians were interested in the approaching performance of "Rigoletto", which was to be given under the patronage of Countess Greffulhe for the benefit of the hospital train of Grand Duchesse Vladimir of Russia. Toward the end of April the performance took place, in the Sarah Bernhardt Theater. Mme. Lina Cavalieri was the Gilda, Maurice Renaud appeared in the rôle of Rigoletto, Vittorio Arimondi was the Sparafucile, and Mme. Thevenet had the small part of Maddalena. Maestro Vigna directed a performance which made Caruso an instant favorite. Gabriel Astruc, the Paris representative of the tenor from the time of that début, said that this appearance was the start of a Caruso furore in Paris which never abated.

Astruc describes how peasants, wearing overalls, appeared at the box office of the Sarah Bernhardt Theater holding 100-franc notes in their hands. They wished to hear the tenor, even at the to them terrific price.

Paris more than compensated for the wounds Barcelona had administered to the sensitive singer. He snapped his metaphorical fingers, and departed for Prague where he had been engaged to appear in the Königliches Deutsch Landestheater by the celebrated impresario Angelo Neumann. On May 4, with Signora Regina Pinkert, Fräulein Schafer, Enrico Pignataro, and Vittorio Arimondi, and Arturo Vigna conducting, Caruso made his Bohemian début as the Duke in "Rigoletto." After an "Elisir" the tenor proceeded to the Königliches Opernhaus, of Dresden, where on May 8, 1904, he appeared in a single presentation of "Rigoletto" with the same cast.

The Prague music reviewers had termed Caruso's voice to be "like gold, clear and brilliant in color, and of extraordinary roundness." They referred to that voice as unique, and remarkable in its warmth. "He (Caruso) is not a thief," wrote one chronicler, "— as are so many others — of *rubati* and *crescendi*. He keeps always the style of the *bel canto* with a noble manner faithful to its traditions."

Writing in Caruso's autograph book Angelo Neumann declared, "After Graziani and Calzolari, I have never heard a voice or an artist as superb and as complete as you are."

Barcelona, if not forgotten, could now be looked

back upon by the tenor with an amused tolerance. He closed the chapter of those particular experiences, then set his face toward Florence.

It was at this time that Caruso purchased from Baron Pucci the Villa Campi, — famous in its section near the village Lastra a Signa, in the province of Florence. First called the Villa Pucci, Caruso renamed it Villa Bellosguardo (Beautiful View). In the course of years the singer spent more than three million *lire* in perfecting the villa itself, beautifying the gardens, and developing the acreage forming the estate. He caused improvements to be made on the several farms; he arranged with *fattori* (farmers) to work the land on *mezzadria* (half and half) shares. It yielded grapes for wine and an abundance of vegetables.

Within the villa the tenor had placed a considerable part of his collections of paintings, furniture, bronzes and enamels, coins, and other *objets d'art*. Another considerable collection gradually was acquired in New York, where at the time of writing it was in the Canessa Galleries.

A long tour confronting Caruso, and Fofò having then reached an age where his education demanded consideration, the singer gave his attention to that important matter. Consultations with friends, and investigations, at length caused him to select the academy La Badia Fiesolana (situated at Fiesole, near Florence) as the most suitable school in which to place his son. The boy remained in this academy until he was fifteen, when he withdrew to live with his aunt Signorina Rina Giachetti.

GARDEN AND REAR ENTRANCE TO CARUSO'S "VILLA BELLOSGUARDO," AT LASTRA A SIGNA, FLORENCE

Photographed by Prof. Gordon E. Davis of Cornell University, by whose kind permission this reproduction was made.

It had been two years since Caruso had sung in Covent Garden. His reappearance there in "Rigoletto", the opera in which he had first been heard by the English, was accomplished on May 17, 1904, with a cast which included Mmes. Melba and Kirkby-Lunn, and Messrs. Renaud and Journet. Luigi Mancinelli, a former Metropolitan Opera Company maestro, was the conductor. The King and Queen of England, the Princess Victoria, and the Duke and Duchess of Connaught were among the assemblage. Not a critic disagreed in the opinion that the tenor's voice and artistry had grown during his absence. During that season Caruso appeared in twenty-six performances, the operas being "Pagliacci", "Bohème", "Aïda", "Traviata", and "Ballo in Maschera." In addition to those artists mentioned the tenor had as associates Mmes. Destinn and Selma Kurz and Messrs. Scotti and Plançon. July 25 relieved Caruso from further immediate opera activities. He needed a real rest, and he went to the Villa alle Panche.

CHAPTER SEVEN

Established

THERE was a reason for lingering at the Villa alle Panche, which on September 7, 1904, became apparent. For on that day a second son was born to Enrico Caruso. Ada Giachetti was the mother. The boy was named Enrico Caruso, Jr., but he was immediately called Mimmi, as he still is.

October of that year promised another new field into which the tenor was to venture, — Germany. He had conquered among Latins and Anglo-Saxons; if he should succeed in a similar measure with a Teutonic public he could rest assured of what might come. It was therefore with real concern that he prepared for his Berlin début, at Des Westens Theater, where once again he was to be tested in the rôle of the Duke in "Rigoletto." With Maestro Roth conducting, and Frau Mary Stoller and Eduard Nawisky in the two other leading characters, Caruso was first heard by a German audience on October 5, 1904. He seems to have had no more difficulty in gaining the approval of that Berlin public than of others. It was by no means an exclusively popular verdict, for the critics wrote of him as an "exponent of the typical Italian art of singing now so rare." Two nights later in "Traviata", with the same singing associates, Caruso faced his second German

ESTABLISHED

assemblage. Then he departed for London, where he had been engaged to appear in an autumn season to be given at Covent Garden by the San Carlo Opera Company, brought from Naples by Impresario Roberto De Sanna.

It must have been balm to Caruso's heart to have been the choice of the San Carlo Theater manager to appear in this pretentious London season as leading tenor. What would Naples think of this honor! Would its people regret having made his 1902 homecoming so disturbing? And would they perhaps hold some wish that before long he might appear before them again? Caruso hoped so. He wanted his fellow Neapolitans to feel his absence and to yearn for his presence among them in the opera. They would hear of his London appearances, as they heard of all those others during the past two years. It became apparent to him that the severest punishment he could administer would be to surpass himself, and this he undertook to do on October 17 of that year when he reappeared before a London audience in "Manon Lescaut." Signorina Rina Giachetti and Sammarco and Arimondi were in the cast, and Cleofonte Campanini presided over the music side of the performance. On eight subsequent occasions the tenor was heard: in this opera, also in "La Bohème", with Miss Alice Nielsen and Signorina Emma Trentini, and Pasquale Amato and Arimondi; in "Carmen", supported by Mme. Bressler-Gianoli, Miss Nielsen, and Amato; and in "Pagliacci", the other artists being Sammarco and Francesco Daddi.

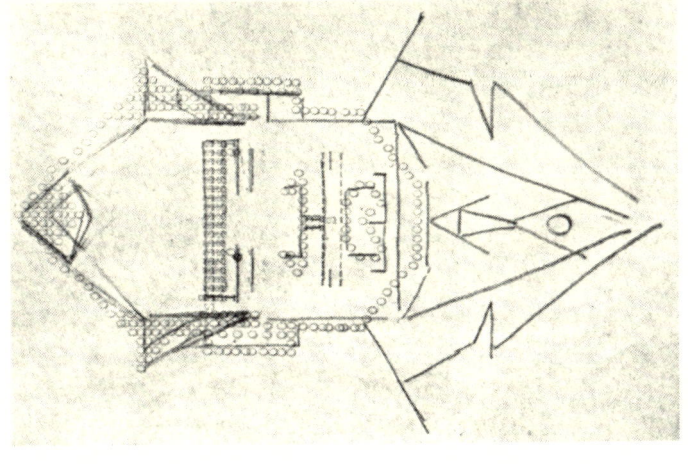

CARICATURES OF CARUSO, DRAWN BY HIMSELF ON A TYPEWRITER

ESTABLISHED

That London season closed November 3 with a performance of "Manon Lescaut", which sent the singer on his New York journey with a light heart. It was to be his second season at the Metropolitan; his *cachet* was fixed for six thousand *lire* an appearance; there was sufficient reason to expect even a more pronounced recognition than before. The singer cabled to his friend Mme. Viafora to have prepared for him the same apartment he had occupied the preceding season, but it had been rented by another. Therefore, on reaching New York, he found quarters in the York Hotel, situated in Seventh Avenue, only two blocks from the opera house.

An altogether different reception from the one given Caruso in 1903 awaited him at his 1904 Metropolitan première appearance. Then he was known and admired; accounts of his European successes had been cabled to New York newspapers and published, and, as invariably occurs in any like circumstance, they added to prestige won. What nervousness the singer may have felt, his inherent self-confidence was growing. Mishaps may come to any opera singer at unsuspected moments; they cannot be avoided. Still, when one's voice is under full command and the rôle thoroughly learned, an experienced artist faces his public with assurance in his heart. Caruso had been gradually expanding in the authority of his delivery; gradually growing in belief in himself. He was always prepared and always in earnest to give the utmost to the public to which he sang. And from the review published in the New York *Sun* of November 24, 1904 — which mentioned that

"Perhaps he imitates Tamagno a little at times" — it would appear that he was yielding to those dramatic instincts to give more and more voice. He had made his season's début in "Aïda" to the general satisfaction of those concerned; and he continued, to his last appearance in 1905, to do so. The fifty-four occasions upon which he sang that season — thirty in New York, five in Philadelphia, three in Boston, two in Pittsburgh, one in Cincinnati, three in Chicago, one in Minneapolis, one in Omaha, one in Kansas City, six in San Francisco, and one in Los Angeles — made Caruso known to the people of the United States. Through the medium of the press glowing reports of him had swept across the land, and for once expectations were realized. From 1905 Caruso was established on his singer's throne. He had his misfortunes — some of them darkly ominous — but as an opera artist, and in concert when he elected so to appear, he was Caruso.

Before that transcontinental tour of the Metropolitan, however, his name was still unfamiliar in at least one city, Los Angeles. Advised that he was to appear there, the local impresario wrote to Conried, "Could n't you substitute Andreas Dippel for Caruso? I am sure Dippel would attract a larger audience; he is far better known here than Caruso."

Caruso, well satisfied by this time with the United States, had begun to look upon its people and customs with a more than superficial eye. As imitative as he was observant, he took to himself the consideration of matters touching dress and deportment. The tailor, the bootmaker, the furnisher were summoned to display their samples and take the singer's measurements; and so the wardrobe increased. It was on December 12, 1904, that Tito Ricordi, addressing Caruso from the Carlton Hotel, London, wrote:

> As I have arranged everything for "Butterfly" at Covent Garden for next season, and since you are to be the first Pinkerton in London, it would seem to me an opportune thing while you are in New York to have your costumes made there. The uniforms are two: a dark blue one, for the first act, and another one of white. Mind, however, that both of them are simple uniforms of a lieutenant of the navy. I would advise you to consult George Maxwell, who was in Brescia at the première of the opera.
>
> I am so happy to hear of your recent successes at the Metropolitan, and I avail myself of the occasion to give you my compliments and best wishes for a Merry Christmas and Happy New Year.
> Yours,
> Tito Ricordi.

The growing consciousness of his professional opportunities and responsibilities had prompted Caruso, during the preceding May while in London, to engage as accompanist and *répétiteur* Richard Barthelemy; and the two worked diligently every day. Recreation the tenor would consider only after the routine of work had been performed. And he was insistent upon detail. Old rôles were refreshed in his memory; new ones were taken up for the sort of study that occupied so many of Caruso's hours. He was beginning, at about this time, to give closer attention to whatever attached to any character in which he was to appear; its history, the period in which an opera was laid, and the costumes. He was to develop a deeper study of these matters as years passed, but the practices which then were becoming more a fixed habit were commencing to show at the opera. Perhaps this conscientious thoroughness was also a factor, if in less degree than the singer's voice and singing talent, for the vogue which he then started to acquire. The public may not have appreciated the broadening artistry due to the labors of which it was not aware; the chances are that it did not. For the Caruso tones were then entering their full glory, and it was the listener's ear which appears to have been chiefly charmed. Yet there can be no doubt that the subsequent days wherein the tenor's supreme art was to rule were being prepared for during that second Metropolitan season.

His consideration for the needs of others was also beginning to show itself in substantial ways. Pasquale Simonelli explained the origin of the annual Metropolitan Opera House performance for the benefit of the Italian Hospital, an undertaking which means so much to the Italian Benevolent Society. "In 1904, after a similar opera representation through which the French Hospital profited, I asked Conried if he would assist, in this same way, the Italians. He consented willingly, and thus encouraged I selected for our proposed performance the three most popular artists of that time, — Mme. Sembrich, Caruso, and Scotti. But Mr. Zanolini, secretary of the Italian Benevolent Society, feared for the expense of such a cast which would bring the total cost of the suggested performance to $4500. Mr. Zanolini doubted the theater could be filled. When I expressed my disappointment to Caruso, he reassured me with the generous offer, 'Tell Mr. Zanolini that I will return to him, intact, my *cachet*.'"

For his part in this charitable undertaking Conried received, through the solicitations of Simonelli and the Italian Consul Tosti, the decoration of Chevalier of the Crown of Italy, and, later, Count Massiglia, Consul General at New York, was instrumental in having conferred on the impresario the order of Officer of the Crown of Italy.

There were moments of relaxation, as for example in a "La Gioconda" presentation, when the playfully inclined Caruso pressed an egg into one hand of the baritone Giraldoni, who was left to get rid of it as best he might. In Boston Caruso succumbed to an attack of mumps; and this gave copy for the newspaper paragraphers and brought the singer still more firmly into the public eye. So the season wore on; Caruso appeared in concerts given in the homes of James H. Smith, Miss Leary, and at a Bagby Waldorf-Astoria musicale. He tried vainly to make "Lucrezia Borgia" interesting; succeeded in his first New York appearances in "Les Huguenots" and "Ballo in Maschera" in strengthening his position, and finished his 1904–1905 appearances at the farewell given on March 3. In the fourth act of "La Gioconda" — with Mmes. Nordica and Homer, and Giraldoni — and the first act of "Pagliacci" — appearing with Mme. Bella Alten and Scotti — Caruso sang as apparently he never had sung before. Throngs of people were turned away from the

Metropolitan box office, unable to gain admission; a laurel wreath was presented to the tenor, who was experiencing his first taste of riotous popularity. Dashing from the stage, Caruso quickly returned, dragging Heinrich Conried with him. Old-time New York opera patrons agreed that it was an unusual scene, a brilliant audience, and a gala conclusion to an interesting season.

II

Earlier in the year Caruso had received from Edoardo Sonzogno a letter concerning a season the publisher-impresario was arranging to give at the Sarah Bernhardt Theater, in Paris. Dated in Milan, this letter ran:

I received from Mr. Higgins a telegram as follows: "Written to Caruso to accept singing with your company in Paris until May 19." I am so glad now that you have the permission and all misunderstandings are out of the question. Dear Caruso, I could not give in Paris a season of opera — in which I wish to give all the best the Italian art can offer — without you, who should be the principal element. You will sing in "Fedora", and Campanini will be the conductor. There is much expectation in Paris for this great season, and I want to give there not only the best artists but the best chorus, and the best orchestra I can possibly find.

By this time you have received the official letter from Mr. Higgins, and it will remain only to arrange the dates you wish to perform the opera, dates which should not be less than four until May 19.

I ask you to please let me know when it will be possible for you to make the first appearance, then

PUCCINI COUNTS ON CARUSO'S COLLABORATION FOR THE SUCCESS OF THE LONDON PREMIÈRE OF HIS "MADAMA BUTTERFLY"

9. 2. 05

Dearest Caruso,

    I learned of Tosca and Bohème at the Metropolitan and it pleased me so much to hear the echoes of the successes — mostly obtained through you and your merits.

    In London you will sing Butterfly. I hope very much for your collaboration together with Destinn and Scotti. . . . I can hear you, I can see you in that part, which not being so lengthy a one (less work for you to learn it) has, notwithstanding, the need of your refulgent voice and of your art for the purpose of putting the rôle in its just and efficacious evidence.

    I thank you and I greet you.

Affectionately

G. Puccini.

I will make the announcement. One rehearsal, I think, will be enough, as each of the selected artists knows already the opera through having sung in it. It will be a perfect ensemble, I am sure.

It is useless to say that I count upon your good will and friendship to make these performances possible, and I thank you in advance.

Believe Me Affectionately Yours,
Ed. Sonzongo

To make this season all he had stated was in truth Sonzogno's earnest desire. With the aid of Gabriel Astruc as chief assistant he laid careful plans and announced a repertory which included besides "Fedora" the same composer's "Siberia", and "Andrea Chenier", "L'Amico Fritz", and "Il Barbiere di Siviglia." But alas! The works which the French public best liked — operas by Verdi, Donizetti, Bellini, and Puccini — were missing from the Sonzogno list. It is true that Caruso was a magnet whenever he appeared; even before the première "Fedora" not a ticket for the six performances was left in the box office. The speculators, as busy in Paris as they are in New York, laid gouging fingers upon every piece of available pasteboard. Prices soared, the public fumed and raged, yet it bought what the speculators had to sell. But on other than Caruso nights there was no such attendance.

The tenor was finding himself in those days. The fire of youth could be quickly lighted by whatever audience chose to apply the match, which lay in spontaneous response to Caruso's preliminary efforts.

Nicola Daspuro, who was present at that introductory "Fedora", on May 13, 1905, said that while the aria *Amor ti vieta* was the beginning of a riot, the real artistic triumph came at the end of the second act, when Caruso delivered the phrase, *La fante mi svela l'immondo ritrovo*. "His voice, and the realism of the anguish and horror he put into the phrases, were as lightning in a terrible storm. The breathing of that assemblage seemed to be the breathing of Caruso; the life of each person appeared to be controlled by the singer's lips. Even to those artistically sophisticated Parisians here was a new experience: one of the most tragic developments of a human character, in which passions we all might know and feel were made so real by this artist that our hearts flew to his feet. At the finale, as Caruso sang the famous *T'amo*, the curtain dropped with the public emitting a kind of ecstatic yell; then from a thousand throats came cries of 'Encore, encore, encore!' Half bewildered, Campanini was compelled to take up his bâton, and again that finale was sung — and for an audience which well knew that from a French impresa no *bis* would have been granted. It wished also another repetition, and clamored until Campanini came before the curtain to say: '*Excusez-moi, excusez-nous. . . . Je vous prie de nous donner cinq minutes de repos, car dans ce moment nous sommes nerveux . . . presque malade.*'"

Each subsequent "Fedora" appears to have provoked like public outbursts. Caruso received twenty thousand francs, — from the total receipts of one hundred thousand francs. It was proof of what Giulio Gatti-Casazza always said: "Any amount you may pay Caruso, he is always the least expensive artist to any management."

A reporter of the Paris *Le Gaulois* asked Caruso, "What do you think of your successes?"

"My successes," replied the singer, "or my unhappiness? What are my successes? I have none. I happen to be a very well-known tenor, a kind of trademark to be exploited by an impresario. I cannot consider my own desires. I dare not even think of catching cold. I have to take care of that delicate watch mechanism which is my throat, and of the rest of my body, in order that not a grain of sand may get into the intricate wheels and interfere with their workings."

There had been other artistic successes than those of "Fedora", in which Mme. Lina Cavalieri and Titta Ruffo participated. Angelo Masini, the one tenor Caruso always revered, sang the farewell performance of "Il Barbiere di Siviglia." Caruso listened to him, then went to his hotel, where a letter from Giordano had been left for him. It read:

My Dearest Caruso.

Before leaving Paris I must tell you again and again how grateful, how sincerely grateful, I am to you for what you have done for me here and for what you will do for me in London. I will wait in Milan for your word calling me. Sonzogno tells me he has sent you all the models for the costumes, as you desired. Again a thousand thanks.

I am   Fraternally yours,
                               U. Giordano

"La Bohème" reintroduced Caruso to Covent Garden patrons on May 22 of that year, and he sang twenty-four times before finishing the season on the following July 25. He reappeared with two standbys, Mme. Melba and Scotti. In "Rigoletto" he appeared with Mme. Selma Kurz and Scotti and Journet; with Mmes. Kurz and Destinn and Clarence Whitehill and Scotti he sang in "Les Huguenots"; "Aïda" presented him with Mmes. Destinn and Donalda and Scotti; and when he appeared in "Ballo in Maschera" the tenor's confrères were Mmes. Destinn and Kurz, and Scotti.

The much anticipated "Madama Butterfly" English première took place on July 10, 1905. Mme. Destinn was the Cio-Cio-San; Scotti sang the rôle of the consul Sharpless, and Mme. Lejeune was the Suzuki. All that Maestro Puccini and Tito Ricordi could have wished was realized in that representation. The duet for soprano and tenor at the close of the first act — with such artists as Mme. Destinn and Caruso — was quite enough to satisfy the heart of any composer. Thereafter the acceptance — to use a phrase of which Caruso was fond — "was enough."

In his "Nights in London" Thomas Burke wrote of that particular "Madama Butterfly", of what the opera in Covent Garden really is, also with vivid pen of Caruso. "What is he? He is not a singer. He is not a voice. He is a miracle. There will not be another Caruso for two or three hundred years; perhaps not then. We had been so accustomed to the spurious manufactured voices of people like de Reszke and Tamagno and Maurel, that when the genuine article was placed before us we hardly recognized it. Here was something lovelier than anything that had yet been heard; yet we must needs stop to carp because it was not quite proper. All traditions were smashed, all laws violated, all rules ignored. Jean de Reszke would heave and strain, until his audience suffered with him, in order to produce an effect which this new singer of the south achieved with his hands in his pockets, as he strolled around the stage.

"The Opera in London is really more of a pageant than a musical function. The front of the house frequently claims more attention than the stage. On Caruso and Melba nights it blazes. Tiers and tiers of boxes race round in a semicircle. If you are early, you see them as black gaping mouths. But very soon they are filled. The stalls begin to leap with light, for everybody who is not anybody, but would like to be somebody, drags out everything she possesses in the way of personal adornment and sticks it on her person, so that all the world may wonder. At each box is a bunch of lights, and with the arrival of the silks and jewelry, they are whipped to a thousand scintillations.

"The blaze of dancing light becomes painful; the house, especially upstairs, is spitefully hot. Then the orchestra begins to tumble in; their gracefully gleaming lights are adjusted, and the monotonous A surges over the house — the fiddles whine it, the golden horns softly blare it, and the wood-wind plays with it.

"But now there is a stir, a sudden outburst of

clapping. Campanini is up. Slowly the lights dissolve into themselves. There is a subdued rustle as we settle ourselves. A few peremptory *Sh-sh-sh!* from the ardent galleryites.

"Campanini taps. His bâton rises . . . and suddenly the band mumbles those few swift bars that send the curtain rushing up on the garret scene. Only a few bars . . . yet so marvelous is Puccini's feeling for atmosphere that with them he has given us all the bleak squalor of the story. You feel a chill at your heart as you hear them, and before the curtain rises you know that it must rise on something miserable and outcast. The stage is in semi-darkness. The garret is low-pitched, with a sloping roof ending abruptly in a window looking over Paris. There is a stove, a table, two chairs, and a bed. Nothing more. Two people are on. One stands at the window, looking, with a light air of challenge, at Paris. Down stage, almost on the footlights, is an easel, at which an artist sits. The artist is Scotti, the baritone, as Marcello. The orchestra shudders with a few chords. The man at the window turns. He is a dumpy little man in black wearing a golden wig. What a figure it is! What a make-up! What a tousled-haired, down-at-heel, out-at-elbows Clerkenwell exile! The yellow wig, the white-out moustache, the broken collar. . . . But a few more brusque bars are tossed from Campanini's bâton, and the funny little man throws off, cursorily, over his shoulder, a short passage explaining how cold he is. The house thrills. That short passage, throbbing with tears and laughter, has rushed, like a

ESTABLISHED

stream of molten gold, to the utmost reaches of the auditorium, and not an ear that has not jumped for joy of it. For he is Rodolfo, the poet; in private life, Enrico Caruso, Knight of the Order of San Giovanni, Member of the Victorian Order, Cavalier of the Order of Santa Maria, and many other things.

"As the opera proceeds, so does the marvel grow. You think he can have nothing more to give you than he has just given; the next moment he deceives you. Toward the end of the first act Melba enters. You hear her voice, fragile and firm as fluted china, before she enters. Then comes the wonderful love-duet — *Che gelida manina* for Caruso and *Mi chiamano Mimì* for Melba. Gold swathed in velvet is his voice. Like all true geniuses, he is prodigal of his powers; he flings his lyrical fury over the house. He gives it all, yet somehow conveys that thrilling suggestion of great things in reserve. Again and again he recaptures his first fine careless rapture. His voice dances forth like a little girl on a sunlit road, wayward, captivating, never fatigued, leaping where others stumble, tripping many miles, with fresh laughter and bright quick blood. There never were such warmth and profusion and display. Not only is it a voice of incomparable magnificence: it has that intangible quality that smites you with its own mood: just like something that marks the difference between an artist and a genius. There are those who sniff at him. 'No artist,' they say, 'look what he sings.' They would like him better if he were not popular; if he concerned himself, not with Puccini and Leoncavallo, but with those pretentiously subtle triflers, Debussy and his followers. But true beauty is never remote. The art which demands transcendentalism for its appreciation stamps itself at once as inferior. True art, like love, asks nothing and gives everything. The simplest people can understand and enjoy Puccini and Caruso and Melba, because the simplest people are artists. And clearly, if beauty cannot speak to us in our own language, and still retain its dignity, it is not beauty at all.

"Caruso speaks to us of the little things we know, but he speaks with a lyric ecstasy. Ecstasy is a horrible word; it sounds like something to do with algebra; but it is the one word for this voice. The passion of him at times almost frightened me. I remember hearing him at the first performance of 'Madama Butterfly', and he hurt us. He worked up the love duet with Butterfly at the close of the first act in such fashion that our hands were wrung, we were perspiring, and I at least was near to fainting. Such fury, such volume of liquid sound could not go on, we felt. But it did. He carried a terrific crescendo passage as lightly as a schoolgirl singing a lullaby, and ended on a tremendous note which he sustained for sixty seconds. As the curtain fell we dropped back in our seats, limp, dishevelled, and pale. It was we who were exhausted. Caruso trotted on, bright, alert, smiling, and not the slightest trace of fatigue did he show."

A personality of such distinction as to be in demand for almost every special occasion, Caruso was commanded to appear on June 8 before the King and Queen of England and King Alfonso of Spain.

ESTABLISHED

The third act of "La Bohème" and the fourth act of "Ugonotti" had been chosen as appropriate operatic bits; and with the tenor, as artists, were Mmes. Melba, Destinn, and Parkina, and Scotti and Whitehill. Just sixteen days later Caruso received the following letter from Lord Farquhar.

Dear Signor Caruso:
   I am desired by Their Majesties, the King and the Queen, to forward to you the enclosed souvenir of your visit to Buckingham Palace, and to thank you especially for the great pleasure you gave Their Majesties and their guests by your beautiful singing.
   I must also congratulate you on the success of the charming concert.
                                        Yours,
                                             Farquhar.
Postscript.
   This letter would have reached you more than a week ago had it not been for the pressure during Ascot week.
                                                       F.

The "enclosed souvenir" proved to be a diamond and ruby pin, with the initials of the king. The tenor was pleased by this remembrance. He had an odd way of expecting thoughtful attentions, and although he was always as delighted as a child when some evidence of consideration arrived, he could be quite put out if, by any chance, the one who should have made known a proper appreciation delayed in so doing. And woe to the person who ever forgot.
   What experiences that London season brought!

In the old courtyard of the Savoy Hotel, on the evening of July 26, a Venetian lagoon appeared almost as if by magic. George A. Kessler, of New York, wished to give a dinner to twenty-four of his friends — a dinner that would be remembered. Caruso was asked to sing, and sing he did — for a fee no other artist probably could have got.

The Covent Garden engagement was over; Ostende was to come, but for a little while the tenor could forget about singing. He strode forth into the streets with his companions, and with them went the rounds. It was summer, there was nothing to do save what one wished; one morning found Caruso, Tosti, and Scotti motoring out to Windsor for luncheon. After the meal there followed the usual Caruso antics. The sound of a motor pausing before the restaurant attracted the musical trio; looking, they became still more attentive, for from the car alighted Adelina Patti, her husband Baron Cederstrom, and the baron's young sister. Standing like three soldiers in a line, their left hands behind them, their right hands holding their hats, and grinning as so many schoolboys, Caruso, Tosti, and Scotti bent from the waist in a salute to the famous prima donna. Before she would permit them to sit at her table she made them pose before her camera, in the very attitudes they had assumed at her appearance.

III

Pleasure-seeking Ostende, which draws thousands each year into Belgium, was waiting for Caruso. **Impresario** Georges Marquet, General Director of the Resort Amusements, reasoned shrewdly what it would mean to inaugurate the Theater Royal with an opera including Caruso in the cast. The news of his coming had touched Ostende with a flare of anticipation. Many already there had heard the tenor; many had not. He was a sort of curiosity — primarily to be heard, of course, but also, one was to bear in mind, to be seen. What was he like? Where was he to stop during that month of August, which was to have Ostende's celebrated bathing beach eclipsed by a singer? Guests at the Continental Hotel were the favored ones who might oftenest catch a glimpse of the tenor. He arrived at that hostelry a few days in advance of August 3, which was the date he was to make his first appearance in Belgium, in "Rigoletto."

Great ladies, famous men, the curious of both sexes who were neither great nor famous, yet for reasons of their own were set down at this distinctive watering place, stared at the stocky figure and the chubby face of the artist. Solitude he was able to find only in his own hotel rooms.

The King and Queen of Belgium, and H.R.H. the Duke of Abruzzi, were in the audience which received "Rigoletto." Mlle. Lalla Miranda and M. Beronne appeared as Gilda and the Jester. French was the language of the country, and of the opera, — for all save Caruso, who was permitted to sing the text of the Duke in Italian. From another having less to offer vocally there might have ensued objections; the critics doubtless would have made the matter a particular point. Instead there was only a repetition of other expert views in the substance of opinions expressed in the newspapers. The Ostende *Carillon*, and *La Reforme*, a leading daily of Brussels which had sent its first music critic to this première, published eulogies, as had other newspapers before them. The Caruso voice was pronounced "a delight, supremely enchanting, which sounds like a clarinet played by an archangel." There was much more, and at length, the quoting of which is needless. The public was even more outspoken if less expert; but what it offered came spontaneously from hearts that, under the spell of the singer, had lost all calm.

A series of concerts at the Kursaal followed the opera representations. These were as crowded by the Caruso-mad throng, which hung on his tones, and then applauded until its strength was spent. Jan Kubelik, the violinist, and an orchestra conducted by Maestro Rinskopf participated in these concerts. At their conclusion the tenor turned from work and set his face to the south, toward his Villa Bellosguardo.

Like other periods of rest he was then experiencing, this one held none of the extended tranquillity which it should. Family gatherings were somehow never quite to be arranged. Marcellino Caruso was content to remain by the side of his wife Maria Castaldi Caruso, who had steadily resisted her son's entreaties to leave, for even brief visits, her Naples home.

But others needed no invitation to cross the threshold of whichever villa the singer was occupying. Often, when it was quiet and rest he wished, some composer or maestro or artist or agent descended upon him. Fond as he was of companionship, there were times when he felt the desperate craving of isolation. Success which was bulking larger each year was his, yet he could not, it appeared, have everything; not the one thing which, as a boy, he had vaguely dreamed of. Outwardly happy, the singer had not always the light heart his face seemed to reflect. Nor was his health, for all his stoutness of body, of the best. For the physical exercise he needed to keep in condition was as repugnant as water to a kitten. He would go about over the land surrounding his villa, conversing with the farmers, but for the most part he preferred lingering in the nearer recesses of his garden.

The change which invariably was wrought at the approach of departing time for the important winter's engagement told the story: Caruso's greatest happiness lay in his work. Then a smile hovered almost constantly about the corners of his mouth; he would hum occasionally; and his eyes would glow as though beholding some scene to come.

November 20, 1905 — and the third Caruso season at the Metropolitan. He was to receive seven thousand francs an appearance ($1344 at the rate of current exchange). As events transpired he sang sixty-four times during that 1905–1906 year: in forty operas and four concerts in New York, the remaining occasions being in other cities. How steadily the Caruso resistance held. Not a single appearance did he miss. Considering his sedentary life and his constant smoking of cigarettes, it seems remarkable.

Still, the act of singing requires no slight physical exertion, and this may possibly have helped. The receipts for his public efforts during that season totaled $87,984 as against $65,664 for the year before, and $29,807.62 for his first season. Since his reputation was increasing at a prodigious rate, his royalties from the sale of his phonograph records were growing at a corresponding pace. Money as well as fame was rolling in upon this favored Neapolitan, and he was investing in securities a comfortable part of what he earned.

New York swept upon the Metropolitan Opera House for that season's première with a zest new and easily explained. Another star, which was fast becoming brighter than any which had shone in the exclusive Metropolitan firmament, seemed moving to a fixed place. Mme. Nordica, Mme. Homer, and Plançon were of the cast in the representation of "La Gioconda" presented on that evening. Maestro Vigna conducted. More compelling than ever, Caruso received an ovation at his first appearance which was an indication of the enthusiasm in store. It was a Caruso night, as each subsequent season première was regularly to become, — not to mention those many others that followed, year after year, until that farewell "La Juive" which none suspected was to be *the* farewell.

New York had now come to regard Caruso as its rather particular property. What mattered if he sang in other countries out of what was in the United States its regular season? From November to the following spring he belonged to the nation's metropolis. His goings and comings, even when of a personal nature, were held to be appropriate for chronicling in the press. He was interviewed for special articles, and often made to say things he never really said or quite understood, as explained to him by those "feature writers" from notes they made. Being "in the news", the tenor was a public character. His daily routine; his diet; what he liked to do and what he did not like to do, were set down in print, and not infrequently the singer was made to appear in a light which annoyed him in the extreme. For it is certain — reading through the mass of clippings taken from the New York newspapers of that season — Caruso was scarcely responsible for much of what was published concerning him; he appears, all too often, to have been the victim of imaginatively inclined newspaper folk intent upon a story that would enlist the approval of some enterprising editor.

If, as happened during a January representation of "Tosca", the tenor gave the impression of kissing the prima donna (Mme. Emma Eames) with evidences of realism, it became the subject of exaggerated newspaper articles. And when during a performance of "L'Elisir d'Amore" he accidentally cut his temple with the bottle containing the supposed elixir, and later narrowly missed being struck by the descending drop-curtain, the reporters plied their pencils in glee over having a "good story" to write.

This season brought its humorous experiences, as well. One of these occurred on the evening of January 4, 1906, when "Faust", without a chorus, was performed. The choristers, denied demands made upon Conried, went on strike. Caruso, Mme. Emma Eames, and Pol Plançon, who were members of the cast, were nervous because of the omission of the customary choruses, but nothing interfered to mar their parts in the performance.

Even a change of domicile could not be accomplished without the news of it getting into the breakfast-table newspaper. It was so in December, 1905, when Caruso moved from the Hotel York to 54 West Fifty-seventh Street. People made it a point to walk past this dwelling, eager to see the exterior, even though an examination of the premises should be denied them.

There was enough for the tenor to do without disturbing himself too seriously over these pryings into his private life, though he rebelled against a curiosity of what he might choose to do outside the theater. Not that he objected to the public's attention. He was aware of what it meant to him professionally. He would have preferred, however, to have been relieved of the stares and comments which increased as his popularity grew. But such a thing was not to be. The frequent publishing of his photographs and cartoons made him easily singled out from others. His round face, upturned moustache, and black hair were peculiarly Caruso-esque. And the individual Caruso gait.

To his valets, Martino, and Mario, who continued faithful members of his household to the day of the tenor's death, he would often say, "Why will they annoy me?" Yet, had he been neglected, he doubtless would have been made unhappy.

"Favorita", "Sonnambula", "Faust", "Marta", and "Carmen" were the operas Caruso added to his New York repertory during the 1905-1906 season. It was a distinguished company, with Mmes. Sembrich, Eames, Nordica, Fremstad, Homer, Edyth Walker, Emma Abbot, Marie Rappold, Bella Alten, Josephine Jacoby, and MM. Campanari, Scotti, Burgstaller, Knote, Dippel, Journet, Dufriche, Reiss, Paroli, Rossi, and Blass among the principals. It was during this season that Miss Geraldine Farrar joined the company of which she was soon to become a foremost member.

The introductory concert in which the tenor appeared that year took place on January 18, 1906, in the home of Mr. James H. Smith. His associates were Mme. Rappold and Miss Lina Abarbanell, sopranos, and Nahan Franko, violinist. The *Salut demeure*, from "Faust", and a group of songs by Tosti comprised the offerings which brought the singer two thousand dollars, of which he was allotted one thousand five hundred.

January 22 marked Caruso's second concert appearance, when he sang at a Bagby Musicale at the Waldorf-Astoria. Victor Herbert and his orchestra had a part in that program. Two days later the tenor journeyed to Washington, where he sang with Miss Abbot and Jean Gerardy, the 'cellist, at a musicale given by Mr. and Mrs. Perry Belmont in their Scott Circle home. Besides the first-act duet from "Bohème", Caruso sang the *Una furtiva lagrima* aria and a song by A. Buzzi-Peccia. His fee for this engagement was two thousand five hundred dollars, and he also was given the use of a private car to and from Washington. A smaller *cachet* came to him for appearing, on February 27, in a concert arranged by Mrs. Orme Wilson in her home, but the entire amount — one thousand five hundred dollars — the Metropolitan management permitted him to retain.

In the midst of these musical activities, and while opera at the Metropolitan was at its height, Director Conried announced the completion of arrangements to send the Metropolitan Opera Company on a tour to the Pacific Coast. Scarcely had this news been made public when Oscar Hammerstein startled New York with a statement carrying still greater import. He declared his intention of launching a season of opera in the Manhattan Opera House the following autumn, and the press carried accounts of the engagement of Alessandro Bonci, and the reported successful negotiation of contracts with the great Battistini, Edouard de Reszke, Giovanni Zenatello, and — possibly — a few farewell appearances of Jean de Reszke himself. Although the de Reszkes and Battistini were destined not to come, the announcement was sufficient to fire public anticipation.

With competition threatening, the Metropolitan organization was moved to still greater endeavors. Caruso — to whom the mere mention of Bonci's name was ever a source of stimulation — sang with renewed fervor. He appeared, with Scotti, at the benefit given in March for the Italian Immigrants and Miss Leary's Italian Settlement; and on March 16 the Metropolitan's New York season came to a

ESTABLISHED

close. "La Gioconda" was the opera; in the cast with Caruso were Mmes. Nordica and Homer, and Scotti and Plançon; Vigna conducted. Twenty-one calls resulted when the final curtain fell. It was a noteworthy night; a noteworthy season as well, for the total receipts were estimated at $1,173,000.

How little did that company of traveling musicians appreciate what fate held for them! Two appearances in Baltimore, two in Washington, three in Pittsburgh, three in Chicago, two in St. Louis, and one in Kansas City had presented Caruso to the people of these cities in "Marta", "Faust", "Lucia di Lammermoor", "Pagliacci", "Carmen", and "Bohème." On the night of April 17 — the eve of the great San Francisco earthquake and fire — the tenor sang Don José in "Carmen."

Antonio Scotti related the Caruso experiences during that terrifying occasion. He occupied quarters in the Palace Hotel near those of the tenor. "I awoke," said the baritone, "at a quarter before five on that unforgettable Wednesday morning, with a feeling of seasickness. Then I heard the sound of falling plaster and cries in the street. I rushed to make lights, but could not; there was no electricity. When I tried to unlock the door, there was no key to be found. It had been jostled to the floor, where I finally discovered it. Once in the outer hallway I saw Martino, Caruso's valet; and almost immediately Caruso himself, fully dressed, came out of his room; and seeing me cried 'Totonno!' I begged him to wait, but he seemed half-crazed and only continued on his way down stairs. I put on my clothing, hurried below and there met Mme. Sembrich and Plançon. Plançon was a sight; he had not had time to dye his beard — as he did each morning — and it was green.

"I walked to the square on which the St. Francis Hotel fronts and here I met several other Metropolitan artists. The scenes I will not undertake to describe; it cannot be told in a way to give one more than a suggestion of the terror and excitement. While I was standing in a dazed state, Caruso unexpectedly appeared. He had a towel about his neck and carried a framed portrait of Theodore Roosevelt, which had been given him by the then president of the United States. I remember that Caruso and I exchanged some words, and that he announced his determination of returning to the Palace Hotel to pack his trunks. I sought to dissuade him, without success. He left me to return to the hotel where, among other adventures, he engaged in a fight with a Chinaman.

"After a time I went looking for some sort of conveyance, and found a wagon. I asked the driver how much he wanted to take some trunks and friends to the home of Arthur Bachman, whom Caruso and I knew. He insisted on being paid three hundred dollars, and I agreed. Anything, I thought, to get to some place of safety.

"We finally got Caruso's trunks, and mine, and some others on this wagon; then we piled on ourselves, and slowly were taken out of the danger zone to the home of Mr. Bachman. That night Caruso could not be induced to occupy a room in the house; he slept under a tree in the Bachman yard.

"The next day we started for the ferry to try to get across the bay to Oakland, where we could board a train to start east. In some way Caruso became separated from us. I recall that he appeared, as we were loaded into a launch, and that we saw him in an altercation with some officers on the dock. He was still carrying the portrait of Roosevelt, which proved to be his passport, for when he showed it — with the inscription of the president to Caruso, — they allowed him to pass, and he joined our party in the launch. That ended our immediate troubles. We were soon safely in the train, but carrying with us recollections we could never forget."

The first word received by Director Conried from the scene of the disaster came from Nahan Franko, concert-master of the Metropolitan Opera Company Orchestra. It read: "Inform families of musicians, through union, of safety of all."

But what a financial loss the opera company sustained. The tour had to be abandoned; thousands of dollars in advance subscriptions were returned to the San Francisco public, and in spite of the insurance the loss of stage settings, properties, and costumes, and orchestra instruments, totaled a large figure.

Caruso reached New York with badly shaken nerves, though grateful for having escaped without injury. Soon after his arrival he sailed for London where he was scheduled to open the Covent Garden season on May 15.

IV

Extraordinary success affects people in different ways. Caruso, for all his gifts, was none the less susceptible. He always said that he was as human as other folk, and in many respects this was indeed true, for he inclined to the same things those about him inclined towards, and was keen in his desire to have the good will of the public. Thus, to be criticized for a personal act hurt him, — often more deeply than an adverse phrase penned by a reviewer for some artistic blemish charged against him in a performance. In view of this sensitiveness it may appear strange that his thirty-third year found him developing a half-swaggering independence, unless it served merely to prove him to have been like the average run of mortals. Whatever the analysis applied, the difficulty of maintaining a level course must appear clear. For distinction and wealth were being piled upon the tenor; men and women made fools of themselves over him; he was treated almost like a monarch. Perhaps tolerance should be exercised in treating some of his behavior at that time; he had been given so much, and in so short a period, it is small wonder if his honors went a bit to his head.

Having the artist's nature, he was then moved by it, despite his naturally well-balanced mind, into exaggerations of public conduct which he completely outgrew in his maturer years. Yet not a little of the criticism that has been directed against the tenor was overdrawn, and some of it, emanating from sources jealous of his success, was downright untrue. At least, it would seem no more than fair to make allowances during that time for one who lacked the advantages many another had, and whose steady growth in qualities of integrity and fineness filled those closing years of his life with deeds which could have come only from a man deserving the just esteem of those who really knew him.

London, in 1906, was as wild over Caruso as New York. And his reappearance in "Rigoletto" during that spring Covent Garden season only piled fresh fuel upon the fires of his popularity. In sheer golden beauty and liquidness of tone, his voice was then probably at its best. It had intensity and power also, but the timbre had not begun to darken, — which happened several years later, as the result of his singing heavy rôles and giving without stint every vocal resource he possessed. The ease of his voice emission, his marvelous breath capacity and control, and the authority with which he delivered a phrase were elements which even the casual listener could apprehend. Nor did one need to be particularly musical in order to appreciate that the Caruso voice and the Caruso singing were more than exceptional. He thrilled, also, quite as much by his inherent talent for song and through the fidelity of his vast understanding of the deepest meanings of composer and poet. A greater artist he was ultimately to become, but according to the lights of some, Caruso, in those days, was the singer supreme. Night after night, in virtually every engagement, he was consistently the same. Doubtless he rose or fell vocally as his spirits or physical condition compelled, yet so slight was this variance that common opinion seldom found the tenor other than the Caruso they knew, or expected to hear.

Mme. Donalda and Scotti and Journet were of the "Rigoletto" cast which, under Campanini's bâton, brought the tenor back to Covent Garden. He appeared, presently, in "Pagliacci", with Mme. Destinn; and soon after was heard in "Tosca", in which Signorina Rina Giachetti sang the title rôle to the Scarpia of Scotti. There followed "Traviata", with Mme. Melba and Battistini; afterward came "Don Giovanni", twice performed to the delight of the London public, and the satisfaction of Mme. Destinn and Battistini and Journet, who also appeared. In all, Caruso sang on twenty-nine occasions before the termination of his contract, July 26.

Out of the theater, however, the singer took whatever time was necessary to attend to the demands made upon him by members of his family. On July 13, in a letter penned in the Hotel Cecil to his brother Giovanni, who had just acquainted him with the news of an expected new arrival in his family, Caruso wrote:

"I am very tired, and long for a real rest. You ask me the name your coming child should bear. Why don't you ask Father? He is still living and he, not I, is the one to be asked. I want you to know that Papa is the only one who should be listened to — not I. Remember, he is still living."

Before that the tenor had agreed to sing for a benefit concert to be given under the auspices of the French Embassy, and this act prompted Paul Cambon to send him the following letter:

"I am told," wrote the ambassador, "that you have consented to sing at the concert organized by this embassy. I express to you all my gratitude and that of the French in London. Your name will be an element of success, and I am sure every one will dispute the pleasure of hearing you sing. I am really touched by the grace with which you have consented to lend your coöperation at our benefit, which has never before received such admirable proof of sympathy."

Here again was evidence of Caruso willingness to aid, wherever he could, a worthy cause. And he was forever putting his hand into his pocket to assist with money persons and undertakings often undeserving of his generosity.

From London he went to Ostende, where he sang in a series of Kursaal concerts with his usual recognition; then he journeyed to Italy for a few weeks' rest at his Bellosguardo Villa.

The second of October, 1906, brought Caruso before a Vienna audience for the first time. The Royal Opera House reflected traditions which had always interested the tenor; and the known discrimination of the Viennese public disturbed him not a little as to how he was to be received. The opera was "Rigoletto", and Caruso's chief associates in the cast were Mme. Kurz and Titta Ruffo. Like many a previous nervous anxiety, this one was blown afar on the winds of triumph. The quiet and tranquillity he had gained in his native land had freshened the Caruso resources. Such a voice and such singing could scarcely be lost upon so keen an assemblage, nor was it. His pulse quickening under this newest approval, the tenor continued on to Berlin, where he sang his introductory Don José in "Carmen."

That appearance sealed for always the Caruso vogue in Berlin. Already had he gained his place, and a secure one it appeared to be. But on this occasion Kaiser Wilhelm was present, listening attentively and indicating in the royal manner his approbation of the Italian visitor before whom the foremost German singers bowed. During the performance the tenor was commanded to appear before the Kaiser, a summons he obeyed with wonderment over what was to occur. Caruso faced the former German ruler at other times, and in other circumstances, though never, as he said, with such a fluttering of his heart. It must have fluttered still more when he had bestowed upon him the title of Imperial Chamber Singer.

Many were the incidents attending that Berlin engagement. In his most jovial mood, after the strain of the première, the tenor plunged into the kind of play which seemed so unfailingly to relieve any tension. One night, following his custom of smoking between the acts, the tenor was accosted by a fireman who informed him he was infringing upon an unbreakable rule. "I am sorry," said the fireman, "but you cannot smoke."

"Then I will leave the theater," replied Caruso, in a jesting tone which was not understood.

Alarmed at what he accepted as an earnestly uttered threat, the fireman reported the matter to his chief. That officer hastened to the stage and gave

ESTABLISHED

Caruso full permission to smoke, with one proviso: he must be followed about constantly by the fireman, carrying a pail of water. And this actually happened, during the remainder of Caruso's engagement.

To Paris the tenor journeyed next, there to sing in a performance given at the Palais du Trocadero on October 25, for the benefit of the Maison de Retraite de Pont-aux-Dames, of which Constant Coquelin was president. An audience of five thousand persons paid one hundred fifty thousand francs to attend this concert. Some time afterward, at the solicitation of Coquelin, France decorated Caruso with the Croix de Chevalier de la Legion d'Honneur.

New York silently beckoned, and the singer sailed away for his fourth successive season at the Metropolitan.

Another change of residence took place for Caruso; and this time he decided to stop at the Savoy Hotel. His suite overlooked Central Park, and there he spent many an hour, driving or walking, and, often, studying some rôle he was to sing. Singled out, because of the conspicuousness of his position, for criticism of various kinds, Caruso, like many another person of eminence, had often to suffer. Thoughtless people who spoke out of slight knowledge or none at all, and the envious, chafed because of the singer's success. He could not in the nature of things please every one: had he been perfect there yet would have gone up many voices in complaint. An experience which Caruso encountered shortly before he was to reappear before a Metropolitan audience was but one of many he had to undergo. But he emerged from it, and his season's début, on November 28, 1906, with Mmes. Sembrich and Alten, and Scotti in "La Bohème", was attended by a reception from the audience which revealed completely the estimation in which he was held.

Caruso's associates have told how, overjoyed at that manifestation of public confidence, he broke down upon reaching his dressing room and cried. There was reason for this display of emotionalism, for a cold or disapproving attitude on the part of that assemblage might easily have sent the singer from American shores forever. The whole affair, drawn out as it had been, was a shock that imparted to Caruso a sobering effect, and it is a fact that thereafter his serious side deepened and continued steadily to prevail.

The incentive to make his artistic self more essential "was redoubled." In voice and song Caruso established himself, with each fresh appearance, more firmly in the good will of his hearers, while on the critics he exerted an even stronger appeal. "Traviata" and "Marta" followed "Bohème" in quick succession; then came the tenor's first "Fedora" in New York. The *cachet* for this season was seven thousand five hundred francs ($1440) an appearance, and for the sixty-two opera performances in which Caruso sang in the United States between November 28, 1906, and April 27, 1907, he received $89,280. If it had not been for his indisposition on six different occasions, the singer would have increased his income for that season by nearly

VILLA FEDORA 12=12=1906=
BAVENO

[handwritten letter in Italian]

THE AUTHOR OF "FEDORA" TO CARUSO AFTER THE PREMIÈRE AT THE METROPOLITAN OPERA HOUSE

12-12-1906

Dear and Great Enrico,
   You have already a telegram signed by Sonzogno and myself. But I feel the necessity of sending you a few lines written by me, to express my *hearty thanks*. You have been and always will be the greatest, the only, Loris. Therefore you can imagine my happiness every time that you will sing in my opera. This means an assured triumph. I am grateful to you. . . . I embrace you.
         Yours,
               U. Giordano.

ten thousand dollars. Still, he had no cause for financial complaint.

After the "Fedora" presentation, which took place in the Metropolitan on December 5, Caruso received from Giordano the following letter, sent December 12 from the Villa Fedora, at Baveno:

Dear and Great Enrico,
You have already a telegram signed by Sonzogno and myself. But I feel the necessity of sending you a few lines written by me, to express my *hearty thanks*. You have been and always will be the greatest, the only, Loris. Therefore, you can imagine my happiness every time that you will sing in my opera. This means an assured triumph.
I am grateful to you. . . . I embrace you.
Yours,
U. Giordano.

Caruso needed such encouraging words as these; he needed, during this specific season, any bit of commendation that might come to him, no matter how small. Persons envious of his success, who stooped to the depths of anonymous communications in efforts to disturb his peace of mind, were not idle. Letters — even postcards — containing threats and filled with abuse were heaped upon him. He needed the stoutest courage to maintain his poise in those days, and to his credit be it said that he bore the burden with a minimum of complaint.

Much of his time he spent in the seclusion of his Savoy suite, which consisted of rooms 94 to 98. There his loyal friends surrounded him; and gradually, as the weeks passed, then the months, the tenor became more his former self in light-hearted moments. But his seriousness did not diminish. Caruso had entered a new phase of his life. He busied himself with what was important, since the Manhattan Opera Company, giving performances aiming at direct competition with the Metropolitan, was something of a factor in New York's operatic field.

The season ran on, presenting Caruso in rôles he had hitherto not sung in the United States, the operas being "L'Africaine", "Manon Lescaut", and "Madama Butterfly." Spring arrived, March 23 sending the tenor up for his season's farewell in "Tosca." The next day the Metropolitan company started on a four weeks' tour. Caruso sang during that month in ten cities; twice in Baltimore, twice in Washington, three times in Boston, on four occasions before Chicago audiences, twice in St. Louis, and one each in Cincinnati, Kansas City, Milwaukee, St. Paul, and Minneapolis.

The engagement was concluded in Milwaukee, April 27. Hurrying to New York, Caruso sailed immediately for London, where he was scheduled to appear at the Covent Garden opening on May 15. After that representation of "La Bohème", with Mme. Donalda and Scotti and Charles Gilibert, and, two evenings later, a second appearance in "Madama Butterfly" with Mme. Destinn and Scotti, the tenor crossed the English Channel. Another hurried effort — this time in concert at the Paris Trocadero, given under the patronage of the Belgian Embassy and the Comtesse of Greuffulhe, for the benefit of the

ESTABLISHED 239

Belgian Charities in France — brought receipts of one hundred fifty thousand francs, — also the decoration of the Cross of the Chevalier of the Order of Leopold.

Following a further rushed journey, which began the day after this concert, the tenor settled himself in London where, beginning again on May 21 in "La Bohème", in which his associates were Mme. Melba and Scotti and Gilibert, he sang continuously until July 30. In all he placed to his credit thirty-one appearances in the operas "Traviata", "Aïda", "Carmen", "Tosca", "Ballo in Maschera", "Fedora", "Andrea Chenier", and "I Pagliacci." In addition to those artists already mentioned, Caruso sang with Mmes. Kurz, Rina Giachetti, Kirkby-Lunn and Severina, and MM. Journet, Sammarco and Scandiani (now impresario at Milan's La Scala).

Easier days, with brighter skies, had come. Settled into the routine, Caruso found happiness in the companionship of his younger son, Enrico Jr., Mimmi. From Italy the boy had been brought to London by his governess, Miss Louise Saer; and established in a house in Ealing (from which the singer later moved to Claringdon Courts, in Maida Vale) Caruso devoted considerable attention to the child he loved. They had barely gotten comfortably settled in Ealing before a gift arrived from the Duke and Duchesse of Vendôme (the latter having been the Princess Henriette of Belgium), accompanied by the following letter, signed by E. de Cartier, Counsellor of the Belgium Legation at London. It read:

At the request of H. E. Leghait, Minister of Belgium in Paris, I have the honour to present to you — enclosed herewith — a cigarette case which Their Highnesses the Duke and Duchesse of Vendôme request you to accept as a souvenir of the concert you gave at the Trocadero in Paris, recently, in favor of the Belgian Charities in France. At the same time M. Leghait requests me to convey to you his thanks, all over again, for your generous coöperation, and his gratitude for the wonderful performance which will leave a memory with all who had the pleasure and good fortune to hear you sing.

The world was getting right again; Caruso relaxed and began to play more. Miss Saer, writing of those and later days, observes:

"Signor Caruso loved his children, and was very ambitious for them. He would often ask the boys what they intended to do when they were old enough to earn for themselves; and he instilled into them the necessity of having to work in order to live.

"The first time the younger boy was left in the charge of his governess, and Signor Caruso was saying good-by, the child said: 'Where are you going, Papa?' The father replied, 'I am going to work, so you can get food to eat and clothes to wear.' Later on, when the child (then four years old) was asked where his father had gone he answered, 'He has gone to get the dinner.'

"This little boy was happy as the day was long, and as a rule was always laughing, talking, singing, and playing with his toys . . . especially soldiers. Photographs, taken from time to time, would be sent to his father to enable him to see how Mimmi progressed. On one occasion a snapshot having been taken on the sands which showed the boy in a serious mood, the governess thought it would be well for the father to see him in this unusual pose. To her surprise a telegram arrived, stating that he did not like the expression, and would come to cheer his boy up.

"At another time, a telegram was received asking if the child were well. It seems that Signor Caruso had had a bad dream about Mimmi which he could not get out of his mind. Nothing, however, was wrong with the boy.

"These incidents show that Signor Caruso was, whenever possible, very solicitous for the welfare of his children; and it was unfortunate for both father and children that they could not be — owing to Signor Caruso's art and engagements — together more than they were. For each would have had a beneficial effect on the other.

"Sometimes, when Signor Caruso heard Mimmi being corrected, he would exclaim, 'Yes, yes; I want you to be a good boy . . . not a bad boy, as I was.'

"He would, too, be very interested in any new clothes that Mimmi would show him; and during Signor Caruso's holidays the governess has known him, in the case of the elder boy who was in boarding school, to go out and buy him clothing, with great discrimination.

"When Signor Caruso used to sing in Covent Garden, he liked Mimmi to go to hear him. Always, in acknowledging the most vociferous applause, he would not forget the box where he knew his child was, but would smile and throw many kisses to him.

"The governess, too, will not forget the look of extreme approbation with which he looked upon Mimmi in his first evening suit, when he was seven years old.

"As an employer, Signor Caruso exhibited keen business traits. He would exact a full day's work for a fair day's pay; but, at the same time, he wished his employé to look upon him as a friend as well as an employer. When one member of his household had outgrown her position and asked him for a recommendation, Signor Caruso said, 'It will be a pleasure for me to give you a reference, and I want you always to look upon me — not as Caruso, but as a friend. Should you need help at any time be sure to write and tell me so. And I want a reference from you, too.'

"The governess remembers one occasion when, leaving Pagani's restaurant in London, after lunch, Signor Caruso caught sight of Queen Alexandra passing.

"With wild enthusiasm he led a cheer. The queen looked up, and recognizing him at once cried, 'Oh! that is Caruso.' The crowd heard, and turning to the great man raised another cheer, and the shouts for the queen and the shouts for the singer became intermingled.

"Signor Caruso was fond of telling what Mr. McCormack's little boy once said to him, during one of their return voyages from America. The child seeing Signor Caruso for the first time, eyed him from head to foot, and then said, 'Well, you may be the greatest Italian singer, but my father is the greatest Irish singer.'"

In the midst of his activities Caruso was the constant recipient of letters from personages. The pleasure he gave seemed to have in it very great usefulness, and recognition was being steadily shown. After a concert given in London that July, for the Italian Charities Association, the then ambassador,

TELEPHONE N° 0420.
TELEGRAPHIC ADDRESS,
"GRAND, FOLKESTONE."

THE GRAND,
FOLKESTONE.

[Handwritten letter in Italian]

AFTER HEARING HIS OWN "IDEALE," RECORDED BY CARUSO,
"CICCIO" TOSTI GIVES THE TENOR HIS APPRECIATION

Saturday, 8 Feb. : 08

Dearest friend,
    I spent a *good* half-hour, today, in listening to you sing, three times. "Ideale."
It is the first time that I have loved the gramophone.
        Affections.
                Yours
                          Ciccio.
Will be in London on Monday.

ESTABLISHED

Di San Giuliano, thanked the tenor in a written communication. It was at about this time that the King of England conferred upon Caruso the order of M.V.O. Charged by Lord Farquhar to present the decoration to his compatriot, the composer, Francesco Paolo Tosti, called on the tenor. Finding him not at home, he left the following letter;

"Carissimo — Sorry not to find you in. Here is the Victorian Order that I was asked to take to you. Please do write me at once assuring me that you have received it. And do please write another letter, in the official style (you can write it in French) to Lord Farquhar, asking him to thank the King for the great honor he has bestowed on you."

It was signed,"Affectionately yours, Ciccio Tosti."

But the letter the singer prized, in some ways, above many he received at this time, was one from Edouard de Reszke. The basso, and also his brother Jean, had visited Caruso in his Covent Garden dressing room on more than one occasion; but the first had always left the deepest impression, when Jean de Reszke had turned to Edouard, saying, "This boy will one day be my successor." On July 16, 1907, Edouard de Reszke sent the tenor the following letter:

Dear Caruso:
 I am so sorry I could not manage to come and bid you good-by before leaving London, and tell you again, viva-voce, all the pleasure I had from hearing you sing. I never heard a more beautiful voice. . . . You sing like a god. You are an actor and a sincere artist, and above all you are modest and without

exaggerations. You were able to draw from my eyes many tears. I was very much touched, and this happens to me very, very seldom. You have heart, feeling, poetry, truth . . . and with these qualities you will be the master of the world.

Please do accept these few words from an old artist who admires you not only as an artist, but as a very dear man. May God keep you in good health for many years. Au revoir, until next year.

Your friend and colleague,
Edouard de Reszke.

CHAPTER EIGHT

Trying Days

An orderly and somewhat set procedure was beginning to dominate the life of Enrico Caruso. It reflected variety enough, and a host of interests due to the meeting of new and important people; but the tenor's professional movements from place to place were beginning to take him to stages which were familiar ground. There was something reassuring in the consciousness that an audience would be made up mainly of old acquaintances; something to be looked forward to in meetings thus renewed. Yet for all the pleasurable part which anticipation held, no one knew better than Caruso what was expected of him. He was popular because of his voice and artistry; he would continue thus only so long as nothing occurred to dim either the one or the other; so the thought of each reappearance, for all the thrill a reappearance gave, was disturbing to his nerves. Once the ice of a performance was broken this tenseness passed, and the tenor became his best self, singing with spontaneity and that individual abandonment of style which were conspicuously his.

He left Italy in late September of 1907 for Budapest where, the evening of October 2, he appeared in the Royal Opera House in "Aïda." Two nights later, in Vienna, Caruso sang in the same opera; and

"Bohème" and "Rigoletto" following on the sixth, ninth, and eleventh of that month. From Vienna the singer journeyed to Leipzig, where the public of that city listened to him in the "Aïda" of Verdi. His vocal condition was excellent, and that alone was sufficient to insure success to his efforts. Confidence having been established through actual accomplishment, Caruso put still more spirit into his work. In Hamburg, on October sixteen, eighteen, and twenty, he appeared in "Rigoletto", "Aïda", and "Pagliacci" with a degree of success that carried him to Berlin in a mood that augured well for the four appearances he was scheduled to make there between October 23 and 29. It is difficult to state in which of the two operas — "Aïda" and "Pagliacci" — the public liked him better. When he finished his tour in Frankfurt, four days later, after having sung in "Pagliacci" and "Rigoletto", there was little doubt that he was likely to experience in New York his most satisfactory season. For that city he sailed almost immediately from Bremen; and he took with him two thousand dollars for every appearance. Although the arrangements had been made by the Metropolitan Opera Company management, each *cachet* was credited under the terms for the 1907–1908 season, which provided that the tenor was to receive two thousand dollars whenever he sang.

New York welcomed its premier artist warmly. He was interviewed by the men of the press, who crowded about him when he came off the ship. This business disposed of, Caruso was driven to the Plaza Hotel; once more had he changed his living place. It is

Photo M. E. Hewitt Studio, N. Y.

MARBLE BAS-RELIEF, BY THE MASTER OF THE MARBLE MADONNAS, XV. CENTURY, IN THE CARUSO COLLECTION

Now in the Caruso Chapel at the Cimitero del Pianto, in Naples.

strange, in the light of his intense superstition, that he should have agreed to being lodged in a suite on the thirteenth floor. But he was soon moved to rooms 1123, 1125, 1127, 1129.

Those who had been accustomed to Caruso with a moustache beheld him at that time clean-shaven. And observant persons must have noticed about him a more serious manner than he had habitually shown before. For it is of record that 1907 brought the tenor back to the United States with a consciousness of his opportunities, which he had decided not to neglect.

Already interested in collecting *objets d'art*, he began, at this period of his life, to devote more time and attention to acquiring new pieces. An artist by nature, he built up his collection as one will who does so because of sheer love of it. Still, his enjoyment did not cease when he had made some new purchase. The singer spent a part of each day with those pieces of art he had about him; and in this he found a special pleasure.

Caruso began by buying a gold coin of Arsinoë II. From this small beginning, about 1906, he was prompted to purchase other coins until, at the time of his death, he owned nearly two thousand different gold coins of all countries, and of dates that ranged from the fifth century B.C. to modern times. But the plastic arts interested him most; and often, in his visits to museums of art, he would stand before some specimen impossible for him to attain, gazing admiringly yet regretfully at what he would have liked to own. He had been particularly drawn to the

J. Pierpont Morgan Collection in the New York Metropolitan Museum of Art; and later, when that collection was broken, came the chance to secure a part of the bronzes and enamels.

Among these purchases were ten pieces of Limoges enamel, containing a plaquette by Nardon Penicaud — "The Adoration of the Magi." Two other plaques which the artist prized highly were by Pierre Raymond, and represented "The Entombment" and "The Descent from the Cross." He also secured from what had been the Morgan Collection a small mortar (Venetian, XVI Century); a door knocker (Venetian, XVI Century); a large mortar (Venetian, XVI Century); a pair of candlesticks by Alessandro Vittorio; the figure of a bear, by Riccio; a Hercules, after Bertoldo; a horse (Paduan work, XVI Century); an equestrian figure (North Italian, XVI Century); and three lamps by Riccio.

In the Caruso Collection of pottery — which numbers some three hundred pieces — were objects dating back to 1000 B.C. and continuing on to the XVI Century, — specimens from Egypt, Greece, Rome, Rhages, Rakka, Sultanabad, Damascus, and Rhodes. He loved each one of them, and knew their respective histories.

Of small vases and plates in glass, the singer gathered in the course of his travels some four hundred pieces. Some were of Egyptian periods, some of Greek, and others of Roman. Not a few were of rare iridescence and colorings; and these the tenor was fond of turning over and over, commenting upon their beauties — if a friend happened near. These glasses were designed for toilet purposes, appreciated in ancient times to such extent that they often were placed upon the tombs of the owners when they died, — a practice which accounted for the excellent preservation of such fragile pieces.

While bas-reliefs interested Caruso he had only a few; but each was very fine. One was by Tullio Lombardi, dated 1526; another was a relief of the Quattrocento, by the *Master of the Marble Madonnas*, and this work so appealed to the singer that his family, knowing of his sentiment for it, has caused it to be placed on the altar of his chapel.

Perhaps one of the most unique parts of Caruso's *objets d'art* consist of about twenty-five enameled gold boxes and fifty gold watches, of the XVIII Century. Some of these boxes were acquired from the Alfred Rothschild Collection, Paris. They are beautifully enameled, and regarded as *chefs-d'œuvre* of French gold-smithing. It was the tenor's wish that this collection should always be kept intact, and so his heirs have arranged that it be made a special bequest to Gloria Caruso.

In the Villa Bellosguardo, at Signa, the entire furniture appointments (excepting one bedroom, which contained eight original French pieces of the period of François I) are of XVI Century Italian. There is also a XVII Century chapel, with a large Presepio which consists of about five hundred figures — personages, animals, *et cetera* — each one in wood, sculptured by distinguished artists of South Italy of the XVII Century among them San Martino, Vaccari, Mosca, and others.

Nor does the Caruso Collection stop here. It includes paintings, as well as other works of art which need not be detailed, and old velvets, embroideries, and other textiles, — two of which are a dalmatic and a chasuble, both regarded as fine examples of XVI Century English embroidery.

It is difficult to determine the sum Caruso had invested in his art collection. Estimates place the amount, conservatively, at $500,000; but the belief exists that, if it were offered for sale, it would bring a still larger sum. The tenor was a wise purchaser. He knew art and its value; and while he undoubtedly paid good prices for many pieces, it is a fact that he occasionally picked up a bargain, and was elated in knowing that he had. One such was a bronze plaquette by Tullio Lombardi, a Venetian artist of the XV Century, which the singer found in a London bric-a-brac shop. Whether the dealer was unwary, it is a fact that Caruso bought it for ten shillings. Its true value was about $500, and when the tenor learned of this, he was wildly delighted.

Although scarcely in the same category, the stamp collection Caruso made was by no means insignificant. He had many books in which, with his own hands, he had pasted rare stamps of almost every country. Burrowing for something out of the ordinary fascinated him; and the more circuitous the course, the more, apparently, did he enjoy it. For he was your true collector. To commission another to gather something rare — unless it chanced to be a piece of art or some stamp he particularly wanted — deprived him of the enjoyment of both acquisition and

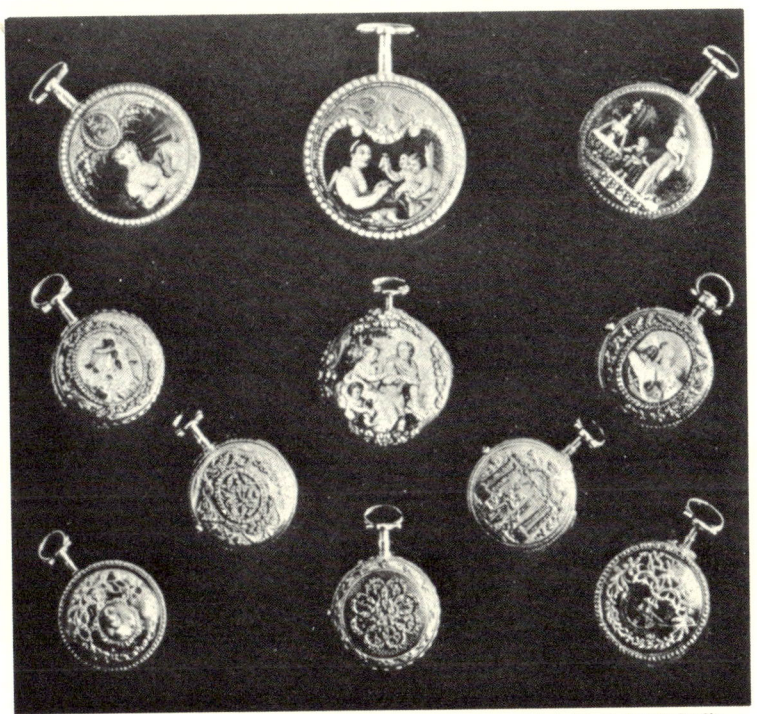

EIGHTEENTH CENTURY GOLD WATCHES, ENAMELED AND JEWELED,
IN THE CARUSO COLLECTION

Gift of Signori E. and A. Canessa to Caruso, on the occasion of his Twenty-Fifth
Operatic Anniversary.

possession. So he browsed among antique shops, and into out-of-the-way spots as well, looking for the unusual. Occasionally he was rewarded in finding what he believed would fit in the collection he gradually was building. But art for its own sake he appreciated. The time he spent in the galleries and museums would seem proof of that. And November, 1907, found him turning with increasing fervor into a channel that was to enrich his artistic sensibilities and serve as an aid in developing that side of him which made his later character interpretations achievements to be remembered.

II

A fortune was earned by Caruso during that 1907–1908 season. Fifteen autumn appearances in Europe, sixty-eight in operas presented in the United States, two New York musicales, and seven concerts (which comprised the tenor's first American tour outside of opera) netted him $187,500, since for his out-of-town concert engagements he had received $2500 each. The new world was assuredly an El Dorado for this Neapolitan who, scarcely ten years earlier, had had to struggle for opportunities to sing at barely a living wage.

The record, from an endurance standpoint, stands forth as unique. Indisposition did not once interfere with the filling of an announced engagement. From November 18, when Caruso made his reappearance in "Adriana Lecouvrer" at the opening of the Metropolitan season, until May 18, when the final concert was sung, the tenor appeared on seventy-seven occasions.

Mme. Lina Cavalieri and Antonio Scotti were associates in the cast which sang during the first presentation of "Adriana Lecouvrer" in the United States. The opera caused no special enthusiasm, and it was given on only two subsequent occasions. More interest was displayed in the "Iris", which Caruso added to his Metropolitan répertoire on December 6 of that year, singing with Mme. Emma Eames. February 26 was an eventful date, because it brought the singer forward in "Il Trovatore", an opera which makes vigorous demands upon the tenor. The resistance and dramatic fiber of Caruso's voice, as shown in his Manrico, indicated clearly the way his career was pointing. It was predicted that he would drift more and more towards heroic rôles, despite his eminent fitness for those of lyric character.

Experts who felt that Caruso was a tenor of pure lyric type regretted seeing him yield to those robust tendencies which he was beginning to disclose, even in music which needed no pronounced dramatic emphasis. Others — realizing the growth of the singer's art and visualizing its promise — admired the readiness with which he was seizing new and larger opportunities. For it is true that a wider range of expressiveness, histrionically as well as vocally, offers in characters of large mold.

Metropolitan patrons listened to Caruso in "Faust", "Manon Lescaut", "Tosca", "Madama Butterfly", "Pagliacci", Puccini's "Bohème", "Fedora", and "Aïda." What tenor could have sung, with such consistency and satisfaction to his hearers, so many rôles of markedly different qualities? And who can forget the enthusiasm he caused in "Bohème", with Miss Geraldine Farrar, who was then at the height of her powers? That season served to cement the ties between the United States public and Enrico Caruso. He had gotten his bearings; his popularity exceeded that of any artist within the recollection of the oldest inhabitant, excepting, possibly, in the opinion of some, Jean de Reszke. But the pertinent fact, which was highly gratifying to the Metropolitan Opera Company board of directors, was the contentedness of this superlatively useful tenor. It mattered little if the devotees of De Reszke declared, as was their frequent wont, the supremacy of their departed idol; Caruso was there; vocally he was the unquestioned superior of his Polish predecessor; and if in finish of art and aristocracy he lagged behind the De Reszke standards, he was a magnet needed to hold the interest of the people. All in all, it is questionable if these directors would have exchanged the Caruso of that season for the De Reszke of a decade before, which had crowned him as first of all tenors. As for the masses (and quite possibly the majority of discriminating, and unprejudiced auditors) Caruso would have been preferable to that rival whose traditions he was forced constantly to meet. For his vocal and inherent singing gifts appear to have been manifestly the superior.

As in other seasons, the Metropolitan made a brief tour after its New York farewell performance of

April 4, when "Il Trovatore" was given, with Mme. Rita Fornia, Mme. Homer, and Riccardo Stracciari in the cast. Three appearances in Boston, two in Baltimore, one in Washington, three in Chicago, and two in Pittsburgh brought the tenor to the beginning of his concert tour. Then he sang — and in most of the cities for the first time — in Columbus, Toronto, Detroit, Buffalo, Cleveland, Rochester, and Montreal.

The tour had been arranged by the Wolfsohn Musical Bureau, the assisting artists being Miss Julia Allen, soprano; Miss Margaret Keyes, mezzo-soprano; Henri Scott, basso, and a youthful violinist, "Sammy" (since become Sergei) Kotlarsky.

Profitable though he found such efforts, and much as he was sought by communities willing to pay almost any price to get him, Caruso disliked to appear on the concert platform. He asserted frankly that it was not his métier; and he was never wholly comfortable before an audience outside a performance of opera. He was intensely nervous before his first aria. And, always, he used music. Asked why he did so, when he sang the airs in opera from memory, he said, "I feel more secure, and I always read both the words and the notes. On the stage I have the prompter to rely on, which reassures me; in concert, if I were to forget the text or the music, I would be lost without the music."

On May 21, 1908, aboard the *Kaiserin Augusta Victoria*, Caruso sailed for Europe. His party consisted of himself, Maestro Tullio Voghera, his accompanist, his valet Martino, and Father Tonello, an old and valued friend. "The day before we sailed," relates Father Tonello, "Caruso gave me the itinerary of our trip. 'We go first to London, where I am to sing at Albert Hall for a benefit concert under the patronage of the King and Queen of England. Two weeks later we will leave for Paris, where I am to appear in "Rigoletto" for the poor artists and composers. Then we will travel directly to Naples, to see my father. He is sick, and I wish to go to his bedside before going on to Florence.'

"I was pleased to learn of Caruso's affection for his aged parent, and surprised also, because he had told me on several occasions that his father had always objected to his musical career, and sometimes had treated him harshly. Had Marcellino Caruso had his way, Enrico would perhaps never have gotten farther than a clerkship.

"Caruso ate in the ship's Ritz restaurant, sometimes with Maestro Voghera, sometimes with me. The first three days out were uneventful. Sunday, the 24th of May, was a glorious day, one of the most perfect I have ever known while at sea. Caruso was particularly happy, and he insisted that Voghera and I dine with him in the Ritz restaurant. While I was in the ship's barber shop a wireless message was brought me. It read, 'Prepare Caruso for the sad news of his father's death.' I scarcely knew what to do. When I reached the promenade deck Caruso greeted me with the words, 'You must be a great man. Several millionaires are on this boat, and some other distinguished people, yet you are the one person who has received a wireless to-day.' Observing my seriousness, Caruso continued to tease me. We dined. Immediately afterward I conferred with the captain of the ship — a particular friend of the singer — and with Voghera and Martino. We decided that I should convey the sad news to Caruso just before he retired.

"It was midnight when the tenor went to his stateroom. He was in high humor, and remarked that he had had 'lots of fun' and was 'looking forward to reaching London in four days more. Then Paris, and — Naples.'

"I trembled at having to begin.

"'By the way,' I said, 'when we sailed you received a quantity of letters and cablegrams; did you, by any chance, receive any information about your father's health?'

"He looked into my eyes, searchingly; then in a voice which betrayed his anxiety he observed, 'I see now that the wireless you received this morning was about my father. Let me see it.'

"When he had read it he collapsed, and in a voice choked with sobs he began to cry out to his father — as though he were actually present. Hours passed before he could be induced to go to bed. But he arose at five o'clock the next morning and wrote out six wireless messages: one to his stepmother, two to Tosti and to Gabriel Astruc, asking that his engagements be canceled, and others to Camille Saint-Saëns, the composer, and other intimate friends, acquainting them with the news and expressing his misery. The message to Maria Castaldi Caruso read: 'Learn middle ocean death adored father. Am desperate, desolate, heart-broken. Am near you, dividing sorrow. Hope having paid all ritual homages his memory as he deserved. Embrace you weepingly.'

"We arrived at Plymouth on Thursday night, May 28," continued Father Tonello. "The following day we went to Mount Avenue House, Ealing, near London. Tosti was there to greet and comfort Caruso; also to inform him that despite his bereavement he must try to meet his engagement at Albert Hall, since the house had been completely sold out."

The situation was one doubly trying to the soul of the singer, for he was saddened by another blow, which followed that caused by the death of his father. The woman he loved, and who had borne his two children, had left his house. He could not at once bring himself to credit the circumstances which took Ada Giachetti out of his life; but facts were not long to be disputed. Perhaps, at another time, the shock would have been less difficult to bear. Coming at that time, it was a loss magnified; and the singer needed the friends who stood loyally at his side.

Father Tonello describes the situation.

"Well," said Tosti, "what shall I announce in the program for to-morrow?"

Caruso looked up at the composer, and replied, "If I can sing at all, it will be *Vesti la giubba, il lamento di Canio nei Pagliacci.*"

When Tosti had departed, the tenor went "with great and fearful hesitation" to the piano and began to vocalize. His voice rang true.

Father Tonello relates that Caruso went the following afternoon to Albert Hall, his face revealing the depth of his agitation. The tenor sang first on the program, which included Mme. Melba, and Mario Sammarco. "He began the recitative to the 'Pagliacci' aria in a voice touched by an emotion deeper than any he had known before. Yet only Paolo Tosti and one other friend, who were of the thousands which thronged the auditorium, realized what Caruso was experiencing during those moments. He sang the lament with a pathos and passion I had never heard him put into the aria before. It was not to be wondered at that the people went mad. If they could only have known! All they saw, as they applauded frantically, was a man, with face unnaturally pale, who came again and again before them."

III

On June 7, while the tenor was still in London, he received from Gaston Calmette, then editor of Paris *Le Figaro*, the following letter:

Dear Friend:

I could not get your address in London until now although I wished to be the first to welcome you back to Europe. You are coming to Paris to add new laurels to those without number which you already have. I will be in the first row to acclaim you, and my *Figaro* will be happy to send throughout the world, to the throng of your admirers, the news of your fresh conquest in Paris. Bravo! Bravo!

This communication was one of several Caruso received at the time which helped steady him in the sorrow that caused his shoulders to droop. After he had read what Gabriel Astruc had to say the tenor wrote him:

My dear Gabriel:
Your telegram touched me very much. Please express my heartiest thanks to the beloved Victorien Sardou, Camille Saint-Saëns, and Jules Massenet. In my deep sorrow I do not forget what I must do to alleviate the sorrow of others. You can announce that I will sing — as I promised — for the benefit performance of the Disabled Artists House.

And on June 11, 1908, Caruso appeared for the first time in the Opera of Paris, in "Rigoletto", under the bâton of Tullio Serafin. Mme. Melba was the Gilda, and Maurice Renaud the Jester. The receipts reached one hundred fifty thousand francs, and the occasion, attended by President Fallieres of France, and Mme. Fallieres, was noteworthy in a number of respects. Afterward Caruso sent his personal check for twelve thousand five hundred francs (the amount of the fee which it had been necessary to remit to the Metropolitan Opera Company management) to Paul Hervieu, president of the Society of Authors and Composers. It was another piece of evidence of the generosity of a singer who, his word once given, could be relied on.

But there was no happiness that summer for Enrico Caruso. A shadow was cast about his villas, and upon his days — wherever he went. It was not in his nature to be embittered, yet he more than once felt his lips sardonically curving. The autumn he welcomed, because it again brought work. As before, he began his 1908-1909 season with a tour of Germany, opening on October 1 in Wiesbaden, where he sang in "Rigoletto." In Frankfurt Caruso appeared in "La Bohème" and "Pagliacci." The tenor went to Bremen for a single appearance in "Pagliacci"; continued to Hamburg, where the operas presented were "Pagliacci" and "Bohème"; and after one "Rigoletto" in Leipzig he concluded his journey in Berlin, where on October 20, 22, and 24 he sang in "Pagliacci", "Bohème", and "Aïda." This tour was under the direction of Herr Ledner, who had been retained by the Metropolitan Opera Company management to make the arrangements.

It was while Caruso was in Hamburg that he received a letter from Constant Coquelin, which read:

My dear Friend:

Through a good and sincere friend I had word of your departure. I had commissioned her with a message to you, which she delivered. I was really disappointed not to have had your answer, as all my hope was in you. I did not look for anything but you, and this year again passes without the Société des Artistes Dramatiques having had for their benefit a matinée.

My comrades reproached me, and I took it all upon my shoulders, not wanting to say I had had no answer from you. I did not doubt for a moment the answer I would have from your big heart so full of fraternal charity; and your kind letter proves it. When I think what you did in the opera, and for those authors, I die of jealousy.

I also hear through the same friend that you were preoccupied; that you had lost your charming gayety, the good humor of the man just glad to be living; that you were melancholy, and a little discouraged. Dear Caruso, you have no right to be that; nothing in this world equals the miracle of your voice — of your talent — and that must console you for the little discomforts of life, usually most unjust. In reasoning, one must judge the things for what they are worth and not suffer except for the relative meaning of it all.

It happened to me, more than once in my life, to be disappointed, disillusioned in friends. . . . I was quite cured — even to not having a regret. We should only regret what is worthy of it. Your triumphs will be a noble distraction for you, and the jealousies of one or the other do not exist when one is indisputably the first. I am sorry not to have been able to spend a few days with you; it would have been good for you to listen to a few of my experiences . . . you would have been amused at more than one, and have reflected upon some of them.

When do you return to Europe? Tell me first that you are feeling better, and then we will talk of a big project. I hope it will be before the month of May. *Pon-aux-Dames* always claims your visit; there you are loved as nowhere. Let me finish by telling you that before November we will have begun rehearsals of "Chantecler."

Give me the news, Dear Caruso. No, you have not lost any of my friendship, which is forever grateful to you and which wishes you all the happiness you so richly deserve.

Your friend,
Coquelin.

Close friends of Caruso, who were often with him during these years, assert that the change which became noticeable in him the previous season had deepened when he reached New York in November, 1908. The loss of his father, and the estrangement between him and Ada Giachetti, had left their mark.

There began, then, those faintly perceptible alterations of contour in the singer's face; and that sleek, pudgy quality of the flesh gradually gave way to firmness. Fortunately, enough demanded Caruso's attention to occupy most of his time. Heinrich Conried had been succeeded as director of the Metropolitan by a dual control consisting of Giulio Gatti-Casazza, as general manager, and Andreas Dippel, as administrative manager; and the advent of Arturo Toscanini, as principal conductor, put new color upon New York's opera. The tenor was aware of the crisis affecting both his private and professional life, and to meet it he bent every effort.

Desiring a new environment, Caruso selected for his New York home that year the Knickerbocker Hotel. It appears to have been a happy choice, for he made it his permanent home while in the United States; and not until the summer of 1920 — when word reached him in Havana of the decision to remodel the Knickerbocker into an office building — did he consider moving.

Although the 1908–1909 season in the Metropolitan Opera House did not open until November 16, Caruso sang in a representation of "Faust" which the company gave in the Academy of Music, Brooklyn, two nights before. It was in "Aïda", however, that the regular opera subscribers welcomed the tenor, under altered conditions which the public was willing enough to accept.

To his friends, it was apparent that Caruso needed to be diverted. He was clearly grieving, and his health not of the best. Singing seemed to be an effort for him; and anxious moments weighed upon those who sought, in various ways, to lift the singer from his gloom. They thronged his hotel apartment, to play cards and gossip with him; and frequently a party would be made up to go to some Italian restaurant, where atmosphere could be had that reminded Caruso of his native land.

In spite of these efforts the tenor continued to droop. On December 18, 1908, he became indisposed — after having sung seventeen times in "Faust", "Aïda", "Bohème", "Butterfly", "Traviata", "Tosca", "Carmen", and "Cavalleria Rusticana" — and he missed two appearances. He missed two more, the middle of the February following, and later that month, three successive opportunities to earn his two thousand dollar *cachet*. Matters appeared to be going from bad to worse when, on March 8, he could not sing his announced performance in "Il Trovatore", nor appear in any of six other operas for which he had been cast. April brought little improvement in Caruso's condition; seven times he was obliged to report his indisposition to the Metropolitan management, — a total of twenty-one for that season.

Yet for all his ill fortune he had sung on forty-four occasions (two being in concert); and his earnings totaled (with his ten October engagements in Germany) $98,350. In addition to the works already mentioned, Caruso sang also in Massenet's "Manon", for the first time in the United States, and in "Pagliacci." He was still in a state of dread not unlike that he had felt when he had written to his brother Giovanni, on April 2, "I did not sing for one month and a half. I will resume singing to-morrow matinée, and you can understand how nervous I am, as I do not know if I will be able to give the performances of the full season or quit and rest one entire year at home. Pray for me."

With feelings of gravest apprehension, the tenor sailed for Italy, where he could consult specialists of his own nationality. He went direct to Milan, and to Professor della Vedova who was celebrated as a throat surgeon. Almost at the beginning of the tenor's career he had developed a node on one vocal chord, which della Vedova had removed. After this expert had examined Caruso, he declared that he had succumbed again to a similar affection.

The singer was taken quietly to a dwelling, and once more an operation was performed; very soon he was able to go to the Hotel Cavour. In spite of pledges of secrecy, della Vedova was alleged by his patient to have informed a representative of the *Corriere della Sera* of what had happened. The story which was immediately sent out to many parts of the world so angered Caruso that he later refused to pay the whole of the sixty thousand *lire* fee Professor della Vedova demanded. The singer asserted that he had never been shown any evidence to prove that a node had actually been removed; and that a young Florentine physician, quite unknown, had relieved him of his trouble — said to have been rheumatic concretions. A scraping of infiltrations from the tenor's vocal chords was stated to have wrought a cure. Weeks of anxious waiting followed; then the singing voice was discovered to have been restored.

TRYING DAYS

Attorneys finally brought about the settlement of Professor della Vedova's claim, which certain of Caruso's fair-minded friends persuaded him was just. The first operation charge had been only fifty *lire;* this second one was at length reduced to thirty thousand *lire* which the singer then paid. Professor della Vedova believed it was a reasonable charge for his services in enabling Caruso to resume his career and earning powers.

After a short stay at his Bellosguardo villa, he went to Salsomaggiore and then to Montecatini, — places celebrated for their medicinal waters. Gradually he improved. By midsummer he was almost cheerful, and his physical condition vastly changed. No longer did he shrink at the thought of an approaching public appearance, for when August 20 arrived he began a concert tour of England, Scotland, and Ireland (under the management of the Quinlan Musical Bureau) with an optimistic air.

With Miss Hilda Saxe, violiniste, as assisting artiste, and Tullio Voghera as his accompanist, Caruso appeared in Plymouth, Blackpool, Glasgow, Edinburgh, Newcastle, Manchester, and Belfast; then at Albert Hall, London, and on September 20, for a second time in Liverpool. No further need to worry about his voice; he had conquered with his audiences, and so with more of his former spirit he departed for eight opera appearances in Germany. Frankfurt, Nurnberg, Hamburg, Berlin, and Bremen heard Caruso that autumn — in "Rigoletto", "Lucia di Lammermoor", "Tosca", "Carmen", "Bohème", and "Pagliacci."

IV

Caruso reached New York in the autumn of 1909 lighter of heart than he had been in eighteen months. He appeared as one relieved of a weight, and his mood turned now and again to jest. The Metropolitan had passed under the sole management of Giulio Gatti-Casazza — Andreas Dippel having withdrawn — and the future seemed to augur well. Nor was there any evidence from the direction of the weakening Manhattan Opera Company to indicate any individual rivalry which Caruso need consider. It looked like a propitious season for the tenor, and such it proved to be. He sang fifty-seven times in the opera, and once in concert. Including his pre-season European concert and operatic engagements, his earnings for 1909–1910 reached $158,350.

The change in the tenor's vocal condition was instantly apparent to the critics and public which greeted him in the Metropolitan on November 15. As in the previous year, he had sung once in another city — this time, as Radames in "Aïda", in Philadelphia. With Mme. Destinn and Pasquale Amato in the cast, Caruso opened the regular New York season in "La Gioconda." From that moment he moved steadily forward, with no mishap to mar his course. "Traviata", "Butterfly", "Pagliacci", "Aïda", "Tosca", "Faust", and "Bohème" served to dispel any doubt the people may have had concerning the possible failing in the singer's resources. And when, on January 22, 1910, he sang in the first

TRYING DAYS

United States representation of Franchetti's "Germania" the experts knew that all was well.

But two experiences of that season were trying affairs: the first, which brought about a meeting between him and Mme. Ada Giachetti, upsetting him completely; the second, threatening his personal safety, causing him mild alarm.

The mother of his two children appeared with sudden unexpectedness in New York, while the tenor was preparing for a rehearsal at the Metropolitan. He was calm enough as he went with his attorney from the Knickerbocker to the York Hotel, where Mme. Giachetti was stopping; it only vanished when he saw the woman who still held, for all the suffering she had caused him, an irresistible appeal. During the private talk they had together Caruso wept. In the end he gave to Mme. Giachetti what she had made the journey to get, — money. A cash payment was made, and a settlement arranged; then the soprano returned almost immediately to Italy. Some time afterward she brought suit against Caruso, in a Milan court. Serious charges were preferred, and the trial caused a commotion; but the tenor was completely vindicated. The depth of his feeling for this woman was such, however, that despite all that had occurred he continued sending her money almost to the day of his death. "Send this to the mother of the children," he would say, after he had written out a chèque; and the last one he ever wrote was returned, when it had been paid, to his New York bank, weeks after his funeral had taken place.

The second experience of that winter was an

attempt made to blackmail Caruso, by alleged members of the so-called "Black Hand." The letter received in February of 1910 demanded the payment of fifteen thousand dollars, if the singer wished to escape the penalty of death. He was instructed to carry a package containing the money at a certain time on his way to the Metropolitan Opera House. A man would appear, to whom Caruso was to hand the package; complying with this demand, his personal safety was assured. Instead, the tenor was provided by the New York detective bureau with an escort; and, although efforts were made to keep the police officers under cover, their presence was discovered by the blackmailers, and nothing happened.

A second letter warned against further efforts to thwart those who wanted money. In it a place in Brooklyn was designated as a spot where the cash was to be left. The police now planned with greater care than before; and on the night stipulated, Martino, one of Caruso's valets, took the package. On the top and bottom bank notes had been placed, but the bulk of the bundle of money consisted of strips of green paper, so cut as to resemble bills.

The entire block in which the designated house stood had been surrounded by detectives. Martino made the trip, unaccompanied, to Brooklyn. He located this house, then placed the package on the steps, according to instructions. A quarter of an hour passed before anything suspicious happened. Then three men appeared. They passed the steps where the package of money lay, returned, passed it

TRYING DAYS 269

again,—then picked it up. Instantly detectives swarmed upon them from every side. One of the three escaped, but two were arrested. Several months later, while Caruso was singing in Paris, Antonio Misiani, the ringleader, was sentenced by Judge Fawcett to seven years' imprisonment and deportation. At a later trial Antonio Cincotta was tried and convicted. The publicity of the affair possibly served as a lesson to others who may have held similar ideas of extorting money from Caruso, for he was never afterwards bothered by threats of like nature. But when a petition for the pardon of the two culprits was prepared, the following year, the signature which headed it was that of Enrico Caruso.

Otto H. Kahn, chairman of the board of directors of the Metropolitan Opera Company, had long wished to have that organization presented in Europe. With Caruso in his best form, and a finer artist than ever, it appeared a propitious time for an undertaking which, once announced, caused a whirl of discussion on both sides of the Atlantic. The press took up the matter; the artists of the Metropolitan were elated at the opportunities certain to be offered; altogether, it was a decision unique in the history of opera, with the consequences a matter of speculation in many quarters.

Besides appearances in Brooklyn and Philadelphia, Caruso had sung in representations given by the Metropolitan in Boston, Chicago, Cleveland, Milwaukee, St. Paul, and St. Louis; and on May 4 and May 7 of 1910 he had received the first indorsement of two Atlanta audiences which, until then, had never heard him.

Gabriel Astruc — guaranteed against loss for one half of the proposed Paris season by Mr. Kahn — was moving assiduously in preliminary preparations; and he had already communicated encouragement in the following letter:

"If we have Caruso — and if Caruso sings 'Aïda', 'Pagliacci', and 'Manon Lescaut'", Astruc had written Mr. Kahn, "the success is assured; and I am positive that it will not be necessary to touch one penny of the money guaranteed by our patrons."

To secure Caruso's pledge, personally, Astruc wrote the singer; and the latter, eager for a satisfactory outcome of the project, replied with:

Mon cher Gabriel:

The season here will be over in a few days, and I am anticipating with much pleasure and joy the moments when I will be in Paris, to interpret my three preferred rôles — "Aïda", "Pagliacci", and "Manon Lescaut" — at the Chatêlet Theater, before the Parisian public that is so dear to me.

Au revoir,
Enrico Caruso.

If Caruso appreciated his Parisian public it was an appreciation returned. When, on April 20, 1910, the advance sale for the announced Metropolitan Opera Company season at the Chatêlet opened, the people clamored only for Caruso tickets. Here was a dilemma. To protect himself financially, Astruc issued a notice that no subscriptions for an "Aïda" performance would be accepted without purchase of

TRYING DAYS

tickets for an "Otello" representation. To secure seats for a "Pagliacci" and "Cavalleria Rusticana" performance it was necessary also to subscribe for a "Falstaff"; while those who wished to attend the "Manon Lescaut" must indicate a similar wish to attend a performance of one of the operas in which Caruso was not scheduled to sing. From the public there arose a howl of objections, of course, but it was of no avail. The capitulation was immediate, for on the morning of May 21 (the day of the season première) the subscription receipts had reached the sum of six hundred thousand francs.

Prior to his Paris reappearance, and with the Metropolitan forces, Caruso had consented to sing once, — at a Trocadero concert given for L'École Menagère. But this affair, in which Mmes. Brozia and Lapeyerette and M. Florexo, and Mlles. Geniat and Robinne assisted, only heightened public interest to hear the tenor in opera; and the one hundred thousand francs receipts added to Caruso's popularity. Again the singer sent his chèque for the amount of his fee — ten thousand francs — to Mme. la Comtesse Greffuhle, head of the organization which was to benefit.

"Aïda" opened the Metropolitan's first and only Paris season, with Caruso, Mmes. Destinn and Homer, and Amato, and Toscanini conducting. Every seat in the Chatêlet Theater was occupied; no other space where one could stand was vacant. The attitude toward the visiting organization was friendly, though not completely so. Some persons chose to interpret the undertaking as a desire to show Paris how opera should be given; and, as might have been expected, the approval was somewhat qualified. Caruso, alone, received a wholehearted indorsement. The audience enthused; the press almost raved. One writer declared that "Caruso has a voice vibrant, magnificent. He is a marvelous tenor who feels the music, and he has the ability to make the listeners feel what he is singing. What a triumph he made last night. The other artists went very well ... but it was a Caruso night. He carried the work of all the opera. Thank God he has strong shoulders."

Fifteen regular representations and two extra ones comprised that season: three each of "Aïda", and "Pagliacci", and five of "Manon Lescaut", with nine of the three other operas. Mlle. Lucrezia Bori, Amato, and de Segurola sang in "Manon Lescaut", and Miss Bella Alten and Amato in "Pagliacci", which Vittorio Podesti conducted. In the three "Otello" performances the principals were Mme. Frances Alda and Leo Slezak and Antonio Scotti; while in "Falstaff" Scotti had the title rôle.

A scrutiny of the receipts indicates the drawing powers which Caruso disclosed. At the opening "Aïda" the return totalled 63,204 francs. Two evenings later, when "Cavalleria Rusticana" and "Pagliacci" were presented, the income dropped to 52,304. But it ascended on May 25 to 64,307 francs, immediately following an "Otello" (without Caruso) which had drawn no more than 48,296 francs. The second double bill, in which "Pagliacci" was the attraction, yielded 64,307 francs; and this sum

Théâtre Réjane
15 Rue Blanche

Quand un artiste a eu
la joie délicate et unique
(grâce à vous
hier) à vous
entendre ; cela n'a plus
d'un à vous dire la
suite cette impression
profonde ; ce devait devenir
un joie prête par vous

connaissant un peu
à peut être vous serrer
la main en vous
remerciant de cette
soirée inoubliable

Réjane

HOW MADAME RÉJANE APPRECIATED A CARUSO PERFORMANCE

"When an artiste has had the delicate and unique pleasure — as I had while listening to you last evening — she has but one desire; to tell it to you at once . . . the profound impression. It is a real joy, and although I know you slightly, I would like to grasp your hand and thank you for that unforgettable evening.

Réjane

TRYING DAYS 273

was exceeded by more than one thousand francs at the second "Aïda." The first "Manon Lescaut" brought 61,391 francs into the Châtelet coffers; a repetition of the opera was rewarded with a slight increase in patronage, while the third one was still more profitable, by two thousand francs. Nor did the rest of the regular performances, in which the tenor participated, yield less than sixty-two thousand francs each. Only when the two extra representations of "Manon Lescaut" were offered did the receipts drop, — to 42,626 and 46,536 francs respectively. These performances, it should be explained, were not subscription affairs; therefore the patronage was really very large.

The gross financial return for the season reached 864,707 francs. Of this amount the ten Caruso performances were worth to the management 594,978 francs (an average of nearly sixty thousand francs an opera); the other nights brought 269,729 francs from the public (almost forty-five thousand francs each). Mme. Olive Fremstad, Herman Jadlowker, and Amato had shared in the "Cavalleria" representations; there had been both the Metropolitan orchestra and chorus, and its settings. Altogether, the effort was one of distinction. The June 25 farewell closed an undertaking which left Paris something to think about; but the Metropolitan has never since repeated its experiment of that year.

For Caruso there had been one extra appearance, — when he sang for the benefit of the survivors of the victims of the lost French destroyer *Pluviôse* — in the third act of "Bohème", with Miss Farrar, then appearing at the Opera Comique, and Scotti, and in the final scene in "Faust."

The effort had, however, been a severe strain. Within eight days, as the close of the Châtelet season drew near, the tenor had appeared six times. Still, he seemed to have been the one who felt grateful, for he wrote to Astruc, addressing him as "My dear Gabriel", on June 28, — "Before leaving Paris permit me to send you, once again, my sincerest, heartfelt thanks for the continued proof of the friendship you have shown me. Be sure that I will never forget all the courtesies you extended me. I will always be grateful to you."

What an experiment to look back upon! Nor was it prestige and money only which Caruso carried away with him. A communication he always valued had come, after one of his Châtelet appearances, from Mme. Réjane.

"When an artiste has had the delicate and unique pleasure — as I had while listening to you last evening — she has but one desire: to tell it to you at once . . . the profound impression. It is a real joy, and although I know you slightly, I would like to grasp your hand and thank you for that unforgettable evening."

CHAPTER NINE

A New Period

THE world was assuming once again a more benign aspect. Health and honors and wealth were heaping upon the singer. He experienced only one deep regret; a single longing still remained unsatisfied. Doubtless it would always so remain. He would have liked to put out of his mind all thought of this person; yet, try as he did, there continued the old gnawing at his heart. Resting in the Bellosguardo Villa did not lessen it; nor hours spent at the Villa Alle Panche. In some respects memories were but kindled anew. Fortunately friends were always near to give the comforting words so needed. One of these — Otto Gutekunst of London — tells of the Caruso he and Mrs. Gutekunst knew.

"A heart of gold, and one of nature's gentlemen, if ever there was one! A big mind and intellect, and simple and playful, like a child. He was ever affectionate and confiding towards his friends. With him have passed, and have we passed, the happiest years of our lives; and the gap he has left can never be filled again . . . as far as we are concerned; neither by artist nor by man, and certainly not by such a combination of both.

"We first got to know him through Selma Kurz, the Vienna prima donna, when they were both singing at Covent Garden. She was then staying with us, in 1904. From then until the war broke out — he last sang in London in 1914 — we were the most intimate friends, and together whenever he and we were disengaged. He dined with us, or we with him, after the performances. We mostly waited for him, and supped together, or we met at Pagani's, with other friends, such as Tosti, Denza, Scotti, Barthélemy, Lecomte (Count Scalzi), now also dead. Sometimes he would dine with us *en petite comité*, with just a few friends, and sing to us or draw caricatures or play 'coon can' or some Italian card game.

"At times we took him for drives, because we thought the air would do him good, for he used to sleep with closed windows! Nature and scenery never — strange to say — seemed to appeal to him, or interest him greatly.

"In those days both he and I used to overindulge at times at table, both being blessed with great appetites; and I advised more exercise and restricted diet. He suffered from headaches, at times, in consequence of these transgressions, or rather from lack of exercise and air. Finally, in New York, he found a doctor who put him on a strict diet and generally took him in hand, with success. He was also forbidden excessive cigarette smoking.

"It was in 1910, I think, that we thought we might interest him in two games which would afford him occasional or regular exercise. We took him to Stoke Pogis, and he played his first round of golf . . . coached by I. Sherlock, the professional. He went around in something like 155. Not bad for

CARUSO'S PENCIL-SKETCH OF LITTLE GLORIA WHEN SHE WAS NINE MONTHS OLD

"Gloria Caruso" is written with the child's own hand, clasped and directed by the hand of her father.

ONE OF CARUSO'S LAST PEN-AND-INK CARICATURES

A NEW PERIOD 277

one who had never held a golf club in his hands. Unfortunately, he was so tired, for some days, that he could scarcely fulfill his engagements; and that was the end to golf. Some time after we induced him to try lawn tennis. His first and only game consisted of — I think — one set. Then he disappeared in the hall and fell fast asleep. There was no more tennis after that. But he enjoyed the games and was as gay as a boy.

"We went with him to Ostende, when he fulfilled his first engagement to sing at the Kursaal. Some 18,000 people usually heard him ... in a space which nominally would hold only 12,000. One had to be in one's place an hour before the commencement in order to be able to get one's seat, as later the auditorium was so packed that it became impossible to move. The enthusiasm was incredible.

"We used to bathe, and take amusing snapshots of one another in the sea, where he used to pose as a Triton, or sea monster, blowing up his cheeks or making grimaces. Barthélemy was with us at that time, and we were very jolly together. The year following we were there again, he insisting that we should be his guests; and he exercised his hospitality in the most touchingly scrupulous and conscientious manner. Voghera and Lecomte (Count Scalzi) were with us that time, and I recollect no end of amusing little episodes and happenings in those happy days. It was interesting to listen for hours, when he studied and practised from the new operas for New York, where he had to sing in one new work every fall. At night there was very little to do. We did not gamble, to speak of, but he used to say, with a wink of the eye, '*Oh! Comme on s'amuse à Ostende!!*'

"In the following years, when his London season was over, he commenced going on continental *tournées;* to Berlin, Dresden, Frankfurt, Munich, Vienna, Stuttgart, where we nearly always accompanied him, I combining business of my own with this pleasure. He used to feel very nervous whenever he sang to new audiences, always wanting to give of his very best.

"And the people worshipped him, everywhere; and there was the keenest competition for tables at supper, after any Caruso performance, near his table. When he entered, with us, everybody would rise as one man and cheer him, just as if a king had entered; only more genuinely and enthusiastically. And then, of course, one felt very proud, being the center of attention and admiration all the time — though it was of course only reflected glory, for our part. There, everybody tried to get him to lunch or dinner, especially at Berlin where we knew many people. Those we knew usually asked us in the first instance, or him through us, knowing that he would be more inclined to accept if we came also. If he did not wish to speak or converse at these entertainments, or was bored by meeting a crowd of people he did not know, or he did not want to eat and drink, he just started sketching portraits and caricatures, to the great delight of the various sitters.

"His eyesight and self possession, when once actually on the stage, were phenomenal. I don't think he once failed to spot us, wherever we might

A NEW PERIOD 279

be sitting, in stalls or box, in any opera house. It was a sort of sport with him.

"We used to look after little Enrico — Mimmi — between the ages of three and ten, especially during Enrico's absence. The boy was very attached to 'Auntie Lina' and 'Uncle Otto.'

"I just recall an example of Enrico's subtle and kindly way of teasing me with regard to my singing. We were staying with him at the Bristol, in Vienna, our apartment being above his. The bathrooms also ran straight up, one over the other to the top floor, all the windows opening on the same air shaft. I used to sing songs and exercises while bathing and dressing; and he said to me, on the second or third morning, with a sly wink of the eye, 'Otto, I wish you would not sing in your bathroom, because people will think it is I.' All the same, we occasionally sang duets together, at home. Nor shall I ever forget, when in Paris, at a performance of the 'Precieuses Ridicules', we went to Coquelin's dressing room after the first act. They embraced affectionately, and Coquelin confessed to a paralyzing fear of having to sing in the next act, with Caruso sitting almost next to him, with us, in the stage box.

"There are hundreds more of these little touches and memories that I could write about. And now — alas! — all is over. It ended practically with the beginning of the war, for after that — or since the summer of 1914 — we never saw him again . . . though our correspondence never ceased, nor our fondest thoughts and memories of the happy past.

"Half our interest in life has gone with him. I might say, with Scotti:

"I don't know when we may have once more the courage to bear the strain of turning on any of his gramophone records! Or of hearing any of the operas of his répertoire."

That summer of 1910 seemed not to have benefited the singer in restoring his vitality, sapped through the continuous effort and strain of a season overlong. If he could have brought himself to regular exercise, taking enough air, and restricting his diet, his peace of mind might have been eased. But he invariably met any such suggestion with a shrug of his heavy shoulders, or would turn irritatingly to light a cigarette. And it was an obstinacy which held to the very end. Considering his sensible attitude toward most matters, this unwillingness to heed what was likely to affect his own welfare may appear strange.

After his vacation period, which he concluded in Paris, Caruso departed for Brussels where, on September 24 and 25, he sang in two representations of "Bohème" at the Théâtre de la Monnaie. Mme. Alda and Pasquale Amato appeared with him, the performance being conducted by Maestro Dupuis.

His 1910 tour in Germany opened October 1, with "Aïda", in Frankfurt. Three nights later he reappeared there in "Carmen"; then came Munich, where the latter opera and "Bohème" were given. Hamburg welcomed the tenor on October 15 in "Rigoletto", and before his departure he was also heard in "Carmen" and "Marta." No mention is made of any apparent vocal indisposition. His

A NEW PERIOD

receptions were of the usual impressive order, but he was not his best physical self. Nevertheless his Berlin accomplishments did not suffer. He himself related a conversation held between two women, who had seats directly back of one of the singer's friends.

"When I made my first appearance of that season, in 'Aïda', one of these auditors — who were both hearing me for the first time — remarked, 'Why he isn't a tenor, his voice is baritone.' At my next effort, three nights later, in 'Carmen', the discussion continued. The ladies agreed that they might possibly be mistaken during that performance; and when 'L'Elisir d'Amore' was presented, my critics no longer questioned that I was a tenor. In explanation of this seeming misunderstanding, I can say that I always use a different character of voice for music which is strictly lyric or dramatic. Radames is a rôle which demands a dark, heavier quality of tone, while Nemorino is just the opposite."

The tenor always insisted that he kept his "different voices" in a chest of drawers; one containing his "Aïda" voice; another the one he used in "Marta"; a third holding the precious instrument with which he sang in "Bohème", — and so on, throughout his entire répertoire. And it is a fact that throughout any day on which a performance was, he governed his actions and his state of mind, to prepare him for the music of the night. If it were to be "Samson et Dalila", "La Juive", "La Forza del Destino", "Le Prophète", or any other heavy work, Caruso would lie down during the day and vocalize very little, — in slow sustained phrases. If, contrarily, he had to sing in such an opera as "L'Elisir d'Amore", he would rise early and move actively about his apartments. Every action, every thought, would be light and swift. Seeking extreme suppleness and agility, he would sing swift scales in the most lyric quality of tone. And when it came time for him to deliver his first phrase in the opera, his voice was invariably the character of voice the composer sought.

So well did Caruso sing his Don José in "Carmen" that he was summoned, at the conclusion of the representation, to the presence of the Kaiser in the Imperial box. The tenor, still under the influence of his tragic final scene in the opera, confessed to an inability to reply, at first, in other than French monosyllables to the remarks of the Kaiser. But when the then ruler of Germany said, "Caruso, why don't you turn your back to America, and stay with us, always in Europe?" the tenor answered, "Your Majesty, my gratitude to America will be extinguished only with my death."

II

Caruso returned to the United States, where he was received as a conqueror. His previous season had been his best, and the memory of his Paris triumphs still clung to the minds of all who had read of them. His place in the Metropolitan was seemingly as fixed as the very foundation upon which the opera house was reared. Back once more amid familiar places and scenes and people, it was like home — and next to Italy, Caruso by that time had come so to regard New York. He liked Fifth Avenue,

A NEW PERIOD

the cosmopolitanism of the crowds, and those little spots to which he had become so accustomed that they almost seemed to greet him with friendly nods. And he was contented in his Knickerbocker apartment. There, with his secretary and his valets Martino and Mario, he lived in solid comfort. His slightest wish had only to be made known, — an attention which secretly meant very much to the singer.

The season began, with Gluck's "Armide." It was not a particularly suitable rôle for Caruso. He always said that Renaud was the one character which gave him so little to do, in both singing and acting, that to appear in the opera was like taking a rest. The public did not care for the classic strains of the work, and three performances sufficed. Very different was the part of Dick Johnson, in Puccini's "La Fanciulla del West", which had its world première at the Metropolitan on December 10, 1910, with the composer present. And yet it could not be saved even by the glorious singing of Caruso and the equally sincere efforts of Mme. Destinn and Pasquale Amato, whose voice and artistry made him a fitting associate for his illustrious compatriot.

It was during this time Amato's singing was considered second only to that of Caruso. The friendship between the two artists was of the closest — few enjoyed Caruso's affection and confidence in such a degree as did Amato.

The New Year came, and Caruso continued his work. He had already appeared in a Philadelphia representation of "Aïda"; he went to Brooklyn for a "Pagliacci" performance, and in mid-January to

Chicago where he sang twice — in "Pagliacci" and "La Fanciulla del West" — with the Chicago-Philadelphia Opera Association, which consisted of the Manhattan organization the Metropolitan had acquired from Oscar Hammerstein and, shortly after, had sold to a group of Westerners and Philadelphians. A single appearance as Canio in Cleveland left the tenor free to return to New York, where he arrived feeling out of sorts.

He resumed his singing, however; and besides a "Gioconda", "La Fanciulla del West", and "Germania", he sang at a musicale given by Mrs. Cornelius Vanderbilt, and at one given in the Waldorf-Astoria.

On February 6, 1911, Caruso made his final appearance of that season, with Mme. Destinn and Amato, in "Germania." It was an unconscious farewell; although indisposed, the tenor confidently expected to resume his place in later performances. The New York newspapers announced Caruso to be suffering from a cold; but as the days passed, and he did not reappear, the concern of the public and press increased.

United States newspapermen have what is termed "a nose for news." Let them suspect something to be hidden, and their ingenuity is instantly challenged to ferret out the truth. As February waned, and Caruso continued absent from the casts of the Metropolitan, the reporters increased their efforts to discover whether the statements that he was suffering from influenza were not covering certain facts. From some source came the rumor that the tenor had, by

CARUSO AS DICK JOHNSON IN "THE GIRL OF THE GOLDEN WEST"

A NEW PERIOD

his continuous and unrestrained singing, developed another node on one of his vocal chords. This rumor was ridiculed by the opera house management; by the artist's physician; by his friends. Still, the story prevailed. And then, one morning, came the word that Caruso had been advised to return to Europe, where the climate and rest might help to restore him to health.

The singer's Knickerbocker apartment had become the objective of a host of daily visitors. Friends, advisers, newspapermen, and others swarmed the place. Nervous over his inability to fill his opera engagement, Caruso's sensitiveness added to his troubles. He feared, intensely, adverse criticism. "Now," he declared, "my enemies will say I have lost my voice." It was a delicate situation, intensified by the singer's own emotionalism. Out of the storm, however, came one whose very poise served to calm the tenor's fears,—Calvin G. Child, of the company which made exclusively Caruso's phonograph records.

Between Caruso and Child there had developed a deep friendship, growing out of an association which had begun in 1903. The first Caruso phonograph records had been made in late 1901 or 1902, in Milan, for the Gramophone Company of London. Soon after the tenor's United States début, he had been visited by Child; and a proposal that ten opera arias be recorded was tendered and accepted. The financial basis was an outright payment; the selections chosen were: *Vesti la giubba* ("Pagliacci"), *Celeste Aïda* ("Aïda"), *Una furtiva lagrima* ("L'Elisir d'Amore"), *La Donna è mobile, Questa o quella* ("Rigoletto"), *E lucevan le stelle* ("Tosca"), *Recondita armonia* ("Tosca"), *La rêve* (Massenet's "Manon"), *Di quella pira* ("Il Trovatore"), and the *Siciliana,* from "Cavalleria Rusticana." Caruso went on February 1, 1904, to the Victor recording laboratories in New York, then located in Carnegie Hall; and in a single afternoon he made all these records. Only one "master" was demanded at that time; later it was Caruso's custom to make two master records of each selection, and frequently he made three. If he were not thoroughly satisfied he would even go to the pains to make a fourth, — in order to secure what he, and Child, deemed was artistically essential.

"I never knew him to make a record which was mechanically defective," said Child, "for he had the one perfect voice for recording. But there was one bad note in the first *E lucevan le stelle* which I pointed out at the time. 'That's emotion,' he said, when he listened to the note; afterward, though, the number was remade.

"During Caruso's third season in the United States, and realizing that a royalty arrangement would be more satisfactory than outright payments, we made a contract with him on the former basis. During his illness in the late winter of 1911, I visited Enrico to discuss a renewal of his contract. It was his way, often, when seeking my opinion of any matter affecting him, to give me the details of a hypothetical case. On this occasion he said:

"'What would be the status of a contract between

A NEW PERIOD 287

an artist and a phonograph company if the artist wished to terminate his contract?'

"'Well,' I replied, 'if, in the instance of your own contract, you preferred not to renew it, you would be privileged to enter into arrangements with any other company; but if you made for that company records you had made for us, on a royalty basis, your interest in such of those records as we might subsequently sell would cease. You could, however, make any records you had not sung for us without in any way affecting your rights in those you did not record elsewhere.'

"'Since we are discussing contracts, your own with the Victor will expire in about sixteen months. You have been ill, and the financial loss due to your absence from the opera and your medical expenses must have been heavy. If you would like to renew your contract with us, I will be glad to pay you an advance of twenty-five thousand dollars against your future royalties.'

"I remember that he looked up sharply as I made the statement. 'You say that your company will advance me twenty-five thousand dollars if I sign a new contract?'

"'Yes.'

"'When could I have the advance?'

"'Well, to-day is Saturday; I will be here at two o'clock on Monday afternoon with a chèque.'

"For reply he turned to the table near him, and picking up a letter from it, handed it to me. 'There,' he said, 'is an offer from a phonograph company offering me more to make records than you offer.

Please answer it. And please make out a contract arranging that Caruso will sing for your company, as long as he lives.'

"I explained that such a contract would scarcely be legal, and suggested a term of years. 'Very well, then make it for twenty-five years; and — never mind about the twenty-five thousand dollar advance.'

"Such an action was typical of Caruso; he had only one way of doing business.

"He never was the slightest trouble. Never did we have any arguments over making a record. He realized, very soon after our first royalty arrangements, the seriousness of the work.

"'You know, Child,' he said, 'recording is different from the opera or concert. On the stage, if you take a note in the wrong way, it is possible to turn quickly away, with a gesture; or one may look angrily at the conductor, thus moving an audience to believe it is his fault, not the singer's. But this you cannot do when you make a record, because what you sing is there for all time. So one must not only approach the task seriously; it is necessary to be in the best vocal condition.'

"Caruso's visits to us for professional purposes were invariably looked forward to with real pleasure. For he was more than a great artist; his consideration of members of the recording staff, and of the orchestra, made every Caruso date anticipated with delight. It was the practise, first, to rehearse the composition to be recorded, then to make a little test of it . . . to determine if everything was correctly adjusted. The actual making of the 'masters' was done with

A NEW PERIOD 289

the utmost zeal and patience, and nothing ever was too slight to be made as perfect as possible.

"Many times, when Caruso appeared with other artists in the securing of concerted compositions, the finished proof record might reveal an unsatisfactory phrase or an incorrect note caused by another singer or the orchestra. In such instances, though blameless himself, Caruso never objected to or complained about a remake. He was always most considerate of singers who worked with him.

"On one occasion, when he was singing the *Cujus animam* from the "Stabat Mater", it was impossible to avoid several rehearsals of the introduction, which has a difficult and trying part for the trumpeter, who plays an obbligato. When the 'masters' were at length finished, Caruso — who always sang with his collar and scarf off — picked up a gold and enamel scarf-holder, and handing it to the trumpet player, he said, 'You deserve a reward; I thought you would surely crack.'

"Often he came to the recording laboratory with little souvenirs for members of the staff and the orchestra; and once he brought each of them a gold medallion with a bas-relief of his head on one side.

"I never knew him to appear among us that, should a change have taken place in the orchestra personnel or if some member were not present, he did not instantly notice the absence and inquire where the missing player was.

"Naturally, he was held in esteem by the musicians. And at times, when it was imperative — because of his opera engagements — to make records on a

Saturday or a Sunday, there was no objection, — because they were working for Caruso.

"After each number, the players would applaud. But when an entire morning, or afternoon, had been devoted to work, there would come a lull in the spontaneity and enthusiasm of such applause. Then the tapping of bows on violins, and other physical demonstrations of approval, would become somewhat perfunctory. Once he turned to me, and with a twinkle in his eye, remarked, 'Tell them they don't have to do that.'

"His interest in the mechanical side of recording was intense. He was the one artist who was taken 'behind the scenes' and shown just how we proceeded mechanically. He was always ready to make experimental tests, to aid us in our advancement in the art; and ever willing with helpful suggestions.

"The procedure, after a proof-pressing was returned from the factory, was for me to take it to him . . . that we might hear it together. Sometimes he would say he doubted if the composition was good material for the public. We always respected his opinions. Our own we considered important, yet until a record had Caruso's acceptance, it could not go to the public.

"For many years I had sought to have him come to the United States well in advance of the time for him to begin his professional duties in public. It seemed only just, to himself and to us, that he devote to his recording several days when he was perfectly fresh, and his mind free from having to think of other music matters. Until the early autumn of 1920

A NEW PERIOD

(he had spent the summer at his leased villa on Long Island), we had usually had to make records a day or two at a time, either in late December or early January, or in the spring, before he left for Europe.

"He said he thought I was right in the suggestion offered; so a lengthy répertoire was prepared in the spring of 1920, and in the following September, before starting on his concert tour, a full week was devoted to recording it. I was so delighted at the results that I commented on them, unconsciously, in the presence of one of the orchestra players, who observed, 'That's right, — to get him when his voice is rested.' It was almost prophetic, for the time he might have planned to come to us found him fighting desperately for his life . . . and never afterwards was he able to sing as he would have wished, to make a record."

The sum of $1,825,000 in talking-machine royalties had been paid to Caruso during the life of his contracts . . . to January 1920, an average of a little more than one hundred twenty-five thousand dollars a year. But for the year from January 1921 to 1922 the royalties received by the Caruso estate reached the sum of four hundred thousand dollars. Thus, a total of $2,225,000 has been earned through this medium. "While the 1921 income does not," declares Child, "establish a figure for the future since it is absolutely unprecedented — it is a fact that with only one new number issued, the gross receipts from the sale of Caruso talking-machine records from January 1, 1922, to the following May were in excess of those for the same period two years previous, when several new compositions were being regularly released; and this four months' income, during the first part of 1922, almost equalled that for the similar length of time one year ago.

"Apart from our business relations," said Child, "those of a personal nature were of two fast friends. When he once said to me, 'Child, everybody is asking me to sing a concert tour; I suggest that you manage my concert affairs, and you and I will divide the profits.' Deeply as I valued this proof of confidence, I explained that my lack of experience in that field was sufficient cause to prompt declining the generous offer. I told him I felt, if I were to accept, that our friendship would end.

"His loss I cannot undertake to estimate, because it is not possible. In life, I held for him affection and admiration. Now that he is gone I realize still more how true a friend he was."

III

Caruso sailed for London in February, 1911, with the people of many countries gravely concerned over his state of voice. The backbiters (among them those who pretended friendship) remarked prophetically that his career was "finished." Experts who had all along discountenanced his tendency toward a prodigality of tone wagged their ears sagely. "He sang too strenuously and too much," they declared. It was the masses, whose hearts the tenor had reached with his singing, who were genuinely distressed.

Copyright Famous Players Lasky Corporation.

CARUSO AS HE APPEARED IN "THE SPLENDID ROMANCE," A FILM MADE IN AMERICA BUT NEVER PRODUCED

The rôle he assumed was that of a prince.

A NEW PERIOD

Having suffered previously from the effects of a nodule, it was the belief in many quarters that the old trouble had returned. Italian newspapermen, in particular, interested themselves in the matter, with the result that rumors got abroad that Professor della Vedova had gone to Caruso, and performed another operation similar to the two previous ones. Thereupon, reports spread that Caruso might never sing again.

He was in London when this news broke; and to the press the following statement was given: "The canard that my vocal chords are giving me trouble is pure invention. The Italian doctor who is said to have started the rumor did so merely to advertise himself; and the story he gave to a reporter about a 'corn' having made its appearance in my throat is absolutely without foundation. Indeed, the Italian doctor has not examined me for two years. For the rest, my voice is in good condition as ever and I will duly keep my continental and other engagements. Doctor William Lloyd, under whose care I have been since my return to London, assures me that my vocal chords are perfectly healthy and normal."

Le Figaro, of Paris, defended the singer in an article published on May 20, 1911, which read: "We wish to put a stop to innumerable pieces of misinformation about Caruso's voice. He has not, thank Heaven! lost it. Our esteemed friend is in London, resting after an attack of la grippe in New York."

By this time much improved, and hoping to allay fears over his condition by appearing conspicuously in public, Caruso went to a fancy-dress charity ball given that spring in the Savoy Hotel. Many distinguished people were present. Among the party of which Caruso was one were Lady O'Hagan; the Hon. Wilfred Edgerton, costumed as a Chinaman; Lady Rosslyn, attired as Lady Hamilton (after Romney); the Earl of Shrewsbury, made up as an American Indian, and Mr. and Mrs. Gutekunst. Caruso was garbed as a Moor, which made him appear much like Nadir, in "The Pearl Fishers."

It was at this time that the London receiver of taxes adjudged the tenor a resident of the British metropolis — since he maintained a domicile in Maida Vale — and assessed him at a figure he considered outrageously high. So incensed was Caruso that he ordered removed from his London residence, almost overnight, all its furnishings; and those he did not send as gifts to friends he had shipped to Italy. By such means did he escape being taxed. And he thereupon moved his son Mimmi, and his governess, Miss Saer, to Criklewood (the home of the Saers), where they remained until 1914. At the outbreak of the war both went to the villa of Signorina Rina Giachetti, at Livorno, and later to the villa at Signa. When Caruso married Miss Dorothy Benjamin, in 1918, Miss Saer and Mimmi went to live at the Hotel Paoli, on the Lungarno, Florence.

It is significant that the tenor refrained wholly from singing until the opening of the 1911–1912 New York Metropolitan season. Europeans did not hear his voice that year. Nervous over his artistic future, Caruso turned in his wretchedness from everything musical. His chief object was to try to forget, and he devoted himself more than had been his wont to efforts to find pleasurable moments. Old friends and acquaintances saw him oftener; new people were met, some of whom he cultivated. Signorina Elisa Ganelli, a Milanese salesgirl, was one of those who attracted the tenor those summer days. She was comely, spirited, and companionable; to be gloomy in her society was no easy matter. So the months passed.

By autumn, Caruso had emerged from his nervous irritability. His health was improved; the voice, tried judiciously now and again, was giving forth its former resonance. His courage regained, the tenor set sail for New York, where he discovered more than one friendship-pretender eager to shake him by the hand. Caruso met them all with philosophic tolerance. He held no delusions over the constancy of certain individuals; but of what use was it to quarrel needlessly? He was convinced of his restored vocal vigor. While that lasted he could afford to smile, even if it disguised his real feelings.

The evening of November 13, 1911, disposed of any doubts the public then held as to the Caruso voice. For his Radames in "Aïda", in which he appeared at the Metropolitan opening with Mmes. Destinn and Margarete Matzenauer, gave the optimists renewed joy. Nor was it any short-lived jubilation. "Gioconda", "La Fanciulla del West", "Pagliacci", "Armide", "Tosca", "Bohème" — as well as repetitions of some of these operas — confirmed evidences that the tenor was his complete artistic self. He made new phonograph records, which are still among the best sellers, and continued with his operatic triumphs. Then something else happened. Keen observers detected an improvement in the singer's acting which hinted at the first blossomings of an unsuspected side of Caruso's art. Hardship, disappointments, sorrow, illness, and the strain of endeavoring to maintain a hard-won position constituted the price for its fruits. But it seems to have been a price necessary to the development of the Caruso resources.

The year 1912 swung the tenor into a series of fresh successes — at the Metropolitan, in Brooklyn, in Philadelphia. Where were the calamity howlers of ten months before? Under cover, apparently; at least, nothing was heard from them.

In the midst of this reëstablished security the singer was disturbed again when, on February 17, suit in Milan was brought against him by Signorina Ganelli, for alleged breach of promise. It proved no more, however, than a temporary annoyance; in less than a month the case was thrown out of court, with damages, in any amount, denied the plaintiff.

Relieved of this threatened trouble, Caruso sang on with increasing powers. Then followed "Rigoletto", and "Manon Lescaut" — in which, according to the New York *Sun*, "Caruso never sang better. . . . The voice . . . is now matched by the grace and significance of his actions. There is no need to say more. For such a delight all lovers of beauty can give thanks. . . ." The season finished on April 27, at Atlanta, with the tenor appearing in

A NEW PERIOD

"Rigoletto." He had sung fifty times, without missing a single performance; and his monetary return was one hundred thousand dollars.

One extra appearance followed, at a benefit concert given in the Metropolitan Opera House for the families of the victims who had perished with the lost steamship *Titanic*. Mme. Lillian Nordica, Misses Mary Garden, Bella Alten, Marie Mattfeld, Bernice de Pasquali, Kathleen Parlow (violiniste), and Andres de Segurola were on the programme which was conducted by Alfred Hertz and Giuseppe Sturani. The patrons and patronesses were President Taft and the Duke and Duchess of Connaught; W. Bourke Cochran delivered the commemorative address. Caruso sang *The Lost Chord*, in English, to the accompaniment of the New York Philharmonic Orchestra, led by Frank Damrosch.

IV

Memories of a victory won in enhancing his place in the hearts of the American public sent the singer that 1912 spring happily upon his voyage to Europe. His confidence, too, had been strengthened; and from it a broadened authority grew. Symptoms of cynicism — a bit mild perhaps, yet none the less clear — also became manifest. For it was inevitable that Caruso was to learn, out of his experiences with life, of human frailties.

On the very day of his sailing he had received from Arrigo Boito a cablegram inviting him to create the tenor rôle in the composer's "Nerone", scheduled for its première at La Scala during the 1913 season, in connection with the celebration of the Verdi centenary. Urged by Giulio Ricordi, the editor, and Toscanini, Caruso accepted this invitation, though to do so it became necessary for him to cancel his planned autumn *tournée* of Germany. Although Herr Ledner released Caruso from his contract, the opera was not finished in time for the proposed date of the première.

Three appearances in "La Fanciulla del West", and three others in the always welcome "Rigoletto" presented the singer at the Paris Opèra for the first time in his career. With Mme. Carmen Melis and Titta Ruffo, and Maestro Pomé conducting, these mid-May performances raised Caruso still higher in the estimation of discriminating Parisians. The Opera management begged him to appear in a few representations of "Il Barbiere di Siviglia", with Feodor Chaliapin, but without avail. He sought rest, and in the following September he began his 1912–1913 season as guest artist in Munich, appearing in "Tosca" and in "Rigoletto", and at the Hof Theater, in Stuttgart. Writing to his brother Giovanni, after his two appearances in "Pagliacci" and "Bohème", Caruso stated that never had he known such an ovation as the one tendered him after he had sung the *racconto*, in the first act of "Bohème", the last part of which he had been compelled to repeat.

"Manon Lescaut" reintroduced the tenor to his New York public, on November 11, with Mlle. Bori and Scotti as his chief associates, and Giorgio Polacco conducting. That 1912–1913 season carried

Copyright H. Mishkin, N. Y.

CARUSO IN 1913, THE YEAR WHICH MARKED THE BEGINNING OF HIS ASCENDANCY

Caruso to still higher ground. He sang only one unfamiliar opera, "Les Huguenots"; little of an uncommon nature occurred to require chronicling. Rôles which he had made almost exclusively his own were those in which the people heard and saw him — in such representative works as "Gioconda", "Pagliacci", "Bohème", "Aïda", the "Manon" of Massenet, "Tosca", "Cavalleria Rusticana", and "La Fanciulla del West." As Raoul, in "Les Huguenots", the tenor attracted attention for the heightened distinction of his bearing; as for his singing of the music, he was impressing more and more upon his audiences the fact that heroic parts were to become a forte.

Forty of the fifty appearances Caruso made in the United States that season took place in the Metropolitan. Brooklyn heard him twice, Philadelphia four times, Boston once, and Atlanta on three occasions. He sang in no concerts; he missed only two appearances; his gross earnings were one hundred thousand dollars.

On his way to London, for the Covent Garden season, he ran down to Paris where, for a fortnight, he stopped at the Élysée Palace Hotel. Then he crossed the English Channel, took up his abode at the Savoy Hotel, and prepared to give Londoners what they had been waiting to hear. "Pagliacci" was the opening opera, with Caruso, Mme. Carmen Melis, and Sammarco. The tenor appeared from May 20 to June 28, the other operas being "Aïda", "Tosca", and "Bohème", and his associate artists were Mmes. Melba, Destinn, and Edvina, and Scotti.

He did not realize, when he visited Vienna the following September for two appearances in "Rigoletto" and one in "Carmen", that he was never to sing there again. Nor — because of the war, and his subsequent illness and death — that the October of 1913, which he spent in Germany, was likewise an unsuspected good-by. Munich had one representation each of "Pagliacci", "Carmen", and "Bohème"; Stuttgart, the last German city in which he ever appeared, enthused over Caruso in "Carmen", "Tosca", and "Rigoletto." From the Hotel Marquardt, Stuttgart, he wrote to his brother Giovanni that not only was he being followed through the streets by crowds, but that they remained under his hotel window at night . . . "watching over him like a precious stone." It was not unlike an earlier demonstration outside his dressing-room windows, at the Berlin Royal Opera. He had arrived early at the theater, as was his custom, and was already costumed and made up for the stage when Martino, one of his valets, pulled aside a curtain to look at the throng below, which was calling loudly for the tenor. "Let us see him," they called, on catching sight of Martino; and the latter told his master of the situation. Touched by this demonstration, the tenor said, "If it were not that I should take care of my voice this evening, I would sing to them." Instead he had to be content with showing himself at the window, and waving a hand.

Tranquil in all important respects was Caruso's 1913–1914 season in the United States. New York, Philadelphia, Brooklyn, and Atlanta were the only

A NEW PERIOD

cities which caught the sound of his voice. He refused point-blank every concert engagement offered. From November 17 until the following April 22 — when he departed for Georgia — New York City was his home. He appeared in one new opera, Charpentier's "Julien"; and with Miss Farrar as chief associate, he interested a certain few. But the opera was not a success; after five representations it was put on the shelf, where it still lies.

"Aïda", "Ballo in Maschera", "Gioconda", "Tosca", "Pagliacci", "Manon", "Manon Lescaut", "Bohème", and "La Fanciulla del West" were the Caruso operas of that year. And the same amount he had earned the season before — one hundred thousand dollars — was the tenor's reward for fifty engagements he sang, without the loss of one.

The winter had been a reasonably happy one for him. He was content to remain in his Knickerbocker apartment; and while, as had been his custom for several years, he lunched frequently at Del Pezzo's restaurant in West Thirty-fourth Street, the routine of life was growing smoother. It would have been wise had he been careful of his diet. Unfortunately, he ate too heartily. Often he would begin a meal with antipasto, soup, and three kinds of spaghetti; then attack a meat course, with various Italian vegetables, and wander on through a salad to fruit and coffee. There would have been much wine, in the course of the eating, and innumerable cigarettes. It is no wonder he put on weight; no wonder, since he shunned exercise and plenty of fresh air, that he should have experienced in frequency and in increasing violence those terrific aches in his head. But friendly remonstrance was of no avail. He would listen, and occasionally nod affirmatively, — and that was an end to the matter. Still, the golden lustre of the Caruso voice was not perceptibly tarnished. It was becoming heavier; less lyric-like in its shimmering quality; and the habit of scooping high notes, in a manner typical of the artist, was becoming more fixed. Experts regretted that the tenor disclosed unmistakable tendencies in the direction of heroic operas. Their conclusions may have been right. For it is possible, had Caruso been satisfied to curb his ambitions, that he would have put less strain upon his matchless voice. Nevertheless, it was a temptation no other artist — in all probability — could have resisted. The larger rôles were his to sing, if he wished, — and to sing them was his keenest desire.

He realized, also, the strategic advantage of his position at the Metropolitan in being able to fill in equal measure, to the satisfaction of a worshiping public, the duties of a lyric and of a dramatic leading tenor. So, he found himself actuated by a threefold desire: to gratify personal aspirations; to continue as the idol of a people who were eager to have him sing in different types of rôles; and to bask in the esteem of a management which was showing an increasing willingness to eat from his hand. After all, it must be admitted that Caruso bore himself amazingly well. He had power, yet never did he abuse it; nor did he abuse the still greater power which was to come. Standing, as he was, upon the

A NEW PERIOD 303

threshold of his most glorious artistic moments, he poised with perfect balance for the leap.

In the spring of 1914 he went to London, — for the last season before a public which prized him as did that of the newer world. He was not aware of this at the time. He did not know that thereafter events were to shape in ways tying him more firmly to the western country across the seas. It is merely a fact that after his opening "Aïda", with Mmes. Destinn and Kirkby-Lunn, and Dinh Gilly, the season sped to a rousing close. "Tosca", "Ballo in Maschera", "Madama Butterfly", and "Bohème," were the other works in which he sang. Mmes. Melba, Muzio, Rosa Raisa, Edvina, and Zeppilli, and Antonio Scotti and Pompilio Malatesta were members of the casts in which the tenor appeared that Covent Garden season. June 29, 1914, marked Caruso's final London appearance. The opera was "Tosca." Fatigued beyond words, the singer went for absolute rest to Bagni di Montecatini, near Lucca. It was one month before he wrote to his brother. In a letter filled with expressions of his discouragement, Caruso admitted to feeling really ill. The doctors, he wrote, called it "a nervous breakdown", and advised him to "go to the mountains." He winced at the thought of going to an unfamiliar spot, and acquainted Giovanni with his determination to proceed to Bellosguardo, where he asked his brother to join him. "But do not tell a soul," he warned. "I cannot be disturbed with either letters or visitors."

Germany's declaration of war, followed soon after by Italy's announced decision to remain neutral, only added to Caruso's agitation. He worried over the future of his country, and the worry did him no good. As the weeks passed, and the tremendous gravity of the situation increased, so did the emotionalism of the half-broken Neapolitan destroy his chances for the tranquillity required for his recovery. When Temistocle Ricceri appealed to Caruso to sing at an affair to be given October 19 in the Costanzi, of Rome, to secure funds to enable Italian workingmen to leave Germany, there could only be one answer.

The great Battistini, and Lucrezia Bori, Giuseppe de Luca, and other illustrious artists sang in excerpts from operas that memorable evening. Toscanini conducted; yet even his aversion to encores melted before the tumult which demanded again the *Vesti la giubba*, delivered by Caruso during the representation of "Pagliacci", in which he participated. For twenty minutes the Costanzi was the scene of enthusiasm akin to riot. Again — as in other previous instances — did this particular one mark an unpremeditated farewell. For never afterward did Enrico Caruso sing to his beloved Romans. Immediately after the performance he was rushed in a special train to Naples, where he took a steamer sailing at once for New York. He had no time even to go to bid his stepmother and sister good-by; they went to the pier to see him off. So he departed westward, — without having had the opportunity of paying his faithful visit to the little Church of Sant Anna alle Paludi, and to the fountain he had made while a boy and which still continued to give drinking water to his fellow Neapolitans.

CHAPTER TEN

GOLDEN DAYS

WAR influences were not materially lessened, though thousands of miles separated the tenor from the actual scenes of conflict. In New York one could, and did, hear quite as much of what was going on as those who were in Europe (in certain respects the news was less restricted and thus more quickly learned). It was Caruso's nature to be patriotic. Although he did not diminish his allegiance to either his art or the Metropolitan, his interest in Italy's attitude stirred, as the weeks passed, with deeper intensity. He was beyond the age limit of those eligible at the first call, should his country decide to throw her fortunes on the side of the Allies. But it was by no means certain which way Italy was to swing. Uncertainty plunged New York's Italian colony into heated discussions; and, amongst his friends, the singer did not hesitate to speak his mind. He rebelled, with all his fervor, against the Austrians. Trieste — in his judgment, no less than in that of many of his compatriots — was truly Italian soil. He was ready to support Italy; and means was not denied. For that was the season in which began a new contract, which yielded him two thousand five hundred dollars an appearance.

"Ballo in Maschera" was the introductory opera.

Mme. Destinn and Pasquale Amato were of the cast. Three evenings later — on November 19 — the singer appeared in "Carmen." "Gioconda", a second "Carmen", another "Gioconda", then "Pagliacci", "Aïda", "Manon", and "Huguenots" followed at intervals. Caruso was appearing regularly twice each week; his singing was clocklike; his hold upon the New York public stronger than ever. Then, with the end of his season drawing near, in mid-February, the newspapers began to speculate whether the tenor and Manager Gatti-Casazza were pulling smoothly together. Although explanations of the Raoul Gunsbourg contract had been made, some people questioned these explanations. Yet it was true that Caruso had promised the Monte Carlo impresario, several years before, to appear at the Casino. The fulfillment of that contract had been postponed repeatedly; in 1914 Gatti-Casazza agreed with his leading tenor that he was right in deciding that the appearances should be no longer delayed. This reason, and no other, sent Caruso to Monte Carlo after his 1915 farewell at the Metropolitan, which he sang on February 17, in "Pagliacci." He had appeared just twenty-eight times, for which he received the sum of seventy thousand dollars. From that time forth he was no longer bound to the New York organization on terms other than those which covered his services when it gave performances. He made, thereafter, his own outside contracts, — and he profited accordingly.

A commission, delegated by the mayor of Caruso's native city, met the steamer *Duca d'Aosta* when it arrived at its Naples berth. A benefit performance was being arranged for the refugees from the Avezzano earthquake, and as usual in like circumstances, the tenor's services were sought. Although he was willing to aid, Gunsbourg declined to delay Caruso's Monte Carlo début; so, instead, the singer contributed some money, and went on his way.

The Monte Carlo colony of connoisseurs were curious to hear the tenor once more. Malicious tongues had spread reports that the golden and velvety beauty of those tones had passed. The audience which assembled in the Casino that March 14 evening was eager, and a bit anxious as well. "Aïda" was the opera; and in the cast were Mme. Felia Litvinne (sister to the brothers De Reszke), Alfred Maguenat, and Marcel Journet. Caruso went apprehensively from the Hotel Paris to the theater, and prepared nervously for the test that was to come. He had not many hours to pass in a state of agitation; before the representation was half finished he had crossed the danger line. Still, these Latins — to whom he had not sung in many years — were not thoroughly convinced.

Camillo Antona Traversi, a Parisian newspaperman and critic of repute and who had been engaged as secretary of Gunsbourg's company, went to see Caruso in an *entr'act* during that representation. "When I entered his dressing room," said Traversi, "Caruso spoke abruptly.

"'Camillo, you know I am an imbecile! I feel a rôle too much. I try always to give my best in interpreting a part. I know that I am a singer and an actor — yet, in order to give the public the impression that I am neither one nor the other, but the *real man* conceived by the author, I have to feel and to think as the man the author had in mind. All the secrets lie in the heart of the artist. The difficulty, the terrible difficulty, does not cease when an artist has reached the pinnacle of perfection — the top of the ladder, as we say. He is haunted, when he gets there, by that never-ending inner question: "When will I go down?" I never step upon a stage without asking myself whether I will succeed in finishing the opera. The fact is that a conscientious singer is never sure of himself, or of anything. He is ever in the hands of Destiny.

"'The public is quick to approve or disapprove. It sometimes happens, because of a trivial frog in the throat, that the voice becomes suddenly weaker. It is nothing to be alarmed at, if the public would only realize. But it is quick to leap to conclusions. So, when we are at the zenith we travel through occasional storms. The Damocles sword is dangling constantly above the head of every great singer. For the unforeseen occurrence may often be the most damaging. If that frog I spoke about happens to come, and the voice, for a time, is veiled, an audience may judge hastily and be at fault.

"'It is too bad that the public expects from me, always, perfection — which it is impossible for me always to attain. I am not a machine. I am a human being. I may sing, one night, to please the people. The same opera, sung by me the following night, is less excellent because I am not in the same

GOLDEN DAYS 309

mood or do not chance to feel as well. Even though I may sing better than somebody else, I am criticised as having been "bad" . . . because I have sung less well than the last time I was heard. Do you see my point?'"

The singer had little to complain of, however, when he appeared in "Pagliacci", with Signorina Alice Zeppilli; and, also, when for his third appearance he was cast with Signorina Graziella Pareto and MM. Maguenat and Journet in "Lucia di Lammermoor." Incidentally, he saved an appearance to Signorina Pareto, when the soprano caught a cold, by supplying some of his own remedies and acting successfully as impromptu physician.

Restored in the minds of the skeptics to his former singing place, Caruso was soon besieged by impresari. One of these was Walter Mocchi, who controlled a season in South America. Wishing to be rid of Mocchi's importunings, Caruso said he would accept an engagement, — if he were paid thirty-five thousand francs in gold for each appearance. How little did the singer, in spite of his steady advancement, suspect his approaching commercial value as an artist. And how complete was his surprise when Mocchi held him to his word, and informed him that within one week would they be on board a steamer, bound for Buenos Aires.

A full twelve years had passed since the tenor had appeared in that city. Even before he sang he must have been reassured, for the advance sale — immediately upon the announcement of Caruso's engagement — had leaped to an unprecedented figure. The début was made during May, at the Colon Theater, in "Aïda", with Mme. Roggeri and Giuseppe Danise. "Pagliacci" followed, with the same artists. No one complained of the bigger, darker voice; it had just the warmth South Americans admired, while the art of the artist thrilled. There was just one opinion,—which coincided with the opinions which had held, and were continuing to hold, in those other parts of the world where Caruso reigned.

Massenet's "Manon", with Mme. Genevieve Vix and Mario Sammarco, which Giuseppe Sturani conducted, was the third opera. The fourth was the "Manon Lescaut" of Puccini, conducted by Gino Marinuzzi, with Signora Gilda Della Rizza and Sammarco in the cast. Two "Lucia di Lammermoor" presentations took place with Signora Amelita Galli Curci. He had been hoisted to a new pedestal; honors which it had seemed could scarce be exceeded had, indeed, been surpassed. Of a sudden had come a fresh impetus to carry the singer still farther in advance of even his most distinguished confrères. For from that engagement must date the period of the Caruso supremacy which set him apart from all others; a supremacy which, as an artist, made him signally and conspicuously unique. He had in fact become the first; thereafter no force was to arrest the solidity of his position, in which he was destined to grow in that measure justifying its attainment.

Mocchi's gratitude to the tenor was expressed in a gift made to him just as he was about to depart,

in August, for Italy. It was a gold cigarette case with the following inscription:
 To Caruso, the dearest of all friends the *least* dear of all the artists.

Just one touch of sadness marked Caruso's stay in Buenos Aires. On June 2, 1915, he received at the Hotel Plaza a cablegram telling him of the death of his sister Assunta.

Another, of a different nature, came to him soon after he had reached his Bellosguardo Villa, at Signa. Accused by the Parisian press of being pro-German, and deploring the actions of Gabriele d'Annunzio, Caruso wrote in heated anger to his friend Camillo Traversi, who was then in Paris. The communication was dated September 12, 1915.

My dear Camillo:
 On my return yesterday from Buenos Aires, I found here your letter, and the clippings of the Paris papers . . . including the article of *Le Matin* in regard to that infamy. The invention was a terrible blow to me. It was not alone the item which caused me such pain, but the unfavorable comments of these Paris papers — which evidently have forgotten what I did for Coquelin's benefits for the House of the Disabled Artists, for the Belgians, for the Society of Journalists, and other French benefits. The infamy did not surprise me as much as the readiness of the learned Parisian people to believe that I could possibly be such a coward, such a mean man.
 Believe me, dear Camillo, I cried of rage; and if some day I can discover the person responsible for it all, then the world will hear me speak something of him and of myself. During the past few years

the press seems to have had a mania of occupying itself with poor me, giving me many troubles. I did not bother, because they were speaking of my voice . . . lost; but now it is of a different subject. Before I die of heart-failure, I wish God to grant me grace — to permit me to give to Satan the soul of this man who intended to make the world believe I was such a vile man . . . not an Italian of blood and flesh.

With greetings, believe me,

Yours,

Enrico Caruso.

The singer's fierce anger had cooled somewhat when he was called on to assist in two performances, planned to be held in the Dal Verme Theater, of Milan, to aid artists in need of work. Those two appearances were in "Pagliacci", on September 23 and 25. Toscanini conducted the opera, and "Il Segreto di Susanna", which was the preceding piece. Signorina Claudia Muzio, Luigi Montesanto, and Angelo Bada were of the "Pagliacci" cast. Since Caruso had not sung in Milan for a number of years, his first endeavor resembled a début. He was intensely nervous; there appears, however, to have been slight cause for worry. The next morning the Milanese newspapers eulogized Caruso and his art. His voice, the writers declared, had not "gone." On the contrary, it remained still the beautiful instrument of those times when he had sung in "Fedora"; perhaps a more dramatic voice, but, if anything, more beautiful than before.

It has been said that in his closing years Caruso did not sing in Italy because his compatriots ob-

Copyright H. Mishkin, N. Y.

CARUSO AS SAMSON IN "SAMSON ET DALILA"

jected to the heavier, darker timbre of the tones they had admired in earlier years, — when their lyric purity had first captivated the Italian people. So far as can be learned, no such general opinion held. The tenor was so constantly in demand, and at fees so much higher than any Italian opera house could afford to pay him, that it appears to have been a mere matter of business for him to have accepted contracts offered elsewhere.

He never sang in Italy after his two appearances in Milan. Who knows that he might not have liked to. It is questionable if such a public demonstration of mourning, as attended his death and funeral, could have come from a people who did not truly feel.

II

No one who heard and saw Caruso during his first Samson in "Samson et Dalila", which opened the Metropolitan's season of 1915–1916, could have doubted his ripened art. Previous admissions had been made by eminent music reviewers of the tenor's developed acting resources. It remained for his Samson to disclose him in a rôle of larger mold and potentialities than any in which New York had known him. The Saint-Saëns opera started the singer toward that final phase of his career. In it he checked — for a time, at least — the remonstrances of those who kept insisting that he was a lyric tenor who had wandered outside his métier. How different a man he had become from the Caruso of a decade before! Experience and associations had not been without their influence. The very shape of his head had changed, — along with the contour of his features. He was jovial of mood to the many who saw him casually in the streets. He enjoyed, if less effusively, indulging in his jokes and pranks. And he turned as often and with as keen a pleasure to that oldtime habit of sketching, — both caricature and portraits. But the serious side of the man was having its way. Those who saw him often in his home observed the gradual transformation of the singer. If only the public which observed him cutting capers before the Metropolitan curtain, or seemingly having the time of his life in "L'Elisir d'Amore", could have seen him in his Knickerbocker apartment, as he actually was! Only in these circumstances could they have fathomed the real Caruso.

There the public might have glimpsed him, following the ceaseless routine of work. For it was work that carried Caruso to the goals he reached. Some people have rather doubted it. To them it was to his voice that all the credit went. Those persons cannot know that for Caruso there were few real vacations. Out of season he slaved. At Signa, he almost invariably coached his rôles — old as well as new — with Maestro Mugnone. Occasionally Barthélemy aided him in this capacity; he respected this accompanist because of his musicianship. Maestri Sarmiento, Gaetano Scognamiglio, Tullio Voghera, Bruni, Dell' Orefice, and Vincenzo Bellezza — all at one time or another accompanists to the tenor — commanded his respect. During his last

GOLDEN DAYS 315

few seasons, with the exception of a break of two years, Salvatore Fucito acted as the tenor's accompanist. Besides "Samson et Dalila", the operas in which Caruso sang at the Metropolitan during 1915–1916 were "Bohème", "Tosca", "Manon", "Pagliacci", "Marta", "Ballo in Maschera", "Aïda", "Manon Lescaut", "Rigoletto", and "Carmen." He missed only one performance that year; and for the forty-nine in which he participated he earned one hundred eighteen thousand dollars.

An indication of the value the Metropolitan board of directors had then come to place upon Caruso's services was shown in a letter written by their chairman, Otto H. Kahn, in a letter dated March 27, 1916. It read:

Mr. Gatti-Casazza has informed me that while you prefer not to sign a contract at this time for an extension of your present contract, you have given him your verbal assurance, which, coming from you is just as good as a written contract, that he may depend upon your remaining with the Metropolitan Opera Company. In taking note of this welcome declaration, may I express my sincerest gratification, not only as Chairman of the Metropolitan Opera Company, not only as one of the public, in the affection and admiration of which you have a unique, an unrivalled place, but also as your personal friend and well-wisher who holds you in the highest esteem for the splendid qualities of character which distinguish you as an artist and as a man. With cordial good wishes, and in the hope that your health and strength and the glory of your incomparable voice and superb art may be preserved for many years to come, I remain — Very sincerely yours.

Caruso went to Signa for a rest. He was continuing to suffer more frequently from those violent headaches. The previous year, while in Buenos Aires, he had at times screamed from the pain; the one Metropolitan appearance he had missed during the 1915–1916 season had been due to a headache attack. Doctor Holbrook Curtis had attributed the source to an affection of the nose; and an operation had been performed. But it brought no relief. The first indications of one of these spells would be hardened swellings at the sides of the singer's neck. Massage and electric treatments never seemed to help. An attack would generally last for three or four hours, then slowly subside. The effect, however, was to leave the tenor limp and nerve-wrought.

Barthélemy joined Caruso at Signa to assist him in preparing the music side of the rôle of Nadir in "The Pearl Fishers", which the tenor expected to sing on the opening night of the Metropolitan's 1916–1917 season. Mme. Frieda Hempel, Giuseppe de Luca, and Leon Rothier were of that representation, which Maestro Polacco conducted. The public, despite Caruso's presence in the cast, displayed slight interest in the opera; it was given only twice thereafter. In other works — those which were ever favorites with New Yorkers, especially if Caruso sang — there was no cause for complaint. "Manon Lescaut", "Samson et Dalila", "Pagliacci", "Marta", "Aïda", "Carmen", "L'Elisir d'Amore", "Rigoletto", and "Bohème" followed. What variety was presented in the leading tenor characters of these operas!

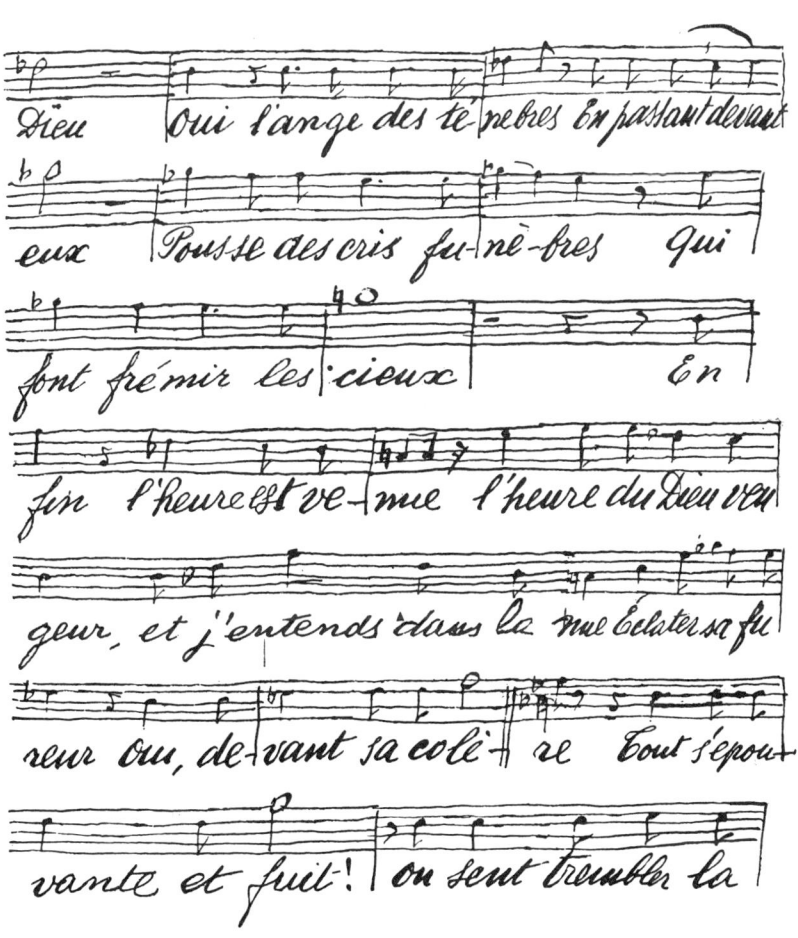

A PAGE OF THE SCORE OF "SAMSON ET DALILA" COPIED BY CARUSO
How he studied the rôle of Samson.

GOLDEN DAYS 317

Success crescendoed for the tenor without a pause. Not once that season did he miss an engagement. His appearances were the same in number as of the year before; his earnings precisely the same. New York, Brooklyn, Philadelphia, and Atlanta were the only cities that heard him in opera; but on May 1 Caruso sang in concert in Cincinnati, beginning a brief tour which took him also to Toledo and Pittsburgh. The Cincinnati Symphony Orchestra participated in these three concerts; and Richard Barthélemy was Caruso's accompanist. For the first two appearances the singer received three thousand five hundred dollars each; five thousand dollars was paid him for the concluding one.

Preparations were made, following Caruso's final United States concert of that year (with the Mozart Society, of New York), for the journey to Buenos Aires. The tenor hesitated about undertaking the trip: the World War had reached an acute stage; ships were being ruthlessly torpedoed; Caruso wondered whether it was a risk to be taken. He went about matters with much foresight, and besides providing himself with numerous life preservers, he had made a suit of clothes which was guaranteed to keep him afloat.

Caruso disembarked from the SS. *Saga* when it reached Rio Janeiro, and boarded the SS. *Indiana* for Buenos Aires. On June 17, and with Mme. Vallin-Pardo as leading soprano, he made his first reappearance at the Colon Theater in "L'Elisir d'Amore." The reception was a repetition of those scenes which had greeted his efforts two years before. "Pagliacci" evoked similar enthusiasm when Caruso sang; and it grew in intensity when he was heard in "Manon", "Tosca", "Bohème", and "Lodoletta", — this last work being new to the tenor at that time. Other South American cities had insisted they be given the then matured Caruso; so a tour was undertaken to Montevideo, Rio de Janeiro, and San Paolo. A return trip had to be made to Rio, for two final appearances. The operas were "Carmen" and "Manon Lescaut"; and, on October 16, 1917, Caruso sang in the latter work for the last time in South America.

Vincenzo Bellezza, one of the Colon Theater conductors, sailed with the tenor for New York in the capacity of accompanist. They worked together on the voyage northwards, and more than one passenger aboard the SS. *Saga* was treated to bits of impromptu concerts. Relief at the safe ending of his long journey overjoyed the singer. He reached New York with his face wreathed in smiles. It had been a hard year, without any extended period of rest, but all that was forgotten. And there was no need to be disturbed over opening the Metropolitan season in a new opera; "Aïda" had been chosen.

It was at this time that Bruno Zirato was invited to accept the post of Secretary to Enrico Caruso. Others had preceded him, though none had served in a full secretarial capacity. Generally it had been an arrangement in which friendship formed a principal part, with the compensation being more in the form of tickets to the opera performances in which the tenor appeared, and occasional "presents", wherein cash sometimes figured. After Count Scalzi — who had been the third person to aid Caruso by writing letters and in other minor ways — there came Luigi Roversi, Enrico Scognamillo, Doctor de Simone, and Constant J. Sperco.

Zirato was the first real secretary Caruso had; for he spent his entire time with the tenor, and made of his position a matter of the strictest and most rigid business. He served his employer faithfully and well, how well those who were close to Caruso during his desperate illness during those dragging final months best know. While between Caruso and Zirato there was a never-ceasing element of friendship (the singer often addressed his secretary by the endearment term of *Compare*), both men inclined naturally toward discipline, and each seemed to take a certain satisfaction in maintaining those niceties which preserved in their relationship a perfect understanding. The best evidence of Zirato's standing with the singer was his uninterrupted continuance in office. For the latter was a difficult man to please. After her husband's death, and when she had returned to New York, Mrs. Caruso wished to have Zirato near her; his presence somehow exerted on her a comforting effect. So he became her secretary.

The United States, having joined the side of the Allies in the war, was then aflame with patriotism. Although opera was the principal interest in the singer's life, he found himself not unwillingly drawn into paths traveled by others who were less emotional than himself. He had already been a large purchaser of Italian bonds; he turned with corresponding readiness to his check-book to add to his store of securities, — this time in the form of United States Liberty Bonds.

His days — and the nights also — were filled with experiences of many kinds. Grateful to a nation which had dealt out such bounty and honors to him, Caruso felt the American side of his nature throbbing in tune with his Italian. He had yielded to an impulse to give lessons to a baritone whose exceptional voice appealed to him; and for an hour or more at a time he would sit at a piano, thumping clumsily a few simple chords, while this only pupil he ever had struggled to imitate the tones the tenor sang. It was not a successful undertaking. After five months Caruso reluctantly gave up the task as an impossible job. Yet it disturbed him that he had failed. His one consolation was the encouragement voiced by his friend, Doctor P. Mario Marafioti, who said, "Remember, Enrico, that you will be judged as a singer, not as a teacher."

The work at the Metropolitan wore on; "L'Elisir d'Amore", "Marta", "Samson et Dalila", "Manon Lescaut", "Pagliacci", "Carmen", and "Tosca" had proved Caruso's expanding artistry; his voice still held; and he could venture a backward glance at a career already distinctive enough to stand as it was. At forty-five, and beginning his fifteenth consecutive season in the foremost opera house of the world, he felt the serene side of his nature coming more to fore. Offers from impresari from all parts of the world poured in upon him. These offers, fantastic in their financial inducements, he read with the most casual interest. They pleased him; that was all. His mind was filled with thoughts of other matters; of persons, and one of these was an American girl, — Miss Dorothy Benjamin. He had met her at the home of Maestro Fernando Tanara, and again at a tea given by Doctor Marafioti. Driving her home, Caruso noticed that she had forgotten her gloves. He urged her to put on the pair he had been wearing, and when they parted insisted she should keep them as a souvenir. Then, for months, he had not seen her again. But he had remembered.

Meanwhile, December gave way to January, and on the 12th of that month, 1918, came the United States première of Mascagni's "Lodoletta." Miss Farrar and Pasquale Amato sang with him; and these artists strove mightily, though in vain, to give the opera some popularity. A real opportunity was on the way, and it arrived on February 7, when the tenor made his first appearance as John of Leyden, in "Le Prophète." What compensation this achievement must have given for those early years of struggle! There were experts who continued to expostulate over the insistence of Caruso in singing such heavy rôles. But others thought they recognized in the man a great artist; a tenor with every kind of voice. Indeed, it has been contended that while Caruso did actually begin with a lyric tenor, his later days found him possessed of an instrument suited for any type of rôle. There was to appear, however, one exception. For when he essayed Avito in "L'Amore dei tre Re", the endeavor met with an indisputable lack of success. Caruso struggled three times after his first appearance in the part, on March 14, 1918, though to no satisfying end. The best evidence that he considered it not for him was the fact that never afterwards did he attempt to sing it.

And one other annoying experience occurred in Boston, at the close of the Metropolitan season in April. The music reviewers of that city criticized the tenor mercilessly. He insisted they were not fair; he himself felt that he had done himself justice. Whatever the facts, Caruso never sang there again.

An income from his opera duties had brought the singer that season the sum of one hundred twenty-five thousand dollars for his fifty appearances; a Biltmore Morning Musicale had yielded four thousand more; and the talking-machine royalties had totaled a huge sum. The gross income, however, was reduced by $59,832.15, — which Caruso paid to the United States Government as income tax. Nor would he avail himself of the courtesy proffered by "Big Bill" Edwards, then Collector of Internal Revenue, to visit the tenor personally at his hotel home. Instead, Caruso went, "like any other citizen," to Edwards's office, to tender in person his check.

With benefit performances of every known sort offered every little while to secure funds for some war-working organization, Caruso was sought out on every side. He was more than good-natured; his responses were made gladly, with a full heart. It was a matter of pride that, beyond the fact that his name had a definite value with the public, influential men and women showed plainly their respect for him as a useful citizen. On April 14, 1918, Caruso contributed his services at a concert given in the Metropolitan Opera House for the benefit of the Italian Reservists; and at the third Liberty Loan Rally, held on May 1 in New York's Carnegie Hall, he sang gratuitously again. Three times during that month he appeared for other worthy causes: for the Italian Relief Fund, at Poli's Theater, Washington, D. C.; at the Metropolitan Opera House at an Italian Red Cross benefit concert; and in the same place, three nights later, for the American Red Cross.

Friends marveled that Caruso continued to remain in the United States; it had been his custom to sail for Europe before the end of each May. But June arrived, finding the singer still established at the Knickerbocker. He sang on the tenth of that month at the Metropolitan for the benefit of the Women's Naval Service, then rested.

Meanwhile, the infrequent and almost casual meetings with Miss Benjamin had been succeeded by visits paid to the young woman in her father's home. When the Benjamin family departed to the Spring Lake, New Jersey, summer place, the tenor's objective lay often in that direction. Those closest to Caruso did not apprehend that he, an Italian, and an artist, might be paying court to an American girl, whose upbringing had been so dissimilar to his own. Yet, whatever the appearances, his fidelity remained unshaken. After Caruso had returned from Ocean Grove, New Jersey, where he sang in late July his

Copyright Underwood & Underwood Studios, N. Y.

MRS. ENRICO CARUSO

a troublesome mental burden. There was good reason. For just before his departure from New York the tenor's proposal of marriage to Miss Benjamin had been followed by an unsuspected outcome. Her father had insisted upon a financial arrangement which neither she nor Caruso could countenance or agree to.

He arrived, still agitated, at the Knickerbocker Hotel in New York, where Miss Benjamin and a woman friend awaited him. What Miss Benjamin had to say was enough to move Caruso to instant decision. "You will return here to-morrow morning at eleven," he said, "and we will be married."

At the appointed hour (August 20) Miss Benjamin was at the Knickerbocker. She had communicated with a friend — Mrs. John S. Keith — who went to her at once. Caruso, Miss Benjamin, Mrs. Keith, and Zirato entered the singer's waiting automobile, — all of them a bit serious of face, for developments had progressed swiftly. A marriage license was thereupon secured, and the party was driven to the Church of the Transfiguration (The Little Church Around the Corner); but the pastor, uncertain as to whether Caruso was already married, preferred not to officiate. The Reverend Oliver Paul Barnhill, of the Marble Collegiate Church, at Fifth Avenue and Twenty-ninth Street, performed the marriage ceremony, with Mrs. Keith and Zirato as witnesses. On one page of his personal account book, in which the tenor himself made every entry, he wrote:

"Expenses for my marriage. . . . $50.00"!

It was not until some time afterwards that

Mrs. Caruso was presented with her engagement ring.

That first summer which the singer ever spent in the United States assumed, then, an aspect different from any he had ever known. His attitude toward the world was that of a man with new responsibilities; his bearing became more than ever one of dignity and reserve. And the Caruso hangers-on — astounded at their patron's marriage — found fewer opportunities to thrust themselves upon him, and partake of the gratuities he had thrown their way. Mrs. Caruso's father was quoted in the newspapers as having said some unpleasant words over which the tenor was distressed; but the storm passed, and work went on even before autumn quite arrived, — the two motion pictures having been finished on September 30.

There had been during August several other benefit concerts in which the tenor had taken part, in one of which Liberty Loan subscriptions secured from among the audience had netted more than four million dollars. He had gone to Buffalo for a regular concert, which was to have been given on October 8 and was only canceled because of the prevalent epidemic of influenza. But before leaving that city he appeared, at the request of Governor Charles Whitman, at a Liberty Loan drive held in the Iroquois Hotel. Mrs. Caruso, who had accompanied her husband, succumbed to the effects of influenza upon reaching New York, on October 12. She insisted, however, that he keep his engagement to sing a special performance of "Pagliacci", given with Miss Claudia Muzio, Pasquale Amato, and Francesco Daddi, under the conductorship of Giorgio Polacco, in Detroit on October 15. The tenor received seven thousand dollars for this one appearance. A fortnight later he aided at a matinée held in New York's Madison Square Garden, promoted by John D. Rockefeller, Jr., for the United War Work; and that same evening — November 3 — he sang, at the special request of Secretary Josephus Daniels, at the concert given in the Hippodrome for the benefit of the Navy Relief Fund.

It had been a trying and somewhat fortuitous summer, yet no rest was in sight. The Metropolitan 1918–1919 opening drew near; rehearsals were in order; yet Caruso found time to earn a five thousand dollar fee by appearing at a Biltmore Morning Musicale. After the Metropolitan première in "Samson et Dalila", with Mme. Louise Homer and Alfred Couzinou, under the music leadership of Pierre Monteux, he made his first appearance anywhere as Don Alvaro in "La Forza del Destino." The occasion introduced Miss Rosa Ponselle to Metropolitan subscribers, and was a memorable affair. Matters thereafter settled into the groove of routine. November and December carried the tenor before his public in "L'Elisir d'Amore", "Le Prophète", "Marta", "Pagliacci", and three times in "Lodoletta", in an attempt to stimulate interest in the Mascagni opera.

For his year of personal work Caruso had reaped an enormous sum. Could he have retained it all, it must have represented a fortune. The income tax had, however, to be considered; it took from the singer the heavy toll of $153,933.70.

IV

The winds of life were becoming tempered. With Mrs. Caruso at his side there was less need for companionship of those previous days which Caruso had not always voluntarily sought; and Bohemianism was thrust into the past. His wife and his home interested him; he spent more time with his *objets d'art*, his stamp albums, and his scrap books which required much attention to keep up to date. Having purchased, the preceding summer, his first automobile for use in the United States, the tenor fell to using it as the easiest means of getting fresh air. His daily accumulation of mail increased; the demands upon him grew; but Zirato relieved him of much which he then felt comfortable in delegating his secretary to perform. He had also his regular caricature to draw, for many do not know that, from 1906, Caruso contributed unfailingly to the columns of *La Follia*, a New York weekly newspaper, a sketch of some kind. Yet there was always time for the tenor to attend personally to whatever was necessary. He maintained, with his own hand, a correspondence with his sons in Italy; and about this time he received from Mimmi (then fifteen years old) the following letter, written February 15, from Florence.

My dear Papa:
The arrival of your letter was a great joy to me. I know from you that my new "mammina" — if I

can call her so, though for the present I will call her sister, for I have heard that she is very young — is, as you say, very adorable; and I hope that we will get along well together.

I am very sorry indeed that I cannot come to America, but as it is your will — "Fiat voluntat tua" — I must abide by it; but I am longing for the time of your arrival here so that, after many years, we will meet and embrace again, and I hope, dear Papa, that you will never leave us, or else take us with you.

In the meantime I will study and try not to lose the year.

I am well and waiting for you. When I see boys riding bicycles I feel I too would like one. Would you permit me to have one? I am a big boy, now, and I feel I need one so much when I go to school, or when I go for a walk. I shall be glad to have your news.

With very much love, dear Papa, from your affectionate son   Enrico

Enrico Jr. got his bicycle; just as a little lame girl, to whom the singer had spoken during a Central Park band concert, received from him a gift of money after he had read a letter written by the child's mother, telling how much joy his greeting had brought. Was he thoughtless? In the midst of the whirl of things he went to the pains to recommend a tenor friend — an American — for a 1919 engagement at Monte Carlo which Raoul Gunsbourg had urgently cabled Caruso to accept. The intention was of the best, but Gunsbourg's reply read, "I regret, dear Enrico, that I cannot engage the tenor you suggest, for my company is quite filled. I have, however, a place for one artist. It is Enrico Caruso. He is a fine chap. Will you talk with him and try to get him to accept my offer?"

It was shortly before this — on December 4, 1918 — that the late Cleofonte Campanini, then general director of the Chicago Grand Opera Company, made quite as flattering an offer, and one even more remunerative. Campanini's letter ran:

Carissimo Enrico:

I spoke to Longone, asking him to see you regarding my proposal to you to sing in our preliminary tournée in the cities of the west, beginning October 12, 1919, for three weeks. I offer nine appearances, all guaranteed. Furthermore, I would like an option for a fourth week, the option to be concluded on or before September 1 next.

The opera would be only one — "Pagliacci." But if you prefer another one, or ones, it is up to you. We will agree on this point later on. I offer you five thousand dollars[1] for each appearance. With Eva's and my best regards for Mrs. Caruso and for you, I am,

Affectionately yours,
Cleofonte Campanini.

Caruso went to Gatti-Casazza in the matter, and the Metropolitan's general manager said frankly that he would not be pleased if the tenor accepted Campanini's proposal, though admitting that Caruso had the right to do so if he wished. Gatti's attitude disposed at once of the proposal. Caruso recognized the impresario's sensitiveness over having him appear with an organization then regarded as a kind of rival — since it had begun to give brief seasons in New

---

[1] This sum was just twice the amount Caruso was receiving for an appearance at the New York Metropolitan.

York, annually. So the singer wrote Campanini, expressing his regret in being unable to accept the invitation.

It was a comforting feeling, being respected both at home and abroad. The singer's manner was undergoing a subtle change — as no one realized better than he. Inwardly he rather delighted in it, but he preserved his dignified exterior until, more and more, it became an accepted thing. Almost before he quite grasped the significance the season neared its end. It was the rounding out of a quarter century of activity on the operatic stage. With "Bohème", "Lodoletta", and "Aïda" added to those operas he had already sung that season, the month of March broke; and on the 8th, Caruso took Mrs. Caruso to St. Patrick's Cathedral, to be baptized. Soon afterwards they were remarried, according to the procedure of the Catholic church. The witnesses were Mrs. Walter R. Benjamin and Bruno Zirato.

The tenor had sung another concert — assisted by Miss Morgana and Elias Breeskin — this time at Ann Arbor, Michigan, arranged by the Metropolitan Musical Bureau for a seven thousand dollar fee. He had also rushed back, on receipt of a telegram from Otto H. Kahn, to sing *The Star Spangled Banner* in the Metropolitan on that distinctive occasion when President Wilson delivered his address on the League of Nations. Although his train did not reach its New York station until 7.45 P.M., Caruso was dressed and ready to go upon the Opera House stage just twenty-five minutes later.

Important as these affairs were to the singer they faded in comparison with the one then drawing near. For a jubilee celebration is something of an event; this one fairly alarmed Caruso as March 22 dawned and he sensed the ordeal he must undergo that night. A host of artists participated in the actual program, which consisted of the third act of "L'Elisir d'Amore", the first of "Pagliacci", and act three from "Le Prophète." Besides Mmes. Muzio, Barrientos, Matzenauer, and Sparkes, there were the baritones de Luca, Scotti, Werrenrath, and Schlegel, the bassos Mardones and Didur, and tenors Diaz and Bada. Maestri Bodanzky, Moranzoni, and Papi conducted; the auditorium was packed at extra prices, and the audience one to cause the heart of almost any man to skip an occasional beat.

The Caruso who came upon a specially set stage after the operatic part of the evening was a pale-faced, nervous man. Surrounded by the entire Metropolitan Opera House personnel, he sat stiffly in a chair at the front center of the stage near the footlights. On a long table, at the rear, were arranged the presents he had received.

James M. Beck had been invited to make the official address of the evening, and this he would have done if political activities had not intervened. But, at actually the eleventh hour, Mayor Hylan sent word that if Beck spoke, Police Commissioner Enright would not present to the singer a flag of the City of New York; so Beck tactfully withdrew (afterwards sending to Caruso a typewritten copy of what he had intended to say), and Enright tendered the flag.

The tenor's reply, delivered with hesitating exactness, in English, was:

"My heart is beating so hard with emotion that I feel that I am afraid I cannot even put a few words together. I am sure you will forgive me if I do not make a long speech. I can only thank you, and beg you to accept my sincerest and most heartfelt gratitude for to-night, and for all the very many kindnesses you have showered upon me. I assure you that I will never forget this occasion, and ever cherish in my heart my affections for my dear American friends. Thank you! Thank you! Thank you! . . ."

Throughout his enunciation of those few sentences the singer clutched with his right hand the staff of the municipal flag he had received. He was white-faced under his emotion, and it was fortunate that Zirato stood just behind, ready to prompt him when his mind searched for an elusive word.

Mr. Kahn, speaking for the Metropolitan board of directors, said:

"In offering you the tribute of our admiration it is not the glory of your voice which I have in mind primarily, though it is the most glorious and perfect voice of a generation, and one which, for having heard, posterity will envy us. But in your case we admire the voice, the art, and the man. I have in mind your boundless generosity, your modesty, kindliness, and simplicity, your unfailing consideration for others.

"Bearing a name which has become a household word throughout the world, you have retained the plain human qualities of a man and a gentleman which have won you the affection of those whose privilege it is to know you personally.

"I have in mind your fine loyalty to this country and this city. A son of a noble country which has taken so glorious a part in the war, you have given abundant proof, again and again, of your warm attachment to America and New York. You have managed even to find a generous thought, a pleasant gesture, and a gracious word in giving through the painful process of paying an income tax into six figures."

The speaker finished by waving one hand toward the table on which lay the gifts from the singer's admirers, among which were: a silver vase from the Metropolitan Opera Company directors; an illuminated parchment from the thirty-five families owning parterre boxes in the Metropolitan, and from the box holders of the Brooklyn Academy of Music, and the Philadelphia Metropolitan Opera House; a gold medal from General Manager Giulio Gatti-Casazza; another from the chiefs of departments back stage; a loving cup presented by the chorus; a silver vase from the orchestra musicians; a platinum watch set with two hundred and eighteen diamonds and sixty-one square-cut sapphires, presented by Caruso's fellow artists; and a silver fruit dish from the Victor Talking Machine Company.

Miss Geraldine Farrar expressed the feelings of her assembled associates when she kissed her confrère on one cheek, and then called for three cheers for America.

His gratitude redoubled, Caruso continued on his

way. A Commodore Hotel Musicale audience listened to him on April 2 during the presentation of a program which included the participation of Miss Mary Garden, Mischa Elman, and Arthur Rubinstein. A week later he appeared at a Buffalo concert; and when the Metropolitan season closed at Atlanta, Caruso prepared for the concert tour under the Metropolitan Musical Bureau management. Miss Morgana and Mr. Breeskin were the assisting artists in the appearances the tenor made in Nashville, St. Louis, Kansas City, St. Paul, Chicago, Milwaukee, and Canton, Ohio. The fee for each concert had been seven thousand dollars, but one for eight thousand dollars was awaiting him at Springfield, Massachusetts, where he appeared with Signora Elena Bianchini-Cappelli, with whom he had not sung since 1895, in Egypt.

For more than eighteen months Caruso had taken no extended rest. He was more weary than even he realized when he and Mrs. Caruso sailed, on May 24, aboard the *Giuseppe Verdi*, for Naples. At Signa there would be an opportunity for the quiet and recuperation he so sorely needed. He arrived there in due course; but the Villa Bellosguardo was not plundered of its wine, oil, and other things, as was erroneously reported in the newspapers, during the trouble with the Italian Reds. That summer of 1919 was peaceful for the singer and his wife. For the first time in years he had about him his family; a new note of respect was reflected in the attentions paid to him by those who visited Signa during those months.

V

Mrs. Caruso was eager that Enrico Jr. should finish his education in the United States; Caruso himself wished to have his younger boy near him, and so on the return voyage he was of the party. They landed in New York on September 3; and after Mimmi had been placed in the Gunnery School, at Washington, Connecticut, preparations were begun for the City of Mexico season of opera in which the tenor had agreed to sing. Since the United States Government had furnished assurance that no violence might be expected en route, the journey, via Laredo, was begun. The private car in which Caruso and his party were traveling was met at the border by an emissary of President Carranza; and when Saltillo was reached, an armored car and a company of soldiers were provided to escort the tenor in safety through a zone regarded as dangerous because of the proximity of the bandit Villa and his men.

The City of Mexico was finally reached, without incidents of an unusual nature, on September 22. Ciro Stefanini, one of Caruso's friends, had already rented for him the pretentious home of the widow of Mariscal de Limantour, former Secretary of the Treasury of Mexico.

Ricardo Cabrera, a newspaperman and respected music chronicler of the City of Mexico, said that although the Caruso train arrived at the station at six o'clock in the morning a throng of people were there waiting.

"He was escorted to the house prepared for his occupancy, at the Avenida Bucareli N. 85, where he breakfasted. Immediately afterwards he went to the office of the impresario, don José del Rivero," declares Cabrera, "where I met him. Since I had been honored to be Special Secretary, to be of assistance in speaking and writing Spanish, I suggested that we take a drink of our national appetizer, the famous *tequila*, which is a liquor made of agave in the province of Jalisco. Caruso was so pleased with this *copita* (glass) that later, if there was no one near to accompany him, he would not infrequently go alone to a saloon bar to have his *copita* of *tequila*.

"The Mexican début of Caruso took place on Monday, September 29, 1919, in 'L'Elisir d'Amore.' One cannot overestimate the occasion; or the responsibility of Caruso to Impresario del Rivero, who had not only guaranteed him seven thousand dollars an appearance for the eleven performances in which he was to sing but had deposited, the preceding March, in the tenor's New York bank, twenty-eight thousand dollars as a guaranty of good faith.

"I remember that when the great artist first appeared on the stage of the Esperanza Iris Theater — which is not of the best acoustically, though the largest and most modern we have — that the audience seemed to be holding its breath. Very evident was their anxiety to discover whether Caruso was really the phenomenon generally reputed, or, as some malicious tongues had gossiped, a 'tenor of the past.'

"The suspense ended very quickly after the first

cavatina, the *Quant' è bella*, had been reached. Only a few bars were sung before the people realized that before them was indeed the most astonishing tenor of all times; and this public, so easily carried off its feet by enthusiasm when it realizes it has not been cheated, rewarded Caruso, after that cavatina, with an ovation. Many others were to come; I doubt, though, if any one meant so much to that conscientious artist. When, in the last act of the opera, he seemed to surpass himself in *Una furtiva lagrima*, the audience appeared as if crazed. Señorita Ada Navarette, who is so popular among us, and who was the Adina, Ramon Blanchard, who sang Dulcamara, and Maestro Gennaro Papi, who conducted, were temporarily forgotten.

"For the second appearance of Caruso, also in the same theater, the management had chosen 'Ballo in Maschera', with Señorita Clara Elena Sanchez, Signorina Gabriella Besanzoni, and Augusto Ordonez appearing in the other rôles, and Maestro Attico Bernabini conducting. A confirmation of the first audience's verdict only excited the populace in their desires to hear this newly acclaimed tenor; and the opportunity for twenty-two thousand came when 'Carmen' was performed on Sunday, October 5, in the El Toreo bull ring. In this representation were Signorina Besanzoni, and MM. Ordonez and de Corabi, with Maestro Papi conducting. Caruso had every opportunity to disclose the many sides of his artistic skill in 'Samson et Dalila', sung in the Esperanza Iris Theater on October 9, and in the pathetic moments during the mill scene he caused some of the auditors to weep. On this occasion Maestro Papi conducted 'Samson', I am told, for the first time in his career.

"'Ballo in Maschera' was repeated, on Sunday, October 12, in the El Toreo bull ring; and the following Friday, in the Iris Theater, the fourth indoor performance took place. The opera was 'Marta,' and in it Caruso moved some to say, 'This must be the way they sing in Heaven.' The theater had been packed with the people an hour before the curtain rose; and many who could not gain admittance begged, almost piteously, not to be sent away without having had a chance to hear Caruso. One could write at length of the singer and his impression upon the thousands who heard him. If we shut our eyes now we can hear him singing Lionel's music . . . and we weep in the thought that never shall we hear him again. We mourn him, as one mourns a departed brother."

There followed after those performances another "Samson et Dalila" in the bull ring; an indoor representation of "Pagliacci", which was preceded (since they would have no other tenor, even in another opera, appearing with Caruso) by a symphonic concert, given as a *serata d'onore* to the star; an open air "Aïda", with Señora Escobar, Signorina Besanzoni, and Ordonez; a concert given for the benefit of the City of Mexico's educational fund, in which Caruso sang gratis; and an indoor farewell, with "Manon Lescaut." The real farewell, however, was taken in the El Toreo. A vote of the people resulted in the choice of the third act of "L'Elisir d'Amore", the first act of "Pagliacci", and act three from "Marta."

Rain began to fall. Before the "Elisir" had been finished many of the twenty-five thousand persons present opened umbrellas . . . and listened to Caruso singing to the accompaniment of pattering rain. "Caruso had to stop," relates Cabrera, "and I recall that when I reached his dressing room he was crying over the disappointment of the people. He asked me to make the announcement that if they would be patient, and wait, he too would wait — until midnight, if necessary — to finish singing to them. Within an hour the rain ceased to fall; and almost miraculously the sky cleared, permitting the performance to go on to its marvelous end. I cannot attempt to even feebly express the delighted madness of the spectators. They would not leave the arena. Instead, they waited until he appeared to go to his automobile; then they charged, and the car had to move very slowly, because even the guard of cavalry soldiers could not keep people from climbing upon it. He left that same night for New York, taking with him the hearts of the Mexican people."

Caruso's own impressions of his reception in the City of Mexico were both vivid and happy.

"I did not meet President Carranza," he said, "because he was at his country home, attending his wife who was ill. Before I first appeared he sent me a courteous letter, expressing his regret that he should not be able to hear me sing. Other officers of the Mexican Government whom I met proved agreeable.

They talked not at all of their affairs, but of mine. They all bowed before music, and seemed to know it well. I loved that foreign land for the reason that it reminded me of my own Italy. I saw only *Mehico* — as they term it — not Mexico.

"When I faced that première audience of three thousand people I realized that they had assembled in the theater to 'be shown', as they say in America. They represented three thousand critics; and, for all my experience, I quaked. I realized that Caruso must prove himself; it was my happy fortune that I could do so. It was strange, to see the men — stony-faced, somber — leaning a trifle forward, each with his right arm advanced slightly, as if it held a pistol . . . pointed at me to shoot, if need be. *Deo gratias* —as they say in Mexico — they did not wish to shoot.

"Although the invitations were many, I accepted as few as I could without causing those desiring to be hosts to feel that I was not grateful. I regretted, particularly, that a sudden illness made it necessary to send word to Governor of the State, Manuel Rueda Magro, of my inability to attend the dinner for which I had sent an acceptance.

"My lungs were strong enough to preserve me from any ill effects from the rarity of the City of Mexico atmosphere. So I experienced no physical inconvenience. As for drinking (there is no prohibition in Mexico) it was, on every side, — 'Will the *Señor Commendador* do me the priceless favor to accept a little drink?' Had I accepted every invitation, I question whether I should have lived to leave the country. Their *pulque* I tried only once, — a single swallow was too much.

"Owing to the Plaza del Toreo being arranged for the opera performances, a smaller toreo was erected in a nearby town, where one bull fight was arranged for me. I occupied President Carranza's box. After a time the people shouted, 'Kill the bull . . . kill the bull, Caruso will pay the fine.'

"'What fine?' I inquired, curiously. Then I was told that it was ordinarily forbidden to kill a bull. On any occasion when the conduct of the bull enrages the people, they insist on having it killed — being willing to have the amount of the fine levied upon them; and something this bull had done had aroused the ill-feelings of the spectators. But the bull was not killed that afternoon, and I escaped having any fine to pay.

"I left the City of Mexico with the most pleasurable thoughts of those who had been so kind to me. And I took away a gold medal given me by the municipality for having sung for their education fund. My stay in the land of *mañana* lingers in my memory as one continuous *fiesta*."

CHAPTER ELEVEN

Twilight

THOSE years which had fallen away were irretrievably gone, yet in their immediate wake lay serenity for Enrico Caruso. He himself probably did not sense how little longer he was destined to sing, but in some vague fashion he may have caught a consciousness that the twilight of his career had begun. Time's touch had become manifest; and though robust he moved, then, with the deliberate heaviness of a man whose physical buoyancy has gone. The once black and abundant hair had thinned; the features had matured in a way to give them authority; the singer's entire manner was that of one who had got somewhere and knew it. Whatever personal criticism may have been leveled against Caruso in earlier days had been gradually obliterated under the softening influences of an inner growth and his accomplishments. The public's estimate of him was a prized thing, and that he meant to keep.

It is true that he was suspicious; he had need to be. His own thoroughness and love of work made him a severe taskmaster, demanding the utmost of every member of his staff; yet he was just. But of administering praise he was chary. It was enough, in his opinion, that an employe was permitted to stay on with him. As for other singers: Caruso rarely commented at all upon them; and if those who would have liked his favorable word were disappointed, they at least were not referred to in fault-finding terms.

Until Zirato went to him, Caruso had made it a practice to keep personally not only his own books of accounts and attend to many minor matters, but he had insisted on cutting the coupons from his bonds. Indeed, one of his diversions was to go with his scissors to the safety deposit vault where such securities were kept. In 1919 he was persuaded to place such matters in the care of a trust company. He would not relinquish to any one else, however, his bookkeeping. His cash credits and debits were entered with his own hand, — each dollar being strictly accounted for. There was no slighting of a single item of outgo. Tips, moderate losses at cards, and purchases of the slightest character, all went into Caruso's cash book; and he drew his own checks, and cast his balances in the various New York and Italian banks where his deposits were kept. He never gambled a penny on the market; instead he bought the bonds of nations, and of corporations whose stability had been long proved. Thus, in spite of his huge current expenditures, Caruso's fortune grew. At the time of writing, his estate had not been completely inventoried; but it was then estimated as one which would probably approximate several millions of dollars.

The singer reached New York from his Mexico journey on November 6, just eleven days prior to the 1919–1920 season opening at the Metropolitan. He appeared in the première performance, which was

"Tosca", with Miss Geraldine Farrar and Antonio Scotti. Intense though the enthusiasm was on that evening, the singer's thoughts were on other and, to him, more important matters. The first was the anticipated addition to the Caruso family; the second, his début in the rôle of Eleazar in Halevy's "La Juive."

Mrs. Caruso said that she never quite comprehended how her husband learned the words and music of his part. There was usually, at the beginning of any day, some immediate bit of study and practice. After he had spent the customary ten minutes or more with his salt and water, and other inhalants and gargles, the singer would turn to his bath. While he proceeded with it either Martino or Mario (his valets) might take to him a low music rack, with some score placed so that, during his splashing, he could read. His accompanist, likely enough, would be playing at the piano in a near-by room, from a duplicate of that same score; and if Caruso felt so inclined he might sing a bit, in half-voice.

Breakfast consisting of a cup of black coffee and one roll would already have been had, in bed, where the mail would have been disposed of; then, after the tub, would come a glance at a morning newspaper, to read cursorily some story his attention had been called to. Business or any pressing matters finally out of the way, the tenor would concern himself with his voice and his music. If he had no performance to prepare for on the approaching evening, his vocal exercises would be brief. Should he be scheduled for an opera, then the score of the work had to be played straight through — every note of it — to the end. It mattered nothing if it were to be "Aïda" in which he was to sing, or any other work in which he had appeared a hundred times or more. He insisted on refreshing perfectly his memory, and of placing in his mind just as firmly the words and music of the rôles his associates were to sing. Is it any wonder that he was always letter perfect? Such preparedness as this enabled him — with his voice, which had such range, color, and dynamic plasticity — to sing any piece of music in an opera he knew with almost the same confidence as though it were part of his own rôle. He did it, to cite a specific instance, during a 1915 Philadelphia representation of "Bohème", when Andres de Segurola stood in need of help. The basso was suffering from laryngitis. On the way from New York to Philadelphia, in the Metropolitan's special train, de Segurola confided to Caruso that he would probably have to "cut" Colline's "song to the coat."

"Don't do that," counseled the tenor, "I will sing it for you; but you would better not speak about it to Polacco." (Polacco was the conductor of the night.)

When Caruso began the air, *Vecchia zimarra*, instead of de Segurola, Polacco was astonished. At the close of the act he rushed back stage, furious because he had not been informed of what to expect. "We did not tell you, Giorgio," said Caruso, "for fear you might say 'No.'"

Accustomed as she was to hearing her husband so constantly at his practise, Mrs. Caruso confesses

Copyright Mishkin, N. Y.

CARUSO AS ELEAZAR IN "LA JUIVE"

This photograph was taken in Caruso's dressing-room at the Metropolitan Opera House, Dec. 24, 1920, the night of his last appearance.

to wonderment over the way the Eleazar rôle grew. "I would hear him occasionally humming some phrases," she said, "and of course there were times when I was present during serious moments with the piano. But Enrico learned the words and music of this character, it seemed to me, with less effort and certainly with much less expenditure of time than he customarily gave to a new part. He wrote the text and notes, and 'business' of the action, in a small book which he could carry about with him,—just as he always did. And I daresay that he spent many an hour with Mr. Bodanzky, to get the maestro's ideas of tempi. For Enrico was careful, always, to get the interpretative ideas any conductor with whom he was to sing might have with respect to his music. His own individuality never was interfered with; on the contrary, he always insisted that he felt freer in singing if he knew the precise attitude of a maestro toward any opera in question. It was so with Maestri Moranzoni and Papi; and I distinctly recall that, while Enrico had previously sung Chenier in 'Andrea Chenier', he asked Maestro Moranzoni to visit him to go over the score which he was preparing for the Metropolitan's 1921 revival. He never was able to sing it, as all of us know; on the night it was first presented at the Metropolitan he lay desperately ill."

It was the consensus of opinion that Eleazar was the crowning effort of Enrico Caruso's career. The critics so wrote; even the public, though some part of it may have preferred him in some other rôle, was impressed as by no other with the artist's vocal, musical, and dramatic artistry. As The Jew, Caruso was a towering figure. He appeared, declared the most competent authorities, so natural and so spontaneous that it was as though one were hearing and seeing, in reality, the character represented.

The tenor had been long in preparing for it. He spent considerable time in the New York Public Library, studying his subject and the character of Shylock from books and plays. Similar attention was given to the costuming side; and Caruso asked a friend — Mrs. Selma Shubart — to assist him in finding a shawl such as a Rabbi wears while saying prayers. This lady at length secured from a New York Rabbi a silken white and black scarf which had been in use; and it was the one the tenor wore in the scene wherein Eleazar presents the unleavened bread to his co-religionists just before the Princess interrupts that ceremony. To other essentials — small as well as large — having to do with the faithful portraiture of the character of the aged Jew, Caruso devoted much effort. How fitting it all was! For this was the last new rôle in which his best-loved and best-loving public was to have him. His associates in that cast were Miss Rosa Ponselle, as Rachel; Miss Evelyn Scotney, in the part of the Princess; Orville Harrold, appearing as Prince Leopold; and Leon Rothier, as Cardinal Brogni. Artur Bodanzky conducted.

On December 18, 1919, in the Knickerbocker Hotel, New York, a girl baby was born to Enrico and Dorothy Caruso. Congratulations flooded the father and mother, in person, and by telegraph and telephone from innumerable parts of the world. The tenor was like a child in this new experience, which brought him delight and joy. The following evening — a Friday — he appeared at the Metropolitan in "L'Elisir d'Amore", where he received from the audience an ovation which said plainly, — "We are happy for you!"

Christened Gloria Caruso, a baby book was at once secured for the tiny newcomer. Giulio Gatti-Casazza was the first person to write in this book. His inscription was: "To Gloria, every glory!" She was baptized on February 7, 1920, in the Caruso Knickerbocker suite, special permission from Monsignor Lavelle having been secured to allow the ceremony to be performed outside the church. Monsignor Gherardo Ferrante officiated; Signora Marchesa Orazio Cappelli was the godmother. Immediate members of both sides of the Caruso families, and a dozen others, were present. Among those who sent gifts were Mr. and Mrs. Henry H. Rogers, Mrs. Ogden Goelet, and Italo Montemezzi, the composer.

The presence of a girl baby in the Caruso household gave the singer a new interest; so deep an interest did it become that he was appreciably affected and influenced in a number of vital respects. Little Gloria thrived; she had as a frequent companion the greatest of tenors, — although she did not appear to be at all awed over the fact. At first he was merely an agreeable and rather attentive person, whom she liked. Later, she called him by some name of her own conjuring.

If Caruso had been responsive in other days to

appeals for financial assistance, the coming of Gloria softened his heart still more. And how well his friends knew him is indicated in a letter written to the tenor that January 12, by Miss Farrar. The body of the letter ran thus:

My dear Enrico:
    If I may beg five minutes of your attention from the young heiress Gloria, may I ask you to let me have your name on a Committee which is making up a fund for our first great American singer, Minnie Hauk, born long before our time and now in her seventieth year, blind, destitute, and in misery? I want to get as much contribution as I can, and I feel that the artists at the head of the Committee are the people who can interest our public in such a thing.
    It is not agreeable to ask charity, and I never do, but in this case it is the first time we have ever had the privilege of helping an American name. I am asking everybody to give one hundred dollars to this subscription as well, but if the calls on your pocket have been too many, my real object is for you to join the Committee.
    With affectionate wishes to you and Madame for 1920.

As ever,
Geraldine.

At the end was a postscript, not the inevitable feminine addenda, but a single sentence which must have caused the tenor to chuckle:

    P. S. Please make check payable to Mr. Waldron P. Belknap, Treasurer, and send it to Mr. Albert Morris Bagby, Vice-President, Waldorf-Astoria, New York City, marked "Minnie Hauk Fund."

Copyright by Keystone View Co., N. Y.

GLORIA

The photograph was taken in the garden of Mrs. Caruso's rented house at No. 144 East 55th Street, New York City.

"Pagliacci", "Samson et Dalila", "Marta", "Manon Lescaut", "Forza del Destino", and five repetitions of "La Juive" had been some of the representations demanding the singer's attention up to the christening date of Gloria. Five days later a slight attack of bronchitis caused him to miss a scheduled appearance in "Manon Lescaut", and he had not recovered in time, one week later, to sing in "Le Prophète." The indisposition had subsided by February 21, for on that evening Caruso appeared in "Le Prophète", and, at the Saturday matinée of that week, in "La Juive." He missed no further performances during that season, for he continued on through to May 1 — in Atlanta — where he sang for the last time there, in "L'Elisir d'Amore." He had forty-seven engagements in all (two less than the preceding season), and his *cachets* totaled $117,500.

But the earnings from Caruso's concert engagements had been large. During the course of the active months at the opera the tenor had managed to find opportunities to sing at the Waldorf-Astoria, and in Detroit, Pittsburgh, Waterbury, Connecticut, and Scranton, Pennsylvania. For these out-of-town appearances Caruso received seven thousand dollars each. One other appearance outside the opera was recorded in New York's Lexington Opera House, on the evening of March 28. The occasion was a drive for the Italian Dollar Loan, and Caruso's associates included Signora Luisa Tetrazzini and Riccardo Stracciari. The tenor sang Tosti's *A Vucchella*, in return for which a man in the audience purchased fifty thousand dollars in bonds.

His Atlanta contract fulfilled, Caruso turned in the direction of Havana. He had never appeared there. The people were insistent that he should be brought to them, — at any price. Adolfo Bracale was the impresario who undertook the venture; and in certain respects it was to be that, for he had had to guarantee Caruso ten thousand dollars for each evening appearance, and five thousand dollars for every matinée. To insure to himself a profit, Bracale charged very high prices for seats, and this, as events proved, was not relished by the Havana public.

II

Caruso reached Cuba's metropolis on May 5, and went to his quarters in the Hotel Sevilla. Signore Maria Barrientos, Carmen Melis, Gabriella Besanzoni, and Escobar, and MM. Mardones, Stracciari and Parvis were of the Bracale Company, of which Maestro Padovani was principal conductor. A full week off was the première, to be given at the Nacional Theater, and in which Caruso was to be introduced to the Cubans in "Marta." The tenor had ordered for every rôle save one a complete set of new costumes, of a lighter material than he ordinarily wore, because of the extreme heat in Havana. "L'Elisir d'Amore" was the opera in which the singer had expected to make his début. When he learned that "Marta", for excellent reasons, had been substituted there was a commotion. It would never do to undertake an important first appearance in a new costume. Fortunately, Punzo (Caruso's wardrobier) had thought to put some old costumes into the trunks; and that of Lionel chanced to be among them.

The Nacional was packed for that opening "Marta" performance. True to form, Caruso was excessively nervous beforehand. He knew something of the Latin temperament; and so much was expected of him that to fail, in even slight measure, was likely as not to arouse a protest. Some experts have insisted that the greatest vocal moments the tenor ever experienced were in Mexico and Havana. "He realized," declared one of them, "that his New York audience — even all the United States audiences — would accept, and be satisfied, with whatever he had to give. But those Mexicans and Cubans . . . they were another people."

Perhaps. Nevertheless, the Lionel of Caruso prompted his listeners that May 12th night to make a demonstration which only a supreme voice and singing could have aroused. On May 16, at a matinée, the opera was repeated; and two evenings later the tenor was heard in "L'Elisir d'Amore." After his "Ballo in Maschera", on the 21st, and "Pagliacci", four days later, the recognition was "enough." Scarcely equal, it must be admitted, to the Mexican ovations, yet sufficient to convince Caruso that the trip southwards had not been made in vain.

"Tosca", a "Pagliacci" matinée, two evening representations of "Carmen", and one of "Aïda" established a Caruso vogue in Havana. The populace clamored for seats, despite the prices. For an orchestra place twenty dollars was the box-office price; and it angered many people, and furnished food for the gossips whose tongues would not be stilled. Even before his arrival in the city, a Havana newspaper had begun upon Caruso a series of violent attacks. His private and professional life were made subjects for extended abuse, and had any of these articles reached the singer's eyes there might have been trouble. They moderated as the season wore on, yet they are felt to have caused some damage.

A testimonial concert of the same nature as the two given Caruso in Mexico — a *Serata d'onore* — preceded, on June 11, a mixed bill which included the third act of "L'Elisir", and the first from "Pagliacci." The auditors put no restraint upon their plaudits, with the result that the singer returned to his hotel in a satisfied frame of mind.

Two nights later came "Aïda", and a crisis in one of the most trying opera engagements Caruso had known. "La Forza del Destino" was to have been given; it was abandoned because of differences between Bracale and the agent of Ricordi and Company, over the payment of copyright fees. The tenor had sung his *Celeste Aïda* in a manner that had wrought the audience to a frenzy. Signore Escobar and Besanzoni had finished their second-act duet; and Caruso was in his dressing room changing into Radames's costume for the Triumphal Scene. There came a sudden explosion from some part of the theater, which threw those present into a panic. It proved to be a bomb (believed, to this day, to have been instigated by some person or persons angered at the alleged excessive prices put upon the tickets).

No lives were lost; no one was seriously injured; no particular property damage was done; but the frightened people rushed for the street. The police and firemen arrived quickly, and aided in preserving sufficient order to see the audience safely out of the theater. The representation stopped at that point; and without waiting to change from his costume into street attire, Caruso went to his waiting automobile and clad as the triumphant Radames was driven through the streets amid cheers from those near by.

This experience in itself would have been enough to unnerve the tenor. Unfortunately, it had come only a few days after a first one which, although of quite a different character, was still sufficient to put Caruso in an uneasy frame of mind. On June 8, at Easthampton, Long Island, where the Carusos had leased a villa for the summer, Mrs. Caruso had been robbed of jewels valued at one hundred and fifty thousand dollars. Indications had pointed to the theft as having been committed by some one well acquainted with the movements of the household, which then consisted of Mrs. Caruso, her sister-in-law, Mrs. Park Benjamin, their children, and servants. A representative for the Associated Press had visited the Nacional Theater, during the first "Aïda" performance, with the news. Zirato succeeded in keeping it from his employer until after the final curtain; he waited until they were supping, at the Sevilla, to relate what had occurred. The tenor sent at once a cablegram of reassurance, and, after passing over the loss as something not to worry about, begged Mrs. Caruso to think only of herself and Gloria.

But the tenor was anxious and restless. He wished to get the Cuban engagement well over with, and after appearing at Santa Clara, in a mixed-bill made up of acts from "L'Elisir d'Amore" and "Pagliacci", and at Cienfuegos, in "Aïda", he refused Bracale's pleadings that he remain and give in Havana two or three additional "popular" performances. He was excessively concerned for the safety of his wife and child; several cablegrams each day were passing between the singer and Mrs. Caruso. And then came another bit of disturbing news, — the sale of the Knickerbocker Hotel. The information made Caruso downcast; he had become attached to the place; it was home to him; now, with all else that had so recently occurred, he regarded it as an omen of ill-fortune to come.

There was still a New Orleans concert appearance which had been arranged for him by the Metropolitan Musical Bureau, — an appearance the tenor felt in honor bound to keep. He would have liked to cancel it; doubtless he would have done so if it had not been for his sense of obligation and his pride that his word, once given, must at all hazards be respected.

He therefore sailed from Havana for New Orleans, on June 23, on board the SS. *Cartago;* and with the New Orleans appearance behind him, he proceeded direct to Atlantic City, where Mrs. Caruso and Baby Gloria were waiting to meet him.

The Atlantic City objective was consequent upon a promise Caruso had made Calvin Child to sing for members of the Victor organization who were assembled there in convention. Fatigued as he was, the tenor sang his arias and songs with a conscientiousness in nowise different than if the occasion had been a regular public appearance. His concern was manifested, after the concert, in his remark about the acoustics of the hotel ballroom in which the concert had been held. Because of the low ceiling he had wondered about the impression he had made; and as he joined Mrs. Caruso, Mr. and Mrs. Child and others of their party he inquired, "How did my voice sound? To me it seemed out of resonance." Only a Caruso could take so modest a view of his own work.

A few days were spent in New York; then the Caruso family left, on July 4, for their Long Island home. With the exception of a single concert the Metropolitan bureau arranged for at Ocean Grove, New Jersey (another seven thousand dollar affair), there was no further singing by the tenor that summer. He had long looked forward to that vacation; the place itself was several miles out of town, — a low and comfortable house set on the shore of a bit of inland water, with woods all about. But the robbery had upset Caruso's peace of mind, and detectives of the insurance companies which had written policies on the stolen jewels were almost too active. They would appear at unexpected moments — to quiz some member of the household — and some of the questions and insinuations were scarcely pleasant. The jewels, at the time of writing, had not been recovered. In 1921 two insurance companies paid

$75,000 and $18,000 respectively on policies Caruso had carried.

Impresario Bracale exerted unsuccessfully every possible influence to induce Caruso to go to Lima, Peru, for the season he had prepared to give in that South American city. Caruso was worried; his health, further aggravated by headaches, gave those close to him more concern than they cared openly to admit.

After the discharge of the chauffeur who had fallen into disfavor with his employer, the atmosphere about the Caruso country place continued laden with oppression. Friends came and went; there were unpretentious dinner parties, and an occasional game of cards. Daytime relaxations included a few tries at lawn tennis, also a bit of boating, since a small craft was moored at the near-by landing. Spontaneous enjoyment, however, seemed rarely to touch the singer during his Easthampton sojourn. Mrs. Caruso had fixed up a study for him in one wing of the house, and he worked there, — when he was not spending his time with her, or playing with Gloria.

July and August passed; September induced thoughts of the coming season, and on the twelfth of that month the Carusos moved into the new apartment they had rented in the Vanderbilt Hotel. It was the one Alfred Gwynne Vanderbilt had planned and, for a time, occupied. On the topmost floor, its roominess and convenience seemed well suited to the Caruso needs. Yet the tenor crossed the threshold with a sense of uneasiness.

TWILIGHT

III

There appeared to be no rest for the weary. An extensive *tournée* had been booked by the Metropolitan Musical Bureau: three at ten thousand dollars each, and eight at seven thousand dollars. The opening one, at Montreal, had been set for September 28; then the route took the little company — which included as assisting artists Miss Alice Miriam, soprano, and Albert Stoessel, violinist — to Toronto, Chicago, St. Paul, and Denver. From this city to Omaha, thence to Tulsa, Oklahoma, and still farther south to Fort Worth and Houston, lay the itinerary, which finished with two concerts at Charlotte, North Carolina, and Norfolk, Virginia.

Such traveling was certain to fatigue the tenor, yet he did not feel, with the income tax burden impending, that he could afford to refuse so enticing a reward. Before he took train for Montreal he went on September 14, to Camden, New Jersey. And there, for several successive days, he made what were to be his final phonograph recordings. The very last record of all was Rossini's *Messa Solennelle*.

If Caruso was tired from his efforts covering almost continuous singing from the middle of September to the end of October, he must have reached New York with the consciousness that others agreed with the substance of a letter Otto H. Kahn had written him, a few seasons before. In it the Chairman of the Metropolitan board had said:

I have so often and so enthusiastically expressed my admiration to you, that I can hardly add anything to what I have already said. And yet — having just heard you in "Marta" — I feel impelled once more to send you a line of thanks and of admiration. Your voice was always by far the most beautiful organ I have ever heard, and your art was always great. But the combination of your God-given voice, in its most splendid form as it is this season, together with the maturity and perfection to which your art has grown, is beyond praise. And to sing, as you do, with the same artistic perfection, heroic parts and lyric parts, is a most astounding artistic feat.

Please do not trouble to acknowledge this letter. It is simply meant as a spontaneous tribute of admiration and gratitude, which is not new to you, but which, under the inspiration of your last few performances, I could not refrain from tendering to you once more.

Believe me, with sincere regards,
Very faithfully yours,
Otto H. Kahn.

The tribute of this art patron would doubtless have been echoed by countless numbers throughout the world, had they known. For the tenor had become an idol. Even persons who were not musical knew who Caruso was and why. What few of the whole vast number even faintly realized was the responsibility Caruso's artistic position had wrought. He was human, and being human he appreciated — as he had so often said — how machine-like he was expected invariably to be. Perhaps this was one cause for his sensitiveness to the sort of criticism which appeared in three New York daily newspapers — the *Herald,* the *Times,* and the *World* — soon after he had made his 1920–1921 première in "La Juive." "L'Elisir d'Amore" had followed, on November 18, "Samson et Dalila", on the 24th and three days later a "Forza del Destino." But the Caruso who had sung in these operas was not, in the judgment of the trio of music chroniclers, the Caruso of the season before. Others, perhaps equally capable of as correct appraisement, had disagreed with the objectors, — who attributed to overwork the tenor's alleged lapse in vocal powers. "He wants too much money," declared one of the three critics.

In his Vanderbilt Hotel study, Caruso read the newspaper articles and was distressed. Matters had certainly gone awry since he had left his long-established home in the Knickerbocker. The singer was superstitious and subject, as are so many having the artistic temperament, to being affected by signs or occurrences. Thus, to meet in the street a nun was a direct order to instantly change the direction of his course; but should chance cause him to see a man hunchback, after having passed a woman so deformed, it portended good; otherwise the former was an indication of some ill-luck. To pass under a ladder, a stage bridge, or any piece of board put up amid the scenery, was a thing Caruso never consciously did. And it was one of his rules to avoid, if possible, starting a new undertaking on either a Tuesday or Friday. That so intelligent a man could be influenced by such superstitions — and many others which he had — is not so strange as may appear. For Caruso was highly emotional, and the premonitions he sometimes experienced seemed in some fashion to be identified with that part of him which can best be analyzed as the outgrowth of an extreme sensitiveness.

Religion, from his earliest youth, had caught and held him. The tenor's own mother taught him to be "devout and prayerful." Father Tonello remembers, as does many another, that Caruso had in his dressing room a little statue of the Madonna, one of St. Anthony, and one of his mother; and his reverence for the Church, its laws, and its priests never relaxed. Above Caruso's bed hung a solid silver crucifix, while near by were his prayer book, and his beads. "I am aware that some, knowing a few facts of Caruso's life," said Father Tonello; "his human weaknesses and shortcomings, have branded his religious sentiments as superstitious. There might have been a light touch of that in Caruso, as in some other men we read of in history. I know that, even in our day, there have been some highly educated and intellectual men who wore charms or talismans to protect themselves from evil. Caruso was not of this type. His religion was neither hypocrisy nor superstition, but was true faith. Besides the fact that occasionally when Caruso and I were alone the topic of religion would come up, in many of his letters which I keep as precious, I have the testimony of his belief and faith in God."

From the many facts at hand it is clear that Caruso lived largely according to the golden rule. His thoughtfulness of others was never spasmodic. Rather was it a thoughtfulness governed, as was his life, by a sort of regularity. At Christmas he never forgot many of the Metropolitan Opera House attachés and employés. Gifts of one kind and another were rarely omitted (he retained, in a book, the names of persons he wished in various ways to remember); and to members of the chorus and to others the tenor tendered money. Some were of course overlooked, but such omission was never intentional; and if Caruso ever learned of a seeming slight, where generosity should have figured, he hastened to make amends. The probabilities are that he did not administer, in every manner of respect, with unfailing justice; few men do. But his heart, oftener than not, was in the right place.

On this account he felt aggrieved that he should have been criticized, that autumn of 1920, in a manner he deemed unjust. In his rundown condition at the time, he may have magnified what others passed over as not worthy of serious thought. For he had been previously subjected to expert consideration which, though appearing in the public press, had not moved him to such despair as these latest critical notices.

"I know when I sing well or badly," he said, in discussing these unfavorable reviews, "and after each of those performances that gave offense to those writers I came home satisfied."

Advised to discontinue reading the criticisms — if they were so disturbing to his peace of mind — the tenor only shook his head. "So long as I feel I am displeasing I must read them."

The climax came not long after the opening of that 1920–1921 season. Caruso must indeed have been far from physical and nervous health to have allowed himself to become so disheartened. Or it may have been that, fearing he might indeed be slipping, he doubted being able to stand up under what, in his agitated state, he feared might be actual failure. His pride and sensitiveness were too keen to enable him to withstand the effects of such a shock. And as the days passed, and his self-doubt threw a still stronger shadow, Caruso finally surrendered to the inner enemy which had pressed persistently upon him.

Few persons knew of it at the time; it was possible to keep the matter secret, and it is perhaps fortunate that the newspapers never learned what happened. For at the zenith of his career, and with the public as completely at his feet as ever, Caruso informed Gatti-Casazza of the Metropolitan that he wished to resign.

"If I sing as those critics say I sing," he wrote to Gatti-Casazza, "it is time I appeared no more before the New York public."

No bomb, thrown in the opera's executive sanctum, could have caused greater consternation. Gatti knew too well the temper of his chiefest asset. What he had said he should do he assuredly would do,—once he became convinced no other course lay open. To arrest that decision was the task the impresario realized must be done, and as quickly as possible; so he went, posthaste, to the Vanderbilt, where he and Caruso had a long talk.

One other friend to the tenor came, fortunately, into the situation a few days afterwards. His knowledge of the conditions, and his counsel, supplementing the appeal Gatti had made, put fresh courage into Caruso. He would try again, he agreed, to show them what Caruso could do. If he failed —.

"Samson et Dalila" was the opera. Who that heard can forget the singing of the tenor on the evening of December 3, 1920! After the second act this friend from whom Caruso hoped to get the truth went to him in his dressing room. The singer was changing costumes; but he instantly waved an arm of dismissal to his valet Mario, and Punzo, his wardrobier. Sitting in his undergarments, the tenor took a deep puff from the cigarette he was smoking.

"Well?" he said, inquiringly.

The visitor shrugged his shoulders; then he replied, "There is nothing to be said you yourself don't know. In the morning the critics will confirm what I say."

And the following day the reviewers for the *Times*, the *Herald*, and the *World* wrote in effect that Caruso had sung gloriously.

IV

Just how did Caruso sing? Innumerable persons have asked the question, — which has been variously answered. From a strictly technical standpoint this matter of curiosity is natural enough; and there can be little doubt that singers and teachers, who often heard the tenor, have explained, more or less satisfactorily, approximately how he controlled that marvelous voice of his. To hear him sing as he sang that "Samson" performance was to hear the Caruso who used a technique quite different from one he might employ for a different type of rôle. For, as has already been set forth in these pages, he summoned at will a quality and volume of voice to suit the mood of text and music of what lay before him; to do this required using his vocal apparatus in a variety of ways.

He was gifted, unquestionably, with vocal resources of a phenomenal order; and not alone in natural beauty of tone, but in compass, flexibility, color, endurance, and power. Laryngologists who have examined the singer's throat and vocal chords state that the length and thickness of the chords gave the capacity to sound extreme notes, both low and high, while their peculiar softness was largely responsible for the richness of timbre. And yet, one eminent authority (who was an intimate friend of the tenor's and a constant companion for a period of years) asserts that Caruso's vocal chords were not only unexceptional, but that they did not give him his unique voice. This may be a matter of opinion, even in scientific circles, yet it would appear that the harmonious working of the entire Caruso vocal mechanism was chiefly responsible for his superb technique.

Since he did not always possess it, there must exist an interest as to just what that technique was, and how it was acquired.

During the singer's early years, as a tenor, it may be recalled that his voice is accurately reported as having been light to the point of thinness, and that the high tones were insecure. That he sang without marked physical effort during a critical period of voice-development was undoubtedly fortunate. And an analysis of the evidence at hand would seem to indicate that Caruso fell, naturally, into a way of breathing which was the correct way, — and, therefore, Nature's own. Such must have been the case; otherwise, when Lombardi took him in hand (in 1896) to develop the needed power of tone and the high notes, the subsequent smoothness and liquid-like quality never would have ensued.

Caruso was probably singing with a constricted throat in those earliest days. From the accounts reported through first-hand sources he could not have sung otherwise. How he succeeded — as he did — in securing a natural relaxation of the muscles of the throat and of the tongue, is something Caruso never satisfactorily explained. It is doubtful if he really knew. Something happened, when he was ripe to take advantage of whatever the combination of circumstances was, to enable him to fall into a vocally safe and secure way of delivering his singing voice.

After that point had been reached it was a matter, merely — so far as vocal technique was concerned — for him to apply his rare singing instinct, and to appear in public as frequently as possible.

Once his entire vocal mechanism (breath, and its control; vocal cords, throat, tongue, jaw, and lips) began to function in complete accord, the development of technique was only a matter of time. Experience brought confidence; and when maturity was added to this, the technique acquired could be (as it always is, by any one markedly proficient in any interpretative branch of an art) forgotten.

Using a minimum supply of breath, and learning after long practice to distribute it with the utmost conservation, Caruso for a long time never forced his tones. To whatever extent he may have done so during the years following 1905, it is a fact that almost never did he "drive" the voice during the period of his fullest vocal glory. He sang beautifully because he sang naturally; and one of the secrets, if there be any in singing technique, was the purity of his vowels, and his clear attack of consonants. Whoever understands the fundamentals which govern correct singing technique realizes the importance of enunciation. The more distinct it is, the freer and more agreeable the tone.

Singing exclusively for years in the Italian language, and having spoken it always, was an added help to the Caruso technique. Every Italian word ends with a vowel and every vowel ends as it is begun, — without a vanishing point, unlike English. It is this vanishing point which causes the singer trained in the English tongue to unconsciously "swallow" the tone, a practice fatal to the emission of a free and pure musical sound.

When Caruso attacked a tone (excepting in later years, when he permitted himself an unnecessary and a regrettable habit of scooping the higher notes), he attacked precisely, with his throat open, the tongue and jaw relaxed, the lips forming perfectly the vowel of the word to be enunciated, and the breath properly supporting the tone — but seldom forcing it. He secured his brilliancy and resonance principally from the spaces of the mouth and head, — especially the latter. They were reinforced by the resonance supplied by Caruso's deep chest (his entire body aided in this respect), but he directed this tone to the front of the face, one might say almost at a sort of disk, made up of that part from the base of the nose to the lower part of the forehead and including the cheek bones.

Many persons will recall that Caruso often frowned when he sang, drawing his eyebrows together until there appeared furrows just above his nose. He always said that this seemed to help in concentrating the tone in a way that was most effective. The base of the nose always expanded sidewise during this physiological singing act; and it gradually enlarged during later years of his life, as a comparing of photographs will show.

But if any one fancies that either the translucent warmth or the robust vigor of Caruso's best tones came from any pronounced physical effort, such belief is incorrect. He was able to reinforce the resonance of each tone through "letting it filter" to the places where it could radiate to all the spaces which yield resonance. To do this — his vocal mechanism coördinating with such smooth perfection — was, for him, simple enough. He was spontaneous and natural in delivering a singing tone. Therefore, his singing, save in moments of greatest dramatic stress when unusual emphasis was required, was no manifestly greater exertion than it was for him to talk. If there were any real secret to the Caruso method, it would seem to lie, to a considerable extent, in the fact that he "talked" his tones.

All the talk, at various times current, that Caruso sang "by the grace of God", was scarcely correct. His very special endowment, extraordinary as it was, for its fullest development required precisely what Caruso supplied: intelligent and ceaseless work. During the first decade of his career he sang almost constantly, no matter where he was. As late as 1912 he continued, if in a lesser degree, to do so; and in his rooms, or when he was engaged elsewhere at some task, or even when strolling, he would exercise his voice in something midway between a hum and a very light tone. Thereafter this practice gradually subsided; and Mrs. Caruso says that during the summer of 1920 she heard the sound of his voice about the Easthampton house only a few times.

Belief that Caruso did not really know how he produced his tones is erroneous. On the contrary he understood exactly what he did, and why. His communicative powers, however, were not marked; his failure to convey to his one pupil the things he sought to convey is striking proof of this. But he could explain clearly under questioning. This really was the one way to extract from him his knowledge of the technique of singing, no less than his knowledge of his own technique. On occasions he has been known to say "yes" to some question about voice when he did not really agree. Such instances invariably arose at being quizzed when he was not in the mood, or when the questioner's ideas on the

A PAGE FROM SECCHI'S "LOVE ME OR NOT," ILLUSTRATING CARUSO'S ORIGINAL METHOD OF TEACHING HIMSELF HOW TO SING IN ENGLISH

His English rendering is spelt according to the Italian rules of pronunciation.

subject matter were so at variance with his own that he did not wish to bother.

He spoke freely and at length about singing technique to only a few persons. Now that he is gone one learns of the claims of certain persons, who profess to have obtained at first hand from Caruso specific information as to how he sang. The only documentary evidence thus far come to light is presented in a book on the scientific side of the singing voice. The material was written by one who was a close friend to the tenor; he personally indorsed it shortly before his death.

Theories expounded by many voice educators to the effect that the human vocal instrument is delicate and requires constant tending were exploded by Caruso. He smoked cigarettes constantly and was careless about his diet. During an *entr'acte* of a performance in which he was appearing, it was his custom to eat an apple; he smoked before going upon the stage, and immediately when he came off. In brief, he treated his voice like the exceedingly durable instrument a well-used singing voice really is.

On the way to the theater Caruso was generally cheerful, and inclined to jest. Once in his dressing room a full two hours before the curtain was scheduled to rise, his attitude changed. Nothing would be right; nobody appeared able to satisfy him. In his nervous irritability which always preceded his appearance before an audience, the tenor would complain about seeming trivialities: some part of his makeup, a wig that did not set as he thought it should, a tie, or shoes and stockings. Often because some trifle he reached for on his dressing table might be mislaid, Caruso would seize the cover and, with an angry jerk, send bottles and all the other paraphernalia on the table flying.

During those two hours which preceded the beginning of any première, the tenor's nervousness would not subside. On such occasions he would warm up his voice with light scales and other simple exercises, to make the instrument pliant and agile. Then would come the inhalant; after that a pinch of Swedish tobacco snuff, to clear the nostrils; and finally a gargle of lukewarm water and salt. He was then ready for the sip of diluted Scotch whisky, — and the stage.

No Metropolitan representation ever began without the visit, several times, of Ludovico Viviani, an assistant stage manager, to inquire if Caruso were ready. And it was always, "May we begin, Mr. Caruso?"

Particular to the last detail about his own costumes and makeup, and the appropriateness of any other matters bearing upon a performance, the singer was easily annoyed if an associate did anything he considered not good in taste. During one "Marta" representation at the Metropolitan, Caruso arrived on the stage after he had been informed by Viviani that all was in readiness for the second act. The curtain should have immediately risen, but there was no soprano. Inquiries disclosed that she had not yet finished curling her hair. Caruso was furious. When the scene had been finished, he told the singer that servants not only did not curl their hair, but that they wore neither silk dresses nor silken stockings. The soprano was wise enough to heed the advice; at the next "Marta" in which she appeared the materials of her garments were simple, her hair quite straight.

Paul Althouse once had an experience with Caruso over a costume. He had paused at the door of the great tenor's dressing room on his way to the stage. Althouse had been cast for Turiddu in "Cavalleria Rusticana", which was to precede "Pagliacci" with Caruso. The latter looked at his younger confrère, then gasped. "What!" he exclaimed, "a first tenor of the Metropolitan dressed like you? What a reflection on this institution! Here, Mario," commanded Caruso, "get out my Cavalleria costume." He ordered Viviani to hold the curtain; took Althouse into his dressing room; the change of costumes was made and, observing the excellent fit, the singer said, "There, you look a Metropolitan first tenor. Caruso gives you that costume. Now go down and sing like Caruso."

At the beginning of any opera appearance, the tenor's nervousness would hold — until he had delivered his first few phrases, and he was satisfied with his reception. Thereupon his anxiety would appear to pass. There were times, however, when an entire first act would go badly. He might be out of voice or humor; it was perhaps more frequently the case than some who idolized him might be willing to admit. The effect seldom failed to stimulate the tenor to supreme endeavor in the ensuing act; and some of his noteworthy achievements and successes occurred after an unpropitious start.

Then it was that the Caruso voice was called on to the limit. To watch him in such circumstances, if the rôle chanced to be heroic, was a rare lesson in the technique of singing, — for those who could apprehend. Those who could not, completely confused some of the things he did. The brilliancy and power of the high tones, delivered with an open throat which, with the palate high and the larynx low, made a large space, could be so easily misleading to the singer or educator; and more than one voice has suffered in fruitless attempts at imitation. The reason was commonly due to ignorance of the how and why; to an unwillingness to proceed slowly in building up a technique modeled on the same natural laws which Caruso obeyed; and to a misconception of the tenor's taking of breath and its regulation. It was safe enough for him to sing with such apparent abandon; he always knew the precise way to form each tone, whatever its pitch; and his scale was even throughout its entire compass. Caruso did not believe in the so-called "registers" of the voice. Each pitch he sounded with his voice had what might be termed a register all its own. Thus every note matched the one immediately next it in pitch, so that the texture of the voice, both high and low, was relatively the same.

Yet even that voice needed occasional coaxing. In the coats of all Caruso's costumes were little pockets, wherein he could slip a tiny vial of salt water, — to be gargled surreptitiously when, with his back to the audience, he found it imperative to clear his throat of mucus. He always managed these matters ingeniously; a gesture, a step one way or another, a momentary tilting of the head, and the thing was done. Sometimes, when the action sent Caruso from the stage for a few minutes, and there was not time enough to go his dressing room, one of his valets would be standing in the wings with a glass of the precious salt and water.

In spite of every precaution to have the throat prepared for singing, such instances would arise. The tenor was faithful in adhering to a specific schedule before each engagement. He always rested for two hours before he went before the public; the rest consisted of playing solitaire, pasting stamps in an album or clippings in a scrap book. During these two hours Caruso would not speak above a whisper: and if his pantomime were not understood *a volo* (quickly) he would declare the person to be unintelligent, and "not good" for him. The cleansing of his throat (*lo strumento*, he called it) was accomplished with the aid of a French inhaler, into which he had placed some glycerine and Dobell solution. The steam from this Caruso would inhale for perhaps a quarter of an hour; then his throat would be *pulita* (clean). A few rapidly sung scales and arpeggios finished the preparations for the appearance. Caruso rarely used many different sets of exercises, at any time.

Invariably, he would reach a place of appointment in advance of the hour. He was never late in his life, for either a performance or a train; and news-stand venders, in the railway stations, found him a patron willing to purchase anything from magazines to chewing gum.

Scrupulous to be ready for any emergency, he was versatile enough to meet many of different sorts. Thus, in Mexico, he virtually directed the rehearsals of every representation. The stage manager was lacking in the quality of experience to which Caruso had been accustomed, so he took charge. In Havana, where neither "Marta" nor "L'Elisir d'Amore" had previously been given, it was the tenor who indicated what should be done. During a "Marta" representation in Mexico, Caruso's quick mind saved an important incident from falling flat. The soprano, Señorita Navarette, who had forgotten to bring with her a rose, prepared to sing *The Last Rose of Summer*. Noticing that she was without the necessary flower, Caruso whispered to her, "Take a rose from your hat and give it to me." The soprano did not hear. His cue having arrived, the tenor began to sing (instead of the words from the score) "Gi-i-ve m-e-ee the r-o-ose, t-a-ake o-o-ne fro-o-om yo-our h-a-at." Still Señorita Navarette did not seem to understand. Whereupon Caruso himself plucked a flower from the lady's hat, placed it in her hand, and soon after received it from her, as the action demanded.

It was this insistence for detail which was partly responsible for the tenor's rounded artistry; and who does not appreciate how completely he gave all he had to give. After the *Vesti la giubba* aria, in "Pagliacci", he always reached the wings in a state of collapse. Martino, Mario, or Punzo — sometimes Zirato — would be waiting to catch him as he came off, panting from his emotion. And it would require smelling salts, very often, to bring him

CARUSO AS CANIO IN "I PAGLIACCI"

back from the half-unconscious condition induced by his exertion. In other heroic operas, too, his exhaustion would require the aid of strong arms. Punzo was the one who could ease him most gently. Giulio Gatti-Casazza considered Caruso in a class quite his own.

"I have heard all the great tenors of my time, over and over again," he said. "Many of them were wonderful artists, with exceptional voices; and all sang, I remember, some marvelous performances. Yet not one, in my judgment, ever sang an entire rôle with the vocal or artistic consistency of Caruso; and certainly no other tenor I can call to mind remotely compares with him in having continued to sing — week after week, and season after season — with the same almost unvarying achievement of supremacy, almost never disappointing an audience through inability to appear.

"I first heard him sing in the autumn of 1898, at the Lirico Theater in Milan, as Marcello in Leoncavallo's 'La Bohème.' During the same season I had a second opportunity, when he appeared as Loris in Giordano's 'Fedora.' In that rôle he had a triumph so indisputable that his celebrity began. I was then general director of La Scala. I was unsuccessful in my effort to engage Caruso for the 1899–1900 season, because he had arranged to go to Petrograd; but we signed a contract for 1900–1901.

"His La Scala début, in Puccini's 'La Bohème', was not lucky; he was suffering from laryngitis. In such a condition he was indeed kind to have consented to sing at all, which he only did, at a personal sacrifice, to avert a postponement of the performance. He did not have the opportunity to show the public of La Scala his superior qualities; in subsequent representations he improved. But it was not until the first 'Le Maschere' of Mascagni, that he had a triumph . . . the more difficult to achieve, since the opera was a failure. That was what prompted me to revive 'L'Elisir d'Amore', in which Caruso had a success that remained a sensation in the annals of the Teatro Alla Scala.

"During the same season, in the quartet from 'Rigoletto', on the program of the concert given to commemorate the death of Giuseppe Verdi, he sang like an angel, moving his hearers to indescribable emotion. Later, he was severely criticised by the newspaper reviewers for his Faust in 'Mefistofele', in which Chaliapin also sang. I always felt that the criticism was unjust. He returned to La Scala the next season, for the performances of 'Germania' — the then new opera by Baron Franchetti — and his recognition was overwhelming.

"In his last years, Caruso had, for me, a voice darker and more voluminous than when I first heard it; a voice with a tendency to baritonal effects. However, I must say that his voice became, during that final period of his career, of more extended range and security. It was of such endurance and responsiveness that Caruso was enabled to sing some performances, under unfavorable health conditions, without causing the great majority of the public to notice that he was not in perfect physical form.

"Throughout his closing seasons at the Metropolitan, Caruso could, moreover, sing rôles of dramatic character — such as John of Leyden in 'Le Prophète', Alvaro in 'Forza del Destino', and Samson in 'Samson et Dalila' — rôles that in the days of his singing in Milan or Bologna (where I heard him in 1900, in 'Tosca' and 'Iris') he would not have dared attempt. He sang in New York those dramatic parts; yet he retained to the end his facility to permit him to keep in his répertoire such rôles as Lionel in 'Marta', Nemorino in 'L'Elisir', and the Duke in 'Rigoletto' . . . all of a purely lyric, almost light, character.

"He was a unique artist, with whom none other compared. I do not see how we can ever have such another."

V

After that December 3d appearance in "Samson" — the matter of his immediate vocal powers disposed of — Caruso might have settled into the confident calm of preceding Metropolitan years. Reassured as to the attitude of those critics who had so upset him, he had regained through his own accomplishment some steadying self-confidence. Had his health been better, and had he been less tortured by the mental anxieties caused by the Havana bomb explosion and the robbery at his Easthampton home, the remainder of that 1920–1921 season need not have brought the tenor any lessened distinction. But physically he was in a miserable state.

On the fourth of December, while driving in his automobile with Mrs. Caruso, he was seized with a chill. Changing their course, a visit was made at once to Doctor Philip Horowitz, Caruso's personal physician; and after examining and prescribing for his patient, Horowitz ordered him to go home and to bed.

Rest and quiet were seemingly helpful. Caruso suffered from an occasional pain in the left side, of which he complained; he coughed, and occasionally spat; but he declined to treat these matters seriously, and since for weeks his temper had been short, those of the household forebore to press upon him their belief that he should take a complete rest.

He went to the Metropolitan, the evening of December 8, to appear in his first "Pagliacci" of the season. There were no outward appearances that anything untoward was to happen: the preparations proceeded in the usual manner; the first act of the opera began, — then came the *Vesti la giubba*. Many of that audience which was present will recall the breaking of a high tone near the close of the aria and how Caruso subsequently tripped (inexactly reported in the newspapers as an accidental fall) on one of the steps leading to the mimic theater. The truth is that just as he gave that full-voiced high A — which demands after all that has gone before, a deal of physical strength to support it — Caruso felt an excruciating pain in his left side. It made him "sick all over" and he momentarily "saw black."

His tripping was deliberately done, in an attempt to divert the attention of the auditors from the interrupted high note. When he staggered through the curtains of the mimic theater, he literally fell into the arms of Zirato. And amidst his sobs he managed to gasp, "My voice . . . I thought . . . it was . . . gone."

Some minutes passed before the pain in his side had subsided enough to allow Caruso to move. He lay crumpled and moaning in the arms of his secretary surrounded by anxious-faced members of the company. Then, supported on both sides, he walked laboriously to his dressing room.

Zirato pleaded with Caruso to abandon the remainder of the performance; vain argument. Then, having been sent for, Doctor Horowitz arrived. He brushed aside the attending opera house physician, Doctor Marafioti, and directly announced that "it was nothing serious." Horowitz diagnosed the ailment as intercostal neuralgia; and, after strapping the singer's left side with adhesive plaster, gave his permission for Caruso to continue with the performance. Though suffering intense pain, the tenor went on. When the curtain fell, he was hurried to his dressing room, into his street garments, and then to his hotel.

Such was the will of the singer that he would not remain in bed; for the next morning he arose, though with swollen eyes and a yellow skin. Entreaties of Mrs. Caruso and Zirato that another physician be summoned were of no avail; they only enlisted from the patient a dogged refusal to consider anything he did not wish, — such as further medical attention. On that day he listened to a Miss Josephine Lucchese sing, and invited his friend Mrs. Shubart to dine with him and Mrs. Caruso. So the days passed, until Saturday evening, December 11, when he prepared to appear in "L'Elisir d'Amore" in the Brooklyn Academy of Music.

It was only a few minutes before the scheduled hour that the tenor, already costumed as Nemorino, began to cough; and looking at his handkerchief, discovered on it red stains. Alarmed, he went to the washstand, where efforts were made to check the hemorrhage. The following half-hour was one of deep anxiety for the little group of watchers; but in the theater an audience sat all unaware of the frantic efforts going on so near, that Caruso might sing to them.

Viviani had held the curtain ten minutes; the hemorrhage appeared to have been stopped. No sooner did the tenor begin to sing than the flow of blood recommenced. Doctor Horowitz, summoned at Mrs. Caruso's order, arrived during the first act; and he too joined those who stood in the wings, with fresh handkerchiefs which were passed, as they were needed, to the suffering artist on the stage. What he endured throughout that scene, the agitation of Mrs. Caruso who sat in the front row, and of others near enough to see evidences of Caruso's condition were unnerving to them all. Then the curtain came down, before some three thousand frightened people.

Back stage, assistant general manager Edward Ziegler, press representative William J. Guard, and others were adding their pleas to those of Mrs. Caruso that the tenor should consent to having the audience dismissed. He finally agreed; and Guard's announcement sent from the theater a serious-faced throng.

Giulio Gatti-Casazza and other friends rushed to the Vanderbilt Hotel as soon as they received the news. Doctor Horowitz declared the hemorrhage to have been due to the bursting of a vein at the base of the singer's tongue (an opinion not concurred in by other physicians who were later called into consultation). At two o'clock Sunday morning Caruso fell asleep.

He seemed better when he awoke the following morning, and although the hemorrhage appeared to have been checked, there were occasional evidences of very dark blood.

On Monday, being scheduled to sing a Metropolitan "La Forza del Destino" that night, Caruso tried his voice. It was apparently as clear as ever, and heedless of all opposition to sing, he did. What a reception his admirers gave him! In the final act he sang almost defiantly, as though to give out to the world — "Caruso is not ill, he will not be ill . . . his voice still holds." After the representation he dictated cablegrams, with a sort of suppressed elation, to friends in many parts of the world, assuring them the report of his throat having been ruptured was untrue.

Nevertheless, solemn days followed; days filled with efforts at cheerfulness, through which Caruso sought, by following a fairly regular routine, to allay the fears of those he loved. But neither his pride nor his stubborn refusal to admit to being ill, could conceal the fact that he really was. During later years he had eaten less heartily, his old-time huge appetite returning only fitfully. With his poor body struggling against the most serious sickness he had known, he took less and less food; finally he refused nourishment altogether. Will power kept him on his feet and going until December 21; then Nature could no longer sustain him. Seized again during the night by that agonizing pain in his side, he got out of bed and bending forward so he might ease his suffering by bearing some of his weight on his hands, he leaned part way out the window, for air. From time to time, at some fresh stab in his side, he would scream aloud. The morning found him haggard and drawn, yet — stubborn still. He was cast to sing that night in "L'Elisir"; he intended to sing, but — he said he thought Gatti should be informed that he wasn't feeling very well. Once more Mrs. Caruso summoned Doctor Horowitz; and again the physician said, after examining his patient, "It is nothing, just intercostal neuralgia." So he put fresh adhesive tape about the sensitive side and departed. At four o'clock that afternoon, after an entire day of severe suffering, Caruso gave up his thought of being able to sing that night. A few hours later the pain eased.

Twenty-four hours passed without recurrence of the former physical agony, although the next day after Horowitz's call — Thursday — Caruso was pale and weak. He had sung with his accompanist bits from "La Juive"; it seemed to encourage him, for when Mrs. Caruso and Zirato begged him to call in physicians for a consultation he became furious.

THIS CHECK IS IN PAYMENT OF ACCOUNT AS LISTED BELOW AND THE ENDORSEMENT THEREON CONSTITUTES A RECEIPT. PLEASE DETACH CHECK BEFORE DEPOSITING. WHEN BILLS ACCOMPANY CHECK, PLEASE RECEIPT THEM PROMPTLY AND RETURN TO COMPANY.

Dec 24 La Juive 3ᵐᵉ Or Dec 24   2500
1920   Less ½ Advance   225
                                       2275
8% US Int Rev.   200
                                       2075

E Caruso

VOUCHER OF CHECK RECEIVED FROM THE METROPOLITAN OPERA HOUSE, FOR CARUSO'S LAST PERFORMANCE, "LA JUIVE," DEC. 24, 1920

The "III" stands for the third performance of "La Juive" during the season, and "10 Recita." means the tenth Caruso performance of 1920. In May of each year the singer received a cash advance of $9000, which was divided into instalments of $225 for each appearance. This explains the "Less ½ Advance." The deduction worded "8% U. S. Int. Rev.," represents the sum left with the management for the United States Internal Revenue Tax.

TWILIGHT

Friday, December 23, dawned. Caruso rose at about eleven and within an hour was singing from "La Juive" in his studio. Both Gatti-Casazza and Horowitz were present. The former turned to the physician, and inquired anxiously, "What do you think?" to which Horowitz replied, "Don't you hear? there is nothing the matter with his voice." Addressing himself to the tenor Gatti said, "This is a matter for you alone. I don't want to make any suggestion. You have always decided about everything concerning your performances; you must do so now."

"Padrone," returned Caruso, "I will sing."

Preparations for Gloria's Christmas tree went on with only the indifferent assistance of the tenor. That was enough to indicate the gravity of his illness, for he had always a boyish eagerness to take part in such affairs. Mrs. Caruso would have kept him at home; if she could have had her way, there would have been physicians conferring on her husband's welfare. Instead she was helpless, and compelled to allow him to depart to sing — that Christmas Eve of 1920 — in the last performance in which he ever took part.

The climax came at one o'clock the next afternoon, when Caruso went to take his bath. His screams brought the entire household running, and writhing in pain, he was carried to a couch in his dressing room. No longer did Mrs. Caruso hesitate to act on her own initiative. She wanted other physicians; and directly Doctor Francis J. Murray, of the Hotel Vanderbilt, responded to the urgent summons.

He gave injections of codeine and morphine. Within a few hours Doctor Evan M. Evans was called. He seemed merely to glance at Caruso before pronouncing his opinion: "A very painful case of pleurisy." Gatti-Casazza and Ziegler reached the apartment at 4 o'clock; not long afterward a consultation was decided upon. On December 26, Doctors Samuel W. Lambert, Evan M. Evans, Antonio Stella, Francis J. Murray, and Philip Horowitz conferred. The diagnosis pronounced the ailment pleurisy: forty-eight hours afterwards broncho-pneumonia developed, and on December 29 half a gallon of liquid was taken from the pleural cavity with an aspirating needle. It was then that a consultation was held, at which the decision was reached to operate for empyema.

Doctor John F. Erdmann was the surgeon selected. On December 30 he operated; and for two days thereafter the tenor's life hung by a thread. Mrs. Caruso slept near by on a hospital bed; shifts of two nurses each were in constant attendance; cablegrams were sent to scores of people. And there was need; X-rays showed that Caruso's left lung had contracted.

But still more serious times lay just ahead. After having recovered sufficiently to receive personal visits from friends, the fever returned. A consultation took place on February 9; three days later a radical operation was performed by Doctor Erdmann, during which it was necessary to remove four inches of one rib. Caruso lapsed into unconsciousness, hovering between life and death.

The relapse of which the whole world knew at

the time came on February 14, and on the fifteenth he was thought to be dying. Only the best of medical and surgical attention, nursing, and the singer's own exceptional vitality carried him over a danger period which even members of his attending staff doubted he would survive. He swung, pendulum-like, gaining and losing; seven minor operations were necessary, the last being a blood transfusion (the donor being Everett Wilkinson, of Meriden, Connecticut) soon after Caruso's birthday, February 27.

The convalescence was attended by widespread rejoicing. The dread atmosphere of the sick room gave way to one optimistic; the news association and New York newspaper reporters, assigned day and night to watch the tenor and transmit his physicians' bulletins, filed out of Caruso's dining room, which had been their headquarters. The balmy May air carried fresh hope to the singer, and on the eighteenth the medical staff held its final consultation.

How the people exulted at seeing their favorite singer in those first automobile rides he took when he had grown strong enough. And what a reception they gave him at the opera house, when, with Mrs. Caruso, he got out of their car and walked slowly towards the entrance to the executive offices. He might be thin and haggard and pale; what did such things matter? Caruso was getting well!

And then — after the doctors had decided that a change of climate would be beneficial — passage was engaged for Italy. Caruso was going home; and the knowledge of it gave him a further push toward health.

CHAPTER TWELVE

THE END

THE journey was nearly finished. Caruso did not know; a gentle Providence may have spared him for those last days, spent mostly in Sorrento, so near to his own Naples. He gathered strength and weight fast, his appetite returned, and a bit of color crept into his cheeks. Indeed, photographs taken within a month after his arrival in Italy (June 10, 1921) showed him looking encouragingly well. It was extraordinary, this recovery; and what news to send abroad to the waiting thousands who continued to hang on anything that seemingly insured to them their singer! Friends who called to see the Carusos reported his progress: his humor was of the best; he was beginning to take daily strolls, to bargain good-naturedly with shopkeepers over the price of some small purchase. In brief, signs reminding one of the old Caruso cropped more and more to the surface.

There were less buoyant moments; that was to be expected. One may not pause literally before the gates of death without traversing, every step of the way, the long backward journey. But as June gave way to oncoming July, Mrs. Caruso grew more hopeful. This hopefulness increased one sunny afternoon, when a youth ventured to seek the tenor's

THE LAST PICTURE. TAKEN AT HOTEL VICTORIA, SORRENTO, ITALY, JULY, 1921

THE END

opinion as to his singing. The boy sang *M'appari* from "Marta", while Caruso listened with glistening eyes. He waited, quite motionless, until the air was finished; then he spoke.

"That is good, though you did not sing it in quite the right way. Let me show you how."

Mrs. Caruso relates how she sat as her husband began to sing. "I was not excited," she insists, "but, on the contrary, perfectly calm. What I heard caused me to grow cold through astonishment, for Enrico's voice was as golden, as liquid-like, and as pure as though he had never known a day's illness. He sang with the perfect ease with which he had always sung. Suddenly he ceased . . . and I realized that he had finished the song."

Each day brought renewed happiness to the tenor after that experience. His voice was his most precious possession; he had guarded it against assaults through his long career; and he felt then — possibly, when no one else was about, he may have tested its power — that the contracted left lung had become normal. He took up with a new zest the little pleasures of each day, and, with Mrs. Caruso and Baby Gloria, lived in a new and utterly happy world.

When his *padrone* (as he always called Gatti-Casazza) visited him at Sorrento on July 8, the tenor behaved like a much indulged child.

All appeared to be moving well until a few days later, when Caruso returned very fatigued from an over-long walk. His name-day, July 15, brought a return of the first pain in his side he had felt in months. Mrs. Caruso's apprehensiveness was fired anew; she sought in vain to cancel the dinner her husband had planned for a party of friends. None of the guests noticed, however, that their host was out of sorts. Suggestions that physicians be called were met with the same former objections. So long as no practitioner was about, Caruso was not ill; it was only when the doctors surrounded him that danger hovered. Such was his strange reasoning, and it was this attitude of mind which caused him to rebel against any proffers of medical aid.

He was not really strong enough to have attempted the trip to Capri and Pompeii, where he wished to visit the Shrine of Our Lady of Pompeii to pour out his thanks for his recovery. But he went, and laying his ten thousand *lire* offering before the sacred Image of the Virgin, the tenor wept in gratitude.

That effort taxed him greatly; how much may be gathered from his feeble resistance, on July 28, to the visit paid by the Bastianelli brothers (Giuseppe and Raffaele), famous Roman doctors, who had come at Mrs. Caruso's call. They discovered the existence of an abscess, and counseled that he go to Rome for an immediate operation. If only there might have been greater haste! Three days elapsed; three days of precious time which should not have been wasted. When, on the following Sunday, Mr. and Mrs. Caruso, Giovanni Caruso and the tenor's son, Rodolfo, departed for Naples, they could go no farther; the singer had grown desperately weak, and a stop had to be made at the Hotel Vesuve.

The indomitable spirit with which Caruso had

fought off the Grim Spectre was weakening. A physician came; then others, after a consultation had been advised.

Caruso was growing feebler; he clung to his wife's hand. Once he roused from unconsciousness to murmur, "Doro . . . Doro, don't let me die."

When the array of Italian physicians and surgeons finally prepared to operate, they agreed it was too late.

Through that Monday night, and on into Tuesday morning of August second, Enrico Caruso hovered. What a struggle he had undergone! What suffering had he not endured! But he was suffering no longer. He was at peace in his own land where he had longed to be. His mind was wandering, — to other places, perhaps, where in those golden days of the past he had sung to rapt audiences of the old and new worlds. And perhaps, in the labyrinths of his consciousness, he glimpsed again the odd boxes which run around La Scala, the stiff interior of Covent Garden, and all those other famous opera houses in which he had been a guiding light. Perhaps it was the red and gold auditorium of his own beloved Metropolitan that his fancy last saw, and that the smile of peace flickered at the imaginary parting sweep of its big yellow curtains.

APPENDICES

COMPILED BY BRUNO ZIRATO

APPENDICES

APPENDIX A

List of Decorations tendered to Enrico Caruso

Italy:
    Order of Chevalier, Commendatore and Grande Ufficiale of the Crown of Italy
France:
    Legion of Honor
    Palm of Academy
Belgium:
    Order of Leopold
Spain:
    Order of St. James of Compostella
England:
    Order of Michael
    Order of British Victoria
Germany:
    Order of Red Eagle of Prussia
    Order of Crown Eagle of Prussia

APPENDIX B

List of Operas in the Répertoire of Enrico Caruso

"Aïda"
"Adriana de Lecouvreur"
"Africana"
"Amore dei Tre Re"
"Armide"
"Ballo in Maschera"
"La Bohème" (Puccini)
"La Bohème" (Leoncavallo)
"Carmen"
"Cavalleria Rusticana"
"Don Giovanni"
"Elisir d'amore"
"Fanciulla del West"
"Faust"
"La Favorita"
"Fedora"
"La Forza del Destino"
"Germania"
"La Gioconda"
"La Juive"
"Julien"
"Iris"
"Lodoletta"
"Lucrezia Borgia"
"Lucia di Lammermoor"
"Madama Butterfly"
"Manon"
"Manon Lescaut"
"Marta"
"Mefistofele"
"Pagliacci"
"Pecheurs de Perles"
"Le Prophète"
"I Puritani"
"Rigoletto"
"Regina di Saba"
"Saffo"
"Samson et Dalila"
"La Sonnambula"
"Tosca"
"La Traviata"
"Il Trovatore"
"Gli Ugonotti"

APPENDIX C

LIST OF THE OPERAS SUNG BY ENRICO CARUSO ONLY A FEW TIMES OR SIMPLY STUDIED AND NEVER PERFORMED

"Amico Francesco," by Morelli
"Arlesiana," by Cilea
"A San Francisco," by Carlo Sebastiani
"Celeste," by Marengo
"Camoens," by Pietro Musoni
"Dramma in Vendemmia," by Vincenzo Fornari
"Romeo e Giulietta," by Bellini
"Hedda," by Ferd. Leborne
"Don Pasquale," by Donizetti
"Flauto Magico," by Mozart
"Fra Diavolo," by Auber
"Jupanki," by Berutti
"Lohengrin," by Wagner
"Mariedda," by Gianni Bucceri
"Malia," by F. P. Frontini
"Profeta Velato," by Daniele Napolitano
"Navarraise," by Massenet
"Voto," by Giordano
"Maria di Rohan," by Donizetti
"Le Maschere," by Mascagni
"Otello," by Verdi
"Guglielmo Tell," by Rossini
"Il Guarany," by Gomes
"Il Duca d'Alba," by Donizetti

APPENDIX D

List of all Appearances from 1894 to 1921 with Dates of First Performance, City, House, and total of Performances given, and Different Impresarios and Managers.

Date of First Performance	City	House	Opera or Concert	Total Performances Given	Remarks
1894 November 16 and 18	Napoli	Nuovo	L'Amico Francesco	2	
1895 April	Caserta	Cimarosa	Cavalleria Faust Camoens		Impresa of Carlo Ferrara
June	Cotrone	Cathedral	High Mass		
June	Napoli	Bellini	Faust		Benefit performance
July	Napoli	Bellini	Rigoletto		
August	Cairo	Esbekieh Gardens	Cavalleria Rigoletto La Gioconda Manon Lescaut		Impresa of Enrico Santini
September					
October	Napoli	Bellini	Rigoletto Faust	1 1	Impresa of Gaetano Scognamiglio
November 29	Napoli	Mercadante (gia' Fondo)	Traviata	15	Double performances occurred on: December 15: Matinée: Romeo e Giulietta; Evening: Traviata. December 26: Matinée: Rigoletto; Evening: Romeo e Giulietta. December 27: Matinée: Traviata; Evening: Rigoletto. December 29: Matinée: Rigoletto; Evening: Traviata. January 1: Matinée: Traviata; Evening: Rigoletto
December 7	Napoli	Mercadante (gia' Fondo)	Romeo e Giulietta	15	
December 25	Napoli	Mercadante (gia' Fondo)	Rigoletto	10	
1896 January 11	Napoli	Mercadante (gia' Fondo)	Faust	10	

APPENDICES

Date of First Performance	City	House	Opera or Concert	Total Performances Given	Remarks
1896 February 18	Napoli	Mercadante (gia' Fondo)			Farewell appearance with Rigoletto
February	Caserta	Cimarosa	Faust		Opera hissed and artists dismissed after II act
April	Napoli	Bellini	Traviata Rigoletto Faust Mariedda		Impresa of Giulio Staffelli
May	Trapani	Comunale	Lucia		Impresa of Cavallaro
June	Marsala		Rigoletto		
First Saturday and Sunday of June	Salerno	Verdi	Rigoletto	2	To celebrate Independence Day (Festa dello Statuto)
August	Salerno	Comunale	Puritani Cavalleria		Impresa of Visciani
September					
October 15	Salerno	Comunale	Traviata Carmen Favorita Pagliacci A San Francisco	20 in all	Impresa of Giuseppe Grassi
November 15					
December	Napoli	Bellini	Gioconda Ugonotti		
1897 January	Napoli	Mercadante	Gioconda Traviata Dramma in Vendemmia		Impresa of A. Landi and Baron Mascia
February					
March 1 to May 4	Salerno	Comunale	Gioconda Manon Lescaut Traviata Profeta Velato	50 in all	Impresa of Giuseppe Grassi
May 15 to June 15	Palermo	Massimo	Gioconda		Impresa of V. Florio and Di Giorgi. Inauguration of the Massimo
July	Livorno	Goldoni	Traviata La Bohème		Impresa of Arturo Lisciarelli
August					

ENRICO CARUSO

Date of First Performance	City	House	Opera or Concert	Total Performances Given	Remarks
1897 September	Fiume	Verdi	La Bohème		
November 20	Milano	Lirico Internazionale	La Navarrese		Impresa of Edoardo Sonzogno
November 27	Milano	Lirico Internazionale	Arlesiana		World première
1898 January 20	Genova	Carlo Felice	Bohème (L)	13	Impresa of Giovanni Massa
February 3	Genova	Carlo Felice	Pescatori di Perle	8	
June 2 to June 26	Trento	Sociale	Pagliacci Saffo		
July and August	Livorno	Politeama Livornese	Pagliacci		Impresa of Arturo Lisciarelli
October 22	Milano	Lirico	Arlesiana	4	Impresa of Edoardo Sonzogno
November 8	Milano	Lirico	Bohème (L)	7	
November 17	Milano	Lirico	Fedora	10	World première
December	Milano	Lirico	Saffo	6	
December 11					Farewell appearance with Fedora
December to 1899 January	Petrograd	Grand Théâtre du Conservatoire	La Bohème Pagliacci Maria di Rohan Cavalleria Traviata		Impresa of Carlo Guidi
March 1 to 28	Milano	Lirico	Fedora	8	Impresa of Edoardo Sonzogno
May 14	Buenos Aires	La Opera	Fedora	3	Impresa of Amelia Ferrari
May 24	Buenos Aires	La Opera	Traviata	2	
June 4	Buenos Aires	La Opera	Saffo	2	
June 8	Buenos Aires	La Opera	Gioconda	1	
June 22	Buenos Aires	La Opera	Iris	7	

APPENDICES 401

Date of First Performance	City	House	Opera or Concert	Total Performances Given	Remarks
1899 July 4	Buenos Aires	La Opera	Regina di Saba	6	
July 25	Buenos Aires	La Opera	Jupanki	3	
August 8	Buenos Aires	La Opera	Cavalleria and I and II acts from Iris		Farewell appearance
August 10	Buenos Aires	La Opera	Cavalleria		Extra: for benefit victims Black River flood
November 4	Roma	Costanzi	Iris	9	Impresa of Eredi Costanzi and Vincenzo Morichini
November 11	Roma	Costanzi	Gioconda	3	
November 22	Roma	Costanzi	Mefistofele	8	
December 15					Farewell appearance with Iris
December to 1900 February	Petrograd	Grand Théâtre du Conservatoire	Aïda Ballo in Maschera Mefistofele		Impresa of Carlo Guidi
March	Moscow	Grand Théâtre	Faust Aïda Mefistofele Ballo in Maschera		Impresa of Carlo Guidi
May 10	Buenos Aires	La Opera	Mefistofele	4	Impresa of Madame Ferrari
May 17	Buenos Aires	La Opera	Iris	6	
June 9	Buenos Aires	La Opera	Regina di Saba	5	
June 23	Buenos Aires	La Opera	La Bohème	5	
July 12	Buenos Aires	La Opera	Cavalleria	1	
July 28	Buenos Aires	La Opera	Manon	1	
August 5	Buenos Aires	La Opera			Farewell appearance with La Bohème
August 9	Buenos Aires	Catholic Cathedral	Sacred Hymns		Commemoration of King Humbert of Italy

Date of First Performance	City	House	Opera or Concert	Total Performances Given	Remarks
1900 August 12	Buenos Aires	Progress Club	Concert		Benefit organized by Dames of Charity
August 16 to September 10	Montevideo	Solis	Iris La Bohème Cavalleria Manon		
October 23 to November 11	Treviso	Sociale	Tosca	12	Impresa of E. Corti
November 15 to December 15	Bologna	Comunale	Tosca Iris		
December 26	Milano	Alla Scala	La Bohème	10	Management of G. Gatti-Casazza
1901 January 17	Milano	Alla Scala	Le Maschere	3	World première
February 1	Milano	Alla Scala	Quartet from Rigoletto		Commemoration of Giuseppe Verdi
February 17	Milano	Alla Scala	Elisir d'amore	12	Revival
March 16	Milano	Alla Scala	Mefistofele	9	
May 18	Buenos Aires	La Opera	Tosca	10	Impresa of Nardi, Bonetti and Company
June 1	Buenos Aires	La Opera	Regina di Saba	2	
June 9	Buenos Aires	La Opera	Rigoletto	4	
June 23	Buenos Aires	La Opera	Elisir d'amore	2	
July 7	Buenos Aires	La Opera	Lohengrin	3	
July 8	Buenos Aires	La Opera	Iris	3	
July 27	Buenos Aires	La Opera	Traviata	4	
July 29	Buenos Aires	La Opera	Rossini's Stabat Mater		Commemoration of King Humbert of Italy
August 17	Buenos Aires	La Opera			Farewell appearance with Tosca

APPENDICES 403

Date of First Performance	City	House	Opera or Concert	Total Performances Given	Remarks
1901 November	Bologna	Comunale	Rigoletto		
December 14 and 16	Trieste	Politeama Rossetti	Elisir d'amore	2	Benefit Italian Benevolent Association
December 30	Napoli	San Carlo	Elisir d'amore	5	Impresa of R. de Sanna
1902 January 13	Napoli	San Carlo	Manon	5	
January 21	Napoli	San Carlo			Last appearance with Manon
February 1	Monte Carlo	Le Casino	La Bohème		Management of Raoul Gunsbourg
February 16	Monte Carlo	Le Casino	Rigoletto		
March 11	Milano	Alla Scala	Germania	14	World première
May 14	London	Covent Garden	Rigoletto	5	Management of H. Higgins
May 24	London	Covent Garden	La Bohème	4	
June 4	London	Covent Garden	Lucia	3	
June 6	London	Covent Garden	Aïda	4	
June 14	London	Covent Garden	Elisir d'amore	2	
June 28	London	Covent Garden	Cavalleria	2	
July 4	London	Covent Garden	Traviata	2	
July 19	London	Covent Garden	Don Giovanni	2	
July 28	London	Covent Garden			Farewell appearance with Rigoletto
November 6	Milano	Lirico	Adriana de Lecouvreur	6	World première
December 10 and 11	Trieste	Politeama Rossetti	Rigoletto	2	Benefit Italian Benevolent Association
December 26	Roma	Costanzi	Rigoletto	5	Impresa of Eredi Costanzi and Vincenzo Morichini
1903 January 10	Roma	Costanzi	Mefistofele	5	
January 20	Roma	Costanzi	Manon Lescaut	6	
January 31	Roma	Costanzi	Aïda	4	

Date of First Performance	City	House	Opera or Concert	Total Performances Given	Remarks
1903 February 8	Roma	Costanzi			Farewell appearance with Manon Lescaut
February 14	Lisbon	San Carlos	Fedora	1	Impresa of Jose' Pacini
February 20	Lisbon	San Carlos	Aïda	1	
February 27	Lisbon	San Carlos	Tosca	1	
March 4	Lisbon	San Carlos	Adriana de Lecouvreur	1	
March 10	Lisbon	San Carlos	Lucrezia Borgia	1	
March 19	Lisbon	San Carlos	Rigoletto	1	
March and April	Monte Carlo	Casino	Tosca	5	
May 19	Buenos Aires	La Opera	Tosca	2	Impresa of Camillo Bonetti
May 21	Buenos Aires	La Opera	Germania	3	
June 4	Buenos Aires	La Opera	Elisir d'amore	3	
June 18	Buenos Aires	La Opera	Iris	4	
June 26	Buenos Aires	La Opera	Mefistofele	1	
July 7	Buenos Aires	La Opera	Adriana de Lecouvreur	3	
July 25	Buenos Aires	La Opera	Manon Lescaut	3	
August 9	Buenos Aires	La Opera			Farewell appearance with Manon Lescaut
August	Montevideo	Solis	Mefistofele Iris Tosca Manon Lescaut		Impresa of Camillo Bonetti
August	Rio de Janeiro	Pedro II	Rigoletto Tosca Iris Manon Lescaut	2 2 2 2	

APPENDICES

Date of First Performance	City	House	Opera or Concert	Total Performances Given	Remarks
1903 November 23	New York	Metropolitan Opera House	Rigoletto	4	Management of Heinrich Conried
November 30	New York	Metropolitan	Aïda	4	
December 2	New York	Metropolitan	Tosca	3	
December 5	New York	Metropolitan	La Bohème	2	
December 9	New York	Metropolitan	Pagliacci	4	
December 23	New York	Metropolitan	Traviata	1	
December 29	Philadelphia	Academy of Music	Rigoletto		
1904 January 8	New York	Metropolitan	Lucia	3	
January 12	Philadelphia	Academy of Music	Pagliacci		
January 14	New York	Home of Mrs. W. P. Whitney	Musicale		
January 19	Philadelphia	Academy of Music	Tosca		
January 21	New York	Home of Mrs. Orme Wilson	Musicale		
January 23	New York	Metropolitan	Elisir d'amore	4	
February 2	Philadelphia	Academy of Music	Aïda		
February 10	New York	Metropolitan			Farewell appearance with Lucia
March	Monte Carlo	Casino	Aïda		Impresa of R. Gunsbourg
April 20 and 23	Barcelona	Liceo	Rigoletto	2	Impresa of Doctor Alberto Bernis
April 27	Paris	Sarah Bernhardt	Rigoletto		Benefit Russian Train Hospital

Date of First Performance	City	House	Opera or Concert	Total Performances Given	Remarks
1904 May 4	Prague	Landes	Rigoletto		Impresa of Angelo Neumann
May 6	Prague	Landes	Elisir d'amore		
May 8	Dresden	Opern Haus	Rigoletto		Impresa of Angelo Neumann
May 17	London	Covent Garden	Rigoletto	4	Impresa of H. Higgins
May 19	London	Covent Garden	Pagliacci	5	
May 28	London	Covent Garden	La Bohème	6	
June 13	London	Covent Garden	Aïda	4	
June 15	London	Covent Garden	Traviata	3	
June 29	London	Covent Garden	Ballo in Maschera	4	
July 25	London	Covent Garden			Farewell appearance with Traviata
October 5	Berlin	Des Westens	Rigoletto		
October 7	Berlin	Des Westens	Traviata		
October 17	London	Covent Garden	Manon Lescaut	3	With San Carlo Opera Company of Naples. Impresa of R. de Sanna
October 21	London	Covent Garden	Carmen	3	
October 27	London	Covent Garden	La Bohème	2	
November 2	London	Covent Garden	Pagliacci	1	
November 3	London	Covent Garden			Farewell appearance with Manon Lescaut
November 21	New York	Metropolitan	Aïda	4	Management of Heinrich Conried
November 23	New York	Metropolitan	Lucia	2	
November 26	New York	Metropolitan	Traviata	3	
November 28	New York	Metropolitan	Gioconda	4	

APPENDICES 407

Date of First Performance	City	House	Opera or Concert	Total Performances Given	Remarks
1904 December 5	New York	Metropolitan	Lucrezia Borgia	1	
December 13	Philadelphia	Academy of Music	Aïda		
December 16	New York	Metropolitan	La Bohème	2	
December 21	New York	Metropolitan	Rigoletto	2	
December 24	New York	Metropolitan	Elisir d'amore	1	
December 26	New York	Metropolitan	Pagliacci	3	
December 27	Philadelphia	Academy of Music	Pagliacci		
1905 January 10	Philadelphia	Academy of Music	Lucia		
January 12	New York	Home of Mr. J. M. Smith	Musicale		
January 16	New York	Metropolitan	Tosca	2	
January 23	New York	Waldorf Astoria Hotel	Concert		Mr. Bagby Morning Musicale
January 24	Philadelphia	Academy of Music	La Bohème		
January 27	New York	Metropolitan	Ballo in Maschera	2	
February 3	New York	Metropolitan	Les Huguenots	4	
February 21	New York	Metropolitan	Pagliacci		Benefit Italian Hospital
February 28	Philadelphia	Academy of Music	Gioconda		
March 3	New York	Metropolitan			Farewell appearance with Act IV from Gioconda and Act I from Pagliacci
March 6	Boston	Boston Theater	Lucia		
March 8	Boston	Boston Theater	Pagliacci		
March 10	Boston	Boston Theater	Gioconda		

Date of First Performance	City	House	Opera or Concert	Total Performances Given	Remarks
1905 March 13	Pittsburgh	Nixon Theater	Lucia		
March 16	Pittsburgh	Nixon Theater	Gioconda		
March 18	Cincinnati	Music Hall	Gioconda		
March 20	Chicago	Auditorium	Lucia		
March 22	Chicago	Auditorium	Pagliacci		
March 24	Chicago	Auditorium	Gioconda		
March 28	Minneapolis	Auditorium	Pagliacci		
March 30	Omaha	Auditorium	Lucia		
April 1	Kansas City	Convention Hall	Pagliacci		
April 6	San Francisco	Grand Opera House	Rigoletto		
April 8	San Francisco	Grand Opera House	Pagliacci	2	
April 10	San Francisco	Grand Opera House	Lucia		
April 12 and 15	San Francisco	Grand Opera House	Gioconda	2	
April 18	Los Angeles	Auditorium	Lucia		
April 26	New York	Waldorf Astoria Hotel	Concert		Benefit arranged by Miss Leary
May 13 to May 20	Paris	Sarah Bernhardt	Fedora	6	First time in France. Management of Edoardo Sonzogno and Gabriel Astruc
May 22	London	Covent Garden	La Bohème	6	
May 26	London	Covent Garden	Rigoletto	3	

APPENDICES

Date of First Performance	City	House	Opera or Concert	Total Performances Given	Remarks
1905 June 3	London	Covent Garden	Ugonotti	3	
June 8	London	Buckingham Palace	Act III from La Bohème Act IV from Ugonotti		Before the King and Queen of England and King of Spain
June 10	London	Covent Garden	Aïda	2	
June 19	London	Covent Garden	Ballo in Maschera	4	
July 1	London	Covent Garden	Don Giovanni	2	
July 10	London	Covent Garden	Madama Butterfly	4	First time in England
July 25	London	Covent Garden			Farewell appearance with La Bohème
July 26	London	Savoy Hotel	Songs		Dinner offered by G. H. Kessler
August 3	Ostende	Royal	Rigoletto		Inauguration of the Theater
August	Ostende	Kursaal	Series of concerts	10	Management of Georges Marquet
November 20	New York	Metropolitan	Gioconda	3	Management of Heinrich Conried
November 24	New York	Metropolitan	Rigoletto	4	
November 29	New York	Metropolitan	Favorita	4	
December 5	Philadelphia	Academy of Music	Favorita		
December 9	New York	Metropolitan	Elisir d'amore	2	
December 15	New York	Metropolitan	Sonnambula	2	
December 18	New York	Metropolitan	La Bohème	4	
December 26	Philadelphia	Academy of Music	Rigoletto		
1906 January 3	New York	Metropolitan	Faust	4	
January 8	New York	Metropolitan	Tosca	1	

Date of First Performance	City	House	Opera or Concert	Total Performances Given	Remarks
1906 January 15	New York	Metropolitan	Aïda	3	
January 18	New York	Home of Mr. J. H. Smith	Musicale		
January 20	New York	Metropolitan	Lucia	3	
January 22	New York	Waldorf Astoria	Concert		Mr. Bagby Musicale
January 23	Philadelphia	Academy of Music	La Bohème		
January 24	Washington	Home of Mrs. Perry Belmont	Musicale		
January 31	New York	Metropolitan	Pagliacci	3	
February 9	New York	Metropolitan	Marta	4	
February 12	New York	Metropolitan	Traviata	1	
February 13	Philadelphia	Academy of Music	Aïda		
February 20	Philadelphia	Academy of Music	Carmen		
February 27	New York	Home of Mrs. Orme Wilson	Musicale		
March 1	Philadelphia	Academy of Music	Faust		
March 5	New York	Metropolitan	Carmen	2	
March 16	New York	Metropolitan			Farewell appearance with Gioconda
March 17	New York	Waldorf Astoria	Concert		Benefit Italian Immigrants
March 19	Baltimore	Lyric	Marta		
March 21	Baltimore	Lyric	Faust		
March 23	Washington	New National	Lucia		

APPENDICES 411

Date of First Performance	City	House	Opera or Concert	Total Performances Given	Remarks
1906 March 24	Washington	New National	Pagliacci		
March 27	Pittsburgh	Nixon	Carmen		
March 29	Pittsburgh	Nixon	La Bohème		
March 30	Pittsburgh	Nixon	Faust		
April 3	Chicago	Auditorium	Faust		
April 5	Chicago	Auditorium	Carmen		
April 7	Chicago	Auditorium	Marta		
April 9	St. Louis	Olympic	Marta		
April 11	St. Louis	Olympic	Faust		
April 12	Kansas City	Convention Hall	Marta		
April 17	San Francisco	Grand Opera House	Carmen		
April 18	San Francisco				Destruction of San Francisco by earthquake and fire. Company disbanded
May 15	London	Covent Garden	Rigoletto	4	
May 17	London	Covent Garden	La Bohème	9	
May 24	London	Covent Garden	Pagliacci	3	
May 26	London	Covent Garden	Madama Butterfly	5	
May 28	London		Concert		Benefit Belgian Charities
June 9	London	Covent Garden	Tosca	2	
June 25	London	Covent Garden	Aïda	2	
July 7	London	Covent Garden	Traviata	2	

Date of First Performance	City	House	Opera or Concert	Total Performances Given	Remarks
1906 July 17	London	Covent Garden	Don Giovanni	2	
July 26	London	Covent Garden			Farewell appearance with La Bohème
August 4	Ostende	Kursaal	Series of Concerts	10	
October 2	Wien	Hof Oper	Rigoletto		
October 6	Berlin	Des Westens	Carmen		
October 25	Paris	Trocadero	Concert		Benefit arranged by C. Coquelin
November 28	New York	Metropolitan	La Bohème	5	Management of Heinrich Conried
December 1	New York	Metropolitan	Traviata	2	
December 3	New York	Metropolitan	Marta	2	
December 5	New York	Metropolitan	Fedora	4	First time in America
December 12	New York	Metropolitan	Lucia	1	
December 21	New York	Metropolitan	Aïda	5	
December 27	Philadelphia	Academy of Music	Fedora		
1907 January 2	New York	Metropolitan	Tosca	4	
January 11	New York	Metropolitan	L'Africana	2	
January 15	Philadelphia	Academy of Music	Marta		
January 16	New York	Metropolitan	Pagliacci	2	
January 18	New York	Metropolitan	Manon Lescaut	3	
February 7	Philadelphia	Academy of Music	Aïda		
February 11	New York	Metropolitan	Madama Butterfly	4	
February 14	Philadelphia	Academy of Music	Madama Butterfly		
February 21	Philadelphia	Academy of Music	Manon Lescaut		

APPENDICES

Date of First Performance	City	House	Opera or Concert	Total Performances Given	Remarks
1907 February 27	New York	Metropolitan	Rigoletto	2	
March 5	Philadelphia	Academy of Music	Pagliacci		
March 7	Philadelphia	Academy of Music	La Bohème		
March 23 matinée	New York	Metropolitan			Farewell appearance with Tosca
March 25	Baltimore	Lyric	La Bohème		With Metropolitan Opera Company
March 26	Baltimore	Lyric	Pagliacci		
March 28	Washington	Belasco	Madama Butterfly		
March 30	Washington	Belasco	Aïda		
April 2	Boston	Boston Theatre	Tosca		
April 4	Boston	Boston Theatre	Marta		
April 6	Boston	Boston Theatre	Aïda		
April 8	Chicago	Auditorium	L'Africana		
April 10	Chicago	Auditorium	Aïda		
April 12	Chicago	Auditorium	La Bohème		
April 13	Chicago	Auditorium	Pagliacci		
April 15	Cincinnati	Music Hall	Aïda		
April 17	St. Louis	Odeon	Aïda		
April 19	St. Louis	Odeon	La Bohème		
April 20	Kansas City	Convention Hall	La Bohème		
April 22	Omaha	Auditorium	La Bohème		
April 24	St. Paul	Auditorium	La Bohème		

Date of First Performance	City	House	Opera or Concert	Total Performances Given	Remarks
1907 April 26	Minneapolis	Auditorium	Aïda		
April 27	Milwaukee	Alhambra	Pagliacci		
May 15	London	Covent Garden	La Bohème	8	
May 17	London	Covent Garden	Madama Butterfly	4	
May 18	Paris	Trocadero	Concert		Benefit Belgian Charities
May 25	London	Covent Garden	Traviata	5	
May 29	London	Covent Garden	Aïda	3	
June 6	London	Covent Garden	Carmen	2	
June 13	London	Covent Garden	Tosca	3	
June 28	London	Covent Garden	Ballo in Maschera	1	
July 3	London	Covent Garden	Fedora	2	
July 18	London		Concert		Benefit arranged by the Italian Embassy
July 20	London	Covent Garden	Andrea Chenier	2	
July 26	London	Covent Garden	Pagliacci	1	
July 30	London	Covent Garden			Farewell appearance with La Bohème
October 2	Budapest	Royal Opera House	Aïda		
October 4	Wien	Stadttheater	Aïda	2	
October 6	Wien	Stadttheater	La Bohème		
October 11	Wien	Stadttheater	Rigoletto		
October 13	Leipzig	Stadttheater	Aïda		
October 16	Hamburg	Stadttheater	Aïda	2	

APPENDICES

Date of First Performance	City	House	Opera or Concert	Total Performances Given	Remarks
1907 October 18	Hamburg	Stadttheater	Rigoletto		
October 20	Hamburg	Stadttheater	Pagliacci		
October 23	Berlin	Staatsoper	Rigoletto		
October 25	Berlin	Staatsoper	Aïda	2	
October 29	Berlin	Staatsoper	Pagliacci		
October 31	Frankfurt a/M	Opernhaus	Pagliacci		
November 2	Frankfurt a/M	Opernhaus	Rigoletto		
November 18	New York	Metropolitan	Adriana de Lecouvreur	2	First time in America
November 21	New York	Metropolitan	Aïda	6	Management of Heinrich Conried
November 23	New York	Metropolitan	La Bohème	2	
December 6	New York	Metropolitan	Iris	5	Revival
December 14	New York	Metropolitan	Madama Butterfly	5	
December 17	Philadelphia	Academy of Music	Madama Butterfly		
December 19	New York	Metropolitan	Fedora	3	
December 21	New York	Metropolitan	Tosca	5	
1908 January 6	New York	Metropolitan	Faust	5	
January 13	New York	Waldorf Astoria	Concert		Mr. Bagby Musicale
January 14	Philadelphia	Academy of Music	Adriana		
January 25	New York	Metropolitan	Manon Lescaut	4	
February 4	Philadelphia	Academy of Music	Iris		

Date of First Performance	City	House	Opera or Concert	Total Performances Given	Remarks
1908 February 6	New York	Metropolitan	Pagliacci	3	
February 26	New York	Metropolitan	Trovatore	6	
March 3	Philadelphia	Academy of Music	Trovatore		
March 17	Philadelphia	Academy of Music	Aïda		
March 31	Philadelphia	Academy of Music	Tosca		
April 3	New York	Waldorf Astoria	Concert		Benefit arranged by Mrs. Chas. Steele
April 4	New York	Metropolitan			Farewell appearance with Trovatore
April 6	Boston	Boston Theater	Iris		
April 8	Boston	Boston Theater	Trovatore		
April 10	Boston	Boston Theater	Manon Lescaut		
April 13	Baltimore	Lyric	Manon Lescaut		
April 15	Baltimore	Lyric	Trovatore		
April 18	Washington	New National	Pagliacci		
April 21	Chicago	Auditorium	Trovatore		
April 23	Chicago	Auditorium	Pagliacci		
April 25	Chicago	Auditorium	Iris		
April 27	Pittsburgh	Nixon	Faust		
April 29	Pittsburgh	Nixon	Trovatore		
May 1	Columbus	Memorial Hall	Concert		Management of Wolfsohn Musical Bureau
May 4	Toronto	Massey Music Hall	Concert		
May 6	Detroit	Light Guard Armory	Concert		

APPENDICES 417

Date of First Performance	City	House	Opera or Concert	Total Performances Given	Remarks
1908 May 8	Buffalo	Convention Hall	Concert		
May 11	Cleveland	Hippodrome	Concert		
May 13	Rochester	Convention Hall	Concert		
May 18	Montreal	Arena	Concert		
May 30	London	Albert Hall	Songs		Benefit under patronage of H. M. the King
June 11	Paris	Academie National de Musique	Rigoletto		Benefit Societé des Auteurs
October 1	Wiesbaden	Staatsoper	Rigoletto		
October 3	Frankfurt a/M	Opernhaus	La Bohème		
October 7	Frankfurt a/M	Opernhaus	Pagliacci		
October 11	Bremen	Stadttheater	Pagliacci		
October 13	Hamburg	Stadttheater	Pagliacci		
October 15	Hamburg	Stadttheater	La Bohème		
October 17	Leipzig	Stadttheater	Rigoletto		
October 20	Berlin	Staatsoper	Pagliacci		
October 22	Berlin	Staatsoper	La Bohème		
October 24	Berlin	Staatsoper	Aïda		
November 14	Brooklyn	Academy of Music	Faust		
November 16	New York	Metropolitan	Aïda	7	Management of Giulio Gatti-Casazza and A. Dippel
November 17	Philadelphia	Academy of Music	La Bohème		

Date of First Performance	City	House	Opera or Concert	Total Performances Given	Remarks
1908 November 19	New York	Metropolitan	Madama Butterfly	1	
November 20	New York	Metropolitan	Traviata	4	
November 21	New York	Metropolitan	Tosca	2	
November 24	Philadelphia	Academy of Music	Faust		
December 1	Philadelphia	Academy of Music	Aïda		
December 3	New York	Metropolitan	Carmen	3	
December 5	New York	Metropolitan	Faust	3	
December 7	New York	Metropolitan	Rigoletto	1	
December 17	New York	Metropolitan	Cavalleria	3	
December 26	New York	Metropolitan	Pagliacci	2	
December 29	Philadelphia	Academy of Music	Madama Butterfly		
1909 January 4	New York	Metropolitan	Trovatore	1	
January 12	Philadelphia	Academy of Music	Carmen		
January 14	Brooklyn	Academy of Music	Carmen		
January 18	New York	Waldorf Astoria	Concert		Mr. Bagby Musicale
January 19	Philadelphia	Academy of Music	Cavalleria		
January 20	Baltimore	Lyric	Madama Butterfly		
January 28	Philadelphia	Academy of Music	Trovatore		
February 3	New York	Metropolitan	Manon	3	Revival
February 5	New York	Home of Mrs. George Gould	Musicale		

APPENDICES 419

Date of First Performance	City	House	Opera or Concert	Total Performances Given	Remarks
1909 March 2	Philadelphia	Academy of Music	Pagliacci		
March 8	Baltimore	Lyric	Pagliacci		
April 7	New York	Metropolitan			Farewell appearance with Aïda. 21 performances lost through illness
August 20	Dublin	Royal Theater	Concert		Management of Thomas Quinlan
August 25	Plymouth	Guild Hall	Concert		
August 29	Blackpool	Winter Garden	Concert		
September 3	Glasgow	St. Andrew's Hall	Concert		
September 7	Edinburgh	McEvan Hall	Concert		
September 10	Newcastle	Town Hall	Concert		
September 13	Manchester	Free Trade Hall	Concert		
September 15	Belfast	Ulster Hall	Concert		
September 18	London	Albert Hall	Concert		
September 20	Liverpool	Philharmonic Hall	Concert		
September 28	Frankfurt a/M	Opernhaus	Tosca		
October 1	Frankfurt a/M	Opernhaus	Carmen		
October 3	Frankfurt a/M	Opernhaus	Pagliacci		
October 7	Nürnberg	Stadttheater	Rigoletto		

Date of First Performance	City	House	Opera or Concert	Total Performances Given	Remarks
1909 October 11	Hamburg	Stadttheater	Lucia		
October 13	Hamburg	Stadttheater	Tosca		
October 15	Hamburg	Stadttheater	Carmen		
October 19	Berlin	Staatsoper	Carmen		
October 21	Berlin	Staatsoper	La Bohème		
October 23	Berlin	Staatsoper	Pagliacci		
October 25	Bremen	Stadttheater	Carmen		
November 9	Philadelphia	Academy of Music	Aïda		
November 15	New York	Metropolitan	Gioconda	6	Management of G. Gatti-Casazza
November 18	New York	Metropolitan	Traviata	2	
November 22	Brooklyn	Academy of Music	Madama Butterfly		
November 24	New York	Metropolitan	Pagliacci	5	
November 30	Philadelphia	Academy of Music	Gioconda		
December 3	New York	Metropolitan	Aïda	4	
December 11	New York	Metropolitan	Tosca	1	
December 17	Baltimore	Lyric	Pagliacci		
December 25	New York	Metropolitan	Faust	1	
December 28	Philadelphia	Academy of Music	Pagliacci		
1910 January 4	New York	Metropolitan	La Bohème	3	
January 15	Boston	Boston Opera House	Pagliacci		
January 17	Brooklyn	Academy of Music	Aïda		

APPENDICES 421

Date of First Performance	City	House	Opera or Concert	Total Performances Given	Remarks
1910 January 22	New York	Metropolitan	Germania	5	First time in America
January 24	New York	Waldorf Astoria	Concert		Mr. Bagby Musicale
February 2	Baltimore	Lyric	Gioconda		
February 10	Philadelphia	Academy of Music	Rigoletto		
February 15	Philadelphia	Academy of Music	Germania		
February 18	New York	Metropolitan	Rigoletto	1	
March 7	Brooklyn	Academy of Music	Gioconda		
March 10	Philadelphia	Academy of Music	Aïda		
March 21	Brooklyn	Academy of Music	Rigoletto		
March 23	New York	Metropolitan			Farewell appearance with Aïda
March 28	Boston	Boston Opera House	Aïda		With Metropolitan Opera Company
March 30	Boston	Boston Opera House	La Bohème		
April 4	Chicago	Auditorium	Gioconda		
April 6	Chicago	Auditorium	La Bohème		
April 9	Chicago	Auditorium	Germania		
April 11	Cleveland	Keith's Hippodrome	Marta		
April 13	Chicago	Auditorium	Aïda		
April 16	Chicago	Auditorium	Pagliacci		
April 18	Milwaukee	Auditorium	Aïda		
April 20	Chicago	Auditorium	Faust		

Date of First Performance	City	House	Opera or Concert	Total Performances Given	Remarks
1910 April 22	St. Paul	Auditorium	Pagliacci		
April 25	St. Louis	Coliseum	La Bohème		
April 27	Chicago	Auditorium	Pagliacci		
April 29	Chicago	Auditorium	La Bohème		
May 4	Atlanta	Auditorium	Aïda		Music Festival Association
May 7	Atlanta	Auditorium	Pagliacci		
May 18	Paris	Trocadero	Concert		Benefit L'École Managère
May 21	Paris	Châtelet	Aïda	3	Management of Metropolitan Opera Company of New York and Gabriel Astruc
May 23	Paris	Châtelet	Pagliacci	3	
June 9	Paris	Châtelet	Manon Lescaut	5	
June 19	Paris	Opera	Excerpts from Faust and La Bohème		Benefit for victims of "Pluviôse"
June 25	Paris	Châtelet			Farewell appearance with Manon Lescaut
September 24 and 25	Bruxelles	La Monnaie	La Bohème	2	
October 1	Frankfurt a/M	Opernhaus	Aïda		
October 4	Frankfurt a/M	Opernhaus	Carmen		
October 8	Muenchen	Staatsoper	Carmen		
October 11	Muenchen	Staatsoper	La Bohème		
October 15	Hamburg	Stadttheater	Rigoletto		
October 18	Hamburg	Stadttheater	Carmen		

APPENDICES

Date of First Performance	City	House	Opera or Concert	Total Performances Given	Remarks
1910 October 20	Hamburg	Stadttheater	Marta		
October 24	Berlin	Staatsoper	Aïda		
October 27	Berlin	Staatsoper	Carmen		
October 30	Berlin	Staatsoper	Elisir d'amore		
November 14	New York	Metropolitan	Armide	3	Revival
November 17	New York	Metropolitan	Aïda	4	Management of G. Gatti-Casazza
November 23	New York	Metropolitan	Gioconda	4	
November 25	New York	Metropolitan	Pagliacci	3	
December 10	New York	Metropolitan	Fanciulla del West	7	World première
December 20	Philadelphia	Metropolitan	Fanciulla del West		
1911 January 3	Brooklyn	Academy of Music	Pagliacci		
January 14	Chicago	Auditorium	Pagliacci		
January 18	Chicago	Auditorium	Fanciulla del West		
January 19	Cleveland	Keith's Hippodrome	Pagliacci		
January 24	New York	Home of Mrs. Cornelius Vanderbilt	Musicale		
January 30	New York	Waldorf Astoria	Concert		Mr. Bagby Musicale
February 1	New York	Metropolitan	Germania	2	
February 6	New York	Metropolitan			Last appearance. Illness prevented him from continuing after performance of Germania on this date

Date of First Performance	City	House	Opera or Concert	Total Performances Given	Remarks
1911 November 13	New York	Metropolitan	Aïda	5	Management of G. Gatti-Casazza
November 16	New York	Metropolitan	Fanciulla del West	5	
November 21	Philadelphia	Metropolitan	Gioconda		
November 24	New York	Metropolitan	Pagliacci	9	
December 7	New York	Metropolitan	Gioconda	5	
December 16	New York	Metropolitan	Armide	4	
December 21	New York	Metropolitan	Tosca	2	
1912 January 2	Brooklyn	Academy of Music	La Bohème		
January 9	Philadelphia	Metropolitan	La Bohème		
January 17	New York	Metropolitan	Cavalleria	1	
January 27	Brooklyn	Academy of Music	Pagliacci		
January 30	Philadelphia	Metropolitan	Pagliacci		
February 6	New York	Metropolitan	Rigoletto	3	
February 19	New York	Metropolitan	La Bohème	1	
March 5	Boston	Boston Opera House	Fanciulla del West		
March 12	Brooklyn	Academy of Music	Aïda		
March 30	New York	Metropolitan	Manon Lescaut	3	
April 12	New York	Metropolitan			Farewell appearance with Pagliacci

APPENDICES

Date of First Performance	City	House	Opera or Concert	Total Performances Given	Remarks
1912 April 17	Boston	Boston Opera House	Pagliacci		
April 19	Philadelphia	Metropolitan	Aïda		
April 22	Atlanta	Auditorium	Aïda		
April 25	Atlanta	Auditorium	Pagliacci		
April 27	Atlanta	Auditorium	Rigoletto		
April 29	New York	Metropolitan	Concert		Benefit "Titanic" victims
May 16 to June 11	Paris	Opera	Fanciulla del West	3	
			Rigoletto	3	
September 26	Muenchen	Staatsoper	Tosca		
September 28	Muenchen	Staatsoper	Rigoletto		
October 1	Stuttgart	Staatsoper	Pagliacci		
October 3	Stuttgart	Staatsoper	La Bohème		
November 11	New York	Metropolitan	Manon Lescaut	5	Management of G. Gatti-Casazza
November 14	New York	Metropolitan	Gioconda	3	
November 20	New York	Metropolitan	Pagliacci	6	
November 25	New York	Metropolitan	Fanciulla del West	4	
November 28	New York	Metropolitan	La Bohème	3	
December 3	Philadelphia	Metropolitan	La Bohème		
December 9	New York	Metropolitan	Aïda	4	
December 24	Brooklyn	Academy of Music	Pagliacci		

426   ENRICO CARUSO

Date of First Performance	City	House	Opera or Concert	Total Performances Given	Remarks
1912 December 27	New York	Metropolitan	Les Huguenots	5	
1913 January 4	New York	Metropolitan	Tosca	4	
January 7	Philadelphia	Metropolitan	Gioconda		
January 22	New York	Metropolitan	Manon	5	
January 27	New York	Waldorf Astoria	Concert		Mr. Bagby Musicale
January 28	Philadelphia	Metropolitan	Manon		
February 17	New York	Metropolitan	Cavalleria		
March 4	Brooklyn	Academy of Music	Tosca	1	
March 18	Boston	Boston Opera House	Pagliacci		
March 25	Philadelphia	Metropolitan	Les Huguenots		
April 18	New York	Metropolitan			Farewell appearance with Tosca
April 18	Atlanta	Auditorium	Manon Lescaut		
April 24	Atlanta	Auditorium	Gioconda		
April 26	Atlanta	Auditorium	Tosca		
May 20	London	Covent Garden	Pagliacci	2	
May 24	London	Covent Garden	Aïda	5	
June 5	London	Covent Garden	Tosca	3	
June 18	London	Covent Garden	La Bohème	3	
June 28	London	Covent Garden			Farewell with La Bohème

APPENDICES 427

Date of First Performance	City	House	Opera or Concert	Total Performances Given	Remarks
1913 September 27	Wien	Staatsoper	Rigoletto	2	
September 29	Wien	Staatsoper	Carmen	1	
October 1, 3 and 5	Muenchen	Staatsoper	Pagliacci	1	
			Carmen	1	
			La Bohème	1	
October 8, 10 and 12	Stuttgart	Staatsoper	Carmen	1	
			Tosca	1	
			Rigoletto	1	
November 17	New York	Metropolitan	Gioconda	4	Management of G. Gatti-Casazza
November 22	New York	Metropolitan	Ballo in Maschera	5	
November 25	Philadelphia	Metropolitan	Aïda		
November 27	New York	Metropolitan	Manon Lescaut	4	
December 5	New York	Metropolitan	Pagliacci	7	
December 8	New York	Metropolitan	Aïda	3	
December 19	New York	Metropolitan	Tosca	4	
December 23	Philadelphia	Metropolitan	La Bohème		
December 31	New York	Metropolitan	Manon	4	
1914 January 27	Brooklyn	Academy of Music	Pagliacci		
January 30	New York	Metropolitan	La Bohème	2	
February 4	New York	Metropolitan	La Fanciulla del West	3	
February 10	Philadelphia	Metropolitan	Tosca		
February 26	New York	Metropolitan	Julien	5	New Opera
March 3	Philadelphia	Metropolitan	Pagliacci		

428   ENRICO CARUSO

Date of First Performance	City	House	Opera or Concert	Total Performances Given	Remarks
1914 March 24	Brooklyn	Academy of Music	Gioconda		
April 22	New York	Metropolitan			Farewell appearance with Tosca
April 27	Atlanta	Auditorium	Manon		
April 30	Atlanta	Auditorium	Ballo in Maschera		
May 2	Atlanta	Auditorium	Pagliacci		
May 14	London	Covent Garden	Aïda	3	
May 16	London	Covent Garden	Tosca	4	
May 25	London	Covent Garden	Madama Butterfly	4	
May 28	London	Covent Garden	Ballo in Maschera	2	
June 6	London	Covent Garden	La Bohème	2	
June 29	London	Covent Garden			Farewell appearance with Tosca. His last in England
October 19	Roma	Costanzi	Pagliacci		Benefit arranged by Comm. Ricceri
November 16	New York	Metropolitan	Ballo in Maschera	2	Management of G. Gatti-Casazza
November 19	New York	Metropolitan	Carmen	7	
November 25	New York	Metropolitan	Gioconda	2	
December 1	Philadelphia	Metropolitan	Gioconda		
December 5	New York	Metropolitan	Pagliacci	4	
December 12	New York	Metropolitan	Aïda	2	
December 15	Philadelphia	Metropolitan	Aïda		
December 24	New York	Metropolitan	Manon	3	

APPENDICES

Date of First Performance	City	House	Opera or Concert	Total Performances Given	Remarks
1914 December 30	New York	Metropolitan	Les Huguenots	3	
1915 January 1	New York	Metropolitan	Manon Lescaut	1	
January 15	Philadelphia	Metropolitan	Pagliacci		
February 2	Brooklyn	Academy of Music	Carmen		
February 17	New York	Metropolitan	Pagliacci		Farewell appearance with Pagliacci
March 14 to April 15	Monte Carlo	Casino	Aïda Pagliacci Lucia		Impresa of R. Gunsbourg
May 20	Buenos Aires	Colon	Aïda	1	Impresa of Walter Mocchi and Da Rosa
May 30	Buenos Aires	Colon	Pagliacci	4	
June 7	Buenos Aires	Coliseo	Songs		Italian Benefit
June 10	Buenos Aires	Colon	Manon Lescaut	3	
June 20	Buenos Aires	Colon	Manon	8	
June 27	Buenos Aires	Colon	Lucia	2	
July 5	Buenos Aires	Coliseo	Songs		French Benefit
July 9	Rosario		Pagliacci		
July 11	Tucuma		Pagliacci		
July 14 and 16	Cordoba		Pagliacci		
August 4	Buenos Aires	Colon	Pagliacci		Benefit Critic Association
August 10	Buenos Aires	Colon			Farewell appearance with Manon
August 11	Buenos Aires	Colon	Lamento from Pagliacci		Benefit Italian and French Red Crosses
August 12 to August 30	Montevideo	Solis	Manon Pagliacci Manon Lescaut	3 3 3	

Date of First Performance	City	House	Opera or Concert	Total Performances Given	Remarks
1915 September 23 and 25	Milano	Dal Verme	Pagliacci	2	Benefit arranged by Toscanini. His last appearance in Italy
November 15	New York	Metropolitan	Samson et Dalila	5	Revival Management of G. Gatti-Casazza
November 19	New York	Metropolitan	La Bohème	4	
November 27	New York	Metropolitan	Tosca	1	
November 30	Philadelphia	Metropolitan	Manon		
December 2	New York	Metropolitan	Pagliacci	4	
December 15	New York	Metropolitan	Marta	4	
December 15	New York	Metropolitan	Manon	2	
1916 January 1	New York	Metropolitan	Ballo in Maschera	2	
January 4	Brooklyn	Academy of Music	Aïda		
January 5	New York	Waldorf Astoria	Concert		Mr. Bagby Musicale
January 6	New York	Metropolitan	Manon Lescaut	3	
January 25	Philadelphia	Metropolitan	La Bohème		
February 9	New York	Biltmore Hotel	Concert		Friday Morning Musicales
February 11	New York	Metropolitan	Rigoletto	5	
February 17	New York	Metropolitan	Carmen	4	
March 14	Philadelphia	Metropolitan	Pagliacci		
March 24	New York	Metropolitan	Aïda	1	
April 1	New York	Metropolitan			Farewell appearance with Carmen

APPENDICES

Date of First Performance	City	House	Opera or Concert	Total Performances Given	Remarks
1916 April 4	Boston	Boston Opera House	La Bohème		With Metropolitan Opera Company
April 7	Boston	Boston Opera House	Aïda		
April 12	Boston	Boston Opera House	Rigoletto		
April 15	Boston	Boston Opera House	Pagliacci		
April 18	Boston	Boston Opera House	Ballo in Maschera		
April 21	Boston	Boston Opera House	Marta		
April 24	Atlanta	Auditorium	Samson et Dalila		
April 28	Atlanta	Auditorium	Marta		
April 29	Atlanta	Auditorium	La Bohème		
November 13	New York	Metropolitan	Pêcheurs de Perles	3	Revival Management of G. Gatti-Casazza
November 16	New York	Metropolitan	Manon Lescaut	3	
November 24	New York	Metropolitan	Samson et Dalila	5	
November 28	Philadelphia	Metropolitan	Samson et Dalila		
December 4	New York	Metropolitan	Tosca	1	
December 15	New York	Metropolitan	Pagliacci	4	
December 19	Philadelphia	Metropolitan	Marta		
December 25	New York	Metropolitan	Marta	3	

Date of First Performance	City	House	Opera or Concert	Total Performances Given	Remarks
1916 December 30	New York	Metropolitan	Elisir d'amore	5	
1917 January 2	Brooklyn	Academy of Music	Aïda		
January 5	New York	Metropolitan	Carmen	5	
January 23	Philadelphia	Metropolitan	La Bohème		
February 7	New York	Metropolitan	Rigoletto	5	
February 12	New York	Metropolitan	Aïda	4	
February 27	Brooklyn	Academy of Music	Marta		
March 6	Philadelphia	Metropolitan	Rigoletto		
March 18	New York	Metropolitan	Concert		Italian War Benefit
March 23	New York	Metropolitan	La Bohème	1	
April 10	Philadelphia	Metropolitan	Pagliacci		
April 20	New York	Metropolitan			Farewell appearance with Rigoletto
April 23	Atlanta	Auditorium	Elisir d'amore		
April 26	Atlanta	Auditorium	Tosca		
April 28	Atlanta	Auditorium	Rigoletto		
May 1	Cincinnati	Music Hall	Concert		Management of Metropolitan Musical Bureau
May 3	Toledo	Terminal Auditorium	Concert		
May 5	Pittsburgh	Syria Mosque	Concert		
May 8	New York	Astor Hotel	Concert		With Mozart Society

APPENDICES

Date of First Performance	City	House	Opera or Concert	Total Performances Given	Remarks
1917 June 17	Buenos Aires	Colon	Elisir d'amore	3	Impresa of W. Mocchi and Da Rosa
June 20	Buenos Aires	Colon	Pagliacci	4	
June 26	Buenos Aires	Colon	Manon	3	
July 2	Buenos Aires	Colon	Songs		Benefit "Caja Dotal"
July 4	Buenos Aires	Colon	Songs		Fourth of July Celebration for benefit U. S. Red Cross
July 6	Buenos Aires	Colon	Songs		Benefit Charing Cross Hospital of London
July 12	Buenos Aires	Colon	Tosca	2	First performance given for benefit Italian Red Cross
July 15	Buenos Aires	Colon	La Bohème	2	
July 20	Buenos Aires	Colon	La Bohème		Extra performance for benefit Belgian Charities
July 27	Buenos Aires	Colon	Elisir d'amore		Extra performance for benefit Press Club of Buenos Aires
July 29	Buenos Aires	Colon	Lodoletta	2	New Opera
July 30	Buenos Aires	Colon	Act III from Lucia		Benefit " Cantine Maternali "
August 6	Buenos Aires	San Martin	Songs		Benefit " Pantheon International Artists "
August 12	Buenos Aires	Coliseo	Pagliacci		Extra performance. Last appearance in opera in Buenos Aires
August 13	Buenos Aires	Colon	Songs		Benefit Italian War Committee
August 16 to August 25	Montevideo	Solis	Manon Lescaut	2	Impresa of W. Mocchi and Da Rosa
			Pagliacci	3	
			Manon	3	
			Carmen	3	
September 3 to 18	Rio de Janeiro	Lirico	Pagliacci Carmen		Impresa of W. Mocchi and Da Rosa

Date of First Performance	City	House	Opera or Concert	Total Performances Given	Remarks
1917 September 3 to 18 continued			Elisir Lodoletta La Bohème Manon		
September 19	Rio de Janeiro	Lirico	Act I Elisir		Benefit Italian Red Cross
September 25 to October 11	San Paulo	Municipale	Elisir d'amore Carmen Tosca La Bohème Manon Pagliacci Lodoletta		
October 8	San Paulo	Municipale	Act I Pagliacci Act III Elisir		Benefit Italian Red Cross
October 13	Rio de Janeiro	Lirico	Carmen		
October 16	Rio de Janeiro	Lirico	Manon Lescaut		His last appearance in South America
November 12	New York	Metropolitan	Aïda	3	Management of G. Gatti-Casazza
November 15	New York	Metropolitan	Elisir d'amore	5	
November 21	New York	Metropolitan	Marta	5	
November 23	New York	Metropolitan	Samson et Dalila	4	
November 27	Philadelphia	Metropolitan	Manon Lescaut		
December 5	New York	Metropolitan	Manon Lescaut	3	
December 7	New York	Metropolitan	Pagliacci	3	
December 10	New York	Metropolitan	Carmen	2	
December 15	New York	Metropolitan	Tosca	1	
December 18	Philadelphia	Metropolitan	Pagliacci		

APPENDICES 435

Date of First Performance	City	House	Opera or Concert	Total Performances Given	Remarks
1917 December 29	New York	Metropolitan	Rigoletto	1	
1918 January 12	New York	Metropolitan	Lodoletta	5	First time in America
January 15	Brooklyn	Academy of Music	Rigoletto		
February 7	New York	Metropolitan	Le Prophète	5	Revival
February 18	New York	Biltmore Hotel	Concert		Friday Morning Musicale
February 19	Philadelphia	Metropolitan	Lodoletta		
March 14	New York	Metropolitan	L'Amore dei Tre Re	4	
March 19	Philadelphia	Metropolitan	L'Amore dei Tre Re		
April 9	Philadelphia	Metropolitan	Samson et Dalila		
April 14	New York	Metropolitan	Concert		Benefit Italian Reservists
April 19	New York	Metropolitan			Farewell appearance with Elisir d'amore
April 22	Boston	Boston Opera House	Le Prophète		
April 25	Boston	Boston Opera House	Pagliacci		
April 27	Boston	Boston Opera House	Samson et Dalila		
May 1	New York	Carnegie Hall	Concert		Third Liberty Loan Rally
May 20	Washington	Poli's	Concert		Benefit under auspices Italian Embassy
May 24	New York	Metropolitan	Concert		Benefit Italian Red Cross
May 27	New York	Metropolitan	Concert		Benefit American Red Cross

Date of First Performance	City	House	Opera or Concert	Total Performances Given	Remarks
1918 June 10	New York	Metropolitan	Concert		Benefit Women Naval Services
July 27	Ocean Grove	Auditorium	Concert		Management of R. E. Johnston
August 17	Saratoga Springs	Convention Hall	Concert		Management of Metropolitan Musical Bureau
August 31	Sheepshead Bay	Open air	Songs		Benefit Police Reserve of New York
September 6	New York	Waldorf Astoria	Hymns of Allied Nations		Commemoration Lafayette Day
September 12	New York	Central Park Mall	Songs		People's concerts arranged by Mayor Hylan. First time he sang where was no charge for admission
September 15	New York	Century Theatre	Songs		Benefit Tank Corps
September 30	New York	Carnegie Hall	Concert		Liberty Loan Rally promoted by Allied Musical Arts
October 5	New York	Madison Square Garden	Songs		Liberty Loan Rally promoted by United Moving Picture Producers of America
October 9	Buffalo	Iroquois Hotel	Songs		IV Liberty Loan Rally
October 12	New York	Metropolitan	Concert		Benefit Italian Blind Soldiers
October 15	Detroit	Arcadia	Pagliacci		Management Central Concert Company
November 3 afternoon	New York	Madison Square Garden	Songs		Benefit United War Works
November 3 evening	New York	Hippodrome	Songs		Benefit Navy Relief Fund
November 7	New York	Biltmore Hotel	Concert		Friday Morning Musicale
November 11	New York	Metropolitan	Samson et Dalila	5	Management of G. Gatti-Casazza

APPENDICES

Date of First Performance	City	House	Opera or Concert	Total Performances Given	Remarks
1918 November 15	New York	Metropolitan	Forza del Destino	6	Revival
November 20	New York	Metropolitan	Elisir d'amore	5	
November 23	New York	Metropolitan	Le Prophète	6	
November 26	Philadelphia	Metropolitan	Elisir d'amore		
December 7	New York	Metropolitan	Marta	5	
December 18	New York	Metropolitan	Lodoletta	3	
December 23	New York	Waldorf Astoria	Concert		Mr. Bagby Musicale
December 25	New York	Metropolitan	Pagliacci	4	
1919 January 8	New York	Metropolitan	La Bohème	2	
January 21	Philadelphia	Metropolitan	Samson et Dalila		
February 12	New York	Metropolitan	Aïda	2	
March 2	Ann Arbor	Hill Auditorium	Concert		Management Metropolitan Musical Bureau
March 3	New York	Metropolitan	The Star Spangled Banner		League of Nations Rally
March 3	Philadelphia	Metropolitan	La Bohème		
March 22	New York	Metropolitan	Act III Elisir Act I Pagliacci Act III Prophète		To celebrate the 25th year of his operatic career
March 25	Philadelphia	Metropolitan	Forza del Destino		
April 2	New York	Commodore Hotel	Concert		Commodore Hotel Musicales

Date of First Performance	City	House	Opera or Concert	Total Performances Given	Remarks
1919 April 6	Buffalo	Broadway Auditorium	Concert		Management Metropolitan Musical Bureau
April 14	New York	Metropolitan	Carmen	1	
April 17	New York	Metropolitan			Farewell appearance with Aïda
April 21	Atlanta	Auditorium	Forza del Destino		
April 24	Atlanta	Auditorium	Marta		
April 26	Atlanta	Auditorium	Pagliacci		
April 29	Nashville	Ryman Auditorium	Concert		Management of Metropolitan Musical Bureau
May 2	St. Louis	Coliseum	Concert		
May 5	Kansas City	Convention Hall	Concert		
May 8	St. Paul	Auditorium	Concert		
May 11	Chicago	Medinah Temple	Concert		
May 13	Milwaukee	Auditorium	Concert		
May 16	Canton, Ohio	Auditorium	Concert		
May 19	Newark	1st Regiment Armory	Concert		
May 22	Springfield, Mass.	Auditorium			Management of Edward Marsh
September 29	Mexico City	Esperanza Iris	Elisir d'amore		Management of José del River
October 2	Mexico City	Esperanza Iris	Ballo in Maschera		
October 5	Mexico City	El Toreo	Carmen		

APPENDICES 439

Date of First Performance	City	House	Opera or Concert	Total Performances Given	Remarks
1919 October 9	Mexico City	Esperanza Iris	Samson et Dalila		
October 12	Mexico City	El Toreo	Ballo in Maschera		
October 17	Mexico City	Esperanza Iris	Marta		
October 19	Mexico City	El Toreo	Samson et Dalila		
October 23	Mexico City	Esperanza Iris	Pagliacci		
October 26	Mexico City	El Toreo	Aïda		
October 28	Mexico City	Esperanza Iris	Songs		Benefit Educational Fund of the City of Mexico
October 30	Mexico City	Esperanza Iris	Manon Lescaut		Serata d'onore
November 2	Mexico City	El Toreo	Act III Elisir Act III Marta Act I Pagliacci		Farewell appearance
November 17	New York	Metropolitan	Tosca	1	Management G. Gatti-Casazza
November 22	New York	Metropolitan	La Juive	7	Revival
November 26	New York	Metropolitan	Pagliacci	5	
November 28	New York	Metropolitan	Forza del Destino	5	
December 2	Philadelphia	Metropolitan	Elisir d'amore		
December 10	New York	Metropolitan	Samson et Dalila	5	
December 13	New York	Metropolitan	Marta	4	
December 19	New York	Metropolitan	Elisir d'amore	5	
December 23	Brooklyn	Academy of Music	Marta		
1920 January 6	Philadelphia	Metropolitan	La Juive		

Date of First Performance	City	House	Opera or Concert	Total Performances Given	Remarks
1920 January 15	New York	Metropolitan	Manon Lescaut	1	
January 19	New York	Waldorf Astoria	Concert		Mr. Bagby Musicale
February 4	New York	Metropolitan	Le Prophète	5	
February 24	Brooklyn	Academy of Music	La Juive		
February 28	Pittsburgh	Syria Mosque	Concert		Management of Metropolitan Musical Bureau
March 2	Philadelphia	Metropolitan	Marta		
March 14	Waterbury	Auditorium	Concert		Management Metropolitan Musical Bureau
March 28	New York	Lexington Opera House	Songs		Italian Loan Rally
March 30	Philadelphia	Metropolitan	Forza del Destino		
April 5	Scranton	Armory	Concert		Management Metropolitan Musical Bureau
April 18	Detroit	Arcadia	Concert		Management Central Concert Company
April 23	New York	Metropolitan			Farewell appearance with La Juive
April 26	Atlanta	Auditorium	Samson et Dalila		
April 29	Atlanta	Auditorium	La Juive		
May 1	Atlanta	Auditorium	Elisir d'amore		
May 12	Habana	Nacional	Marta		Impresa of Adolfo Bracale
May 16	Habana	Nacional	Marta		
May 18	Habana	Nacional	Elisir d'amore		
May 21	Habana	Nacional	Ballo in Maschera		
May 25	Habana	Nacional	Pagliacci		
May 28	Habana	Nacional	Tosca		

APPENDICES

Date of First Performance	City	House	Opera or Concert	Total Performances Given	Remarks
1920 May 30	Habana	Nacional	Pagliacci		
June 2	Habana	Nacional	Carmen		
June 5	Habana	Nacional	Carmen		
June 8	Habana	Nacional	Aïda		
June 11	Habana	Nacional	Act III Elisir Act I Pagliacci		Serata d'onore
June 13	Habana	Nacional	Aïda		Last appearance. Performance suspended after scene I of Act II because of explosion of a bomb
June 17	Santa Clara	La Caridad	Act III Elisir Act I Pagliacci		Impresa of Adolfo Bracale
June 19	Cienfuegos	Terry	Aïda		Impresa of Adolfo Bracale
June 26	New Orleans	Athenæum	Concert		Management Metropolitan Musical Bureau
June 30	Atlantic City	Ambassador Hotel	Concert		Promoted by Victor Talking Machine Dealers Association
August 14	Ocean Grove	Auditorium	Concert		Management Metropolitan Musical Bureau
September 27	Montreal	Mt. Royal Arena	Concert		
September 30	Toronto	Massey Hall	Concert		
October 3	Chicago	Medinah Temple	Concert		
October 6	St. Paul	Auditorium	Concert		
October 9	Denver	Auditorium	Concert		
October 12	Omaha	Auditorium	Concert		
October 16	Tulsa	Convention Hall	Concert		
October 19	Fort Worth	Coliseum	Concert		
October 22	Houston	City Auditorium	Concert		

Date of First Performance	City	House	Opera or Concert	Total Performances Given	Remarks
1920 October 25	Charlotte	City Auditorium	Concert		
October 28	Norfolk	Tabernacle	Concert		
November 15	New York	Metropolitan	La Juive		Management of G. Gatti-Casazza
November 18	New York	Metropolitan	Elisir d'amore		
November 24	New York	Metropolitan	Samson et Dalila		
November 27	New York	Metropolitan	Forza del Destino		
November 30	Philadelphia	Academy of Music	La Juive		
December 3	New York	Metropolitan	Samson et Dalila		
December 8	New York	Metropolitan	Pagliacci		Stricken with acute pain on side during aria. Performance continues after twenty minutes rest
December 11	Brooklyn	Academy of Music	Elisir d'amore		Hemorrhage attacks him. Audience dismissed after Act I
December 13	New York	Metropolitan	Forza del Destino		
December 16	New York	Metropolitan	Samson et Dalila		
December 22	New York	Metropolitan	Elisir d'amore		Performance canceled at the last moment on account of illness
December 24	New York	Metropolitan	La Juive		Last appearance in his life.

INDEX

INDEX

ABARBANELL, LINA, 225.
Abbot, Miss, 225.
"Adriana de Lecouvreur", Caruso creates rôle in, 165, 166; in America, 252.
"Aïda", Caruso sings at Petrograd in, 118, 119; in New York, 185; in Monte Carlo, 190, 307; in Germany, 246; in Paris, 271.
Alda, Frances, 272, 280.
Allen, Julia, 254.
Alten, Bella, 207, 236, 272.
Althouse, Paul, experience with Caruso in regard to costume, 373.
Amato, Pasquale, in various operas, 201, 266, 271–273, 280, 284, 306, 327; Caruso plays trick on, 202; friendship for Caruso, 283.
"Amico Francesco", L', 46–48.
"Amore dei tre Re", L', 321.
Angelini, Signor, 95, 126.
Annunzio, Gabriele d', 311.
Arachite, Sergeant Angelo, 41.
Arcangeli, Alessandro, 130, 135, 142, 167.
Argenti, Signor, theatrical agent, 79.
Arimondi, Vittorio, in various operas, 118, 122, 176, 190, 196, 197, 201; helpful of advice to Caruso, 103; his account of experiences at Petrograd, 119; tells of Caruso at Monte Carlo, 191; Caruso plays trick on, 202.
"Arlesiana", L', 94, 100.
"Armide", 283.
Arnoldson, Sigrid, 103, 118.
Astruc, Gabriel, Paris representative of Caruso, 196, 209; on the Caruso furore in Paris, 196, 197; letter to Caruso, 258, 259; lays plans for engagement of Metropolitan in Paris, 270; Caruso writes to, on Paris engagement, 274.

BADA, ANGELO, 312.
Bagby Musicales, 207, 225.
"Ballo in Maschera, Il", 119.
Barcelona, engagement at, 193–196.
Baretti, Rosa, Caruso's nurse, 10.
Barnhill, Rev. Oliver Paul, 325.
Baroni, Alice, 101.
Baroni, Giuseppe, 194.
Barthélemy, Richard, 314, 316, 317.
Bastianelli brothers (Giuseppe and Raffaele), 390.
Bathori, Jane, 158.
Battistini, Mattia, in various operas, 103, 118, 119, 122, 232.
Beck, James M., 332.
Bellezza, Vincenzo, 314, 318.
Bellincioni, Gemma, 43, 101, 107, 108; her judgment of Caruso, 99.
Belmont, Mr. and Mrs. Perry, 225.
Bel Sorel, Signora, 101.
Benjamin, Dorothy, marriage to Caruso, 321, 323–326. *See* CARUSO, MRS. ENRICO.
Benjamin, Mrs. Park, 355.
Benjamin, Mrs. Walter R., 331.
Bensaude, Maurizio, 169.
Bensberg, Kate, 57.
Benvenuti, Signora, 167.
Berlin, engagements in, 200, 234, 265, 300.
Bernis, Doctor Albert, impresario of Liceo Theater, Barcelona, 193–195.
Beronne, Mr., 219.
Berriel, Enrico, 194.
Berutti, Arturo, 108.
Bevignani, Vincenzo, 161, 162.
Bianchini-Cappelli, Elena, 50, 54.
"Black Hand", the, attempts blackmail on Caruso, 268, 269.
Bodanzky, Arturo, 348.

"Bohème, La", story of Caruso's first appearance in, 84–88; said to be too strong for Caruso's voice, 91; at Genoa, 95; at Milan, 100, 130–134; in Russia, 103; at Monte Carlo, 156; in New York, 236, 253; in Germany, 298.
Boito, Arrigo, commends Caruso, 116; invites Caruso to create rôle in "Nerone", 297.
Bonci, Alessandro, 128, 129.
Bonetti, Camillo, his first impression of Caruso's singing, 74, 75; takes place of Mme. Ferrari, 143.
Bonini, Signor, 59.
Borelli, Nedea, 82.
Borelli, Signor, 147, 152.
Borgatti, Signor, 143; rivals Caruso at Bologna, 128, 129.
Bori, Lucrezia, 272, 298.
Borlinetto, Signora, 82.
Borucchia, Signor, 114, 168.
Boston, Caruso severely criticized in, 322.
Bracale, Adolfo, 352, 358.
Brambilla, Linda, 135, 142.
Brancaleone, Signor, 74.
Breeskin, Elias, 331, 335.
Bressler-Gianoli, Mme., 201.
Brombera, Signor, 103.
Bronzetti, Giuseppe, his school, 13–18.
Brozia, Mme., 271.
Bruno, Elisa, 169.
Bucalo, Emanuele, 152, 153.
Buenos Aires, engagements at, 107, 108, 124–127, 142–146, 174–177, 309–311, 317, 318.
Burke, Thomas, his description of Caruso's singing, 212–216.

CABRERA, RICARDO, his account of Caruso's singing in Mexico City, 336–340.
Calmetti, Gaston, letter to Caruso, 258.
Calvé, Emma, 160.
Cambon, Paul, letter to Caruso, 232, 233.
Campanari, Giuseppe, 189.

Campanelli, Alfredo, 16.
Campanini, Cleofonte, 165, 169, 201; makes offer to Caruso in behalf of Chicago Grand Opera Company, 330.
Candida, Federico, 57, 100.
Canessa, Achille, his bust of Caruso, 97.
Cappelli, Elena Bianchini, 335.
Cappelli, Marchesa Orazio, 349.
Carbonetti, Federico, in "L'Elisir d'Amore", 136–139.
Carelli, Emma, in various operas, 59, 114, 124, 126, 130, 135, 142.
"Carmen", Caruso experiences difficulty in Flower song, 70; in Berlin, 234, 282.
Carobbi, Silla, 114.
Carotini, Signora, 118, 122.
Carozzi, Signor, 95.
Carrera, Signora, 126.
Cartier, E. de, 239.
Caruso, Anna Baldini, mother of Enrico, 10–13, 18, 19, 23.
Caruso, Assunta, sister of Enrico, 10; death, 311.
Caruso, Enrico, his farewell to America, 1–6; the telling of his life, 6–9; birth, 10; schooling, 11; companionship with mother, 11, 12; early capriciousness of, 13; in Father Bronzetti's school, 13–16; his first training in singing and music, 14; how he learned the words and notes of his opera rôles, 16, 76, 122; further instruction in music received by, 17; influence of his mother, 18, 19; end of his schooling, 20; enters Meuricoffre plant, 21; his first operatic venture, 21; his disposition, 22; death of mother, 23; his singing of church music, 23, 24; love for his stepmother, 25, 26; advancement in business, 26; sings at cafés and baths, 27, 28; first meeting with Edoardo Missiano, 28; comes under the instruction of Vergine, 28; Vergine's method with, 29–31; not a musician, 31; incident of his

INDEX 447

Majori engagement and Baron Zezza's overcoat, 32–34; his military experiences, 34–40; celebrates release from military service, 41; in amateur representation of "Cavalleria Rusticana", 42; fails in trial for the Mercadante Theater, 43–45; his début in "L'Amico Francesco", 46–48; his appearance at Caserta, 50, 51; substitutes in "Faust" at the Bellini Theater, 51, 52; sings in Cairo, 52–55; sings in "Rigoletto" at the Bellini Theater, 56; at the Mercadante, 57–59; sings twice a day, 58; failure at Caserta, 59; his Sicilian tour, 60–65; sings at Salerno, 65–73; commended by de Lucia, 68; and Josephine Grassi, 68, 69, 79, 80; the breaking of his voice, 70–72; his vocal endurance and dependableness, 72, 73; progress of, 74; acquires greater poise, 75, 76; second Salerno season, 76–80; at the Massimo Theater, Palermo, 81, 82; engaged for the Lirico, Milan, 82, 83; four periods of his career, 84; visits Puccini and is chosen to sing in "La Bohème", 84–88; alliance with Ada Giachetti, 89; difficulties with Sonzogno répertoire, 90–94; his Genoa engagement, 95–97; more serious work, 98; his success in "La Fedora", 99–101; son born to, 100; Russian engagement of, 102–104; sings before the Czar, 104; South American engagement, 104–108; at home, 109–112; engagement at Costanzi Theater, Rome, 112–117; contract with Vergine annulled, 115; charmed by smoothness and purity of singing, 115; second Russian engagement, 118–123; arrangement of his day, 121, 122; further study, 123; second South American engagement, 124–127; Treviso engagement, 127; Bologna engagement, 128, 129; his first production of "La Bohème" at La Scala, 129–134; his singing of "L'Elisir d'Amore", 135–140; hostility toward, 141; third South American engagement, 142–146; never read books, 145; sings in charity performances at Trieste, 147; his experiences at the San Carlo, Naples, 145–153; at Monte Carlo, 154–157; creates tenor rôle in "Germania", 156–158; at Covent Garden, 158–161; engages for Metropolitan Opera House, 161–165; reluctance to do business through agent, 163, 164; loath to concede that others had helped him, 166, 167; at Trieste and Rome, 167; Metropolitan engagement canceled owing to retirement of Grau, 168; at Lisbon, 169; makes new engagement with Metropolitan, 170–172; purchases Villa alla Panche, near Florence, 173; in South America again, 174–177; arrival in New York, 177–180; first meeting with Conried, 181, 182; his first appearance at the Metropolitan, 183; newspaper comments on, 184–187; sets up his own establishment, 187; regards America as possible future home, 188; proposal of Conried to, 188; sings in private musicales, 189; at Monte Carlo again, 190, 191; his liking for pranks, 191, 202, 207; asked by Leoncavallo to create rôle in "Rolando", 191–193; his experience at Barcelona, 193–196; sings at Paris, Prague, and Dresden, 197; purchases Villa Campi, 198; again at Covent Garden, 199; birth of second son, 200; sings at Berlin, 200; sings with San Carlo Company at Covent Garden, 201; tour of the United States with the Metropolitan, 203, 204; his conscientious thoroughness in the details of his characters, 205, 206; his generosity, 206, 207, 232, 233, 259, 322, 323; enthusiasm for, 207, 208; successes at Paris, 208–

211; at Covent Garden, 212-218; his singing described by Thomas Burke, 212-216; sings at Court and receives gift from King and Queen, 216; at Ostende, 218-220; not quite happy when at leisure, 221; beginning of his third season at the Metropolitan, 221; his receipts, 221, 222; featured by the press, 223, 224; humorous experiences of, 223, 224; sings at concerts, 225; in the San Francisco earthquake, 227-229; guilty of certain exaggerations of public conduct, 230; at the height of powers as singer, 231; letter to his brother, Giovanni, 232; in Vienna and Berlin, 233, 234; receives title from Kaiser Wilhelm, 234; decorated by France, 235; fourth season with the Metropolitan, 235-238; receipts, 236; in London and Paris, 238, 239; decorated by Belgium, 239; letters to, 239-244; pleasure in his children, 239-242; decorated by the King of England, 243; life beginning to be dominated by orderly procedure, 245; in Germany, 246; his collection of objects of art, 247-251; receipts, 251; his endurance, 251; as fitted for heroic and lyric rôles, 252, 299, 302, 313, 321, 360, 379; compared to De Reszke, 253; disliked to appear in concerts, 254; why he used music in concerts, 254; learns of the death of his father, 255-257; deserted by Ada Giachetti, 257; letter of Gaston Calmette to, 258; letter of Coquelin to, 260, 261; illness of, 261-264; receipts, 263; makes concert tour of England, Scotland, and Ireland, 265; in Germany, 265; receipts, 266; interview with Ada Giachetti, 267; his feeling for Ada Giachetti, 267, 274; threatened by the "Black Hand", 268, 269; and the Paris trip of the Metropolitan, 269-274; Otto Gutekunst's reminiscences of, 275-280; his "different voices", 281, 282, 366; friendship for Amato, 283; unable to complete 1911 engagement with Metropolitan, 284, 285; sings for records, 285-292; income from records, 291; rumors concerning, 292, 293; at fancy-dress charity ball in London, 294; adjudged resident of London, 294; his improved art in 1911-1912 engagement at Metropolitan, 295, 296; sings in benefit performance for families of victims of *Titanic*, 297; growing cynicism of, 297; invited to create tenor rôle in "Nerone", 297; first appearance at Paris Opera, 298; enthusiasm for, in Germany, 298, 300; his diet, 301; final London appearance, 303; suffers from nervous breakdown, 303; sings for Italian workingmen in Germany, 304; his feelings opposed to the Austrians in the War, 305; at Monte Carlo, 306-309; terms of picture engagements with the Metropolitan, 306; his views on the uncertainty of his profession, 307-309; in Buenos Aires again, 309-311; his anger at being accused of pro-Germanism, 311; sings in Milan, for last time in Italy, 312; hard study put upon his parts, 313-315; letter of Otto Kahn to, 315; suffered from headaches, 316; the 1916-1917 season in New York, 316, 317; his final engagement in South America, 317, 318; his secretaries, 318, 319; buys Liberty Bonds, 320; gives lessons, 320; meets Dorothy Benjamin, 321; sings in "Lodoletta", "Le Prophète", and "L'Amore dei tre Re", 321, 322; criticised severely in Boston, 322; income, 322; courts Miss Benjamin, 323, 324; in motion pictures, 324, 326; sings at Saratoga Springs, 324; married to Miss Benjamin, 325; sings at various concerts, 326, 327; contributes sketches to *La Follia*, 328; refuses offer of Chicago Grand Opera Com-

INDEX

pany, 329–331; remarried to Mrs. Caruso with Catholic rites, 331; his jubilee celebration, 332–334; concert tour, 335; in Mexico, 336–342; beginning of the twilight of his career, 343; kept his own accounts, 344; the estimated value of his estate, 344; his daily habits, 345; his part in "La Juive", 345–348; perfect in his operas, 346; daughter born to, 349; asked to subscribe for Minnie Hauk, 350; concerts, 351; sings in Cuba, 352–356; in New Orleans, 356; spends summer at Long Island home, 357, 358; moves to Vanderbilt Hotel, 358; season of concerts, 359; makes final phonograph records, 359; tribute of Otto Kahn to, 359, 360; criticism of, in New York papers, 360, 361; sensitive to criticism, 360, 363; superstition of, 361; a religious man, 362; lived largely according to the golden rule, 362, 363; informs Gatti-Casazza that he wishes to resign from the Metropolitan, 364; makes final trial and remains, 365; his technique, 365–371, 374; had vocal resources of phenomenal order, 366; never forced his voice, 368; his brilliancy and resonance, how secured, 369; made no pronounced physical effort in singing, 369; his nervousness before and after the beginning of a performance, 371–373; how he prepared for singing, 372, 375; particular in regard to costumes, 372, 373; how he coaxed his voice, 374, 375; his insistence for detail, 376; gave, in singing, all he had, 376; considered by Gatti-Casazza in a class by himself, 377–379; illness and final performances, 379–387; last days and death, 388–391; list of decorations tendered to, 395; list of operas in répertoire of, 396; list of operas sung rarely or simply studied by, 397; list of appearances of, 398.

Caruso, Mrs. Enrico, marriage, 321, 323–326; remarried with Catholic rites, 331; her account of how Caruso studied the rôle of Eleazar, 347; robbed of jewels, 355, 357; in Caruso's last illness, 379–391.

Caruso, Enrico, Jr., birth, 200; his father's delight, 239–242; letter to his father, 328, 329; put to school in America, 336.

Caruso, Giovanni, brother of Enrico, 10; birth of son, 232; present at Enrico's last illness, 390.

Caruso, Marcellino, father of Enrico, 10, 24, 25.

Caruso, Maria Castaldi, stepmother of Enrico, 25.

Caruso, Rodolfo (Fofò), 100, 390.

Caruso, Gloria, daughter of Enrico, 349.

Caruson, G., 147.

Caserta, Caruso sings at, 50, 59.

Castagneto, Prince Adolfo di, 149–153.

Castaldi, Maria, 25.

Cavalieri, Lina, 196, 211, 252.

"Cavalleria Rusticana", Caruso's first appearance in, 50; in Salerno, 68; in South America, 108, 126.

Chaliapin, Feodor, 142, 298.

Chicago Grand Opera Company, makes offer to Caruso, 330.

Child, Calvin G., his reminiscences of Caruso, 285–292.

Cincinnati Symphony Orchestra, 317.

Cincotta, Antonio, of the "Black Hand", 269.

Clasenti, Signor, 176, 194.

Cochran, W. Bourke, 297.

Connaught, Duke and Duchess of, 297.

Conried, Heinrich, engages Caruso for the Metropolitan, 170–172; Caruso's first meeting with, 181, 182; decorated, 207; succeeded by Gatti-Casazza and Dippel, 262.

Coquelin, Constant, letter to Caruso, 260, 261.

Corsi, Emilia, 95.

Corti, Enrico, 127.

Costanzi Theater, Rome, engagement of Caruso at, 112–117.

INDEX

Couzinou, Alfred, 327.
Covent Garden, engagements of Caruso at, 158–161, 199, 201, 212, 232, 238, 239, 299, 303; opera in, as described by Thomas Burke, 212–216.
Cuba, engagement of Caruso in, 352–356.
Cucini, Signora, 118, 119, 143.

DADDI, FRANCESCO, 201, 327.
Dalmaro, Mary, 114.
Danesi, Mlle., 43.
Danise, Giuseppe, 310.
Darclée, Ericlea, 143, 169.
Daspuro, Nicola, Caruso sings to, 43–45; engages Caruso for season at Lirico Theater, Milan, 77, 78, 82, 83; insists that Caruso's accomplishment was due to his own instinct, 166; on Caruso's appearance in "Fedora", 210.
Decorations tendered to Caruso, 395.
Della Riza, Gilda, 310.
Dell' Oreficé, Maestro, 314.
Depuis, Maestro, 280.
De Simone, Doctor, 319.
Destinn, Mme., in various operas, 199, 212, 217, 232, 238, 266, 271, 283, 284, 295, 299, 303, 306.
Dippel, Andreas, administrative manager of the Metropolitan, 262; withdraws, 266.
Di San Giuliano, 243.
Domprowitch, Mme., 74.
Donalda, Mme., 212, 232, 238.
"Don Giovanni", 232.

EAMES, EMMA, 252.
Edgerton, Hon. Wilfred, 294.
Edvina, Mme., 299.
"Elisir d'Amore, L'", revived at La Scala, 135–140; at Naples, 151, 152; at Buenos Aires, 317; in Mexico, 337–340.
Elman, Mischa, 335.
Enright, Police Commissioner, 332.

Ercolani, Signor, in various operas, 124, 126, 143, 174.
Erdmann, Dr. John F., 386.
Evans, Dr. Evan M., 386.

FALCO, SIGNOR DE, 77.
"Fanciulla del West, La", 283.
Farneti, Maria, 176.
Farquhar, Lord, 217, 243.
Farrar, Geraldine, joins Metropolitan Company, 225; sings with Caruso, 253, 273, 301; at Caruso's jubilee celebration, 334; seeks aid for Minnie Hauk, 350.
Fasanaro, Alessandro, 14.
"Faust", Caruso's first appearance in, 51, 52; in Naples, 59; in Caserta, 59, 60; in Russia, 122; without chorus, 223, 224.
"Fedora, La", Caruso's first appearance in, 99–101, 106, 107; in Paris, 203–211; in New York, 237.
Ferraguti, Vittorio, 54, 59.
Ferrante, Gherardo, 349.
Ferrara, Carlo, impresario, 48.
Ferrari, Signora, impresaria, 105–107, 124.
Ferraris, Teresa, 158.
Figueras, Luis Piera, 193–196.
Florexo, Mr., 271.
Florio, Ignazio, 82.
Fornari, Vincenzo, 74.
Fornia, Rita, 254.
"Forza del Destino, La", 327.
Franco, Annina, 59, 69.
Franko, Nahan, 225.
Fremstad, Olive, 273.
Fucito, Salvatore, 315, 324.

GADSKI, JOHANNA, 185.
Galante, Filippo, 124, 145.
Galassi, Maestro, 59.
Ganelli, Elisa, 295, 296.
Garden, Mary, 335.
Gatti-Casazza, Giulio, director of La Scala, 129; at rehearsal of "La Bohème", 133, 134; produces

INDEX 451

"L'Elisir d'Amore", 135, 136; becomes general manager of the Metropolitan, 262; writes in Gloria's book, 349; urges Caruso to remain in the Metropolitan, 364, 365; his estimate of Caruso, 377–379; in Caruso's last illness, 385, 386, 389.
Gatto, Amelia, 16.
Gatto, Giovanni, 13–16.
Geniat, Mlle., 271.
Genoa, engagement of Caruso in, 95–97.
Gerardy, Jean, 225.
"Germania", Caruso creates rôle in, 156–158.
Germany, 197, 234, 246, 265, 298, 304.
Ghibaudo, Signora, 142.
Giachetti, Ada, in rôle of Mimì, 85; lives with Caruso, 89, 94; sails for South America, 102; joins Caruso in Petrograd, 119–121; in "Tosca", 127, 128; goes with Caruso to New York, 179, 187; abandons Caruso, 257; final interview of Caruso with, 267.
Giachetti, Rina, 201, 232, 239.
Giacomo, Salvatore di, 69, 73.
Gilbert, Charles, 238, 239.
Gilly, Mme. Dinh, 303.
"Gioconda, La", success of Caruso in, 74, 78, 81, 207, 222, 226.
Giordano, Signor, secretary of Caruso, 191.
Giordano, Umberto, Caruso in his "La Fedora", 99–101; letters to Caruso, 211, 237.
Giorgio, Cavalier C. di, 82.
Giraldini, Giraldino, 147, 167.
Giraldoni, Eugenio, 126, 128, 143, 169, 174, 207.
Giraud, Fiorello, 169.
Grassi, Josephine, 68, 79, 80.
Grassi, Peppo, 68–73.
Grau, Maurice, Caruso's first arrangement with, 161–164; retires from Metropolitan, 168.
Greffulhe, Countess, 196, 238, 271.
Guard, William J., 382.
Guarini, Signor, 74.

Guarnieri, Antonio, 127.
Guerrini, Virginia, 169, 176, 190.
Gunsbourg, Raoul, 156, 329.
Gutekunst, Otto, 294; his reminiscences of Caruso, 275–280.

HAMMERSTEIN, OSCAR, proposes to give operas in Manhattan Opera House, 226.
Harowitz, Dr. Philip, 380–386.
Harrold, Orville, 348.
Havana, Caruso sings in, 352–356.
Hempel, Frieda, 316.
Herbert, Victor, 225.
Higgins, Henry V., 154, 155.
Homer, Mme., in various operas, 207, 222, 254, 271, 327.
"Huguenots, Les", 299.
Hylan, Mayor, 332.

"Iris", 114, 115, 125, 126, 129, 252.

JADLOWKER, HERMAN, 273.
Journet, Marcel, in various operas, 159, 160, 199, 212, 232, 239, 307, 309.
"Julien", 301.
"Juive, La", 345–348.

KAHN, OTTO H., suggests that Caruso sing in "L'Elisir d'Amore", 140; favors having the Metropolitan Opera Company sing in Europe, 269; letter to Caruso, 315; his address at Caruso's jubilee celebration, 333, 334; tribute to Caruso, 359, 360.
Keith, Mrs. John S., 325.
Kessler, George A., 218.
Keyes, Margaret, 254.
Kirkby-Lunn, Mme., 199, 239, 303.
Kotlarsky, "Sammy", 254.
Krusheniska, Salomea, 118, 119.
Kubelik, Jan, 220.
Kurz, Selma, 199, 212, 233, 239.

INDEX

Labia, Fausta, 168, 169.
La Côte d'Or, 43.
Lambert, Dr. Samuel W., 386.
Landi, Alberto, 74.
Lapeyerette, Mme., 271.
La Puma, Signor, 143.
Lasciarelli, Arturo, and Caruso, 84–88.
Lasky, Jesse L., 324.
Lavelle, Monsignor, 349.
Leary, Miss, 207.
Lejeune, Mme., 212.
Leonardi, Signor, 108.
Leoncavallo, Ruggero, asks Caruso to create rôle in "Rolando", 191–193.
Lerma, Maria de, 108, 122.
Le Volpi della Scozia, 62–65.
Lisbon, engagement of Caruso at, 169.
Litvinne, Felia, 307.
Livorno, engagement of Caruso at, 84–89.
"Lodoletta", Caruso sings in, 318, 321.
"Lohengrin", Caruso in, 145, 146.
Lombardi, Vincenzo, 30, 66–73, 77.
London, Covent Garden. *See* Covent Garden.
Lorello, Enrico, 66; becomes Caruso's secretary, 112.
Lorini, Elvira, 108.
Luca, Giuseppe de, 95, 165, 174, 176, 316.
Luca, Salvatore de, laboratory of, 17.
Lucchese, Josephine, 381.
Lucente, Signor, 167.
Lucia, Fernando de, praises Caruso, 68.
"Lucia di Lammermoor", Caruso in, 61–65.
Luppi, Oreste, 130, 135.
Lutio, Raffaele de, 17.
Luzzatto, Attilio, 117.

"Madama Butterfly", 212–217.
Magini-Coletti, Antonio, 127, 137, 138.
Magni, Ludovico, 57.
Maguenat, Alfred, 307, 309.
Majori, engagement of Caruso at, 32, 33.
Mancinelli, Luigi, 199.
Manhattan Opera Company, 266.
"Manon", 126, 153.
"Manon Lescaut", 53–55, 79, 176.
Mansueto, Gaudio, 169.
Marafioti, Doctor P. Mario, 320, 321, 381.
Marchi, Emilio de, 114.
Marconi, Francesco (Checco), 118.
Mariacher, Signor, 143.
"Mariedda", 60.
Marinuzzi, Gino, 310.
"Marta", 175, 353, 376.
"Maschere, Le", Caruso creates rôle in, 135, 141.
Mascheroni, Edoardo, 107, 151.
Mascia, Baron, 74.
Masini, Angelo, 43, 118, 211.
Masola, Signora, 69, 77.
Massa, Giovanni, 95, 97, 98.
Massiano, Edoardo, first meeting of Caruso with, 28.
Matzenauer, Margarete, 295.
'Mefistofele", 116, 119, 120, 124, 125, 142.
Melba, Nellie, at Covent Garden, 155, 159, 160, 199, 212, 232, 239, 299; at Monte Carlo, 156, 157; sings before King of England, 217; in Paris, 259.
Melis, Carmen, 298, 299.
Mendiorez, Signor, 126.
Menotti, Delfino, 101, 107.
Mercadante Theater, Naples, 43–45, 57.
Metropolitan Opera Company, Caruso makes engagement with, 161–165; engagement canceled owing to retirement of Grau, 168; Caruso concludes new engagement with, 170–172; Caruso's first appearance with, 182; first season with, 182–189; other seasons with, 203–208, 221–229, 236–238, 246, 251–254, 262–264, 266–269, 282–284, 295–301, 305, 306, 313–315, 318–323, 327, 344–351; travels to Pacific Coast, 226–229; gives opera in Paris, 269–274.
Mexico, Caruso sings in, 336–342.

INDEX 453

"Mignon", 45.
Milan. See SCALA, LA.
Mingardi, V., 124.
Miranda, Lalla, 219.
Misiani, Antonio, of the "Black Hand", 269.
Mocchi, Walter, 309, 311.
Modrone, Duke of, 133, 138.
Monaco, Cavalier Alfredo (Monaciello), 149–153.
Monte Carlo, Caruso sings at, 154–157, 306–309.
Montesanto, Luigi, 312.
Monteux, Pierre, 327.
Montevideo, 127, 176, 318.
Monti-Baldini, 114.
Morgana, Nina, 324, 331, 335.
Morichini, Vincenzo, 111–114.
Moscate-Ferrara, Mme., 50.
Moscow, 122, 123.
Mugnone, Leopoldo, 79, 81, 82, 114, 117, 129.
Murray, Dr. Francis J., 385, 386.
Muzio, Claudia, 312, 327.

NAGLIATI, MAJOR, 36–40.
Naples, Caruso sings in, 57–59, 147–153.
Napolitano, Daniele, 77.
Navarette, Señorita, 376.
"Navarraise, La," 92–94.
Nawisky, Eduard, 200.
"Nerone", 297.
Neumann, Angelo, 197.
New Orleans, Caruso sings in, 356.
Nielsen, Alice, 201.
Niola, Amelia Tibaldi, 20.
Niola, Doctor Raffaele, 20.
Nordica, Lillian, 160, 207, 222.
Nuovina, Signora de, 93, 94.

ODDO, SIGNOR, 64.
O'Hagan, Lady, 294.
Operas, in répertoire of Caruso, 396; rarely sung or simply studied by, 397.
Ormeville, Carlo d', 105.
Ostende, Caruso sings at, 218, 219.

PACINI, REGINA, 160, 169.
Pacini, Signor, 126, 167.
Padovani, Adelina, 147.
Pagani, Signor, 69, 72, 73.
"Pagliacci, I", Caruso in, 72, 73, 246, 304, 312, 326, 327; effectiveness of Caruso's singing in, 258; energy required by, 376.
Palermo, Massimo Theater, Caruso sings at, 81, 82.
Palmieri, Giuseppe, establishment of, 17.
Pandolfini, Angelica, 165, 169.
Paolicchi-Mugnone, 82.
Pareto, Signorina, 309.
Paris, Caruso sings at, 196, 197, 208–211.
Parkina, Mme., 217.
Pasini-Vitale, Lina, 168.
Patiti, at the San Carlo, 148–153.
Patti, Adelina, 218.
"Pearl Fishers, The", 95, 97.
Penchi, Signora, 74.
Petri, Elisa, 108.
Petrograd, Caruso sings in, 102–104, 118–122.
Pignataro, Enrico, 50, 69, 77, 197.
Pini-Corsi, Antonio, 85, 95, 169.
Pinkert, Regina, in various operas, 95, 137, 138, 151, 152, 197.
Pinto, Amelia, 142–144, 158.
Plançon, Pol, 160, 185, 199, 222.
Podesti, Vittorio, 118, 119, 272.
Polacco, Giorgio, 298, 316, 346.
Pomé, Maestro, 298.
Ponselle, Rosa, 327, 348.
Potenza, Signor, 57.
Prague, Caruso at, 197.
Procida, Baron Saverio, 152.
"Prophète, Le", 321.
Puccini, Giacomo, selects Caruso to sing in "La Bohème", 84–88; gives rôle of Cavaradossi to de Marchi, 114.
"Puritani, I", 66, 67.

RAPPOLD, MME., 225.
Rapponi, Ida, 126.
Réjane, Mme., writes to Caruso, 274.

Renaud, Maurice, in various operas, 157, 159, 160, 190, 196, 199, 259.
Reszke, Edouard and Jean de, 243, 244, 258.
Ricceri, Temistocle, 304.
Ricordi, Giulio, 298.
Ricordi, Tito, letter to Caruso, 205.
"Rigoletto", Caruso in, in Naples, 56, 59; in Salerno, 65, 66; at Buenos Aires, 144; at Monte Carlo, 157; in London, 159; in Rome, 167; in Spain, 194–196; in Paris, 196, 259; in London, 199, 231; in Berlin, 200; in Belgium, 218–220; in Vienna, 233.
Rinskopf, Maestro, 220.
Rio de Janeiro, 177.
Riso, Signora, 59.
Robinne, Mlle., 271.
Roggeri, Mme., 310.
"Rolando", 192, 193.
Rome, engagement of Caruso at, 112–117.
Rossato, Signor, 59.
Rossi, Giulio, 169.
Rosslyn, Lady, 294.
Roth, Maestro, 200.
Rothier, Leon, 316, 348.
Roversi, Luigi, 319.
Royer, Mary, 156.
Rubinstein, Arthur, 335.
Ruffo, Titta, 211, 233, 298.
Russ, Giannina, 190.
Russia, 102–104, 118–123.

SAER, LOUISE, governess of Caruso's children, 239–242.
Salerno, Caruso sings in, 65–73, 76–80.
Sammarco, Mario, 143, 158, 201, 239, 299, 310.
"Samson et Dalila", 313, 365.
San Carlo, Naples, Caruso sings at, 147–153.
San Francisco earthquake, 227–229.
Santarelli, Signora, 101.
Santini, Maestro, 55.
Saratoga Springs, Caruso sings at, 324.

Sarmiento, Alfredo, 53, 314.
Scala, La, Milan, Caruso's first appearance at, 129–142.
Scalise, Maestro, 74.
Scalzi, Count, 319.
Scandiani, Signor, 239.
Schafer, Fraülein, 197.
Scheff, Fritzi, 160.
Schirardi, Ernesto, 17.
Scognamiglio, Gaetano, 314.
Scognamillo, Enrico, 319.
Scotney, Evelyn, 348.
Scott, Henri, 254.
Scotti, Antonio, in various operas, 74, 75, 154, 160, 161, 168, 183, 185, 199, 207, 212, 217, 227, 232, 236, 238, 239, 252, 272, 298, 299.
Sebastiani, Maestro, 57, 59, 69.
Segurola, Andreas de, 143, 195, 272, 346.
Sembrich, Marcella, 183, 189, 236.
Serafin, Tullio, 259.
Severina, Mme., 239.
Shrewsbury, Earl of, 294.
Sicily, tour of, 60–65.
Sicofanti, at the San Carlo, 148–153.
Simonelli, Giovanni, 168.
Simonelli, Pasquale, 170–172, 179, 181.
Siracusa, Maestro, 60.
Slezak, Leo, 272.
Smith, James H., 207, 225.
Sonzogno, Edoardo, publishing house of, 43; Caruso member of his company, 82, 83, 90–94, 98; letters to Caruso, 106, 208, 209; generous offer of Caruso to, 165.
Sormani, Maestro, 136, 137.
South America, engagements of Caruso in, 104–108, 124–127, 142–146, 173–177, 309–311, 317, 318.
Spain, Caruso sings in, 193–196.
Spasiano, Giuseppe, 15, 16.
Sperco, Constant J., 319.
Spoto, Signor, 169.
Staffelli, Giulio, 60.
Stagno, Roberto, 43, 99.
Stefanini, Ciro, 336.
Stehle, Adelina, 43.
Stella, Dr. Antonio, 386.

INDEX

Stoller, Mary, 200.
Storchio, Rosina, 95.
Stracciari, Riccardo, 169, 254, 351.
Sturani, Giuseppe, 310.

TABOGO, SIGNOR, 108.
Taft, President, 297.
Tanara, Fernando, 321.
Tango, Egisto, 127.
Terzi, Signor, 82.
Tetrazzini, Eva, 169.
Tetrazzini, Luisa, 103, 118, 351.
Thevenet, Mme., 196.
Thos, Constantino, 153.
Tomagno, Francesco, 43.
Tonello, Father, his account of how Caruso received the news of his father's death, 254-258; on Caruso's religion, 362.
Torresella, Fanny, 167.
"Tosca", the tenor rôle in, 112-114; Caruso's success in, 129; in South America, 143, 144, 174; in New York, 186, 223.
Toscanini, Arturo, 298, 312; conductor at La Scala, 129-138, 158; in Buenos Aires, 174, 176; principal conductor of the Metropolitan, 262-271.
Traversi, Camillo Antona, reports interview with Caruso, 307-309; letter of Caruso to, 311, 312.
"Traviata, La", 57, 58, 84, 188.
Trentini, Emma, 147, 201.
Trieste, 147, 167.

VALLIN-PARDO, MME., 317.
Vanderbilt, Mrs. Cornelius, 284.

Vedova, Professor della, 264, 265, 293.
Vendôme, Duke and Duchess of, 239, 240.
Vergine, Guglielmo, his methods with the young Caruso, 28-31; recommends Caruso to Daspuro, 44; advises Caruso to sing in "L'Amico Francesco", 46; his faith in Caruso, 77, 78; and Milan engagement of Caruso, 83; annuls contract with Caruso by adjustment, 115.
Viafora, Gina, 187.
Vienna, 233.
Vigna, Arturo, 156, 183, 190, 196, 222.
Villani, Peppino, 21.
Visciani, Impresario, 67.
Vitale, Edoardo, 167, 169.
Viviani, Ludovico, 372.
Vix, Genevieve, 310.
Voghera, Tullio, 254, 314.

WADLER, MAYO, 324.
Whitehill, Clarence, 212, 217.
Whitney, Mrs. W. Payne, 189.
Wilkinson, Everett, 387.
Wilson, President, 331.
Wilson, Mrs. Orme, 189, 226.

ZANOLINI, MR., 206, 207.
Zeppelli, Alice, 309.
Zezza, Baron, 33, 34.
Ziegler, Edward, 382, 386.
Zirato, Bruno, Secretary to Caruso, 318, 319, 325, 331.
Zuccani, Giovanni, 44, 45.
Zucchi-Ferregni, Signora, 77.
Zucchi, Francesco, theatrical agent, 48, 49, 59, 65.